EDVANTAGE
INTERACTIVE

MW01701962

# AP® PHYSICS 1

South Delta Secondary School

**Authors**

**Dr. Gordon Gore**
BIG Little Science Centre (Kamloops)

**Stephen Fuerderer**
Burnaby SD#41

**Lionel Sandner**
Edvantage Interactive

*AP® Physics 1: South Delta Secondary School*


ISBN 978-1-77430-000-8

Care has been taken to trace ownership of copyright material contained in this text. The publishers will gladly accept any information that will enable them to rectify any reference or credit in subsequent printings.

**Vice-President of Marketing:** *Don Franklin*
**Director of USA Sales:** *Brad Magnes*
**Production Support**: *Ryan Chowdhry*

**Photos:** *p. 10, K. Jung; p. 11, Bureau international des poids et mesures (BIPM)*

*The AP Big Ideas at the beginning of each chapter are quoted from AP Physics: Course and Exam Description, revised edition, effective Fall 2014, published by the College Board, New York, NY. Advanced Placement, AP and College Board are registered trademarks of the College Board.*

**QR Code — What Is This?**
The image to the right is called a QR code. It's similar to bar codes on various products and contains information that can be useful to you. Each QR code in this book provides you with online support to help you learn the course material. For example, find a question with a QR code beside it. If you scan that code, you'll see the answer to the question explained in a video created by an author of this book.
You can scan a QR code using an Internet-enabled mobile device. The program to scan QR codes is free and available at your phone's app store. Scanning the QR code above will give you a short overview of how to use the codes in the book to help you study.
**Note:** We recommend that you scan QR codes only when your phone is connected to a WiFi network. Depending on your mobile data plan, charges may apply if you access the information over the cellular network. If you are not sure how to do this, please contact your mobile provider or us at info@edvantageinteractive.com

COPIES OF THIS BOOK MAY BE OBTAINED BY CONTACTING:

Edvantage Interactive

E-MAIL:
info@edvantageinteractive.com

TOLL-FREE FAX:
866.275.0564

TOLL-FREE CALL:
866.422.7310

Please quote the ISBN and title when placing your order.

# Contents

## AP® Physics 1

# Welcome to AP® Physics 1

**AP® Physics 1** is a print and digital resource for classroom and independent study, aligned with the AP curriculum. You, the student, have two core components — this write-in textbook or WorkText and, to provide mobile functionality, an interactive Online Study Guide.

## AP® Physics 1 WorkText

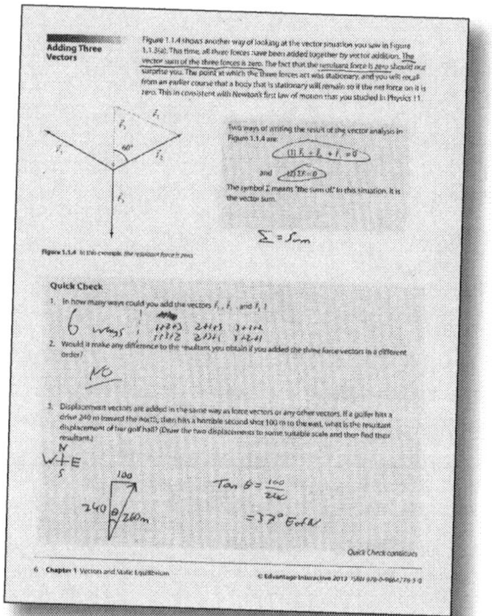

### What is a WorkText?

A WorkText is a write-in textbook. Not just a workbook, a write-in **textbook**.

Like the vast majority of AP students, you will read for content, underline, highlight, take notes, answer the questions — all in this book. **Your book.**

Use it as a textbook, workbook, notebook, AND study guide. It's also a great reference book for post secondary studies.

Make it your own personal WorkText.

### Why a write-in textbook?

Reading is an extremely active and personal process.

Research has shown that physically interacting with your text by writing margin notes and highlighting key passages results in better comprehension and retention.

Use your own experiences and prior knowledge to make meaning, not take meaning, from text.

### How to make this book work for you:

1. Scan each section and check out the shaded areas and bolded terms.
2. Do the Warm Ups to activate prior knowledge.
3. Take notes as required by highlights and adding teacher comments and notes.
4. Use Quick Check sections to find out where you are in your learning.
5. Do the Review Questions and write down the answers. Scan the **QR codes** or go to the **Online Study Guide** to see YouTube-like video worked solutions by *AP Physics 1* authors.
6. Try the **Online Study Guide** for online quizzes, PowerPoints, and more videos.
7. Follow the six steps above to be successful.
8. Need extra support? ASK AN AUTHOR! Go to edvantagescience.com.

**For more information on how to purchase your own personal copy — info@edvantageinteractive.com**

# AP Physics 1 Online Study Guide (OSG)

## What is an Online Study Guide?

It's an interactive, personalized, digital, mobile study guide to support the WorkText.

The **Online Study Guide** or OSG, provides access to online quizzes, PowerPoint notes, and video worked solutions.

Need extra questions, sample tests, a summary of your notes, worked solutions to some of the review questions? It's all here!

Access it where you want, when you want.

Make it your own personal mobile study guide.

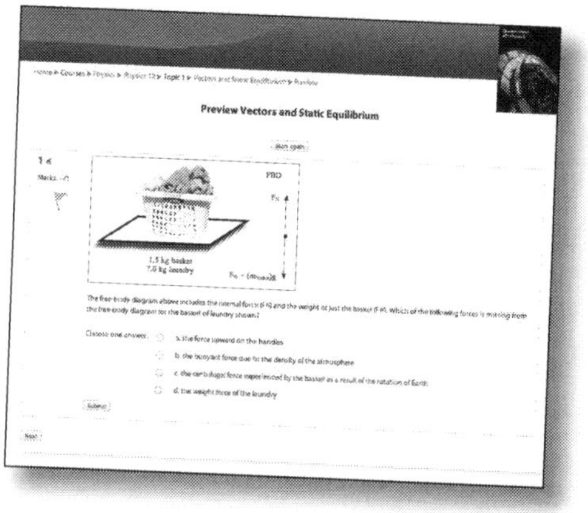


## What's in the Online Study Guide?

- Online quizzes, multiple choice questions, provincial exam-like tests with instant feedback
- PowerPoint notes: Key idea summary and student study notes from the textbook
- Video worked solutions: Select video worked solutions from the WorkText

*Scan this code for more on the OSG*

If you have a smart phone or tablet, scan the QR code to the right to find out more.
Color e-reader WorkText version available.

## Where is the Online Study Guide located?

edvantagescience.com

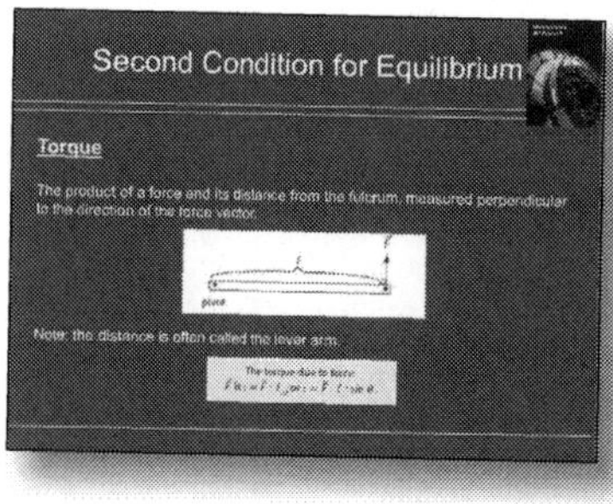


## Should I use the Online Study Guide?

***YES... if you want to do your best in this course.***

The OSG is directly LINKED to the activities and content in the WorkText.

The OSG helps you learn what is taught in class.

**If your school does not have access to the Online Study Guide and you'd like more information — info@edvantageinteractive.com**

# Introduction
## Skills, Methods, and the Nature of Physics

Using the skills developed in this chapter, you should be able to do the following:

- Describe the nature of physics
- Apply the skills and methods of physics including:
  - conduct appropriate experiments
  - systematically gather and organize data from experiments
  - produce and interpret graphs
  - verify relationships (e.g., linear, inverse, square, and inverse square) between variables
  - use models (e.g., physics formulae, diagrams, graphs) to solve a variety of problems
  - use appropriate units and metric prefixes
  - perform vector analysis in one or two dimensions

---

By the end of this chapter, you should know the meaning to these key terms:

- accuracy
- dependent variable
- experimental error
- independent variable
- law
- linear function
- model
- precision
- scalar quantities
- scientific method
- scientific notation
- slope
- uncertainty
- vector quantities
- *y*-intercept

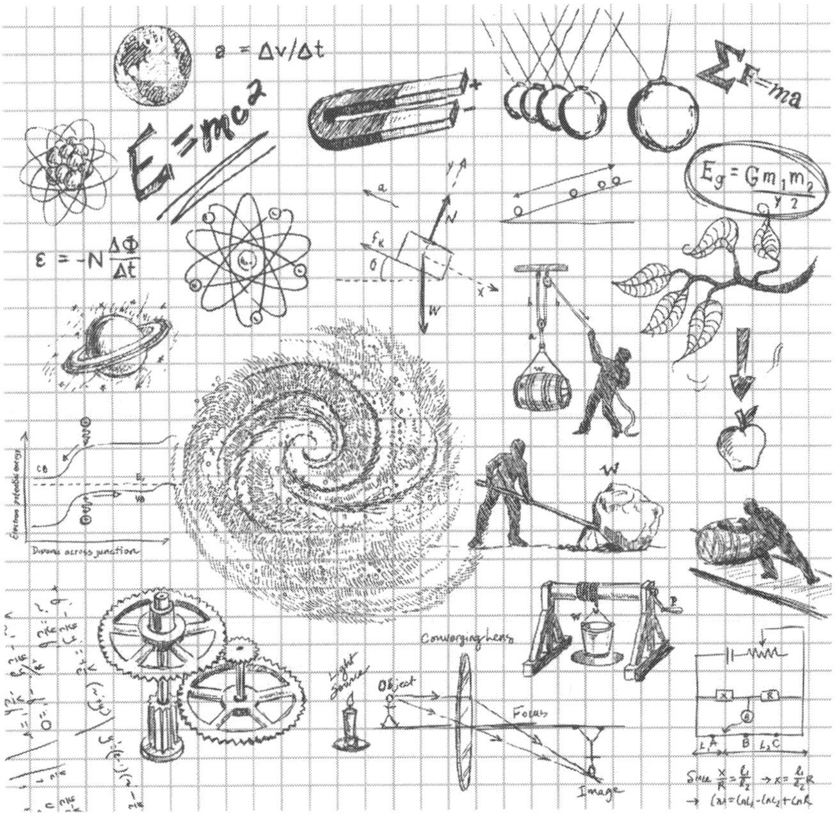


*In this chapter, you'll learn about the tools, skills, and techniques you'll be using as you study physics and about the nature of physics itself.*

# i.1 What is Physics?

## Warm Up

This is probably your first formal physics course. In the space below, describe your definition of physics.

______________________________________________

______________________________________________

______________________________________________

### Physics Explains the World

We live in an amazing place in our universe. In what scientists call the Goldilocks principle, we live on a planet that is just the right distance from the Sun, with just the right amount of water and just the right amount of atmosphere. Like Goldilocks in the fairy tale eating, sitting, and sleeping in the three little bears' home, Earth is just right to support life.

Yet there is much that we don't know about our planet. To study science is to be part of the enterprise of observing and collecting evidence of the world around us. The study of physics is part of this global activity. In fact, from the time you were a baby, you have been a physicist. Dropping food or a spoon from your baby chair was one of your first attempts to understand gravity. You probably also figured out how to get attention from an adult when you did this too, but let's focus on you being a little scientist. Now that you are a teenager you are beginning the process of formalizing your understanding of the world. Hopefully, this learning will never stop as there are many questions we do not have answers to and the wonder of discovering why things happen the way they do never gets boring. That is part of the excitement of physics — you are always asking why things happen.

Physics will give you many opportunities to ask, "Why did that happen?" To find the answers to this and other questions, you will learn skills and processes to help you better understand concepts such as acceleration, force, waves, and special relativity. You will learn how to apply what you have learned in math class to solve problems or write clear, coherent explanations using the skills from English class. In physics class, you can apply the skills and concepts you have learned in other classes. Let's begin by looking at one method used to investigate and explain natural phenomena: the scientific method.

### The Scientific Method

How do you approach the problems you encounter in everyday life? Think about beginning a new class at the start of the school year, for example. The first few days you make observations and collect data. You might not think of it this way, but when you observe your classmates, the classroom, and your teachers, you are making observations and collecting data. This process will inevitably lead you to make some decisions as you consider the best way to interact with this new environment. Who would you like for a partner in this class? Where do you want to sit? Are you likely to interact well with this particular teacher? You are drawing conclusions. This method of solving problems is called the **scientific method**. In future courses you may have an opportunity to discuss how the scientific method varies depending on the situation and the type of research being undertaken. For this course, an introduction to the scientific method is provided to give you a foundation to develop habits of thinking scientifically as you explore our world.

**Figure i.1.1** *Galileo (top) and Newton*

Four hundred years ago, scientists were very interested in understanding the world around them. There were hypotheses about why the Sun came up each day or why objects fell to the ground, but they were not based on evidence. Two physicists who used the scientific method to support their hypotheses were the Italian Galileo Galilei (1564–1642) and the Englishman Sir Isaac Newton (1642–1727).

Both Galileo and Newton provided insights into how our universe works on some fundamental principles. Galileo used evidence from his observations of planetary movement to support the idea that Earth revolved around the Sun. However, he was forced to deny this conclusion when put on trial. Eventually, his evidence was accepted as correct and we now consider Galileo one of the fathers of modern physics. Sir Isaac Newton, also considered one of the fathers of modern physics, was the first to describe motion and gravity. In this course, you will be introduced to his three laws of motion and the universal law of gravitation. Both ideas form a foundation for classical physics. Like many others that followed, both Galileo and Newton made their discoveries through careful observation, the collection of evidence, and interpretations based on that evidence.

Different groups of scientists outline the parts of the scientific method in different ways. Here is one example, illustrating its steps.

**Steps of the Scientific Method**

1. **Observation**: Collection of data. **Quantitative** observation has numbers or quantities associated with it. **Qualitative** observation describes qualities or changes in the quality of matter including, for example, a substance's color, odor, or physical state.
2. **Statement of a hypothesis**: Formulation of a statement in an "if...then..." format that explains the observations.
3. **Experimentation**: Design and carry out a procedure to determine whether the hypothesis accurately explains the observations. After making a set of observations and formulating a hypothesis, scientists devise an experiment. During the experiment they carefully record additional observations. Depending on the results of the experiment, the hypothesis may be adjusted and experiments repeated to collect new observations many times.
   Sometimes the results of an experiment differ from what was expected. There are a variety of reasons this might happen. Things that contribute to such differences are called **sources of error**. They can include random errors over which the experimenter has no control and processes or equipment that can be adjusted, such as inaccurate measuring instruments. You will learn more about sources of error in experiments in section i.3.
4. **Statement of a Theory**: Statement of an explanation for the hypotheses being investigated. Once enough information has been collected from a series of experiments, a reasoned and coherent explanation called a theory may be deduced. This theory may lead to a **model** that helps us understand the theory. A model is usually a simplified description or representation of a theory or phenomenon that can help us study it. Sometimes the scientific method leads to a **law**, which is a general statement of fact, without an accompanying set of explanations.

## Quick Check

1. What is the difference between a law and a theory?

2. What are the fundamental steps of the scientific method?

3. Classify the following observations as quantitative or qualitative by placing a checkmark in the correct column. **Hint:** Look at each syllable of those words: quantitative and qualitative. What do they seem to mean?

| Observation | Quantitative | Qualitative |
|---|---|---|
| Acceleration due to gravity is 9.8 $m/s^2$. | | |
| A rocket travels faster than fighter jet. | | |
| The density of scandium metal is 2.989 $g/cm^3$. | | |
| Copper metal can be used for wire to conduct electricity. | | |
| Mass and velocity determine the momentum in an object. | | |
| Zinc has a specific heat capacity of 388 J/(kg·K). | | |
| The force applied to the soccer ball was 50 N. | | |

4. Use the steps of the scientific method to design a test for the following hypotheses:
   (a) If cardboard is used to insulate a cup, it will keep a hot drink warmer.

   (b) If vegetable oil is used to grease a wheel, the wheel will turn faster.

   (c) If hot water is placed in ice cube trays, the water will freeze faster.

 

## The Many Faces of Physics

There are many different areas of study in the field of physics. Figure i.1.2 gives an overview of the four main areas. Notice how the areas of study can be classified by two factors: size and speed. These two factors loosely describe the general themes studied in each field. For example, this course focusses mainly classical mechanics, which involves relatively large objects and slow speeds.

A quick Internet search will show you many different ways to classify the areas of study within physics. The search will also show a new trend in the study of sciences, a trend that can have an impact on your future. Rather than working in one area of study or even within one discipline such as physics, biology, or chemistry, inter-disciplinary studies are becoming common. For example, an understanding of physics and biology might allow you to work in the area of biomechanics, which is the study of how the human muscles and bones work. Or maybe you will combine biology and physics to study exobiology, the study of life beyond the Earth's atmosphere and on other planets.

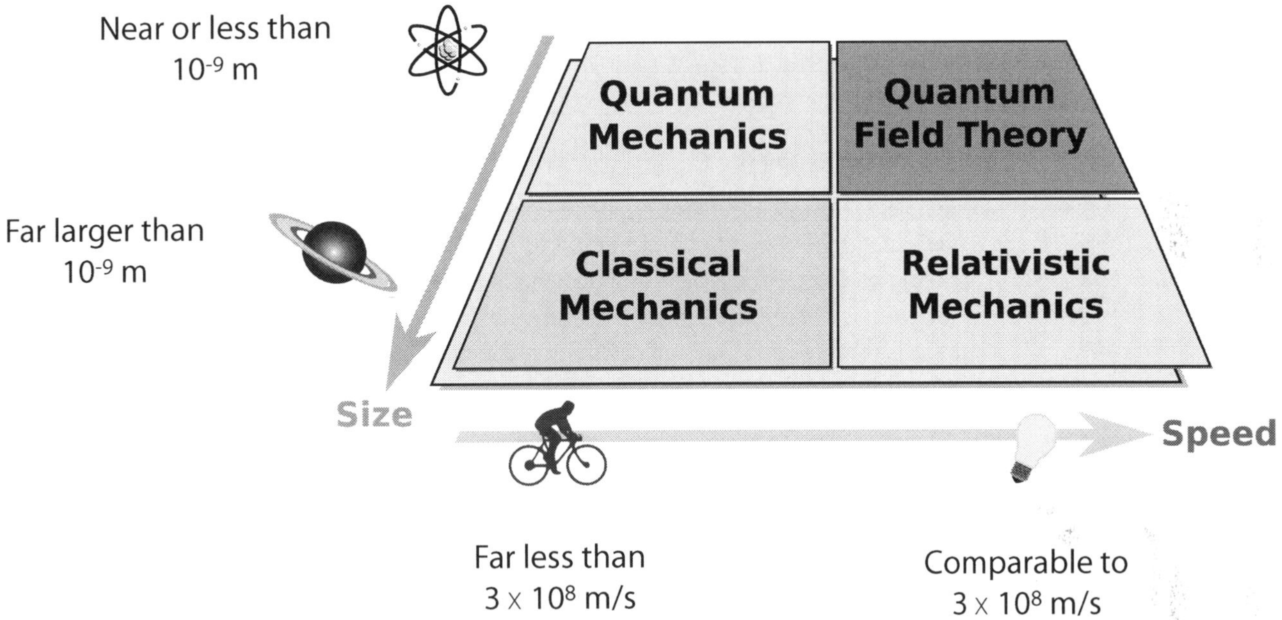


**Figure i.1.2** *The four main areas of physics. (Credit: Yassine Mrabet)*

# i.2 Equipment Essentials

## Warm Up

Your teacher will give you a pendulum made from some string and a washer. One swing of the pendulum back and forth is called a period and measured in seconds. Work with a partner to determine the period of your pendulum. Outline your procedure and results below. When you are done, identify one thing you would change in your procedure to improve your answer.

### Using a Calculator

A calculator is a tool that helps you perform calculations during investigations and solving problems. You'll have your calculator with you for every class. At the same time, however, you are not to rely on it exclusively. You need to understand what the question is asking and what formula or calculation you need to use before you use your calculator. If you find yourself just pushing buttons to find an answer without understanding the question, you need to talk to your teacher or a classmate to figure it out. Many times you'll just need one concept clarified and then you can solve the problem.

Every calculator is different in terms of what order of buttons you need to push to find your answer. Use the Quick Check below to ensure you can find trigonometric functions and enter and manipulate exponents. If you cannot find the answers for these questions, check with your teacher immediately.

### Quick Check

Using your calculator, what are the answers to the following mathematical statements?

1. $\sin 30°$ ________________
2. $\tan^{-1} .345$ ________________
3. $34^2$ ________________
4. $(3.2 \times 10^{-4}) \times (2.5 \times 10^6)$ ________________
5. pi – $\cos 60°$ ________________

### Measuring Time

For objects that have a regularly repeated motion, each complete movement is called a **cycle**. The time during which the cycle is completed is called the **period** of the cycle. The number of cycles completed in one unit of time is called the **frequency** ($f$) of the moving object. You may be familiar with the frequencies of several everyday objects. For example, a car engine may have a frequency of several thousand rpm (revolutions per minute).

The turntable of an old phonograph record player may have frequencies of 33 rpm, 45 rpm, or 78 rpm. A pendulum 24.85 cm long has a frequency of one cycle per second. Tuning forks may have frequencies such as 256 vibrations per second, 510 vibrations per second, and so on.

Any measurement of time involves some sort of event that repeats itself at regular intervals. For example, a year is the time it takes Earth to revolve around the Sun; a day is the time it takes Earth to rotate on its axis; a month is approximately the time it takes the Moon to revolve around Earth. Perhaps *moonth* would be a better name for this time interval.

All devices used to measure time contain some sort of regularly vibrating object such as a pendulum, a quartz crystal, a tuning fork, a metronome, or even vibrating electrons. With a pendulum you can experiment with the properties to make it a useful timing device. When a pendulum undergoes regularly repeated movements, each complete movement is called a cycle, and the time required for each cycle is called its period.

A frequency of one cycle per second is called a **hertz** (**Hz**). Higher frequencies (such as radio signal frequencies) may be expressed in kilohertz (kHz) or even megahertz (MHz), where 1 kHz is 1000 Hz, and 1 MHz is 1 000 000 Hz.

### The Recording Timer

In Investigation i-1, you will use a device called a recording timer like the one in Figure i.2.1. The timer is a modified electric buzzer. A moving arm driven by an electromagnet vibrates with a constant frequency, and each time it vibrates, it strikes a piece of carbon paper. The carbon paper makes a small dot on a moving piece of ticker tape. The small dots are a record of both time and distance. If you know the frequency of vibration of the timer, you can figure out the period of time between the dots, because period ($T$) and frequency ($f$) are reciprocals of one another.

$$T = 1/f, \text{ and } f = 1/T$$

**Figure i.2.1** *A recording timer that uses ticker tape to record time and distance*

If you measure the distance between the dots, this will tell you how far the object attached to the tape has moved. Knowing both distance and time, you can also calculate speed, since the speed of an object is the distance travelled divided by the time.

## Using a Motion Probe

Another method for recording motion is a motion probe. There are several different models that can be used, but they all follow the same basic principles. Using a computer or graphing calculator, the probe is plugged in and run via a software program. The software program collects data on the motion you are studying and represents them as a graph on your computer screen.

Using the data collected, you can analyze the motion. Your teacher will demonstrate how to use the motion probe in your lab.

# i.3 Physics Essentials

## Warm Up

What is the difference between accuracy and precision? Explain your answer with real life examples.

______________________________________________

______________________________________________

______________________________________________

### Significant Digits

Imagine you are planning to paint a room in your house. To estimate how much paint you need to buy, you must know only the approximate dimensions of the walls. The rough estimate for one wall might be 8 m × 3 m. If, however, you are going to paste wallpaper on your wall and you require a neat, precise fit, you will probably make your measurements to the nearest millimetre. A proper measurement made for this purpose might look like this: 7.685 m × 2.856 m.

Significant digits ("sig digs") are the number of digits in the written value used to indicate the **precision** of a measurement. They are also called significant figures ("sig figs"). In the estimate of the wall size for determining how much paint is needed to cover a wall, the measurements (8 m × 3 m) have only one significant digit each. They are accurate to the nearest metre. In the measurements used to install wallpaper, the measurements had four significant digits. They were accurate to the nearest millimetre. They were more precise.

If you are planning to buy a very old used car, the salesman may ask you how much you want to spend. You might reply by giving him a rough estimate of around \$600. This figure of \$600 has one significant digit. You might write it as \$600, but the zeros in this case are used simply to place the decimal point. When you buy the car and write a cheque for the full amount, you have to be more precise. For example, you might pay \$589.96. This "measurement" has five significant digits. Of course, if you really did pay exactly \$600, you would write the check for \$600.00. In this case, all the zeros are measured digits, and this measurement has five significant digits!

You can see that zeros are sometimes significant digits (measured zeros) and sometimes not. The measurer should make it clear whether the zeros are significant digits or just decimal-placing zeros. For example, you measure the length of a ticker tape to be 7 cm, 3 mm, and around ½ mm long. How do you write down this measurement? You could write it several ways, and *all* are correct:

7.35 cm, 73.5 mm, or 0.0735 m.

Each of these measurements is the same. Only the measuring *units* differ. Each measurement has *three significant digits*. The zeros in 0.0735 m are used only to place the decimal.

 

In another example, the volume of a liquid is said to be 600 mL. How precise is this measurement? Did the measurer mean it was "around 600 mL"? Or was it 600 mL to the nearest millilitre? Perhaps the volume was measured to the nearest tenth of a millilitre. Only the measurer really knows. Writing the volume as 600 mL is somewhat ambiguous. To be unambiguous, such a measurement might be expressed in **scientific notation**. To do this, the measurement is converted to the product of a number containing the intended number of significant digits (using one digit to the left of the decimal point) and a power of 10. For example, if you write $6 \times 10^2$ mL, you are estimating to the nearest 100 mL. If you write $6.0 \times 10^2$ mL, you are estimating to the nearest 10 mL. A measurement to the nearest millilitre would be $6.00 \times 10^2$ mL. The zeros here are measured zeros, not just decimal-placing zeros. They are significant digits.

If it is not convenient to use scientific notation, you must indicate in some other way that a zero is a measured zero. For example, if the volume of a liquid is measured to the nearest mL to be "600." mL, the decimal point will tell the reader that you measured to the nearest mL, and that both zeros are measured zeros. "600. mL" means the same as $6.00 \times 10^2$ mL.

The number of significant digits used to express the result of a measurement indicates how precise the measurement was. A person's height measurement of 1.895 m is more precise than a measurement of 1.9 m.

## Accuracy and Precision

Measured values are determined using a variety of different measuring devices. There are devices designed to measure all sorts of different quantities. The collection pictured in Figure i.3.1 measures temperature, length, and volume. In addition, there are a variety of precisions (exactnesses) associated with different devices. The micrometer (also called a caliper) is more precise than the ruler while the burette and pipette are more precise than the graduated cylinder.

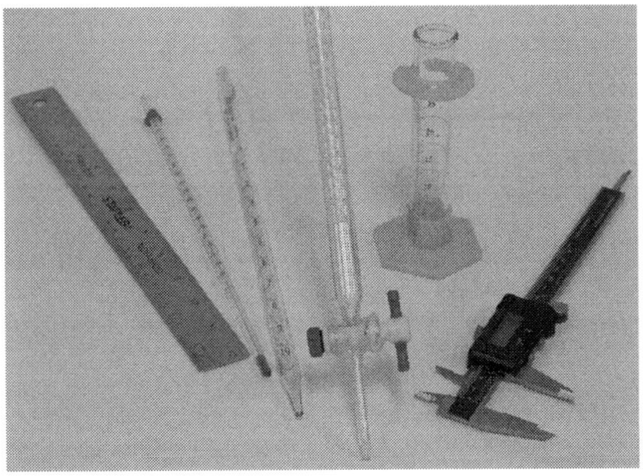

**Figure i.3.1** *A selection of measuring devices with different levels of precision*

Despite the fact that some measuring devices are more precise than others, it is impossible to design a measuring device that gives perfectly exact measurements. All measuring devices have some degree of **uncertainty** associated with them.

The 1-kg mass shown in Figure i.3.2 is kept in a helium-filled bell jar at the BIPM in Sèvres France. It is the only exact mass on the planet. All other masses are measured relative to this and therefore have some degree of uncertainty associated with them.

**Figure i.3.2** *This kilogram mass was made in the 1880s. In 1889, it was accepted as the international prototype of the kilogram. (©BIPM — Reproduced with permission)*

**Accuracy** refers to the agreement of a particular value with the *true value.*

Accurate measurements depend on careful design and calibration to ensure a measuring device is in proper working order. The term **precision** can actually have two different meanings.

*Precision* refers to the reproducibility of a measurement or the agreement among several measurements of the same quantity.

*– or –*

*Precision* refers to the exactness of a measurement. This relates to uncertainty: the lower the uncertainty of a measurement, the higher the precision.

A measurement can be very precise, yet very inaccurate. In 1895, a scientist estimated the time it takes planet Venus to rotate on its axis to be 23 h, 57 min, 36.2396 s. This is a very precise measurement! Unfortunately, it was found out later that the period of rotation of Venus is closer to 243 days! The latter measurement is much less precise, but probably a good deal more accurate!

## Experimental Error

There is no such thing as a perfectly accurate measurement. Measurements are always subject to some uncertainty. Consider the following sources of experimental error.

### Systematic Errors

Systematic errors may result from using an instrument that is in some way inaccurate. For example, if a wooden metre stick is worn at one end and you measure from this end, every reading will be too high. If an ammeter needle is not properly "zeroed," all the readings taken with the meter will be too high or too low. Thermometers must be regularly checked for accuracy and corrections made to eliminate systematic errors in temperature readings.

### Random Errors

Random errors occur in almost any measurement. For example, imagine you make five different readings of the length of a laboratory bench. You might obtain results such as: 1.626 m, 1.628 m, 1.624 m, 1.626 m, and 1.625 m. You might average these measurements and express the length of the bench in this way: $1.626 \pm 0.002$ m. This is a way of saying that your average measurement was 1.626 m, but the measurements, due to random errors, range between 1.624 m and 1.628 m.

## Quick Check

Four groups of Earth Science students use their global positioning systems (GPS) to do some geocaching. The diagrams below show the students' results relative to where the actual caches were located.

1. Comment on the precision of the students in each of the groups. (In this case, we are using the "reproducibility" definition of precision.)

   ______________________________

2. What about the accuracy of each group?

   ______________________________

3. Which groups were making systematic errors?

   ______________________________

4. Which groups made errors that were more random?

   ______________________________

### Other Errors

Regardless of the accuracy and precision of the measuring instrument, errors may arise when you, the experimenter, interact with the instrument. For example, if you measure the thickness of a piece of plastic using a micrometre caliper, your reading will be very precise but inaccurate if you tighten the caliper so much that you crush the plastic with the caliper!

A common personal error made by inexperienced experimenters is failing to read scales with eye(s) in the proper position. In Figure i.3.3, for example, only observer B will obtain the correct measurement for the length of the block.

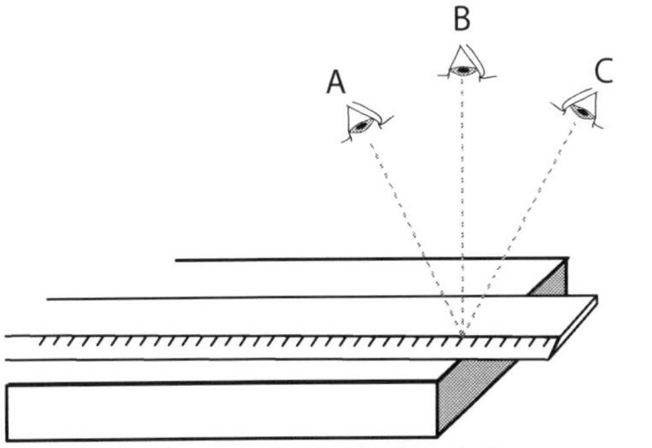


**Figure i.3.3** *Observers A and C will make incorrect readings because of their positions relative to the ruler.*

## Scientific Notation

**Scientific notation** is a convenient way to express numbers that are very large or very small. For example, one ampere of electric current is a measurement of 6 240 000 000 000 000 000 electrons passing a point in a wire in 1 s. This same number can be written, in scientific notation, as $6.24 \times 10^{18}$ electrons/second. This means 624 followed by 16 zeros.

Any number can be expressed in scientific notation. Here are some examples:

$$0.10 = 1.0 \times 10^{-1}$$
$$1.0 = 1.0 \times 10^{0}$$
$$10.0 = 1.00 \times 10^{1}$$
$$100.0 = 1.000 \times 10^{2}$$
$$1\,000.0 = 1.0000 \times 10^{3}$$

### Quick Check

1. Write the following measurements in scientific notation.

   (a) 0.00572 kg ______________________

   (b) 520 000 000 000 km ______________________

   (c) 300 000 000 m/s ______________________

   (d) 0.000 000 000 000 000 000 16 C ______________________

   (e) 118.70004 g ______________________

2. Simplify.

   (a) $10^{3} \times 10^{7} \times 10^{12}$ ______________________

   (b) $10^{23} \div 10^{5}$ ______________________

   (c) $10^{12} \times 10^{-13}$ ______________________

   (d) $10^{-8} \times 10^{-12}$ ______________________

   (e) $10^{5} \div 10^{-7}$ ______________________

   (f) $10^{-2} \div 10^{-9}$ ______________________

# Review of Basic Rules for Handling Exponents

## Power of 10 Notation

| | |
|---|---|
| $0.000001 = 10^{-6}$ | $1 = 10^{0}$ |
| $0.00001 = 10^{-5}$ | $10 = 10^{1}$ |
| $0.0001 = 10^{-4}$ | $100 = 10^{2}$ |
| $0.001 = 10^{-3}$ | $1\,000 = 10^{3}$ |
| $0.01 = 10^{-2}$ | $10\,000 = 10^{4}$ |
| $0.1 = 10^{-1}$ | $100\,000 = 10^{5}$ |
| $1 = 10^{0}$ | $1\,000\,000 = 10^{6}$ |

## Multiplying Powers of 10

Law of Exponents: $\mathbf{a^m \cdot a^n = a^{m+n}}$

(When multiplying, ***add*** exponents.)

Examples: $100 \times 1\,000 = 10^2 \cdot 10^3 = 10^5$

$$\frac{1}{100} \times 1\,000 = 10^{-2} \times 10^3 = 10^1$$

$$2500 \times 4000 = 2.5 \times 10^3 \times 4.0 \times 10^3 = 10 \times 10^6 = 1.0 \times 10^7$$

## Dividing Powers of 10

Law of Exponents: $\mathbf{a^m \div a^n = a^{m-n}}$

(When dividing, ***subtract*** exponents.)

Examples: $\frac{10^5}{10} = 10^{5-1} = 10^4$

$$\frac{100}{1000} = \frac{10^2}{10^3} = 10^{-1}$$

$$\frac{1.00}{100\,000} = \frac{10^0}{10^5} = 10^{-5}$$

# i.4 Analysis of Units and Conversions in Physics

## Warm Up

Place a check by the larger quantity in each row of the table.

| Metric Quantity | | Imperial Quantity | |
|---|---|---|---|
| A kilogram of butter | | A pound of butter | |
| A five-kilometre hiking trail | | A five-mile mountain bike trail | |
| One litre of milk | | One quart of milk | |
| A twelve-centimetre ruler | | A twelve-inch ruler | |
| A fifteen-gram piece of chocolate | | A fifteen-ounce chocolate bar | |
| A temperature of 22°C | | A temperature of 22°F | |

## Measurement Through History

Units of measurement were originally based on nature and everyday activities. The grain was derived from the mass of one grain of wheat or barley a farmer produced. The fathom was the distance between the tips of a sailor's fingers when his arms were extended on either side. The origin of units of length like the foot and the hand leave little to the imagination.

The inconvenient aspect of units such as these was, of course, their glaring lack of consistency. One "Viking's embrace" might produce a fathom much shorter than another. These inconsistencies were so important to traders and travellers that over the years most of the commonly used units were standardized. Eventually, they were incorporated into what was known as the English units of measurement. Following the Battle of Hastings in 1066, Roman measures were added to the primarily Anglo-Saxon ones that made up this system. These units were standardized by the Magna Carta of 1215 and were studied and updated periodically until the UK *Weights and Measures Act* of 1824 resulted in a major review and a renaming to the **Imperial system of measurement**. It is interesting to note that the United States had become independent prior to this and did not adopt the Imperial system, but continued to use the older English units of measure.

Despite the standardization, development of this system from ancient agriculture and trade has led to a vast set of units that are quite complicated. For example, there are eight different definitions for the amount of matter in a ton. The need for a simpler system, a system based on decimals, or multiples of 10, was recognized as early 1585 when Flemish mathematician Simon Stevin (1548–1620) published a book called *The Tenth*. However, most authorities credit Frenchman Gabriel Mouton (1618–1694) as the originator of the metric system nearly 100 years later. Another 100 years would pass before the final development and adoption of the metric system in France in 1795.

The International Bureau of Weights and Measures (BIPM) was established in Sévres, France, in 1825. The BIPM has governed the metric system ever since. Since 1960, the metric system has become the International System of Units, known as the SI system. SI is from the French *Système International*. The SI system's use and acceptance has grown to the point that only three countries in the entire world have not adopted it: Burma, Liberia, and the United States (Figure i.4.1).

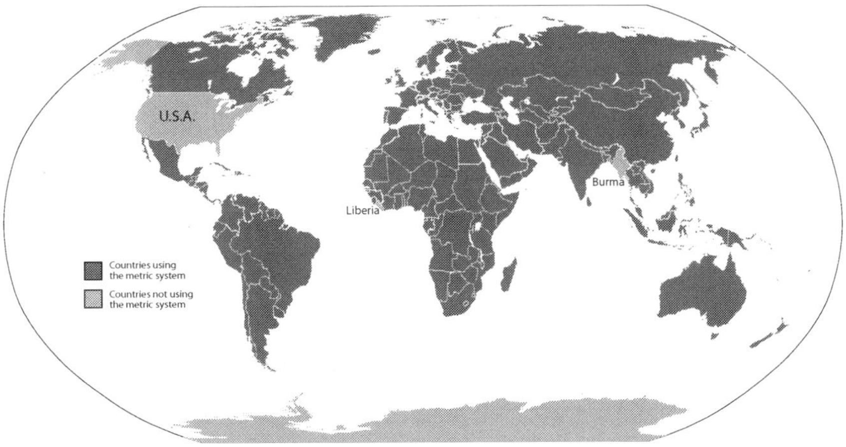


**Figure i.4.1** *Map of the world showing countries that have adopted the SI/metric system*

## Dimensional Analysis

Dimensional analysis is a method that allows you to easily solve problems by converting from one unit to another through the use of conversion factors. The dimensional analysis method is sometimes called the factor label method. It may occasionally be referred to as the use of unitary rates.

A **conversion factor** is a fraction or factor written so that the denominator and numerator are equivalent values with different units.

One of the most useful conversion factors allows the user to convert from the metric to the imperial system and vice versa. Since 1 inch is exactly the same length as 2.54 cm, the factor may be expressed as:

$$\frac{1 \text{ inch}}{2.54 \text{ cm}} \text{ or } \frac{2.54 \text{ cm}}{1 \text{ inch}}$$

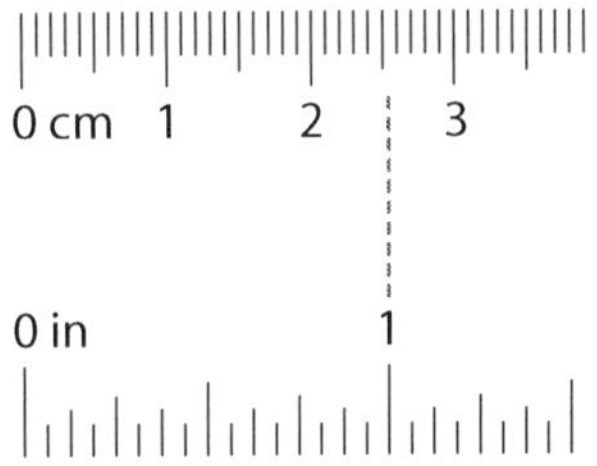


**Figure i.4.2** *A ruler with both imperial and metric scales shows that 1 inch = 2.54 cm.*

These two lengths are identical so multiplication of a given length by the conversion factor will not change the length. It will simply express it in a different unit (Figure i.4.2).

Now if you wish to determine how many centimetres are in a yard, you have two things to consider. First, which of the two forms of the conversion factor will allow you to *cancel* the imperial unit, converting it to a metric unit? Second, what other conversion factors will you need to complete the task?

Assuming you know, or can access, these equivalencies: 1 yard = 3 feet and 1 foot = 12 inches, your approach would be as follows:

$$1.00\ \cancel{\text{yards}} \times \frac{3\ \cancel{\text{feet}}}{1\ \cancel{\text{yard}}} \times \frac{12\ \cancel{\text{inches}}}{1\ \cancel{\text{foot}}} \times \frac{2.54\ \text{cm}}{1\ \cancel{\text{inch}}} = 91.4\ \text{cm}$$

Notice that as with the multiplication of any fractions, it is possible to cancel anything that appears in both the numerator and the denominator. We've simply followed a numerator-to-denominator pattern to convert yards to feet to inches to cm.

The number of feet in a yard and inches in a foot are defined values. They are not things we measured. Thus they do not affect the number of significant digits in our answer. This will be the case for any conversion factor in which the numerator and denominator are in the same system (both metric or both imperial). Interestingly enough, the BIPM has indicated that 2.54 cm will be exactly 1 inch. So it is the only multiple-system conversion factor that will not influence the number of significant digits in the answer to a calculation. As all three of the conversion factors we used are defined, only the original value of 1.00 yards influences the significant digits in our answer. Hence we round the answer to three sig digs.

## Converting Within the Metric System

The metric system is based on powers of 10. The power of 10 is indicated by a simple prefix. Table i.4.1 is a list of SI prefixes. Your teacher will indicate those that you need to commit to memory. You may wish to highlight them.

Metric conversions require either one or two steps. You will recognize a one-step metric conversion by the presence of a *base unit* in the question. The common base units in the metric system are shown in Table i.4.2.

**Table i.4.1** *SI Prefixes*

| Prefix | Symbol | $10^n$ |
|---|---|---|
| yotta | Y | $10^{24}$ |
| zetta | Z | $10^{21}$ |
| exa | E | $10^{18}$ |
| peta | P | $10^{15}$ |
| tera | T | $10^{12}$ |
| giga | G | $10^{9}$ |
| mega | M | $10^{6}$ |
| kilo | k | $10^{3}$ |
| hecto | h | $10^{2}$ |
| deca | da | $10^{1}$ |
| deci | d | $10^{-1}$ |
| centi | c | $10^{-2}$ |
| milli | m | $10^{-3}$ |
| micro | µ | $10^{-6}$ |
| nano | n | $10^{-9}$ |
| pico | p | $10^{-12}$ |
| femto | f | $10^{-15}$ |
| atto | a | $10^{-18}$ |
| zepto | z | $10^{-21}$ |
| yocto | y | $10^{-24}$ |

**Table i.4.2** *Common Metric Base Units*

| Measures | Unit Name | Symbol |
|---|---|---|
| length | metre | m |
| mass | gram | g |
| volume | litre | L |
| time | second | s |

One-step metric conversions involve a base unit (metres, litres, grams, or seconds) being converted to a prefixed unit or a prefixed unit being converted to a base unit.

Two-step metric conversions require the use of two conversion factors. Two factors will be required any time there are two prefixed units in the question. In a two-step metric conversion, you must always convert to the base unit first.

 

## Unit Conversions

A **derived unit** is composed of more than one unit.

Units like those used to express rate (km/h) or density (g/mL) are good examples of derived units.

Derived unit conversions require cancellations in two directions (from numerator to denominator as usual AND from denominator to numerator).

### Sample Problem i.4.2 — Unit Conversions

Convert 55.0 km/h into m/s.

| What to Think About | How to Do It |
|---|---|
| 1. The numerator requires conversion of a prefixed metric unit to a base metric unit. This portion involves one step only and is similar to sample problem one above. | $\frac{55.0\ \text{km}}{\text{h}} \times \frac{\text{m}}{\text{km}} \times \frac{\text{h}}{\text{min}} \times \frac{\text{min}}{\text{s}}$ |
| 2. The denominator involves a time conversion from hours to minutes to seconds. The denominator conversion usually follows the numerator. Always begin by putting all conversion factors in place using *units only*. Now that this has been done, insert the appropriate numerical values for each conversion factor. | $= \frac{\text{m}}{\text{s}}$ <br> $\frac{55.0\ \cancel{\text{km}}}{\cancel{\text{h}}} \times \frac{10^3\ \text{m}}{1\ \cancel{\text{km}}} \times \frac{1\ \cancel{\text{h}}}{60\ \cancel{\text{min}}} \times \frac{1\ \cancel{\text{min}}}{60\ \text{s}}$ |
| 3. As always, state the answer with units and round to the correct number of significant digits (in this case, three). | $= 15.3\ \frac{\text{m}}{\text{s}}$ <br> The answer is 15.3 m/s. |

## Graphing

In Figure i.4.3, a variable $y$ is plotted against a variable $x$. Variable $y$ is the **dependent** variable and variable $x$ is the **independent** variable. In this particular situation, the graph is a straight line. (You might say that variable $y$ is a **linear function** of the variable $x$.)

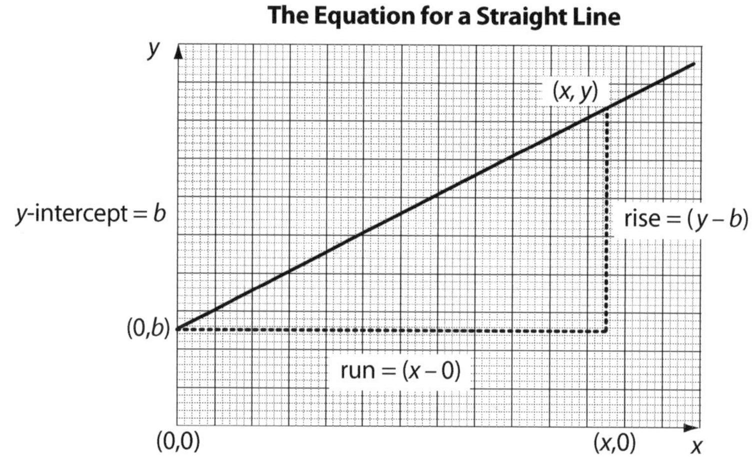


**Figure i.4.3** *In a straight line graph like this one, the variable y is a linear function of the variable x*

The **slope** of the graph is given the symbol $m$, where $m = \frac{\text{rise}}{\text{run}}$.

To find the value of the slope, the two points with coordinates $(0,b)$ and $(x, y)$ will be used. The value of $y$ where the graph intercepts the $y$-axis is called the ***y*-intercept**, and it is given the symbol $b$.

$$\text{Since } m = \frac{\text{rise}}{\text{run}} = \frac{(y-b)}{(x-0)},$$

Therefore, $mx = y - b$, or

$$y = mx + b$$

This is a general equation for any straight line. The slope of the line is $m$ and the $y$-intercept is $b$.

To write an equation for any straight-line graph, you need only determine the value of the $y$-intercept by inspection and the slope by calculation. You can then substitute these values into the general equation.

For the linear graph in Figure i.4.4, the $y$-intercept, by inspection, is 1.4. ($b = 1.4$) The **slope** is calculated using the two points with coordinates (0, 1.4) and (10.0, 4.4).

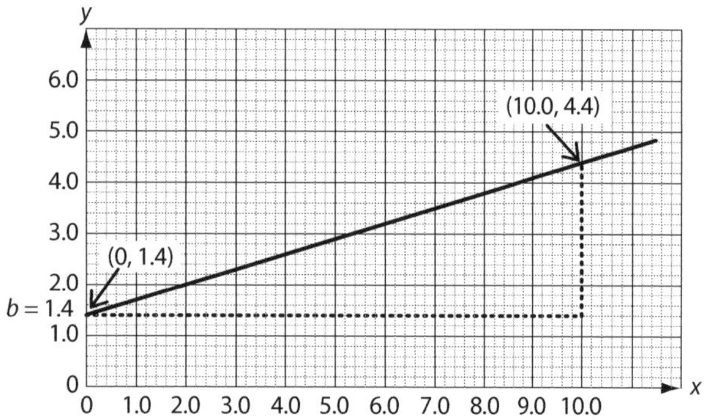


**Figure i.4.4** *The slope of a line can be calculated using just two points.*

$$m = \frac{(4.4 - 1.4)}{(10.0 - 0)} = \frac{3.0}{10.0} = 0.30$$

The equation for this straight line is therefore: $y = 0.30\,x + 1.4$

In these examples, the units of measure of the variables have not been included, in order to simplify the explanation. In experiments, the observations you make are frequently summarized in graphical form. When graphing experimental data, always include the measuring units and the specific symbols of the variables being graphed.

The three most common types of graphic relationships are shown in Figure i.4.5.

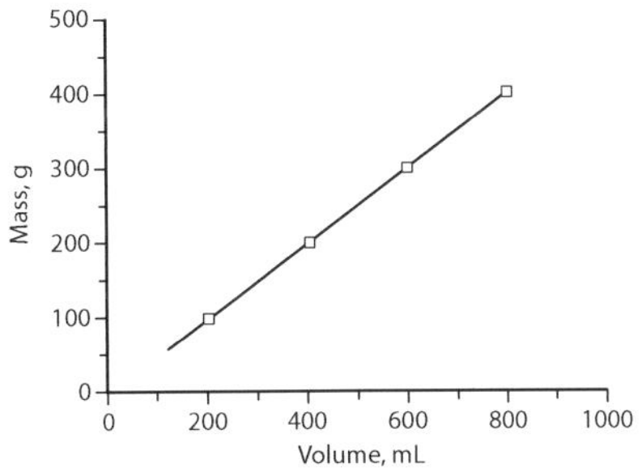


Direct: $y = mx$
($y$ and $x$ increase in direct proportion)

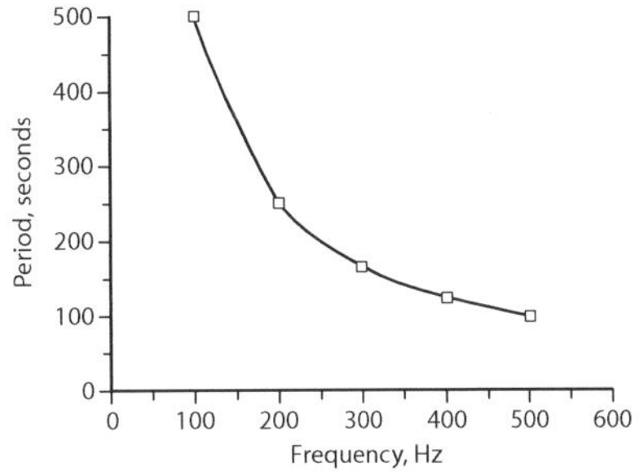


Inverse: $y = m/x$
(as $x$ increases, $y$ decreases)

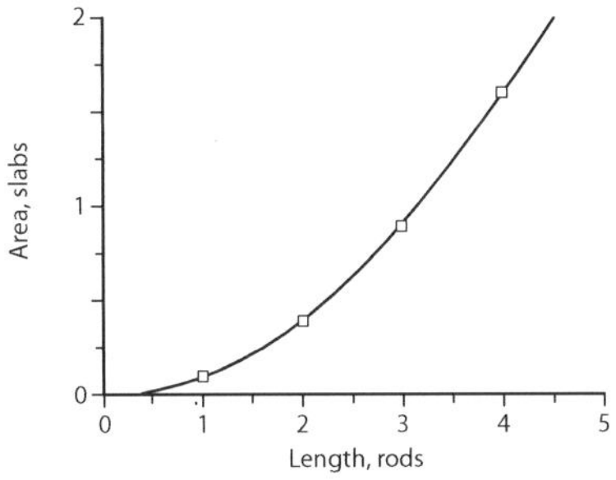


Exponential: $y = mx^n$
(as $x$ increases, $y$ increases more quickly)

**Figure i.4.5** *Three common types of graphic relationships*

## Sample Problem i.4.5 — Determination of a Relationship from Data

Find the relationship for the graphed data below:

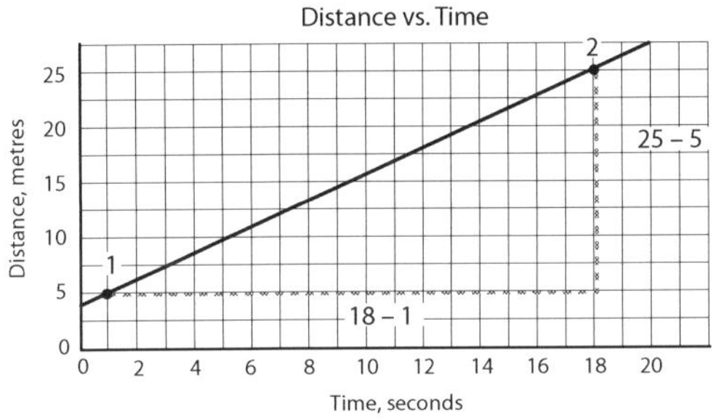


### What to Think About

1. Determine the slope for the straight line. To do this, select two points on the line of best fit. These should be points whose values are easy to determine on both axes. *Do not use data points* to determine the constant.
   Determine the change in $y$ ($\Delta y$) and the change in $x$ ($\Delta x$) including the units.
   The constant is $\Delta y / \Delta x$.

2. Determine the relationship by subbing the *variable names* and the constant into the general equation, $y = mx + b$.

   Often, a straight line graph passes through the origin, in which case, $y = mx$.

### How to Do It

$\Delta y$ is $25 - 5 = 20$ m
$\Delta x$ is $18 - 1 = 17$ s

$$\frac{20 \text{ m}}{17 \text{ s}} = 1.18 \text{ m/s}$$

distance = (1.18 m/s)time + 4.0 m.

## Practice Problems i.4.5 — Determination of a Relationship from Data

1. Examine the following graphs. What type of relationship does each represent? Give the full relationship described by graph (c).

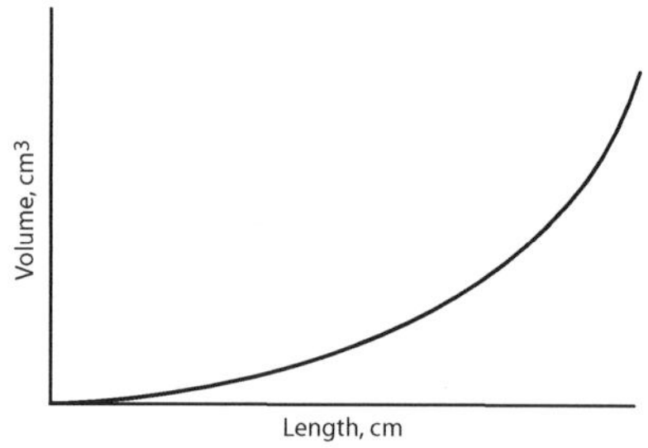


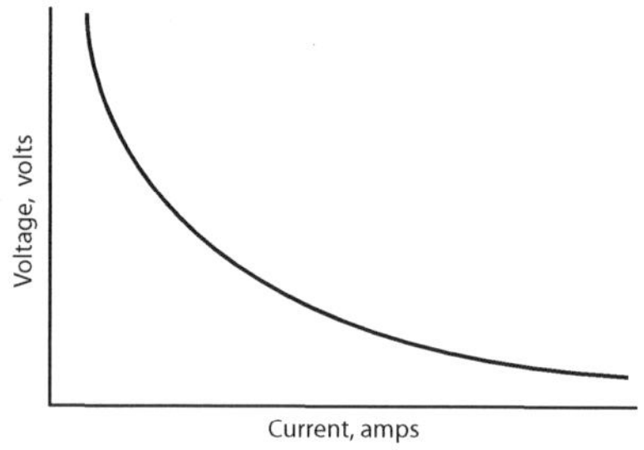


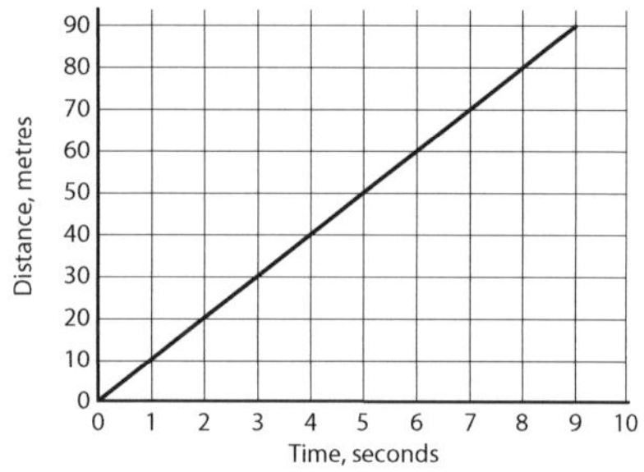


2. A beaker full of water is placed on a hotplate and heated over a period of time. The temperature is recorded at regular intervals. The following data was collected. Use the following grid to plot a graph of temperature against time. (Time goes on the *x*-axis.)

| Temperature (°C) | Time (min) |
|---|---|
| 22 | 0 |
| 30 | 2 |
| 38 | 4 |
| 46 | 6 |
| 54 | 8 |
| 62 | 10 |
| 70 | 12 |

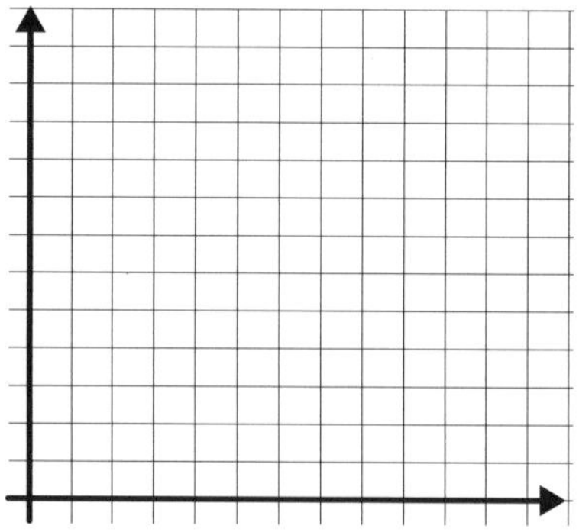

*Continued on the next page*

 

**Practice Problems i.4.5 — Determination of a Relationship from Data (Continued)**

(a) What type of relationship was studied during this investigation?

(b) What is the constant (be sure to include the units)?

(c) What temperature was reached at 5 min?

(d) Use the graph to determine the relationship between temperature and time.

(e) How long would it take the temperature to reach 80°C?

(f) What does the *y*-intercept represent?

(g) Give a source of error that might cause your graph to vary from that expected.

# i.5 Vectors

## Warm Up

Your teacher will place an object in the classroom. Use only written directions that could be used to verbally explain to someone who is blindfolded how to get from your chair to the object.

______________________________________________________________________________

______________________________________________________________________________

______________________________________________________________________________

## Introduction to Vectors

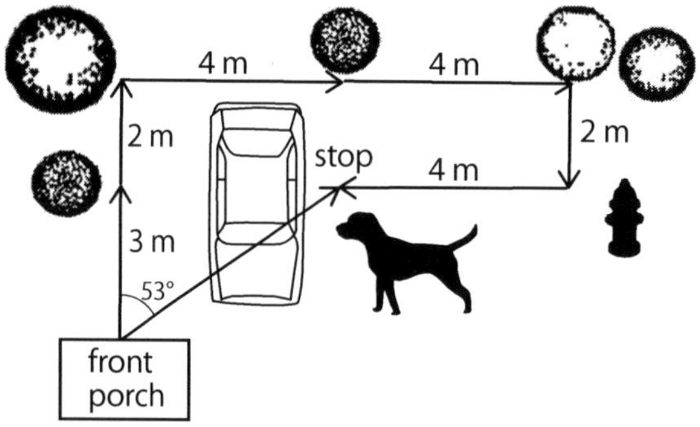


**Figure i.5.1** *Buddy's trip around the front yard*

In Figure i.5.1, notice a series of arrows drawn on the map of a physics teacher's front lawn. Each arrow shows the *magnitude* (size) and *direction* of a series of successive trips made by Buddy, the teacher's dog. Buddy was "doing his thing" before getting into the car for a trip to school. These arrows, showing both magnitude and direction of each of Buddy's displacements, are called **vectors**.

To identify the direction of vectors, two common conventions are used: numerical and compass. Sometimes compass directions are also called cardinal directions.

Numerical directions use a positive and negative sign to indicate direction. If you think of a graph, the "up" direction on the *y*-axis and the "right" direction on the *x*-axis are positive. "Down" on the *y*-axis and "left" on the *x*-axis is negative. For example, a person walking 2 km right is walking +2 km and a person walking 2 km left is walking −2 km. The sign indicates direction.

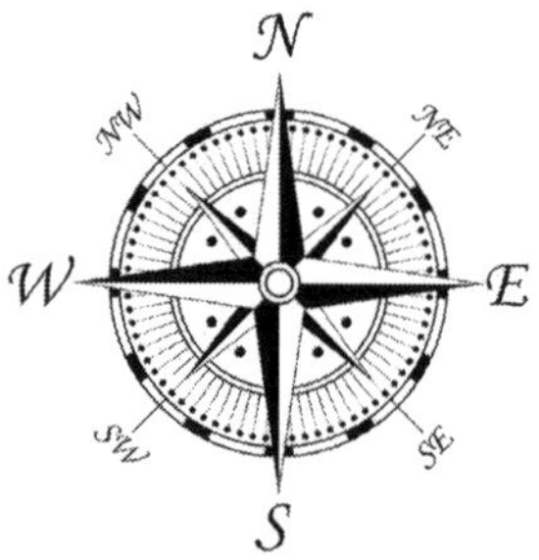


**Figure i.5.2** *The cardinal directions are north, east, south, and west, as shown on this compass.*

Compass or cardinal directions are another way of indicating vector directions. As Figure i.5.2 shows, there are four main directions on the compass: north, east, south, and west. North and east are usually positive, and south and west are negative. For example, if a person walking north encounters a person walking south, the two people are walking in opposite directions.

To determine the angle $\theta$, you use trigonometric ratios. Three trigonometric ratios are particularly useful for solving vector problems. In the right-angled triangle ABC, consider the angle labelled $\theta$. With reference to $\theta$, AC is the opposite side ($o$), BC is the adjacent side ($a$), and AB is the hypotenuse ($h$). In any right-angled triangle, the hypotenuse is always the side opposite to the right angle.

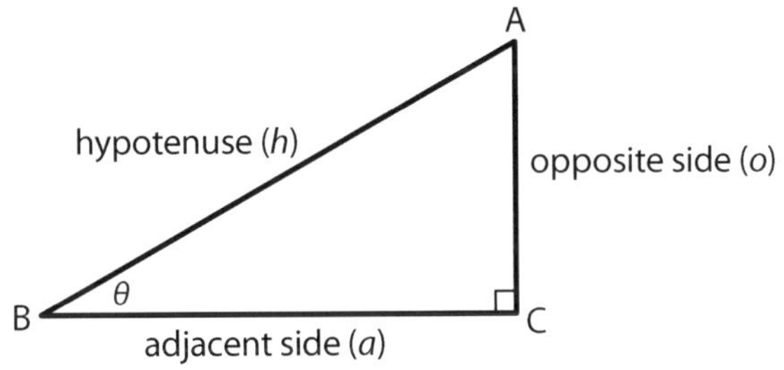


**Figure i.5.3** *The sides of a right-angled triangle are used to define trigonometric ratios.*

The three most commonly used trigonometric ratios are defined as follows:

$$\text{sine } \theta = \frac{\text{opposite side}}{\text{hypotenuse}} = \frac{o}{h}$$

$$\text{cosine } \theta = \frac{\text{adjacent side}}{\text{hypotenuse}} = \frac{a}{h}$$

$$\text{tangent } \theta = \frac{\text{opposite side}}{\text{adjacent side}} = \frac{o}{a}$$

Trigonometric ratios can help you solve vector problems quickly and accurately. Scientific calculators can provide you with the ratios for any angle.

Now, back to Figure i.5.1. When Buddy reaches his final spot near the car door, how far has he walked since he left the front porch? This question has two answers, depending on what "How far?" means. The distance Buddy has travelled is the arithmetic sum of all the short distances he has travelled between the shrubs, trees, and fire hydrant while he visited them. This is simple to calculate.

$$\text{total distance} = 3.0\text{ m} + 2.0\text{ m} + 4.0\text{ m} + 4.0\text{ m} + 2.0\text{ m} + 4.0\text{ m} = 19.0\text{ m}$$

If, however, you want to know how far Buddy has travelled from the porch, the bold line in Figure i.5.1, then you want to know Buddy's **displacement**. It turns out that Buddy's displacement from the front porch is 5.0 m. The bold arrow represents the magnitude (5.0 m) and the direction (53° to the right of his starting direction) of Buddy's displacement, and is called the **resultant displacement**. The resultant displacement is not the arithmetic sum, but the vector sum of the individual displacement vectors shown on the diagram.

There are two ways to indicate that a quantity is a vector quantity. The best way is to include a small arrow above the symbol for the vector quantity. For example, $\Delta\vec{d}$ symbolizes a displacement **vector**. If it's not possible to include the arrow when typing, a vector quantity may be typed in *bold italics*. For example, $\boldsymbol{\Delta d}$ also symbolizes a displacement **vector**. If only the magnitude of the vector is of importance, the symbol $\Delta d$ (no arrow or not bold) is used.

## Scalar and Vector Quantities

If you add 5 L of water to another 5 L of water, you end up with 10 L of water. Similarly, if you add 5 kg of salt to 5 kg of salt, you will have 10 kg of salt. Volumes and masses are added by the rules of ordinary arithmetic. Volume and mass are **scalar quantities**. Scalar quantities have magnitude (size) only. Other scalar quantities with which you may be familiar are: length, energy, density, and temperature.

If you add a 5 N force to another 5 N force, the two forces together *may* add up to 10 N, but they may also add up to 0 N or to any value between 0 N and 10 N! This is because forces have *direction* as well as magnitude. Quantities that have both direction and magnitude are called **vector quantities.** Forces and other vector quantities must be added by the special rules of **vector addition,** which take into account direction as well as magnitude.

In addition to forces, other vector quantities you will encounter in this course include: velocity, displacement, acceleration, momentum, electrical field strength and magnetic field strength.

When you describe velocity, displacement, acceleration, force, momentum, or any other vector quantity, you must specify both magnitude and direction.

## Watch Your Language

There are a few quantities where a different word is used for the scalar and the vector measurements. In day-to-day life, most people use one or both terms without wondering which term is correct. It is very important that you use them correctly from now on. This is important because some new concepts will seem much harder than they actually are if you use the terms incorrectly.

For now, there are two sets of scalar and vector quantities to focus on: distance and displacement, and speed and velocity. Distance and speed are scalar quantities. They only have an amount or magnitude. Think of a road sign that says 200 km to Vancouver or shows a speed limit of 30 km/h. Displacement and velocity are vector quantities and include both magnitude and direction. For example, to get to the arena, go 2 km [north].

## Adding Vectors

In Figure i.5.4, an object is hanging from a spring balance. Two forces pull on the object. Earth exerts a 10 N force of gravity downward on it, and the spring balance exerts a 10 N force up on it. Both Earth and the spring balance exert the same *size* of force on the object. The **net force** on the object is not 10 N or 20 N as one might expect. It is, in fact, 0 N!

To understand why the **net** or **resultant force** is zero in this situation, you must know (a) what a vector is and (b) how vectors are added.

 

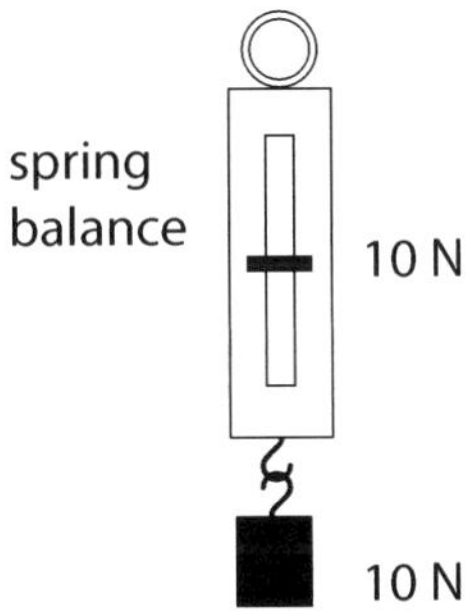


**Figure i.5.4** *The object hanging from this spring balance has forces acting on it in two directions, up and down.*

To show a vector, you must draw a line segment whose length is proportional to the magnitude of the quantity being represented. In Figure i.5.5, this quantity is a force. You draw a segment in the direction the quantity is acting, and place an arrow tip at one end of the line segment to show its direction. The line segment, drawn to an appropriate scale complete with arrow tip, is a **vector.**

Figure i.5.5 shows how the two forces in Figure i.5.4 can be represented with vectors. Figure i.5.5 (a) shows vectors representing the upward force $\vec{F}_1$ exerted by the spring balance and the downward gravitational force $\vec{F}_2$ individually. Figure i.5.5(b) shows the two forces added together by **vector addition**.

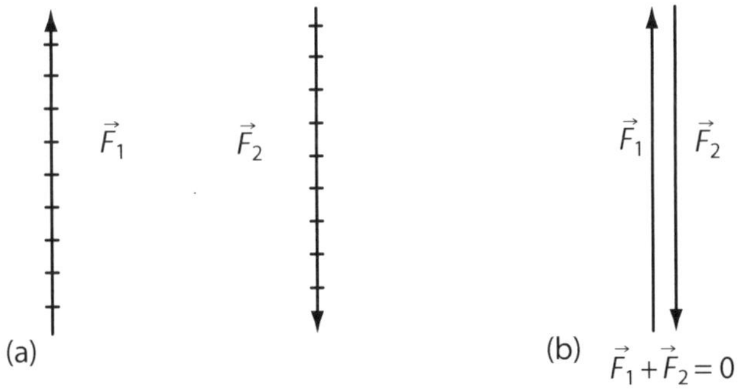


**Figure i.5.5** *Representing forces with vectors*

Note: There are two ways to indicate that a quantity is a vector quantity. In diagrams or in handwritten notes, a small arrow may be drawn above the symbol for the quantity. For example, $\vec{F}$ indicates that a force vector is being discussed. In some textbooks, the symbol for a vector quantity may be typed in ***bold italics***, like this: ***F***. This symbol also indicates that a force vector is being discussed. If only the *magnitude* of a vector is of importance, the symbol *F* (*italics*, but not bold) is used.

To add vector $\vec{F}_1$ to vector, $\vec{F}_2$ draw vector $\vec{F}_1$ first, to scale and in the proper direction. Then draw vector $\vec{F}_2$ so that its tail begins at the tip of vector $\vec{F}_1$ and the line segment of $\vec{F}_2$ points in the proper direction. Be sure to draw the tip of an arrow to show which way $\vec{F}_2$ points. The net or resultant force is the vector going from the tail of $\vec{F}_1$ to the tip of $\vec{F}_2$ .

In Figure i.5.5, the resultant is clearly zero. When two or more forces acting on a body have a resultant of zero, the body is said to be in **equilibrium.** In this example, $\vec{F}_2$ is a force that balances one or more other forces and creates a condition where there is no net force. This type of force is called the **equilibrant.**

In Figure i.5.6(a), strings connected to two different spring balances suspend a 10 N object. The strings form an angle of 120° where they are attached to the object. Notice that *both* scales read 10 N. Can the object possibly be in equilibrium if there are *two* 10 N forces pulling it up, and just *one* 10 N force pulling it down?

To find out what the **resultant** of the two upward forces is, use the rule for adding vectors again. In Figure i.5.6(b), vectors $\vec{F}_1$, $\vec{F}_2$, and $\vec{F}_3$ have been drawn acting at a single point where the three strings meet. The vectors are all drawn to a suitable scale and are aimed in the proper directions relative to one another.

Vector $\vec{F}_1$ (dashed line) has been added to vector $\vec{F}_2$. The tail of vector $\vec{F}_1$ starts at the tip of vector $\vec{F}_2$ and vector $\vec{F}_1$ is aimed in the direction it acts, which is 60° left of the vertical.

The resultant of $\vec{F}_1$ and $\vec{F}_2$ starts at the tail of $\vec{F}_2$, and ends at the tip of $\vec{F}_1$. The resultant is drawn with a bold line and is labeled $\vec{F}_R$. Notice that $\vec{F}_R$ is equal in magnitude but *opposite in direction* to $\vec{F}_3$. (You could call $\vec{F}_R$ the *equilibrant* of $\vec{F}_3$.)

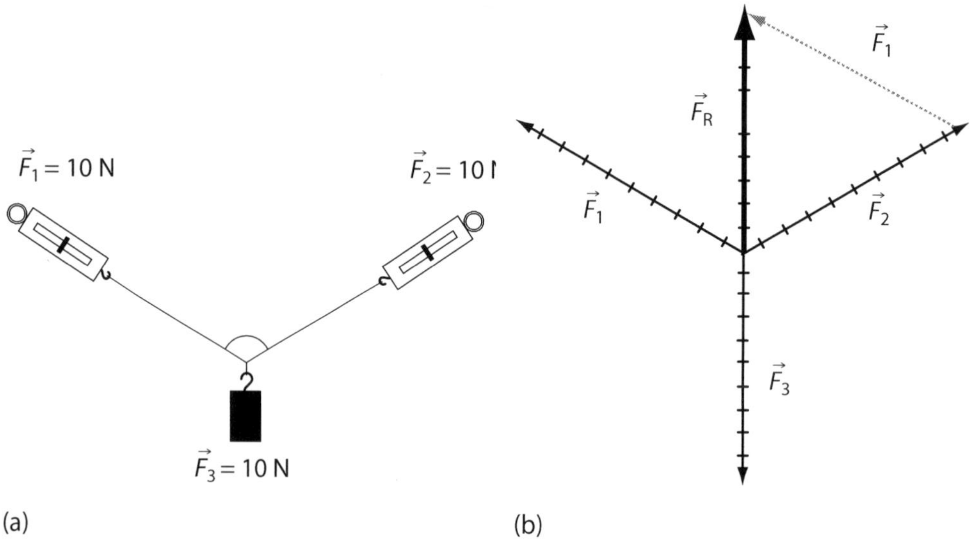


**Figure i.5.6** *Finding the resultant of two upward forces*

## Adding Three Vectors

Figure i.5.7 shows another way of looking at the vector situation you saw in Figure i.5.6(a). This time, all three forces have been added together by vector addition. The vector sum of the three forces is zero. The fact that the resultant force is zero should not surprise you. The point at which the three forces act was stationary, and you will recall that a body that is stationary will remain so if the net force on it is zero. This in consistent with Newton's first law of motion.

## Quick Check

1. What would the resultant be in Figure i.5.6(b) if you added $\vec{F}_2$ to $\vec{F}_1$ instead of $\vec{F}_1$ to $\vec{F}_2$ ?

2. What would the resultant be if you added $\vec{F}_R$ to $\vec{F}_3$ ?

3. (a) When you draw the three vectors in Figure i.5.6(b) tip to tail, what kind of triangle do you get?

   (b) What if the three forces were 6 N [E], 8 N [S], and 10 N. What kind of triangle would they form when added together?

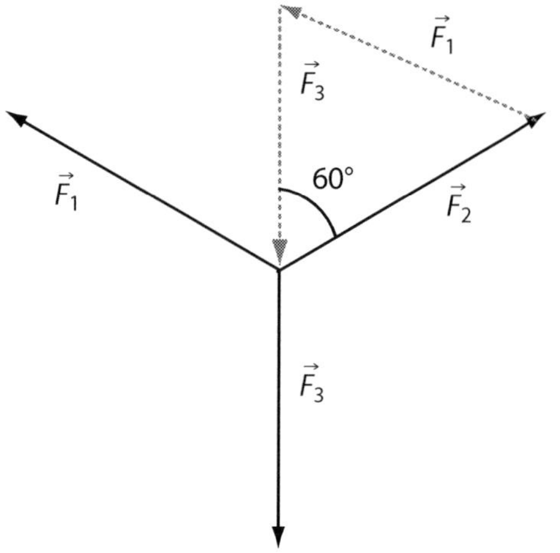


**Figure i.5.7** *In this example, the resultant force is zero.*

Two ways of writing the result of the vector analysis in Figure i.5.7 are:

$$(1)\ \vec{F}_1 + \vec{F}_2 + \vec{F}_3 = 0$$

and

$$(2)\ \Sigma F = 0$$

The symbol Σ means "the sum of." In this situation, it is the vector sum.

## Quick Check

1. In how many ways could you add the vectors $\vec{F}_1$, $\vec{F}_2$, and $\vec{F}_3$?

2. Would it make any difference to the resultant you obtain if you added the three force vectors in a different order?

3. Displacement vectors are added in the same way as force vectors or any other vectors. If a golfer hits a drive 240 m toward the north, then hits a horrible second shot 100 m to the east, what is the resultant displacement of her golf ball? (Draw the two displacements to some suitable scale and then find their resultant.)

*Quick Check continues*

4. A dancer does the following Physics Jig move: 3 steps north, 2 steps west, 5 steps east, and 7 steps south. What is his
   (a) resultant displacement?

   (b) total distance travelled?

## "Subtracting" Vectors

### Method 1

Sometimes, you will have to find the difference between two vectors. For example, if the velocity of a body changes from $\vec{v}_1$ to $\vec{v}_2$, you may need to calculate the *change in velocity,* $\Delta v$. A vector *difference* is defined as the vector *sum* of the second vector and the *negative* of the first vector:

$$v = \vec{v}_2 + (-1)\vec{v}_1$$

or

$$v = \vec{v}_2 - \vec{v}_1$$

When "subtracting" vectors, simply remember that the negative of any vector is a vector of the same magnitude (size) but pointing in the opposite direction. The difference of two vectors is the sum of the first vector and the *negative* of the second vector. See Figure i.5.8.

$$v = \vec{v}_2 - \vec{v}_1 = \vec{v}_2 + (-\vec{v}_1)$$

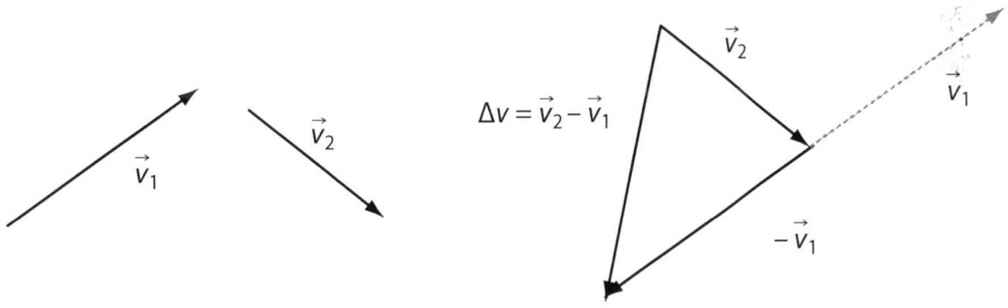


**Figure i.5.8** *Method 1 for "subtracting" vectors*

### Method 2

The difference between two vectors can also be found by drawing the vectors "tail to tail," as shown in Figure i.5.9. The resultant $\Delta v$ is the vector drawn from tip to tip. From Figure i.5.9,

$$\vec{v}_1 + v = \vec{v}_2$$

$$v = \vec{v}_2 - \vec{v}_1$$

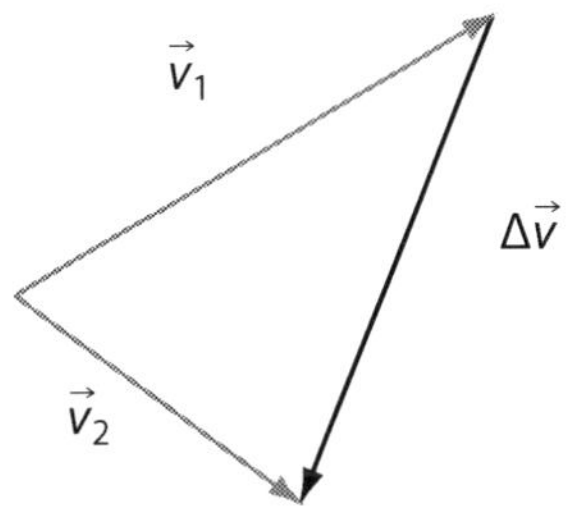


**Figure i.5.9** *Method 2 for "subtracting" vectors*

## i.5 Review Questions

1. Two boys are pulling a girl along on a toboggan. Each boy pulls on a rope attached to the same point on the front of the toboggan with a force of 360 N. Using a scale diagram, determine the resultant of the two forces exerted by the boys if their ropes form each of these angles with each other:

   (a) 0°

   (b) 60°

   (c) 120°

   (d) 180°

2. What is the *magnitude* of the resultant of the three forces acting at point X?

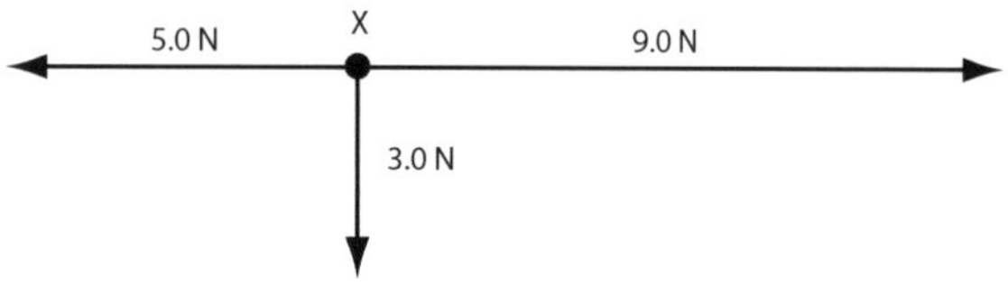


3. A football player is pushed by one opponent with a force of 50.0 N toward the east. At the same time, a second tackler pushes him with a force of 120.0 N toward the north. What is the magnitude and direction of the resultant force on the first player?

4. The following three forces act simultaneously on the same point: 100.0 N toward the north, 50.0 N toward the east, and 220.0 N toward the south. What will their resultant be?

# i.6 Vectors in Two Dimensions

## Warm Up

An airplane is flying north at 200 km/h. A 25 km/h wind is blowing from the east. Will this crosswind speed up, slow down, or have no effect on the plane? Defend your answer.

______________________________________________

______________________________________________

______________________________________________

### Defining Vector Components

Figure i.6.1 shows three ways you could travel from A to B. The vectors are displacement vectors. In each of the three "trips," the resultant displacement is the same.

$$\vec{D}_1 + \vec{D}_2 = \vec{D}_R$$

Any two or more vectors that have a resultant such as $\vec{D}_R$ are called **components** of the resultant vector. A vector such as $\vec{D}_R$ can be **resolved** into an endless number of component combinations. Figure i.6.1 shows just three possible combinations of components of $\vec{D}_R$.

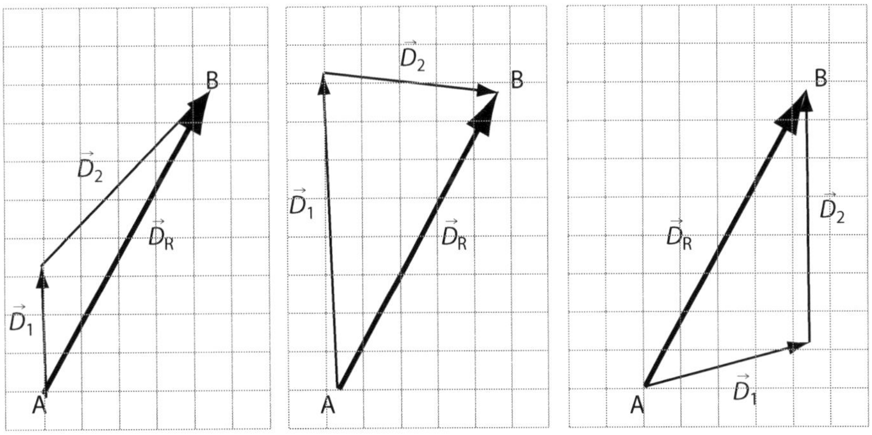


**Figure i.6.1** *Examples of possible components of* $\vec{D}_R$

## Trigonometric Ratios Used in Vector Problems

In many problems, the most useful way of resolving a vector into components is to choose components that are perpendicular to each other. Let's review trigonometric ratios so you can recall how to do this.

Three trigonometric ratios are particularly useful for solving vector problems. In the right-angled triangle ABC in Figure i.6.2, consider the angle labeled with the Greek symbol $\theta$ (theta). With reference to $\theta$, AC is the **opposite side**, BC is the **adjacent side**, and AB is the **hypotenuse**. In any right-angled triangle, the hypotenuse is always the side opposite to the right angle.

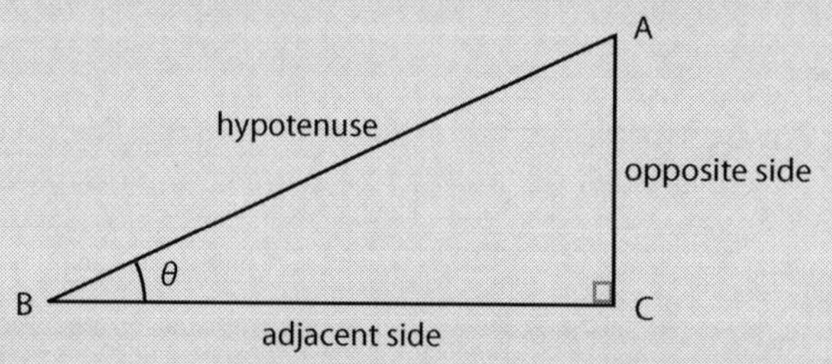


**Figure i.6.2** *A right-angled triangle with the labels you need to know for the trigonometric ratios you'll be using in vector problems*

The three most commonly used trigonometric ratios are defined as follows:

$$\textbf{sine}\ \theta = \frac{\text{opposite side}}{\text{hypotenuse}} = \frac{\text{o}}{\text{h}}$$

$$\textbf{cosine}\ \theta = \frac{\text{adjacent side}}{\text{hypotenuse}} = \frac{\text{a}}{\text{h}}$$

$$\textbf{tangent}\ \theta = \frac{\text{opposite side}}{\text{adjacent side}} = \frac{\text{o}}{\text{a}}$$

Trigonometric ratios, available with the push of a button from your calculator, can help you solve vector problems quickly. Following is a sample vector question involving velocities. The rules for adding velocity vectors are the same as those for displacement and force vectors or any other vector quantities.

 

## Resolving Vectors into Vertical and Horizontal Components

Figure i.6.3 shows one situation where it is wise to use perpendicular components.

In Figure i.6.3(a), a 60.0 N force is exerted down the handle of a snow shovel. The force that actually pushes the snow along the driveway is the **horizontal component** $\vec{F}_x$. The **vertical component** $\vec{F}_y$ is directed perpendicular to the road (Figure i.6.3(b)).

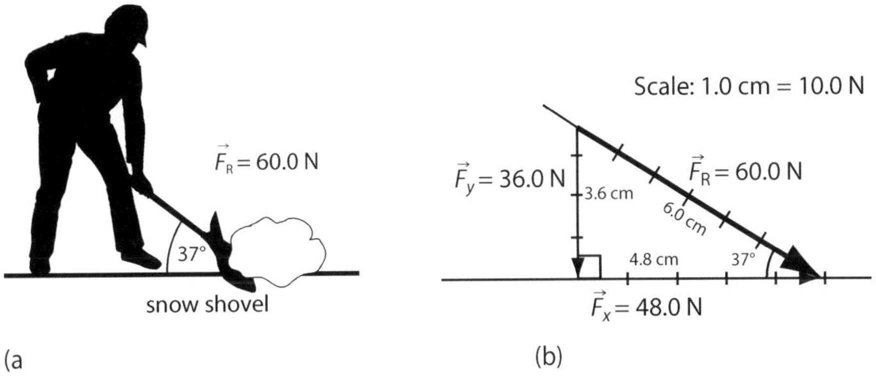


**Figure i.6.3** *The force the man exerts on the snow shovel can be resolved into horizontal and vertical components.*

## Method 1: Solving By Scale Diagram

To find out what the horizontal component $\vec{F}_x$ is, you can use a scale diagram like Figure i.6.3(b). First, draw a horizontal reference line. Then draw a line forming an angle of 37° with the horizontal reference line, because this is the angle formed by the snow shovel handle with the road.

Using a scale of 1.0 cm for each 10.0 N, draw a force vector to represent $\vec{F}_R$, where $\vec{F}_R$ = 60.0 N. Next, drop a line down from the tail of $\vec{F}_R$ meeting the horizontal reference line at an angle of 90°. This gives you both the vertical and the horizontal component forces. Label these $\vec{F}_y$ and $\vec{F}_x$, and place arrows on them to show their directions.

Since the horizontal component vector has a length of 4.8 cm, and each 1.0 cm represents 10.0 N, then $\vec{F}_x$ = 48.0 N. The vertical component vector is 3.6 cm long, therefore $\vec{F}_y$ = 36.0 N.

## Method 2: Resolve into Components

Figure i.6.3(b) shows the force vector $\vec{F}_R$ = 60 N at an angle of 37° to the surface or horizontal. This vector is then resolved into its vertical component $\vec{F}_y$ and horizontal component $\vec{F}_x$. How do we find the magnitude of these component vectors without the aid of a scale diagram?

Recall from your math class that the three angles in a triangle add up to 180°. (See, you would use that fact one day!) So, the unknown angle in Figure i.6.3 is 53°. Remember that a right angle is 90°. So the unknown angle is equal to 180 – (90° + 37°), which is 53°.

Then to find $\vec{F}_y$, we know $\vec{F}_R$ and the angle between $\vec{F}_R$ and $\vec{F}_y$. Using cos $\theta$, we can calculate $\vec{F}_y$:

$$\cos 53° = \frac{\vec{F}_y}{60}$$

$$\vec{F}_y = \cos 53° \times 60$$

$$\vec{F}_y = 36 \text{ N}$$

To find $\vec{F}_x$, we use sin $\theta$ to calculate the horizontal component:

$$\sin 53° = \frac{\vec{F}_x}{60}$$
$$\vec{F}_x = \sin 53° \times 60$$
$$\vec{F} = 48 \text{ N}$$

To check that we have the right answers, we use the Pythagorean theorem as the three vectors form a right angle triangle:

$$F_R = \sqrt{F_x^2 + F_y^2}$$
$$F_R = \sqrt{(36)^2 + (48)^2}$$
$$F_R = 60 \text{ N}$$

## More than One Vector: Using a Vector Diagram

Figure i.6.4 shows a typical force vector situation, where there are three forces acting, but no motion resulting. Two strings support a 36.0 N object. One string makes an angle of 30° with the vertical, and the other string is horizontal. The question is, "What is the tension in each string?" The tension in a string is simply the force exerted along the string. To find the answer to this question, we must first represent the forces in a vector diagram.

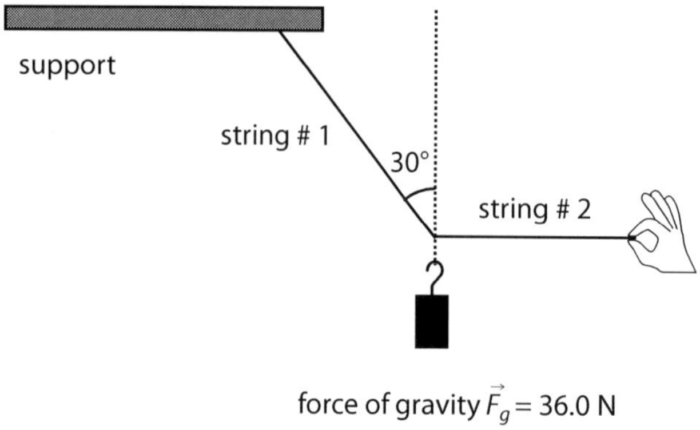


**Figure i.6.4** *Two strings support an object. You want to find the tension in each string.*

Figure i.6.5 shows one way to look at this problem. The 36.0 N object is not moving, so the three forces acting on it must have a resultant of zero. That means the vector sum of the three forces acting on the object is zero.

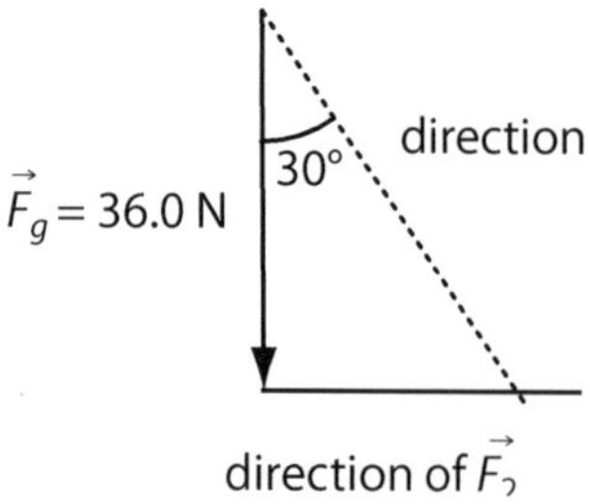


**Figure i.6.5** *Vector diagram representing the three forces acting on the object in Figure i.6.4*

The vector to draw first is the one for which you have the most complete information. You know that the force of gravity $\vec{F}_g$ has a magnitude of 36.0 N and is directed down.

You do *not* know the *magnitude* of the tension along string #1 ($\vec{F}_1$) but you know its *direction,* which is 30° to the vertical. You do *not* know the *magnitude* of the tension in string #2 ($\vec{F}_2$), but you know that it acts in a direction *perpendicular to* $\vec{F}_g$. You also know that vectors $\vec{F}_1$, $\vec{F}_2$, and $\vec{F}_g$ form a closed triangle since their resultant is zero.

In Figure i.6.5, dashed lines show the directions of $\vec{F}_1$ and $\vec{F}_2$. To complete the vector triangle of forces, arrows must be added to show that $\vec{F}_1$ ends at the tail of $\vec{F}_g$, and $\vec{F}_2$ starts at the tip of $\vec{F}_g$. If $\vec{F}_g$ has been drawn to scale, then both $\vec{F}_1$ and $\vec{F}_2$ will have the same scale.

Figure i.6.6 shows what the completed vector diagram looks like. To solve for tension forces $\vec{F}_1$ and $\vec{F}_2$, you must know to what scale $\vec{F}_g$ was drawn. In the next sample problem, the tension will be found using this diagram and components.

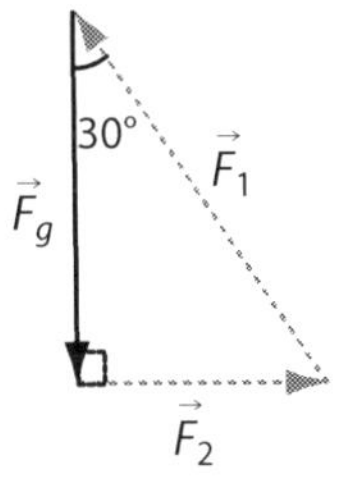


**Figure i.6.6** *Completed vector diagram from Figure i.6.5*

## Sample Problem i.6.1 — Using a Vector Diagram

Use components to find the tension in the two strings shown in Figure i.6.4.

### What to Think About

1. Draw a vector diagram to identify all the forces in the problem.
2. Identify what to solve.
3. For $\vec{F}_1$, find the horizontal and vertical components and use the Pythagorean theorem to solve for $\vec{F}_1$.

### How to Do It

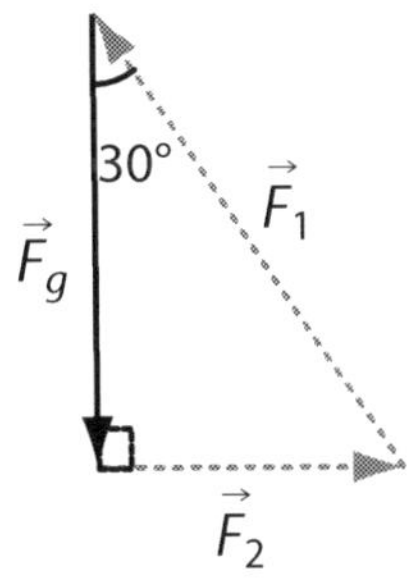


Find $\vec{F}_1$ and $\vec{F}_2$

$$\cos 30° = \frac{\vec{F}_g}{\vec{F}_1} = \frac{36.0\text{ N}}{\vec{F}_1}$$

$$\vec{F}_1 = \frac{36.0\text{ N}}{\cos 30°} = 41.6\text{ N}$$

*Sample Problem continued*

## Sample Problem i.6.1 — Using a Vector Diagram (Continued)

| What to Think About | How to Do It |
|---|---|
| 4. Repeat for $\vec{F}_2$. | $\tan 30° = \frac{\vec{F}_2}{36.0\text{ N}}$<br>$F_2 = (\tan 30°)(36.0\text{ N})$<br>$F_2 = 20.8\text{ N}$ |
| 5. Check that $\vec{F}_g = \vec{F}_1 + \vec{F}_2$. | $\vec{F}_g = \vec{F}_1 + \vec{F}_2$<br>$F_g = \sqrt{(41.6\text{ N})^2 - (20.8\text{ N})^2}$<br>$F_g = 36.0\text{ N}$ |

## Practice Problems i.6.1 — Using a Vector Diagram

1. The graph below shows three force vectors.

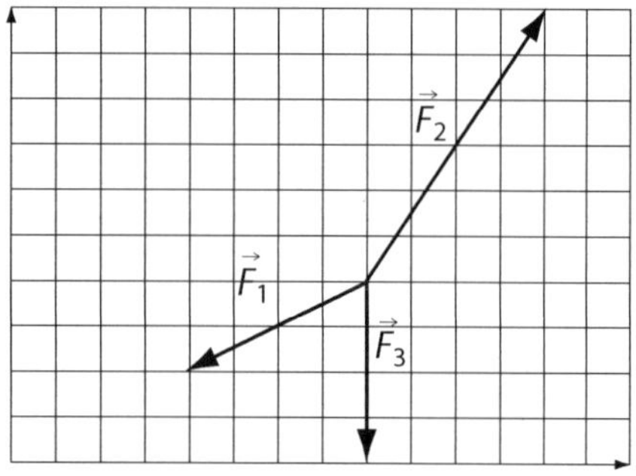


(a) What is the resultant of the three force vectors, added "head-to-tail"?

(b) What is the resultant of the three horizontal components?

(c) What is the resultant of the three vertical components?

*Practice Problems continued*

## Practice Problems i.6.1 — Using a Vector Diagram (Continued)

2. Using the empty graph below (b) and by any logical method, find the force $F_4$ that must be added to $F_1$, $F_2$, and $F_3$ (shown in (a)) to obtain a resultant of zero.

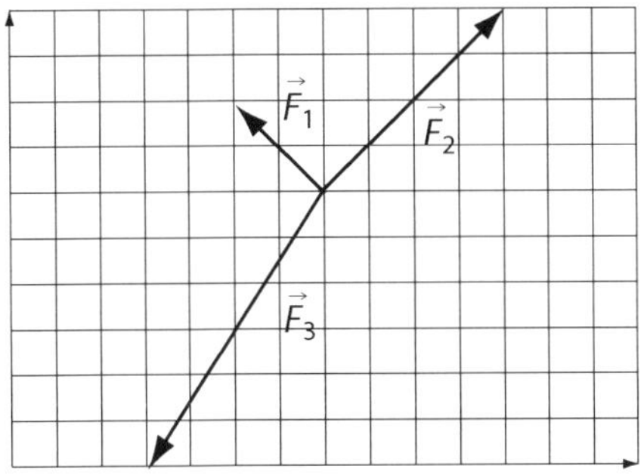


(a)

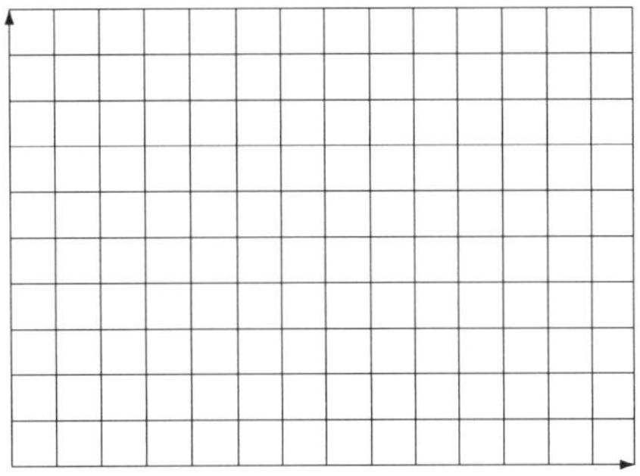

(b)

3. A dedicated physics student pulls his brand new shiny red wagon along a level road such that the handle makes an angle of 50° with the horizontal road. If he pulls on the handle with a force of 85 N, what is the horizontal component of the force he exerts along the handle? Draw a neat, labeled vector diagram. Use a scale of 1.0 cm for every 10.0 N. Why is the horizontal component more useful information than the force he exerts along the handle?

### A Velocity Vector Problem — Vectors in Action!

It might not seem at first glance to be a vector problem, but a boat crossing a river or a plane flying into a strong wind are both examples of more than one vector acting on an object. Commonly called boat or airplane vector problems in physics, these situations involve the object moving through a medium that is also moving. For a boat, this medium is the river that has a current and, for an airplane, it is the air.

Both water and air are mediums that have a velocity and can be represented with a vector. This motion is usually compared to a reference point like the ground. For example, a person watching a boat cross a river observes the boat's motion as a combination of boat speed and river speed. A person in the boat experiences only the boat's speed. This is an example of relative motion. The motion observed is relative to where the person is located.

Let's first look at a motorboat crossing a river. In Figure i.6.7 an observer sees the boat crossing the river at an angle. This is the boat's speed relative to the ground. But a person in the boat measures the speed of the boat relative to the water. This is the boat's speed relative the water. And the current, which is pushing the boat, is the speed of the water relative to the ground. This is summarized in Figure i.6.8. Now we can apply this to a boat vector problem.

**Problem:** A motorboat operator is trying to travel across a fast-moving river, as shown in Figure i.6.7. Although he aims his boat directly across the stream, the water carries the boat to the right. If the boat's resultant velocity, as seen by an observer on the bank, is 15.0 m/s in the direction shown, how fast is the boat moving

(a) in a direction downstream?

(b) in a direction across the river?

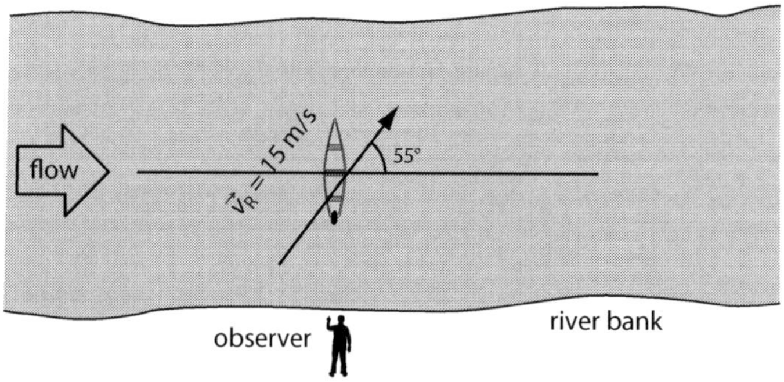


**Figure i.6.7** *The boat is aiming straight across for the shore but is moving diagonally because of the river's current.*

**Solution:** Consider the resultant velocity to have two component velocities: $\vec{v}_y$, the boat's velocity relative to the water, and $\vec{v}_x$, the water's velocity relative to the bank.

Component $\vec{v}_y$ is directed across the river, perpendicular to the bank, while component $\vec{v}_x$ is directed down the stream. For your vector diagram, only a neat sketch is needed, since you will be using trigonometric ratios rather than a scale diagram. See Figure i.6.8.

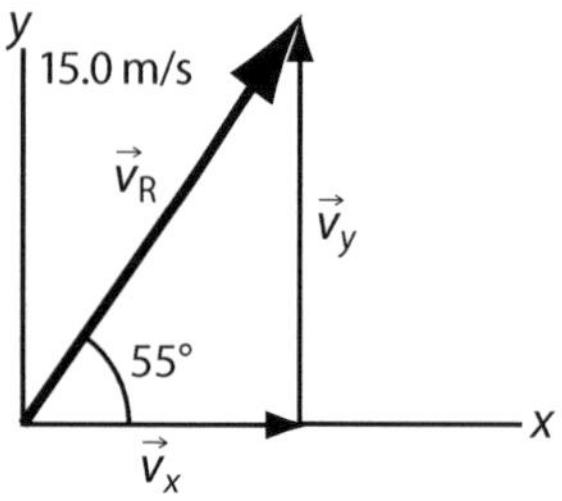


**Figure i.6.8** *Vector diagram showing the direction of the boat*

To solve for $\vec{v}_y$, use

$$\sin 55° = \frac{v_y}{15 \text{ m/s}}$$

$$\vec{v}_y = (15.0 \text{ m/s})(\sin 55°) = (15.0 \text{ m/s})(0.8192) = 12.3 \text{ m/s}$$

To solve for $\vec{v}_x$, use

$$\cos 55° = \frac{v_x}{15 \text{ m/s}}$$

$$\vec{v}_x = (15.0 \text{ m/s})(\cos 55°) = (15.0 \text{ m/s})(0.5736) = 8.60 \text{ m/s}$$

To summarize:

| | | |
|---|---|---|
| Velocity of the boat relative to the ground | $\vec{v}_R$ | 15.0 m/s |
| Velocity of the boat relative to the water | $\vec{v}_B$ or $\vec{v}_y$ | 12.3 m/s |
| Velocity of the water relative to the ground | $\vec{v}_C$ or $\vec{v}_x$ | 8.60 m/s |

An airplane vector problem is similar except, instead of water flowing down a river, you must consider wind speed that can come from any direction. The simplest situation is a plane flying with the wind in the same direction (tail wind) or in the opposite direction (head wind). While the plane will have an air speed, which is the speed of the plane relative to the air around it, a person from the ground would see the ground speed being a combination of air speed and wind speed. Figure i.6.9 demonstrates both of these situations.

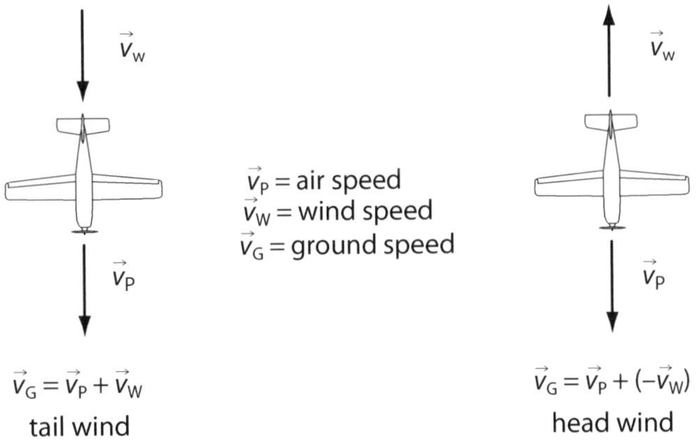


**Figure i.6.9** *The effects of a tail wind and a head wind on an airplane's velocity*

Now, what happens if the wind is moving at an angle to the plane?

## Sample Problem i.6.2 — Relative Motion

What is the ground speed of a plane flying 200 km/h north if the wind is blowing from the east at 40.0 km/h?

| What to Think About | How to Do It |
|---|---|
| 1. Identify what you know and what you are solving. | $\vec{v}_P = 200$ km/h [N]<br>$\vec{v}_W = 40.0$ km/h [W]<br>$\vec{v}_G = ?$ |
| 2. Represent the problem with a diagram. | 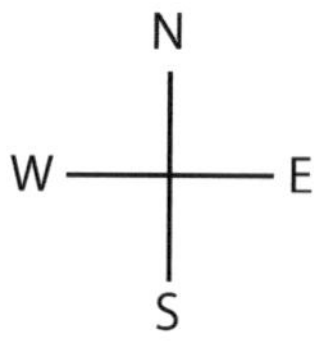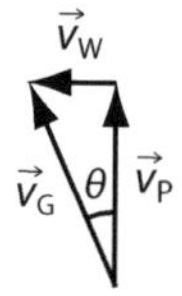 |
| 3. Solve using the Pythagorean theorem. | $\vec{v}_G = \vec{v}_P + \vec{v}_W$<br>$v_G = \sqrt{(200\text{ km/h})^2 + (40\text{ km/h})^2}$<br>$v_G = 204$ km/h<br>$\text{Tan } \theta = \frac{40}{200}$<br>$\theta = 11°$ W of N |

## Practice Problems i.6.2 — Relative Motion

1. What is the tailwind a plane experiences if the groundspeed is 350 km/h and the air speed is 320 km/h?

2. A plane flying 275 km/h [W] experiences a 25 km/h [N] wind. At what angle does an observer see the plane flying?

3. What airspeed would a plane have to travel to have a groundspeed of 320 km/h [S] if there is a 50.0 km/h wind coming from the northwest?

## i.6 Review Questions

1. It is 256 m across the river in Figure i.6.7, measured directly from bank to bank.
   (a) If you wished to know how much time it would take to cross the river, which of the three velocity vectors would you use to obtain the answer most directly?

   (b) What is the magnitude of this vector?

   (c) How long would it take to cross the river?

2. You wish to calculate how far down the bank the boat in Figure i.6.7 will land when it reaches the other side.
   (a) Which velocity vector will give you the answer most directly?

   (b) What is the magnitude of this vector?

   (c) How far down the bank will the boat travel?

3. You absolutely *must* land your boat directly across from your starting point. This time, your resultant velocity will be 15.0 m/s, but in a direction straight across the river. In what direction will you have to aim the boat to end up straight across from your starting point?

4. A girl is mowing her lawn. She pushes down on the handle of the mower with a force of 78 N. If the handle makes an angle of 40° with the horizontal, what is the horizontal component of the force she exerts down the handle?

5. A hunter walks 225 m toward the north, then 125 m toward the east. What is his resultant displacement?

6. An airborne seed falls to the ground with a steady terminal velocity of 0.48 m/s. The wind causes it to drift to the right at 0.10 m/s. What is the magnitude and direction of the resultant velocity?

7. A helium balloon is released and rises with a steady vertical velocity of 12 km/h. A wind from the east blows the balloon toward the west at 18 km/h.
(a) What is the resultant velocity of the balloon?

(b) How far west will the balloon drift in five minutes?

8. (a) In the diagram below, what horizontal force must the boy exert to hold his friend on the swing still?

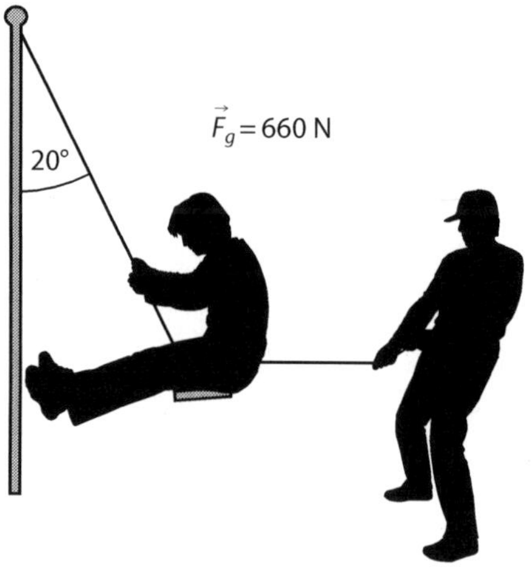


(b) What is the tension in each of the two ropes of the motionless swing, if the two ropes share the load equally?

9. A hockey player is moving north at 15 km/h. A body check changes her velocity to 12 km/h toward the west. Calculate the change in velocity of the hockey player

# Investigation i-1 Measuring the Frequency of a Recording Timer

### Purpose

To measure the frequency of a recording timer and calculate its period

### Procedure

1. Load the recording timer with a fresh piece of carbon paper. Pass a piece of ticker tape through the guiding staples, so that the carbon side of the paper faces the ticker tape. When the timer arm vibrates, it should leave a black mark on the tape.
2. To measure the frequency of the recording timer, you must determine how many times the arm swings in 1 s. Since it is difficult to time 1 s with any reasonable accuracy, let the timer run for 5 s, as precisely as you can measure it, then count the number of carbon dots made on the tape and divide by 5. Practise moving the tape through the timer until you find a suitable speed that will spread the dots out for easy counting, but do not waste ticker tape.
3. When you are ready, start the tape moving through the timer. Have your partner start the timer and the stopwatch simultaneously. Stop the timer when 5 s have elapsed. Count the number of dots made in 5 s and then calculate the frequency of your timer in hertz (Hz).

### Concluding Questions

1. What was the frequency of your recording timer in Hz?
2. Estimate the possible error in the timing of your experiment. (It might be 0.10 s, 0.20 s, or whatever you think is likely.) Calculate the percent possible error in your timing. To do this, simply divide your estimate of the possible error in timing by 5.0 s and then multiply by 100.

   Example: If you estimate your timing error to be 0.50 s, then

   $$\text{percent possible error in timing} = \frac{0.50\text{ s}}{5.0\text{ s}} \times 100\% = 10\%$$

3. Your calculated frequency will have the same percent possible error as you calculated for your timing error. Calculate the range within which your timer's frequency probably falls.

   Example: If you calculate the frequency to be 57 Hz, and the possible error is 10%, then the range is 57 Hz $\pm$ 5.7 Hz, or between 51.3 Hz and 62.7 Hz. Rounded off, the range is between 51 Hz and 63 Hz. You might therefore conclude that the frequency of your timer is 57 $\pm$ 6 Hz.

4. If your timer operates on household voltage, its frequency (in North America) should be 60 Hz. Is 60 Hz within your estimated range for your timer?
5. (a) What is the period of your timer?
   (b) How many dots on the ticker tape represent
   (i) 1.0 s?
   (ii) 0.10 s?

# Investigation i-2 Making a Pendulum Clock

## Purpose

To learn how a pendulum can be used as a clock

## Procedure

1. Prepare a simple pendulum by tying a string to a pendulum bob, either a large washer, as in the image below or a drilled metal ball. Feed the string through the opening of the pendulum support. Avoid winding the string around the support rod. If you do this, the length of the pendulum changes during a swing.

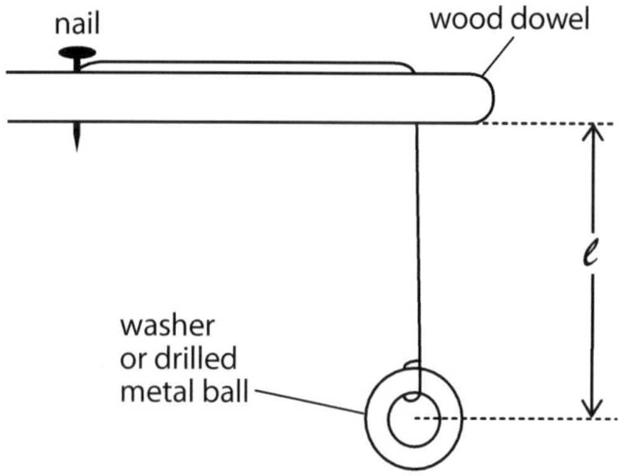


**Setup for Investigation i-2**

2. Start by adjusting the length *l* of the pendulum so that it is as close to being 10.00 cm as you can make it. Measure *l* from the bottom of the pendulum clamp to the centre of the bob, as shown in the image above.
3. Push the bob a small distance, about 2 cm, to one side and let it swing freely. To get a rough idea of how long the pendulum takes to make one swing, use a stopwatch to measure the time it takes for the bob to swing from the highest point on one side of the swing to the highest point on the other side, then back to its starting position. The time it takes the pendulum bob to complete a full swing like this is called the period (*T*) of the pendulum. Try measuring the period of one swing several times with your stopwatch. Why do you think your measurements are so inconsistent?
4. To obtain a more reliable measurement of the period of the pendulum, you will now measure the time for a large number of swings (50) and find the average time for one swing by dividing by 50. Set your 10.00 cm pendulum swinging through a small arc, as before. Start counting backward (3, 2, 1, <u>0</u>, 1, 2, 3, 4, etc.) and start your stopwatch at 0. Stop your watch after 50 swings and record the time your pendulum took to complete 50 swings.
5. To figure out the period of the pendulum, divide the time for 50 swings by 50.0. Record the period, *T*, in your table similar to the Table on the next page. Check your result by repeating the measurement. If necessary, repeat a third time.

6. Measure the period of your pendulum for each of the lengths and record them in the Table below.
7. Prepare a graph with headings and labels like those in graph below. In this experiment, the period of the pendulum depends on its length, so the period is called the **dependent variable.** The dependent variable goes on the *y*-axis. Length is the **independent variable.** We chose what its values would be. Length is on the *x*-axis. Plot period against length using all your data from the Table below. Use a small dot with a circle around it to make each position more visible. See graph below for a sample point. When you have plotted all the points, draw one smooth curve through as many of the points as possible. If one or two points are obvious errors, ignore them when drawing your curve.
8. Make pendulums with the lengths you obtain from your graph for pendulums with periods of 1.0 s and 2.0 s. See if the lengths predicted by the graph actually do produce 1.0 s and 2.0 s "clocks."

**Data Table**

| **Length of Pendulum,** $\ell$ (cm) | **Time for 50 Swings** (s) | **Time for 1 Swing, Period,** *T* (s) |
|---|---|---|
| 10.00 | | |
| 15.00 | | |
| 20.00 | | |
| 25.00 | | |
| 30.00 | | |
| 40.00 | | |
| 50.00 | | |
| 60.00 | | |
| 70.00 | | |
| 80.00 | | |
| 90.00 | | |
| 100.0 | | |

Period vs. Length of a Pendulum

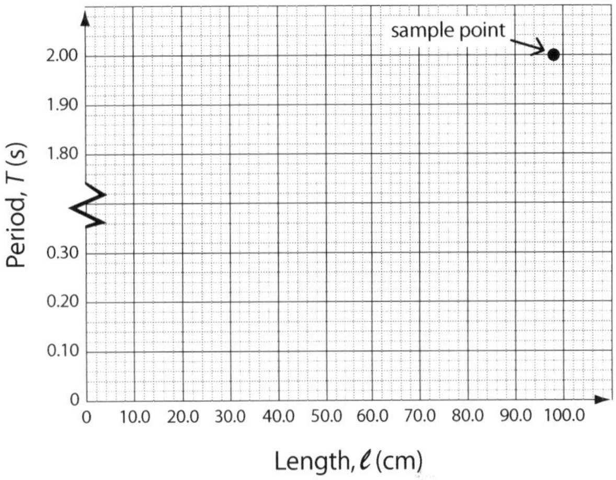


## Concluding Questions

1. According to your graph of period vs. length, how long must your pendulum be if it is to be used as (a) a "one-second clock"? (b) a "two-second clock"? (Such a pendulum takes 1s to swing one way, and one second to swing back.)
2. To increase the period of your pendulum from 1 s to 2 s, by how many times (to the nearest whole number) must you increase its length?

## Challenges

1. Predict what length a 3.0 s pendulum clock would have to be. Test your prediction by experiment.
2. Predict what will happen to the period of a pendulum if you double the mass of the pendulum bob. Test your prediction.

# 1 Kinematics

This chapter focuses on the following AP Physics 1 Big Ideas from the College Board:

**BIG IDEA 3:** The interactions of an object with other objects can be described by forces.

By the end of this chapter, you should know the meaning to these **key terms**:

- acceleration
- average velocity
- constant acceleration
- displacement
- distance
- final velocity
- initial velocity
- instantaneous velocity
- projectile motion
- scalar quantity
- speed
- vector quantity
- velocity

By the end of the chapter, you should be able to use and know when to use the following formulae:

$v = \frac{\Delta d}{\Delta t}$ $a = \frac{\Delta v}{\Delta t}$ $d = \bar{v}t$ $v = v_0 + at$

$\bar{v} = \frac{v + v_0}{2}$ $d = v_0 t + \frac{1}{2}at^2$ $v^2 = v_0^2 + 2ad$

*A roller coaster is an exciting example of kinematics in action.*

# 1.1 Speed and Velocity

## Warm Up

Imagine you are on a hike from a parking lot to a waterfall 2 km away. Is there a way you could describe to someone that the hike was 4 km long and 0 km long? Explain your answer.

___

___

___

___

### The Study of Motion

How far did it travel? How long did it take? How fast did it move? Did it speed up or slow down? These are typical questions one might ask about any object that moves, whether it is a car, a planet, an electron, or a molecule. All of these questions fall under the heading of **kinematics:** the study of the motion of objects, without reference to the cause of the motion. In kinematics, we learn how to describe the motion of objects in terms of measurable variables such as time, distance, speed, and acceleration.

### Distance and Displacement

When you take a trip a road sign will tell you the distance you have to travel to reach your destination. This distance is usually measured in kilometres. Other distances you are familiar with include metres, centimeters, and millimetres. Each of these measurement units tells you how far two points are apart. Because magnitude, or amount of distance covered, and not direction is stated, distance is a scalar quantity. The symbol for distance is *d*.

In the vector section, two methods for determining direction were described. The first method involved the use of positive (+) and negative (–) signs to indicate direction. Any motion right or up is usually considered positive. Any motion left or down is usually considered negative. The second method uses compass points. North and east are usually considered positive, and west and south are negative. Sometimes this can change depending on the question. For example if all the motion is downward, you may consider using down as positive so the math calculations do not involve negative signs.

When a direction is added to a distance, the position of an object or person is described. For example, if you are 5 km [east] of your home you are describing your position. **Position** is the shortest distance between the origin and where the person or object is located. Position is a vector quantity and includes magnitude and direction. The symbol for position is $\vec{d}$.

If you change your position by moving another position 5 km [east] of your original position, then you have a displacement. **Displacement** is a change in position and is a straight line between initial and final positions. It includes magnitude and direction. The symbol for displacement is $\Delta\vec{d}$. It is calculated by determining the change from one position to another. Or put mathematically:

$$\Delta\vec{d} = \vec{d}_f - \vec{d}_0$$

The $\Delta$ sign is important because it indicates a change. In this situation, displacement is defined as the change between the initial position and final position, not the displacement from the origin, which is your home.

**Sample Problem 1.1.1 — Calculating Displacement**

A person is 2.0 m to the left of a viewpoint sign enjoying the view. She moves 4.5 m to the right of the sign to get a better view. What is the person's displacement?

| What to Think About | How to Do It |
| --- | --- |
| 1. Assume right is positive and identify the positions. | $\vec{d}_o = 2.0 \text{ m [left]} = -2.0 \text{ m}$<br>$\vec{d}_f = 4.5 \text{ m [right]} = 4.5 \text{ m}$ |
| 2. Find the displacement. | $\Delta\vec{d} = \vec{d}_f - \vec{d}_o$<br>$\Delta\vec{d} = 4.5 \text{ m} - (-2.0 \text{ m})$<br>$= 6.5 \text{ m}$<br><br>The person's displacement is 6.5 m [right] |

**Practice Problems 1.1.1 — Calculating Displacement**

1. A woman walking her dog travels 200 m north, then 400 m west, then 500 m south.
   (a) What was the total distance she travelled?

   (b) What was the magnitude of her displacement for the entire trip?

*Continued on the next page*

## Practice Problems 1.1.1 — Calculating Displacement (Continued)

2. The diagram below shows the displacements of a golf ball caused by a rookie golfer attempting to reach hole number 7 on Ocean View Golf and Country Club. The golfer requires six shots to put the ball in the hole. The diagram shows the six displacements of the ball.

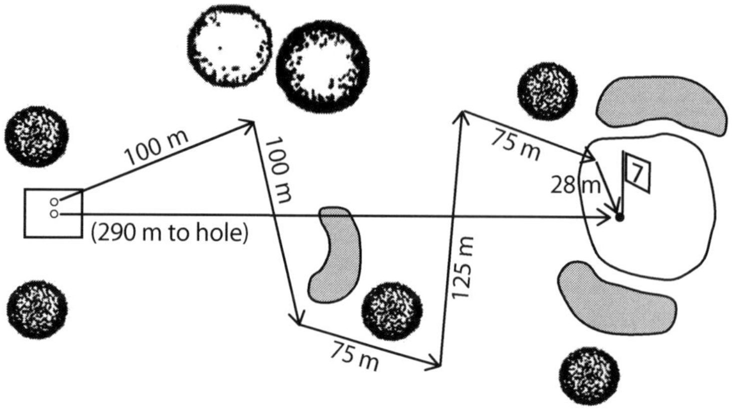


(a) What is the total distance the golf ball travelled while the golfer was playing the seventh hole?

(b) What is the resultant displacement of the ball?

3. What is the total distance and displacement the dog (*aka Buddy*) takes after it leaves the front porch?

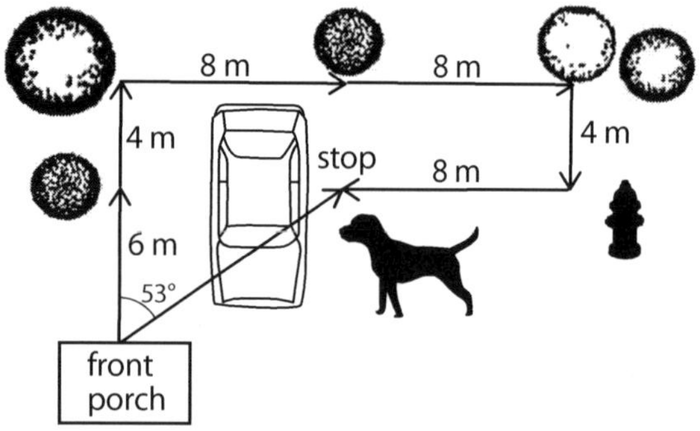

## Speed

The **speed** of an object such as a car is defined as the distance it travels in a unit of time. For highway traffic, speeds are measured in kilometres per hour (km/h). Typical highway speed limits are 80 km/h, 100 km/h, and 120 km/h. Within city limits, speed limits may be 60 km/h, 50 km/h, or 30 km/h (school zone or playground). The average speed of an athlete in a 100 m dash might be approximately 9.0 m/s. The speed of sound is 330 m/s, while the speed of light is approximately 300 000 000 m/s or 300 000 km/s.

If you make a long journey by car, you might be interested in calculating your **average speed** for the trip. For example, if you travel a distance of 450 km in a time of 6.0 h, you would calculate your average speed by dividing the total distance by the total time.

$$\text{average speed} = \frac{\text{total distance}}{\text{total time}} = \frac{450\text{ km}}{6.0\text{ h}} = 75\text{ km/h}$$

The symbol used for speed is *v*, and for average speed, $\bar{v}$. Note that it is a line above the *v* is not an arrow. The formula for calculating average speed from distance (*d*) and time (*t*) is therefore:

$$\bar{v} = \frac{d}{t}$$

If you are driving along the highway and spot a police car parked beside the road with its radar aimed at your car, you will be less interested in your average speed and more concerned with your **instantaneous speed**. That is how fast your car is going at this instant in time! Your speedometer will indicate what your instantaneous speed is.

### Quick Check

1. (a) What is the difference between average speed and instantaneous speed?

   (b) Under what condition may average speed and instantaneous speed be the same?

2. A tourist travels 320 km in 3.6 h. What is her average speed for the trip?

3. A trucker travels 65 km at an average speed of 85 km/h. How long does the trip take?

4. If your car averages 92 km/h for a 5.0 h trip, how far will you go?

## The Difference Between Speed and Velocity

You learned that speed is distance travelled in a unit of time. Average speed is total distance divided by time, and instantaneous speed is the speed of an object at a particular instant. If an object moves along at the same speed over an extended period of time, we say its speed is uniform or constant.

Uniform speed is uncommon, but it is possible to achieve nearly uniform speed in some situations. For example, a car with "cruise control" may maintain fairly constant speed on the highway. Usually, however, a vehicle is making small changes in speed and direction all the time.

If an object is not travelling in a straight line all the time, then its direction becomes important and must be specified. When both the size and the direction of a speed are specified, we call the two properties (speed and direction) the **velocity** of the object. The symbol for velocity is $\vec{v}$. If you say your car is moving 80 km/h, then you are describing your car's speed. If you say your car is travelling 80 km/h in a northerly direction, then you are describing your car's velocity. The difference between speed and velocity becomes important in situations where direction changes during a trip. For example, when a ball is thrown into the air, both its speed and its direction change throughout its trajectory, therefore velocity is specified in this situation. Velocity is calculated by finding the displacement of an object over a period of time. Mathematically this is represented by:

$$\vec{v} = \frac{\Delta\vec{d}}{\Delta t} = \frac{\vec{d}_f - \vec{d}_0}{\Delta t}$$

## Position-Time Graphs

Speed and velocity can be graphically represented. The slope of a position-time graph gives the velocity of the moving object. A positive slope indicates positive velocity. A negative slope indicates negative velocity. When an object is not moving, the position does not change, so the slope is zero. That is, the line is horizontal.

Sometimes it can be confusing to determine the direction and the sign to use. It is important to remember what point of view or frame of reference you are using to observe the action. For example, if you are riding a bike toward your friend at a velocity of 10 km/h [west], your friend sees you coming at 10 km/h [east]. Both of you observe the same situation, it's just the direction that is different. That is why it is important to know which direction is positive and which direction is negative before you start. Usually, if all the motion is in one direction, positive values will be used unless indicated. That will be the case in this book.

The next sample problem describes how the motion of a skateboarder can be solved mathematically and graphically and the velocity of the skateboarder determined.

 

## Sample Problem 1.1.2 — Solving Motion Problems Mathematically

You are on a skateboard and moving to the right covering 0.5 m each second for 10 s. What is your velocity?

| What to Think About | How to Do It |
|---|---|
| 1. Motion is uniform so the velocity is the same for each time interval. Right will be positive. | $\Delta \vec{d}_o = 0.0\ m$<br>$\Delta \vec{d}_f = 0.5\ m$<br>$\Delta t = 1.0\ s$ |
| 2. Solve for velocity. | $\vec{v} = \dfrac{\Delta \vec{d}}{\Delta t} = \dfrac{\vec{d}_f - \vec{d}_o}{\Delta t}$<br>$= \dfrac{0.5\ m - 0.0\ m}{1.0 s}$<br>$= 0.5\ m/s$ |
| 3. Include direction in the answer, which is right since the answer is positive. | $\vec{v} = 0.5\ m/s$ [right] |

## Sample Problem 1.1.3 — Solving Motion Problems Graphically

You are on a skateboard and moving to the right covering 0.5 m each second for 10 s. What is your velocity?

**What to Think About**

1. Collect data and record in table. Moving right will be considered positive.

**How to Do It**

| d (m) | 0 | 0.5 | 1.0 | 1.5 | 2.0 | 2.5 | 3.0 | 3.5 | 4.0 | 4.5 | 5.0 |
|---|---|---|---|---|---|---|---|---|---|---|---|
| t (s) | 0 | 1.0 | 2.0 | 3.0 | 4.0 | 5.0 | 6.0 | 7.0 | 8.0 | 9.0 | 10 |

2. Graph data and draw best fit line.

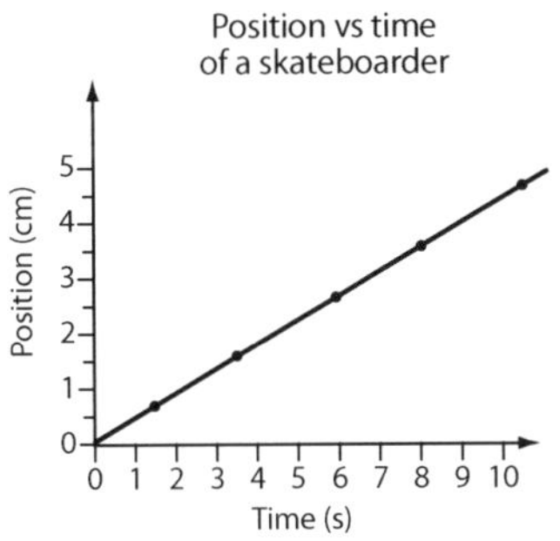


3. Find slope as it is equal to the velocity of the skateboarder.

$$\text{slope} = \frac{\Delta \vec{d}}{\Delta t} = \frac{\vec{d}_f - \vec{d}_o}{\Delta t} = \vec{v}$$

$$\vec{v} = \frac{5.0\ m - 0.0\ m}{10\ s}$$

$$= 0.5\ m/s$$

4. The slope is positive, so the direction is to the right.

$\vec{v} = 0.5\ m/s$ [right]

## Practice Problems 1.1.3 —Solving Motion Problems Graphically

1. Describe the motion represented in each of the following position-time graphs.

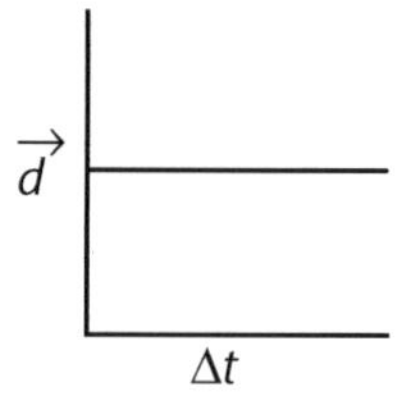


(a)

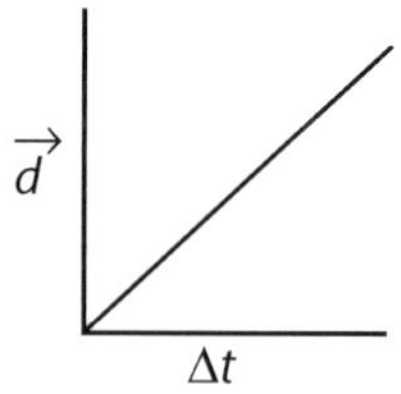


(b)

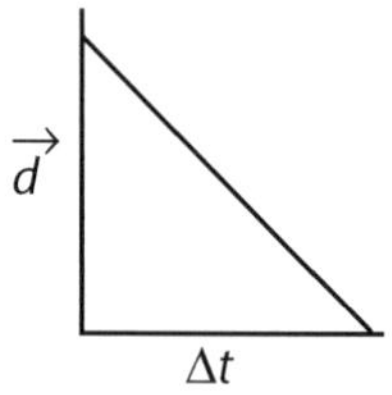


(c)

2. Sketch a graph of each of the following situations.
   (a) A golf ball is rolling towards a cup at 1.5 m/s [west].

   (b) A person is watching from the view of the cup and seeing the ball roll 1.5 m/s [east].

   (c) A person is traveling at 1.5 m/s [west] watching the ball roll towards the cup.

3. (a) Fill in the data table if a car is traveling at 30 km/h through a school zone.

| Time (s) | 1.0 | 2.0 | 3.0 | 4.0 | 5.0 | 6.0 | 7.0 | 8.0 |
|---|---|---|---|---|---|---|---|---|
| Distance (m) | | | | | | | | |

   (b) Graph this data on a distance vs. time graph.

## 1.1 Review Questions

1. Can objects with the same speed have different velocities? Why or why not?

2. What are two ways of describing the direction of an object's motion?

3. If you run with an average speed of 12.0 km/h, how far will you go in 3.2 min?

4. If the average speed of your private jet is $8.0 \times 10^2$ km/h, how long will it take you to travel a distance of $1.8 \times 10^3$ km?

5. A red ant travels across a driveway, which is 3.5 m wide, at an average speed of 2.6 cm/s. How long will the ant take to cross the driveway? Express your answer (a) in seconds and (b) in minutes.

6. If your car moves with a steady speed of 122 km/h for 20.0 min, then at a steady speed of 108 km/h for 30.0 min, what is the average speed of your car for the entire trip?

7. A car moves with a steady speed of 84 km/h for 45 min, then 96 km/h for 20 min.
   (a) What was the total distance travelled during the whole trip?

   (b) What is its average speed for the whole trip?

8. After a soccer practice, Gareth and Owen are heading home. They reach the corner, where they go separate ways. Gareth heads south to the bus stop. Owen walks north to his house. After 5.0 min, Gareth is 600 m [S] and Owen is 450 m [N].
   (a) On the same graph (below), graph the position of each boy after 5.0 min and find the velocity of each boy.

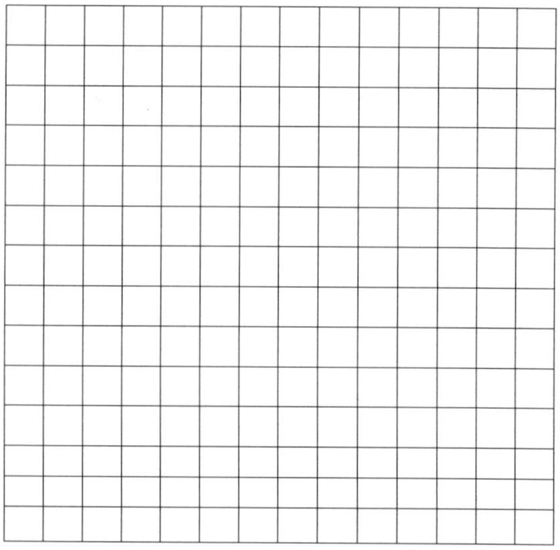

(b) Find the velocity of each boy using algebra.

# 1.2 Acceleration

## Warm Up

Below are two blank speed-time graphs.
On graph (a), sketch the slope that represents a sports car traveling at constant speed.
On graph (b), sketch the slope of the same car starting from rest and speeding up at a constant rate.

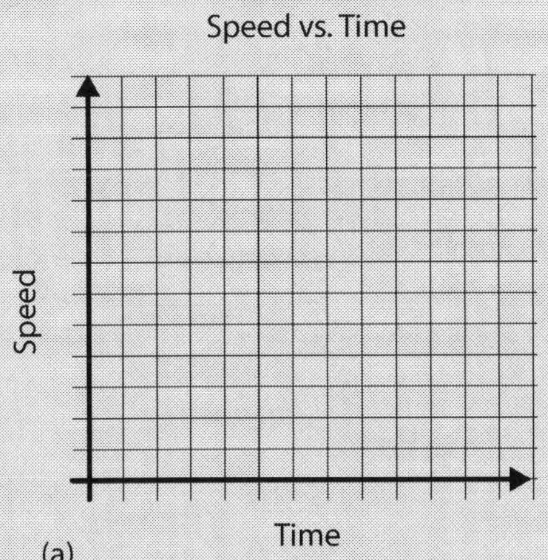

(a)

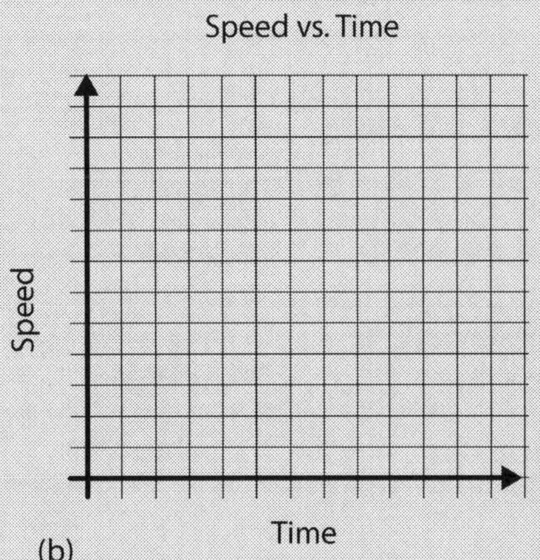

(b)

### Changing Velocity

Whenever the velocity of an object changes, the object experiences **acceleration.** Acceleration is a change in velocity over a period of time:

$$\textbf{acceleration} = \frac{\textbf{change in velocity}}{\textbf{change in time}}$$

The symbol for acceleration is $a$. Velocity has the same symbol as speed, which is $v$. If the velocity at the start of the time interval is $v_0$, and at the end of the time interval is $v_f$, then the change in velocity will be $v_f - v_0$. If the time at the beginning of the time interval is $t_0$, and the time at the end of the time interval is $t_f$, then the change in time, the time interval, is $t_f - t_0$. Using these symbols, acceleration can be defined as:

$$a = \frac{v_f - v_0}{t_f - t_0} \text{ or } a = \frac{\Delta v}{\Delta t}$$

where the Δ symbol is shorthand for "change in" or "interval."

Since velocity has two aspects to it, both speed and direction, acceleration can occur under three conditions:
(a) if speed changes,
(b) if direction changes or
(c) if both speed and direction change.

The standard unit for expressing acceleration is $m/s^2$. An object is accelerating at a rate of 1 $m/s^2$ if its speed is increasing at a rate of 1 m/s each second.

**Sample Problem 1.2.1 — Calculating Acceleration**

A runner racing in a 100 m dash accelerates from rest to a speed of 9.0 m/s in 4.5 s. What was his average acceleration during this time interval?

| What to Think About | How to Do It |
|---|---|
| 1. Determine the correct formula. | $a = \frac{\Delta v}{\Delta t} = \frac{v_f - v_o}{t_f - t_o}$ |
| 2. Solve for acceleration. Note that runner's average acceleration was 2.0 m/s/s, which is usually written 2.0 m/s$^2$ | $= \frac{9.0\ m/s - 0\ m/s}{4.5\ s - 0\ s}$<br>$a = 2.0\ m/s^2$<br>The runner's average acceleration was 2.0 m/s$^2$. |

**Practice Problems 1.2.1 — Calculating Acceleration**

1. What is the average acceleration for the following?
   (a) A car speeds up from 0 km/h to 60.0 km/h in 3.00 s.

   (b) A runner accelerates from rest to 9.00 m/s in 3.00 s.

2. What is the average acceleration of a truck that accelerates from 45.0 km/h to 60.0 km/h in 7.50 s?

3. A car travelling 120 km/h brakes hard to avoid hitting a deer on the road, slowing to 60 km/h in 4.0 s. What is its acceleration? Why is it negative?

## Negative Acceleration

Sometimes you will find a situation where the acceleration is negative. You may think this implies that an object is slowing down, but that is not always the case. Consider the situations shown in Figure 1.2.1.

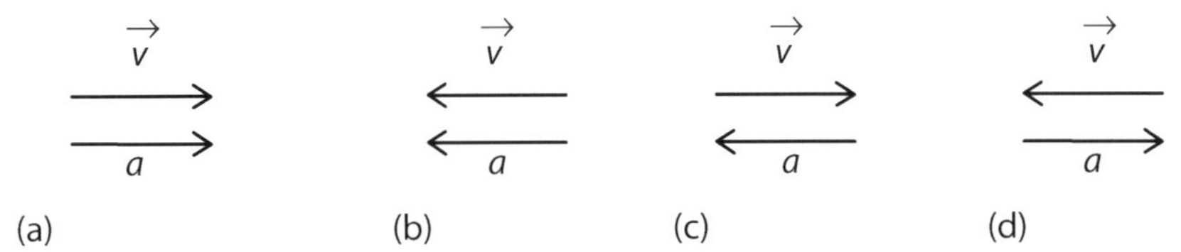


**Figure 1.2.1** *The vectors represent the velocity and acceleration of a car in different situations.*

In (a) and (b) the velocity of the car and the acceleration are in the same direction. This means the car is speeding up, even though the acceleration is negative in (b). In (c) and (d) the velocity and acceleration are in opposite directions and the car is slowing down. We can summarize that this way:

> When the velocity and acceleration are in the same direction, the object is speeding up, even if the acceleration is negative. When the velocity and acceleration are in opposite directions, the object is slowing down.

## Graphing Acceleration

In Figure 1.2.1, fictitious data is used to show how your results from Investigation 1-1 might have been graphed. In this figure, the average speed of the cart is plotted on the *y*-axis, since it is the dependent variable. Time is on the *x*-axis, because it is the independent variable.

Notice that in Figure 1.2.1 the speeds are plotted halfway through each time interval. For example, the average speed of 11 cm/s, which occurs in the first time interval of the sample tape, would be plotted at 0.05 s, not at 0.10 s. This is because the average speed during the interval will occur halfway through it, not at the end of the interval. This assumes, of course, that the speed is increasing at a constant rate and therefore acceleration is constant. The average speed for each interval is the same as the instantaneous speed half way through the interval, if acceleration is constant.

The graph you see in Figure 1.2.1 is, in fact, a graph of the instantaneous speed of the cart vs. time, although average speeds were used to obtain it. To write an equation describing the line in this graph, you need to know the *y*-intercept and the slope.

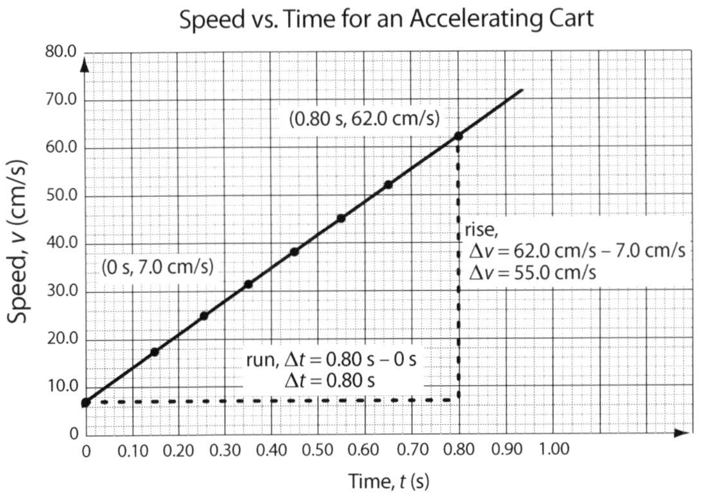


**Figure 1.2.1** *An example of a graph showing acceleration*

By inspection, the *y*-intercept, *b*, equals 7.0 cm/s. The slope *m* is found by using the points (0 s, 7.0 cm/s) and (0.80 s, 62 cm/s). Notice that the "rise" of the line is equal to the change in the speed of the cart, $\Delta v$, and $\Delta v = v_f - v_0$. The "run" of the graph is the change in time $\Delta t$, and $\Delta t = t_f - t_0$.

$$\text{slope} = m = \frac{\Delta v}{\Delta t} = \frac{v_f - v_0}{t_f - t_0} = \frac{62.0\ \text{cm/s} - 7.0\ \text{cm/s}}{0.80\ \text{s} - 0\ \text{s}} = \frac{55.0\ \text{cm/s}}{0.80\ \text{s}} = 69\ \text{cm/s}^2$$

Notice that the slope has units of acceleration. This is because the slope of the speed-time graph *is* acceleration! Remember that acceleration is equal to the change in speed of the cart per second. The slope $m = \Delta v/\Delta t$, which is the acceleration of the cart.

The equation for the line in Figure 1.2.1 will have the same form as the general equation for a straight line, which is $y = mx + b$. When describing experimental results from a graph, however, we substitute the specific symbols for the variables used in the experiment. We also use the numerical values for the *y*-intercept and slope, complete with their measuring units. The equation for the line in Figure 1.2.1 is therefore

$$v = (69\ \text{cm/s}^2)t + 7.0\ \text{cm/s}$$

where $v$ is the speed of the cart at any time $t$.

# 1.2 Review Questions

1. A policeman travelling 60 km/h spots a speeder ahead, so he accelerates his vehicle at a steady rate of 2.22 m/s$^2$ for 4.00 s, at which time he catches up with the speeder.
   (a) How fast was the policeman travelling in m/s?

   (b) How fast is the police car travelling after 4.00 s? Give your answer in both m/s and km/h.

2. A motorbike accelerates at a constant rate from a standing start. After 1.2 s, it is travelling 6.0 m/s. How much time will have elapsed (starting from rest) before the bike is moving with a speed of 15.0 m/s?

3. The graph below shows lines representing speed vs. time for an accelerating aircraft, prepared by observers at two different locations on the runway.

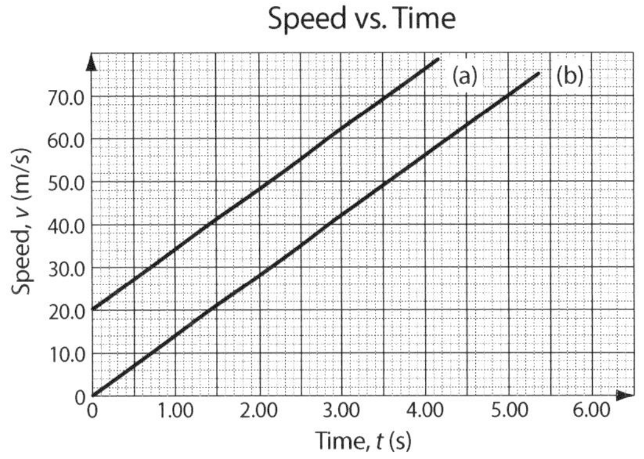


   (a) What is the equation for line (a)?

   (b) What is the equation for line (b)?

   (c) What is the acceleration of the aircraft according to line (a)?

   (d) What is the acceleration of the aircraft according to line (b)?

   (e) Explain why the *y*-intercept for line (b) is different than the intercept for line (a).

4. A racing motorbike's final velocity is 38 m/s in 5.5 s with an acceleration of 6.0 $m/s^2$. What was the initial velocity of the motorbike?

5. While starting your car, which is a standard gearshift, you coast downhill getting to a speed of 2.0 m/s before the engine starts. This takes a total of 3.0 s. If downhill is the positive direction, what is the average acceleration of your car?

6. The graph below describes the motion of a vehicle whose acceleration changes twice. Find the acceleration of the vehicle for the parts of the graph labeled (a), (b) and (c), by finding the slope of each part of the graph.

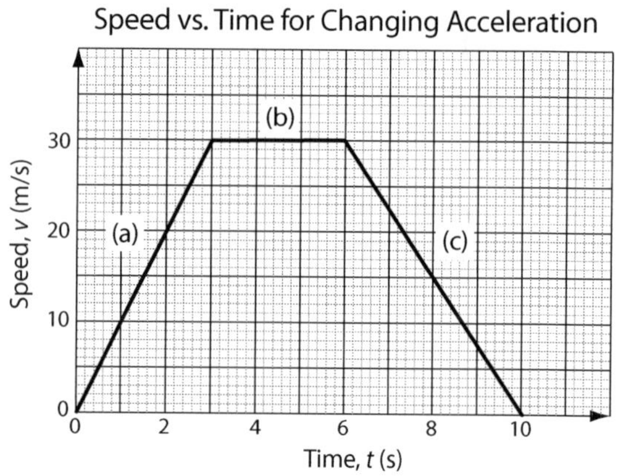


(a)

(b)

(c)

# 1.3 Uniform Acceleration

## Warm Up

In your own words, describe the difference between average velocity, initial velocity, final velocity, and a change in velocity.

______________________________________________

______________________________________________

______________________________________________

______________________________________________

### Graphing Acceleration

In a situation where the speed of a moving body increases or decreases at a uniform rate the acceleration is considered uniform. This motion can be graphed on a speed vs. time and will be linear (Figure 1.3.1). Since speed is the dependent variable, it is plotted on the *y*-axis. Time, the independent variable, will be on the *x*-axis.

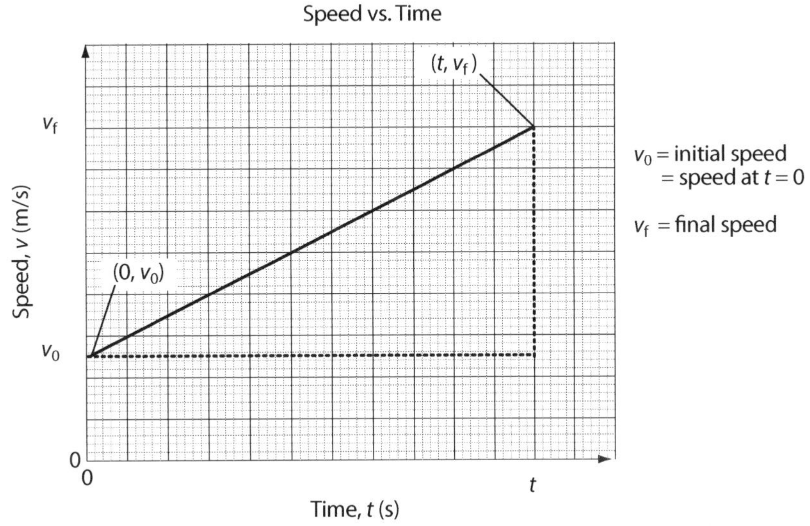


**Figure 1.3.1** *This graph shows speed changing at a uniform rate.*

The *y*-intercept for the speed-time graph is $b = v_0$, where $v_0$ is the speed of the object at time $t = 0$. In Figure 1.3.1, the initial time is zero and the final time is $t$, so the time interval is simply $\Delta t = t - 0 = t$.

The slope of the graph is $m = \dfrac{\Delta v}{\Delta t} = a$, since acceleration is change in speed divided by change in time.

$$\text{If } a = \frac{v_f - v_0}{t}$$

$$\text{Then } at = v_f - v_0 \text{ and}$$

$$\mathbf{v_f = v_0 + at} \qquad \textbf{(1)}$$

This is a general equation for any object that accelerates at a uniform rate. It says that the final speed of the accelerating object equals the initial speed plus the change in speed ($at$).

**Sample Problem 1.3.1 — Determining Uniform Acceleration**

The graph below shows the uniform acceleration of an object, as it was allowed to drop off a cliff.

(a) What was the acceleration of the object?

(b) Write an equation for the graph.

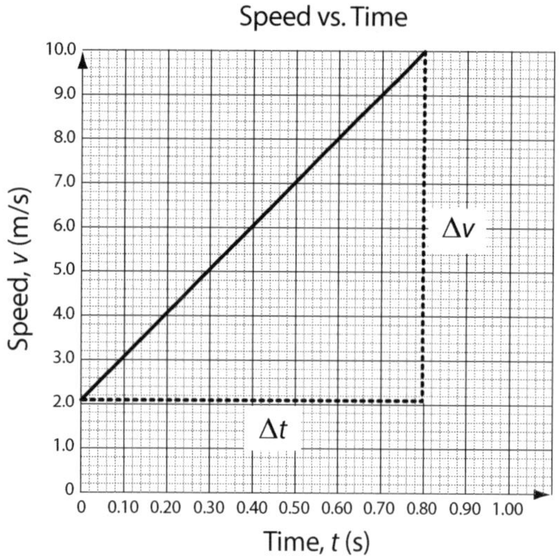


$\Delta v = v_f - v_0$

$\Delta t = t_f - 0$

| What to Think About | How to Do It |
|---|---|
| **(a)** 1. The acceleration is determined by finding the slope of the speed-time graph. | $a = \frac{\Delta v}{\Delta t} = \frac{v_f - v_o}{t_f - t_o}$ <br> $= \frac{10.0\ \text{m/s} - 2.0\ \text{m/s}}{0.80\ \text{s} - 0\ \text{s}} = \frac{8.0\ \text{m/s}}{0.80\ \text{s}}$ <br> $a = 1.0 \times 10^1\ \text{m/s}^2$ |
| **(b)** 1. Determine the general equation for any straight line. | $y = b + mx$ |
| 2. For this line, the slope *m* is the acceleration. Inspection of the graph reveals that the *y*-intercept, *b*, is 2.0 m/s. | $m = 1.0 \times 10^1\ \text{m/s}^2$ <br> $b = 2.0\ \text{m/s}$ <br> $x = t$ <br> $y = v_f$ |
| 3. Derive the specific equation for this line. Note that the final, specific equation for this graph includes the actual numerical values of the *y*-intercept and slope, complete with their measuring units. Once this equation is established, it can be used in place of the graph, since it describes every point on the graph. | $v_f = 2.0\ \text{m/s} + (1.0 \times 10^1\ \text{m/s}^2) \cdot t$ |

## Practice Problems 1.3.1 — Determining Uniform Acceleration

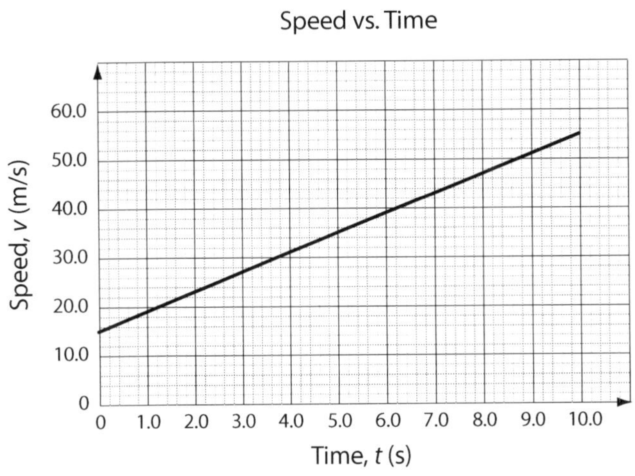


1. (a) What is the *y*-intercept ($v_0$) for the graph shown above?

   (b) What is the slope of the graph?

   (c) What property of the moving object does this slope measure?

   (d) Write the specific equation for the graph, using symbols *v* for speed and *t* for time.

2. The following equation describes the motion of a ball thrown straight down, by someone leaning out of the window of a tall building:

$$v_f = 5.0 \text{ m/s} + (9.8 \text{ m/s}^2) \cdot t$$

   (a) At what speed was the ball initially thrown out of the window?

   (b) What was the acceleration of the ball?

   (c) How fast was the ball moving after 1.2 s?

## Calculating Distance from Uniform Acceleration

Consider an object that is accelerating uniformly from initial speed $v_0$ to a final speed $v_f$ in time $t$. as shown in Figure 1.3.2. How would you calculate the distance travelled by the object during this time?

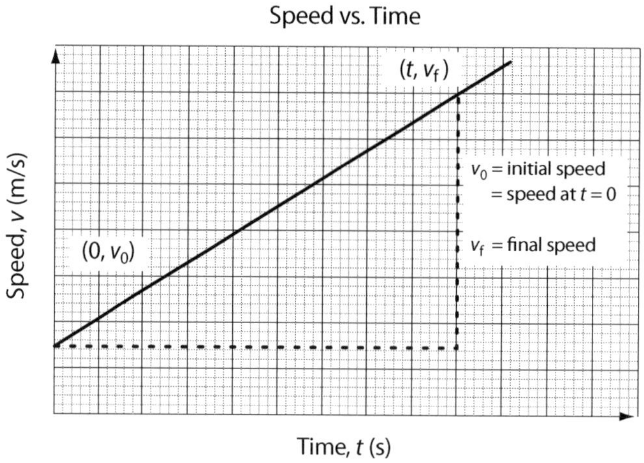


**Figure 1.3.2** *This graph represents an object accelerating at a uniform rate.*

The total distance $d$ travelled in time $t$ will equal the average speed $\bar{v}$ multiplied by time $t$. The average speed $\bar{v}$ is just the average of the initial speed $v_0$ and the final speed $v_f$, which is:

$$\bar{v} = \frac{v_0 + v_f}{2}$$

Distance travelled is $d = \bar{v} \times t$ or $$d = \frac{v_0 + v_f}{2} \cdot t \qquad \textbf{(2)}$$

However, it has already been shown that $$v_f = v_0 + at \qquad \textbf{(1)}$$

Therefore, $$d = \frac{v_0 + v_0 + at}{2} \cdot t$$

and $$d = \frac{2v_0 + at}{2} \cdot t = \frac{2v_0 + at^2}{2}$$

Finally, $$\mathbf{d = v_0 t + \frac{1}{2} at^2} \qquad \textbf{(3)}$$

Sometimes you encounter situations involving uniform acceleration where you have no information about the time interval, $t$, during which the motion occurred. If you know the initial speed $v_0$ and the final speed $v_f$, you can still calculate the distance travelled if you know at what rate the object is accelerating.

For uniform acceleration, $$d = \frac{v_0 + v_f}{2} \cdot t, \text{ and } v_f = v_0 + at$$

Therefore, $$t = \frac{v_f - v_0}{a}$$

Substituting for $t$ in the first equation, $$d = \frac{v_0 + v_f}{2} \cdot \frac{v_f - v_0}{a}$$

Thus, $$2ad = v_f^2 - v_0^2$$

Therefore, $$\mathbf{v_f^2 = v_0^2 + 2ad} \qquad \textbf{(4)}$$

## The Four Uniform Acceleration Equations

Four equations describing uniform acceleration were introduced above. These four equations are extremely useful in this course and in future courses you might take in physics. For your convenience, they are summarized here:

$$(1)\quad v_f = v_0 + at$$

$$(2)\quad d = \frac{v_0 + v_f}{2} \cdot t$$

$$(3)\quad d = v_0 t + \frac{1}{2}at^2$$

$$(4)\quad v_f^2 = v_0^2 + 2ad$$

### Quick Check

1. What is the initial velocity of a car accelerating east at 3.0 m/s$^2$ for 5.0 s and reaching a final velocity of 25.0 m/s east?

2. If we assume acceleration is uniform, how far does a plane travel when it lands at 16.0 m/s west and comes to rest in 8.00 s?

3. What is the stopping distance of a car if it accelerates at –9.29 m/s$^2$ and has an initial velocity of 100 km/h.

## 1.3 Review Questions

1. Use the following graph to answer the questions below.

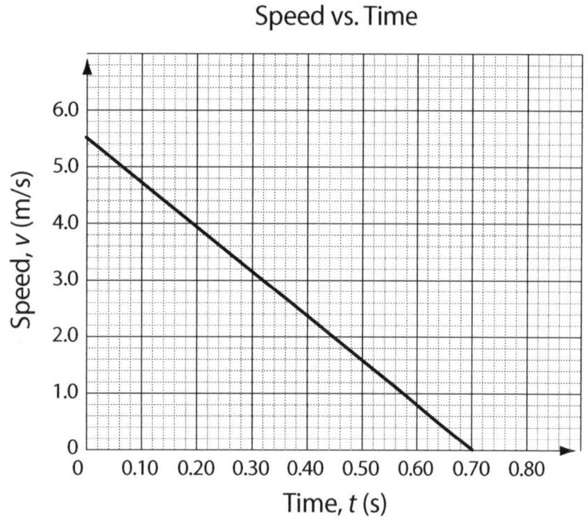


(a) What is the y-intercept ($v_0$) of the speed-time graph shown above?

(b) What is the acceleration of the moving object?

(c) What is the specific equation for this graph?

2. A cyclist coasting along a road allows her bike to come to rest with the help of a slight upslope in the road. The motion of the bike is described by the equation:

$$v_f = 6.6\ \text{m/s} - (2.2\ \text{m/s}^2)\cdot t$$

(a) What was the initial speed of the bike?

(b) At what rate did the bike accelerate while coming to rest?

(c) How long did the bike take to come to rest?

3. What is the rate of acceleration of a mountain bike, if it slows down from 12.0 m/s to 8.0 m/s in a time of 3.25 s?

4. A truck parked on a down slope slips its brakes and starts to coast downhill, accelerating from rest at a constant rate of 0.80 $\text{m/s}^2$.

(a) How fast will the truck be moving after 5.0 s?

(b) How far will the truck coast during the 5.0 s?

5. An aircraft starts from rest and accelerates at a constant rate down the runway.
   (a) After 12.0 s, its speed is 36.0 m/s. What is its acceleration?

   (b) How fast is the plane moving after 15.0 s?

   (c) How far down the runway will the plane be after 15.0 s?

6. A truck is moving along at 80.0 km/h when it hits a gravel patch, which causes it to accelerate at –5.0 km/h/s. How far will the truck travel before it slows to 20.0 km/h?

7. A very frustrated physics student drops a physics textbook off the top of a tower. If the tower is $5.3 \times 10^2$ m high, how long will the book take to reach the ground, assuming there is no air resistance?

8. If an electron accelerates in a space of 5.0 cm from rest to 1/10 *c*, (where *c* is the speed of light, $3.0 \times 10^8$ m/s), what is its acceleration?

# 1.4 Acceleration of Bodies Due to Gravity

## Warm Up

Take a piece of paper and book in each hand and raise them to about the height of your shoulder. Predict which one will hit the ground first if they are both dropped at the same time. Drop both and record results. Now crumple the same piece of paper and repeat. Describe and suggest reasons for any differences between the two events.

______________________________________________

______________________________________________

______________________________________________

______________________________________________

### Free Fall

One of the most common situations involving uniform acceleration is the phenomenon known as **free fall**. For example, if a coin drops out of your pocket, it accelerates toward the ground. If the effects of air resistance are ignored, the acceleration of the coin toward the ground is uniform. The coin starts its downward fall with zero speed, but gains speed as it falls toward Earth. Since gravity is the cause of the acceleration, we call the acceleration during free fall the **acceleration of gravity.** The acceleration of gravity is given a special symbol, $g$.

**Figure 1.4.1** *These sky divers are in free fall until they open their parachutes to slow their descent.*

The magnitude of $g$ depends on your location. At Earth's surface, $g$ is approximately 9.81 m/s$^2$. At higher altitudes, $g$ decreases. For our present purposes, $g$ is assumed to be constant at Earth's surface and to be 9.81 m/s$^2$. On the Moon, the magnitude of $g$ is approximately 1/6 of what it is here on Earth's surface. A body in free fall near the Moon's surface has an acceleration of gravity of only 1.60 m/s$^2$.

Of course, the four equations for uniform acceleration apply to free fall as well as other uniform acceleration situations. The symbol $g$ may be substituted for $a$ in those equations.

**Sample Problem 1.4.1 — Free Fall**

A golf ball is dropped from the top of a tower. Assuming that the ball is in true free fall (negligible air resistance), answer these questions:

(a) How fast will the ball be falling after 1.0 s?

(b) How far down will the ball have fallen after 1.0 s?

| What to Think About | How to Do It |
|---|---|
| **(a)** | |
| 1. Determine initial conditions in the problem so you can choose the correct formula. | The ball starts from rest, so $v_0 = 0.0$ m/s<br>The rate of acceleration is $g = 9.8$ m/s$^2$<br>The time of fall is $t = 1.0$ s |
| 2. Determine which formula to use. | The first uniform acceleration equation (1) applies to this question. |
| 3. Solve. | $v_f = v_0 + at$<br>$v_f = 0 \text{ m/s} + (9.8 \text{ m/s}^2)(1.0 \text{ s})$<br>$v_f = 9.8$ m/s<br>The ball will be falling 9.8 m/s after 1 s. |
| **(b)** | |
| 1. Determine which formula to use. | The third uniform acceleration equation (3) applies to this question. |
| 2. Solve. | $d = v_0 t + \frac{1}{2}at^2$<br>$d = (0 \text{ m/s})(1.0 \text{ s}) + \frac{1}{2}(9.8 \text{ m/s}^2)(1.0 \text{ s})(1.0 \text{ s})$<br>$d = 4.9$ m<br>The ball will have fallen 4.9 m after 1 s. |

**Practice Problems 1.4.1 — Free Fall**

1. (a) How fast will the golf ball in the Sample Problem be moving after it has fallen a distance of 530 m, which is the height of the tower? (Assume free fall.)

   (b) Why does the ball not reach this speed when it hits the ground?

**Practice Problems 1.4.1 — Free Fall**

2. How high is the cliff if you toss a small rock off of it with an initial speed of 5.0 m/s and the rock takes 3.1 s to reach the water?

3. (a) At the Pacific National Exhibition in Vancouver, one of the amusement park rides drops a person in free fall for 1.9 s. What will be the final velocity of the rider at the end of this ride?

   (b) What is the height of this ride?

4. At an air show, a jet car accelerates from rest at a rate of $3g$, where $g$ is 9.81 m/s$^2$. How far does the jet car travel down the runway in a time of 4.0 s?

## Projectiles

There are different types of projectile motion. From throwing a ball up and having it land on your hand to a golf ball being hit off a tee to throwing a rock off a cliff. The golf ball and rock examples require analysis of motion using two dimensions and will be studied in later courses. The example of throwing a ball up in the air and having it land back in your hand is an example of projectile motion in one dimension. This type of projectile motion will be studied next.

Recall that acceleration is a vector quantity with both magnitude and direction. In situations where the acceleration is caused by the force of gravity, the direction of acceleration is downward. This is a negative direction. In gravitational acceleration problems, therefore, you use $a = -9.81$ m/s$^2$.

If a body is thrown into the air, it accelerates downward ($a = -9.81$ m/s$^2$) at all times during the trajectory, whether the velocity is upward (+), zero, or downward (–).

You throw a baseball straight up. It leaves your hand with an initial velocity of 10.0 m/s. Figure 1.4.2 is a graph showing how the velocity of the ball varies with time, starting when you begin to throw the ball and ending when you finish catching it. At A, the ball has just left your hand. At C, the ball has just reached the glove in which you will catch the ball. Notice that between A and C, the velocity is changing at a uniform rate. If you take the slope of this graph, you will obtain the acceleration of the ball due to gravity alone.

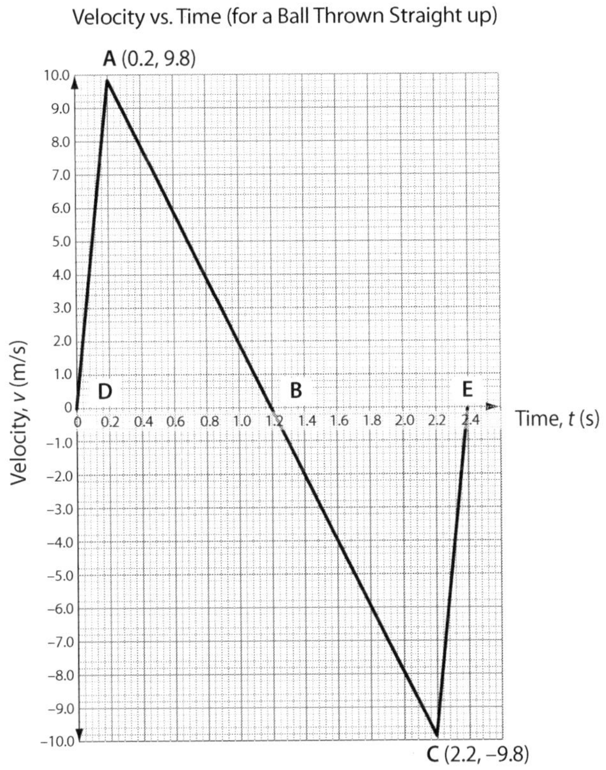


**Figure 1.4.2** *This graph represents the velocity of a ball as a function of time, when you throw a ball straight up in the air.*

## Quick Check

1. In Figure 1.4.2, what was the acceleration of the ball
   (a) while it was being thrown?

   (b) while it was in free fall?

   (c) while it was being caught?

2. What point on the graph corresponds with the instant when the ball reached the "peak" of its flight? Explain how you know this.

3. What altitude did the ball reach? **Hint:** The distance the ball travels equals the average speed multiplied by the time elapsed when it reaches its "peak" altitude. What property of the graph would give you $d = \bar{v} \cdot t$?

## 1.4 Review Questions

1. On a certain asteroid, a steel ball drops a distance of 0.80 m in 2.00 s from rest. Assuming uniform acceleration due to gravity on this asteroid, what is the value of $g$ on the asteroid?

2. The graph below represents the velocity of a ball thrown straight up by a strong pitcher as a function of time. In the first part of the graph ending at A, the ball is accelerated to 39.2 m/s in a time of 0.20 s. After the ball leaves the pitcher's hand, it experiences only the acceleration due to gravity until it is caught in a glove and brought to rest in the hand of the catcher.

Velocity vs. Time for a Ball Thrown Straight up

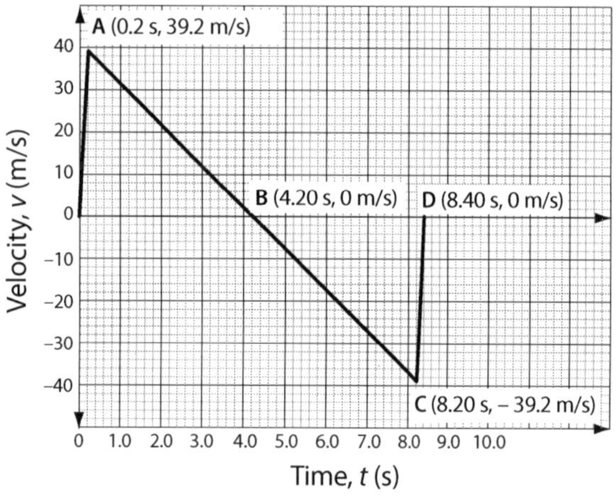


(a) What is the acceleration of the ball while it is being thrown?

(b) What is the acceleration of the ball after it leaves the pitcher's hand? (ABC)

(c) What is the acceleration of the ball while it is being caught? (CD)

(d) What point on the graph (A, B, C, or D) corresponds with the instant when the ball is at the peak of its flight? Explain your answer.

(e) Why is the slope of the graph negative as soon as the ball leaves the pitcher's hand?

(f) Why is the graph labelled velocity rather than speed?

(g) How far up did the ball travel?

(h) How far down did the ball fall?

(i) What is the average velocity of the ball for the whole trip from pitcher's hand to catcher's hand?

3. A body in free fall accelerates at a rate of 9.81 $m/s^2$ at your latitude. How far does the body fall during (a) the first second? (b) the second second? (Think first!)

# 1.5 Projectile Motion

## Warm Up

Place the bottom of a bill in line with your friend's hand as shown in the drawing. Without warning, release the bill. Can your friend grab the bill? Human reaction time is about one seventh of a second. How long would the bill have to be to make it "catchable"?

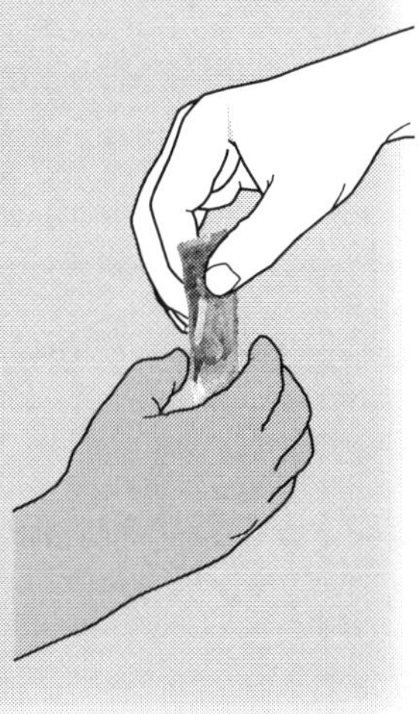

### Describing Projectile Motion

If you throw a baseball, your arm exerts a force on the ball until the ball leaves your hand. Once the ball is free of your hand, it continues moving because of its inertia, and it will follow a curved path unless you throw it straight up. A baseball thrown into the air is a good example of a **projectile**. If a marble rolls off the edge of a table, it follows a curved path to the floor. The marble, too, is a projectile.

Any object (a rock, a ball, or a bullet) that is projected by some method and then continues moving because of its inertia, is a projectile. Figure 1.5.1 shows the path taken by a baseball thrown by a highly skilled fielder. The dashed line shows the path the baseball would take if there were no force of gravity. The solid line shows the actual path taken by the baseball.

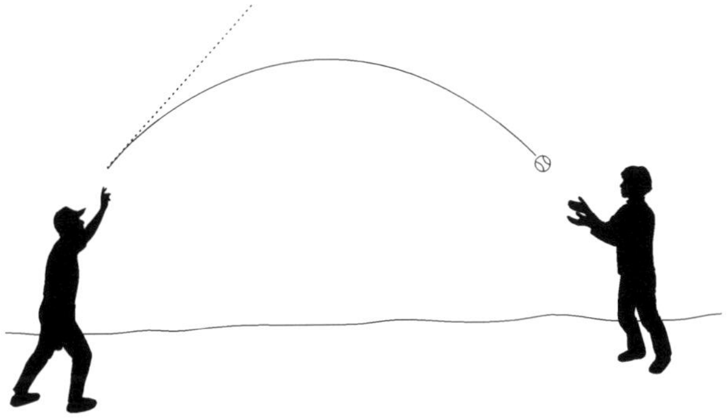

**Figure 1.5.1** *The baseball follows a curved path rather than a straight one from the fielder's hand because of the force of gravity.*

At first glance, it may appear to be a complicated matter to describe the motion of a projectile. After you have done Investigation 1.5.1, you will understand that the motion of a projectile can be described very simply if you look at the vertical motion and the horizontal motion separately.

## Vectors and Projectile Problems

You will use the four equations for uniform acceleration frequently when solving problems involving projectile motion. For your convenience, these laws are summarized here:

| | |
|---|---|
| I | $\vec{v}_f = \vec{v}_0 + \vec{a}t$ |
| II | $d = \frac{v_0 + v_f}{2} \cdot t$ |
| III | $d = v_0 t + \frac{1}{2}at^2$ |
| IV | $v_f^{\,2} = v_0^{\,2} + 2ad$ |

When solving projectile problems, you must remember that velocities, displacements, and accelerations are vector quantities. Upward motion is generally considered positive (+) and downward motion is negative (–). On or near Earth's surface, the magnitude of the acceleration due to gravity is $\vec{g} = 9.80 \text{ m/s}^2$, and since it is always acting downward, you should use

$$\vec{a} = -9.80 \text{ m/s}^2$$

When analyzing the motion of a projectile, the velocity is almost always resolved into its *horizontal* and *vertical* components. The laws of uniform acceleration may be applied to the vertical motion of the object. The horizontal motion is simple to deal with, since horizontal velocity is constant (ignoring air resistance).

## The Parabolic Nature of Projectile Motion

When a projectile is fired, its path is *parabolic* if air resistance is negligible. This can be shown quite simply for a situation where an object is thrown horizontally (Figure 1.5.2).

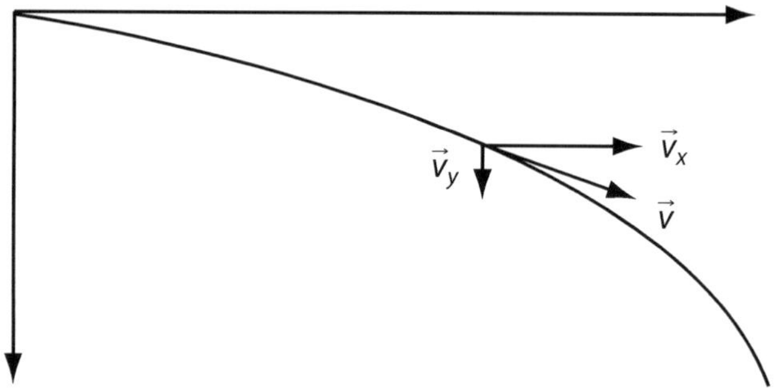


**Figure 1.5.2** *Parabolic motion can be resolved into an x component and a y component for motion.*

Let the magnitude of the horizontal displacement of an object thrown horizontally be $x$. Horizontal velocity, which has magnitude $v_x$ is constant.

$$v_x = \frac{x}{t} \text{ so } t = \frac{x}{v_x}$$

Let the magnitude of the vertical displacement be $y$. Assuming the object starts from rest so that $\vec{v}_0 = 0$, then

$$y = \tfrac{1}{2}at^2 \text{ or } y = \frac{1}{2}a\left[\frac{x}{v_x}\right]^2$$

 

Now, ½, $a$, and $v_x$ are all constant, therefore we can say that $y = kx^2$.

This is the simplest possible equation for a *parabola*. A ball thrown out by a pitcher, or a stream of water issuing from a hose will follow a parabolic path. If air resistance is negligible, any object, given a horizontal motion in a gravitational field, will move along a parabolic path.

## Sample Problem 1.5.1 — Projectile Motion

A golf ball was struck from the first tee at Lunar Golf and Country Club, a private golf course for astronauts stranded on the Moon. It was given a velocity of 48 m/s at an angle of 40° to the horizontal. On the Moon, the magnitude of $g = 1.6\ \text{m/s}^2$.

(a) What is the vertical component of the golf ball's initial velocity?
(b) For what interval of time is the ball in flight?
(c) How far will the ball travel horizontally?

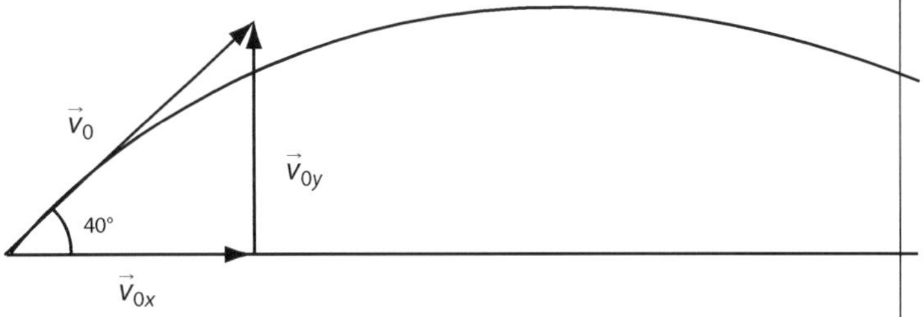


**Figure 1.5.3**

| What to Think About | How to Do It |
|---|---|
| **(a)** | |
| 1. Since the velocity of the ball is initially 48 m/s, find $\vec{v}_{0y}$. (*Keep one extra significant figure for now.) | $\vec{v}_{oy} = \vec{v}_o \sin 40°$<br>$\vec{v}_{oy} = (48\ \text{m/s})(0.6428)$<br>$\vec{v}_{oy} = 30.9\ \text{m/s}$* |
| **(b)** | |
| 1. The most direct way of solving for time is to use Equation III for uniform acceleration. | $d = v_o t + \frac{1}{2}at^2$ |
| 2. Since the ball will eventually return to ground level, its displacement for the entire trip, in a vertical direction, is zero ($d = y = 0$). (*Keep one extra significant figure for now.) | Therefore,<br>$0 = (30.9\ \text{m/s})t + \frac{1}{2}(-1.6\ \text{m/s}^2)t^2$<br>or $(0.80\ \text{m/s}^2)t^2 = (30.9\ \text{m/s})t$<br>$t = \dfrac{30.9\ \text{m/s}}{0.80\ \text{m/s}^2} = 38.6\ \text{s}$* |
| **(c)** | |
| 1. Horizontal displacement: $x = v_{0x}t$<br>Horizontal velocity remains constant:<br>$v_{0x} = v_0 \cos 40°$ | $x = (v_0 \cos 40°)t$<br>$x = (48\ \text{m/s})(0.7660)(38.6\ \text{s})$<br>$x = 1.42 \times 10^3\ \text{m}$ |
| **Summary**<br>Round the final answers to two significant figures.<br><br>The golf ball would travel 1.4 km on the Moon! | (a) 31 m/s<br>(b) 39 s<br>(c) $1.4 \times 10^3$ m or 1.4 km |

**Practice Problems 1.5.1 — Projectile Motion**

1. A girl throws a rock horizontally from the top of a cliff 98 m high, with a horizontal velocity of 27 m/s.
   (a) How many seconds will the rock be in the air?

   (b)How far out from the base of the cliff does the rock land?

2. A golfer gives a golf ball a velocity of 48 m/s at an angle of 45° with the horizontal.
   (a) What is the vertical component of the ball's initial velocity?

   (b) How long is the ball in the air?

   (c) What is the horizontal distance covered by the ball while in flight?

## 1.5 Review Questions

Use $\vec{g} = -9.80\ m/s^2$

1. A rescue pilot has to drop a package of emergency supplies so that it lands as close as possible to a downed aircraft. If the rescue plane travels with a velocity of 81 m/s and is flying 125 m above the downed craft, how far away (horizontally) from the downed craft must the rescue pilot drop his package? (Assume negligible air resistance.)

2. An archer standing on the back of a pickup truck moving at 28 m/s fires an arrow straight up at a duck flying directly overhead. He misses the duck. The arrow was fired with an initial vertical velocity of 49 m/s relative to the truck.
   (a) For how many seconds will the arrow be in the air?

   (b) How far will the truck travel while the arrow is in the air?

   (c) Where, in relation to the archer, will the arrow come down? (Ignore air friction.) Will the archer have to "duck"? Explain.

3. A bullet is fired with a horizontal velocity of 330 m/s from a height of 1.6 m above the ground. Assuming the ground is level, how far from the gun, measured horizontally, will the bullet hit the ground?

4. A ball is thrown with a velocity of 24 m/s at an angle of 30° to the horizontal.
   Assume air friction is small enough to be ignored.
   (a) What is the horizontal component of the initial velocity?

   (b) What is the vertical component of the initial velocity?

   (c) How long will the ball be in the air?

(d) What horizontal distance (range) will the ball travel?

(e) To what maximum height will the ball rise?

5. Solve question 4 for angles of (i) 45° and (ii) 60°. Which of the three angles results in the greatest range? It can be shown that, for a given initial velocity, this angle is the best of all angles for obtaining the maximum range in the ideal, "no air resistance" situation.
   (i) 45°
      (a) What is the horizontal component of the initial velocity?

      (b) What is the vertical component of the initial velocity?

      (c) How long will the ball be in the air?

      (d) What horizontal distance (range) will the ball travel?

      (e) To what maximum height will the ball rise?

   (ii) 60°
      (a) What is the horizontal component of the initial velocity?

      (b) What is the vertical component of the initial velocity?

      (c) How long will the ball be in the air?

      (d) What horizontal distance (range) will the ball travel?

      (e) To what maximum height will the ball rise?

6. A student measured the horizontal and vertical components of the velocity of a projectile in a laboratory situation. The data is given below. Times and velocities are "true" (not scaled).

| **Time, *t* (s)** | **Horizontal velocity, $v_x$ (m/s)** | **Vertical velocity, $v_y$ (m/s)** |
|---|---|---|
| 0.10 | 2.12 | 3.58 |
| 0.20 | 2.12 | 4.56 |
| 0.30 | 2.13 | 5.54 |
| 0.40 | 2.11 | 6.52 |
| 0.50 | 2.12 | 7.50 |

(a) Plot vertical velocity vs. time.

(b) Find the slope and *y*-intercept of your graph.

(c) Write an equation specifically describing your graph.

(d) On the same graph sheet, plot horizontal velocity vs. time.

(e) Write an equation specifically describing your second graph.

# Chapter 1 Conceptual Review Questions

1. Give an example in which there are clear distinctions among distance traveled, displacement, and magnitude of displacement. Specifically identify each quantity in your example.

2. Under what circumstances does distance traveled equal magnitude of displacement? What is the only case in which magnitude of displacement and displacement are exactly the same?

3. There is a distinction between average speed and the magnitude of average velocity. Give an example that illustrates the difference between these two quantities

4. If you divide the total distance traveled on a car trip (as determined by the odometer) by the time for the trip, are you calculating the average speed or the magnitude of the average velocity? Under what circumstances are these two quantities the same?

5. Is it possible for speed to be constant while acceleration is not zero? Give an example of such a situation.

6. Is it possible for velocity to be constant while acceleration is not zero? Explain.

7. Give an example in which velocity is zero yet acceleration is not.

# Chapter 1 Review Questions

1. What is the difference between velocity and speed?

2. A traveller drives 568 km in 7.2 h. What is the average speed for the trip?

3. The following distances and times, for consecutive parts of a trip made by a red ant, were recorded by different observers. There is considerable variation in the precision of their measurements.

   A. 4.56 m in 12 s  B. 3.4 m in 6.89 s
   C. 12.8 m in 36.235 s

   (a) What total distance did the ant travel?

   (b) What was the total time for the trip?

   (c) What was the average speed of the ant?

4. Light travels with a speed of $3.00 \times 10^5$ km/s. How long will it take light from a laser to travel to the Moon (where it is reflected by a mirror) and back to Earth? The Moon is $3.84 \times 10^5$ km from Earth.

5. Under what condition can acceleration be calculated simply by dividing change in speed by change in time?

6. A high-powered racing car accelerates from rest at a rate of 7.0 m/s$^2$. How fast will it be moving after 10.0 s? Convert this speed to km/h.

7. The graph below is a speed-time graph for a vehicle.

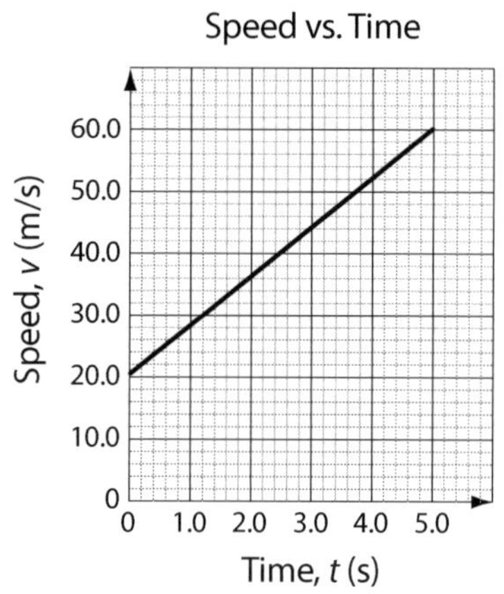


(a) What was the acceleration of the vehicle?

(b) What was the average speed of the vehicle during its 5.00 s trip?

(c) What distance did the vehicle travel during the 5.00 s?

(d) Write a specific equation for this graph.

8. A child on a toboggan slides down a snowy hill, accelerating uniformly at 2.8 m/s$^2$. When the toboggan passes the first observer, it is travelling with a speed of 1.4 m/s. How fast will it be moving when it passes a second observer, who is 2.5 m downhill from the first observer?

9. A space vehicle is orbiting the Earth at a speed of $7.58 \times 10^3$ m/s. In preparation for a return to Earth, it fires retrorockets, which provide a negative acceleration of 78.4 m/s$^2$. Ignoring any change in altitude that might occur, how long will it take the vehicle to slow down to $1.52 \times 10^3$ m/s?

10. Snoopy is taking off in his World War I biplane. He coasts down the runway at a speed of 40.0 m/s, then accelerates for 5.2 s at a rate of 1/2 $g$, where $g$ is the acceleration due to gravity (9.81 m/s$^2$). How fast is the plane moving after 5.2 s?

11. A woman biker (leader of the local chapter of *Heck's Angels*) is driving along the highway at 80.0 km/h, in a 60.0 km/h speed zone. She sees a police car ahead, so she brakes and her bike accelerates at −8.0 km/h/s. How far along the road will she travel before she is at the legal speed limit?

12. Spiderman is crawling up a building at the rate of 0.50 m/s. Seeing Spiderwoman 56 m ahead of him, he accelerates at the rate of 2.3 m/s$^2$.
   (a) How fast will he be moving when he reaches Spiderwoman?

   (b) How much time will he take to reach Spiderwoman?

   (c) When he reaches Spiderwoman, Spiderman discovers that she is a Black Widow and, as you know, Black Widows consume their mates! He is 200.00 m from the road below. How long will it take him to fall to the safety of the road, if he drops with an acceleration of $g = 9.81$ m/s$^2$?

13. A stone is dropped from the top of a tall building. It accelerates at a rate of 9.81 m/s$^2$. How long will the stone take to pass a window that is 2.0 m high, if the top of the window is 20.0 m below the point from which the stone was dropped?

14. An aircraft, preparing for take-off, accelerates uniformly from 0 m/s to 20.0 m/s in a time of 5.00 s.
   (a) What is the acceleration of the aircraft?

   (b) How long will the plane take to reach its take-off speed of 36.0 m/s?

15. At an air show, a jet car accelerates from rest at a rate of $3g$, where g is 9.81 m/s$^2$. How fast is the jet travelling after 0.25 km?

16. To start a soccer game, the referee flips a coin that travels 50 cm into the air.
    (a) What was the coin's initial speed?

    (b) How long was the coin in the air before landing back in the hand of the referee?

17. A glider on an air track is made to accelerate uniformly by tilting the track at a slight angle. The distance travelled by the glider was measured at the end of each 0.10 s interval, resulting in the following data:

| | | | | | | | |
|---|---|---|---|---|---|---|---|
| DISTANCE | $d$ (cm) | 0 | 0.025 | 0.100 | 0.225 | 0.400 | 0.625 |
| TIME | $t$ (s) | 0 | 0.100 | 0.200 | 0.300 | 0.400 | 0.500 |

(a) Plot a graph with distance $d$ on the $y$-axis and time $t$ on the $x$-axis.
(b) Plot a second graph with distance $d$ on the $y$-axis and $t^2$ on the $x$-axis.
(c) Use the slope of your second graph to figure out the acceleration of the glider on the air track. HINT: Think about the third equation for uniform acceleration.

18. A youngster hits a baseball, giving it a velocity of 22 m/s at an angle of 62° with the horizontal. Ignoring air friction, how far will the ball travel before a fielder catches it? Would this hit be a likely home run? Explain.

19. A disgruntled physics student sees the front end of his teacher's car directly below him at the base of a cliff. See the drawing below. If the student is 5.00 m above the car, which is 3.00 m long and travelling only 3.00 m/s to the right, will the apple the student drops hit the teacher's car? (Will physics be a "core" subject?) Show all details of your argument.

20. A pebble is fired from a slingshot with a velocity of 30.0 m/s. If it is fired at an angle of 30° to the vertical, what height will it reach? If its fall is interrupted by a vertical wall 12 m away, where will it hit the wall in relation to the starting position of the pebble in the slingshot?

21. A firefighter is standing on top of a building 20.0 m high. She finds that if she holds the hose so that water issues from it horizontally at 12.0 m/s, the water will hit a burning wall of an adjacent building, at a height of 15.0 m above the ground. What is the horizontal distance from the firefighter to the burning wall?

22. The firefighter in question 21 wants the water from the same hose to reach the burning wall at the same level above the ground as she is standing. At what angle must she aim the hose relative to the horizontal?

23. An observer records time ($t$), displacement ($d$), and velocity ($v$) of a skier sliding from rest down a ski slope, with uniform acceleration. Sketch graphs using the following different variables.

(a) $d$ vs. $t$

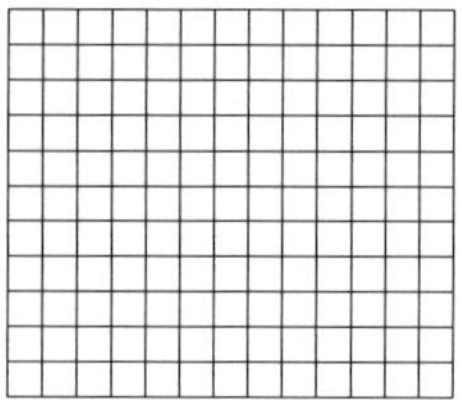

(b) $d$ vs. $t^2$

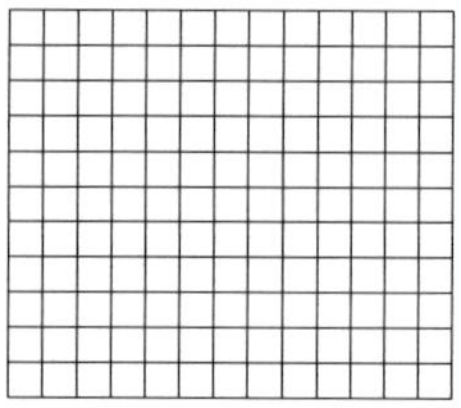

(c) $v$ vs. $t$

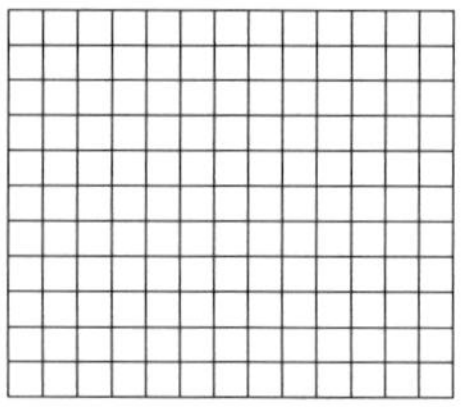

(d) $v^2$ vs. $d$

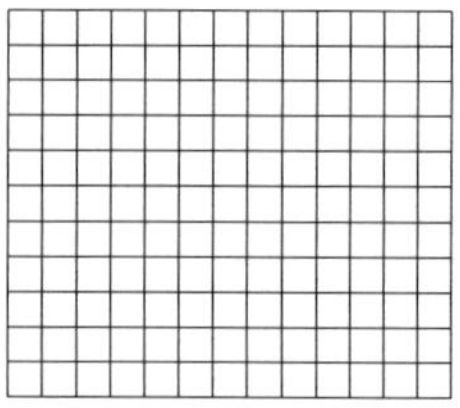

(e) In which case will the observer not obtain a straight line?

24. You drop a penny down a very deep well and hear the sound of the penny hitting the water 2.5 s later. If sound travels 330 m/s, how deep is the well?

25. A stone is thrown straight up with a speed of 15.0 m/s.

(a) How fast will it be moving when its altitude is 8.0 m above the point from which it was thrown? How much time elapses while the stone is reaching that height?

(b) Is there one answer or are there two answers? Why?

26. A small, free-falling pebble takes 0.25 s to pass by a window 1.8 m high. From what height above the window was the pebble dropped?

# Investigation 1-1 Measuring the Speed of a Model Car

### Purpose

To measure the speed of a model car, such as a radio-controlled vehicle

### Procedure

1. Remove a 5.0 m length of ticker tape from a roll. Pass one end of it through a recording timer, and then tape it to a battery-powered toy car. (Figure 1.1)

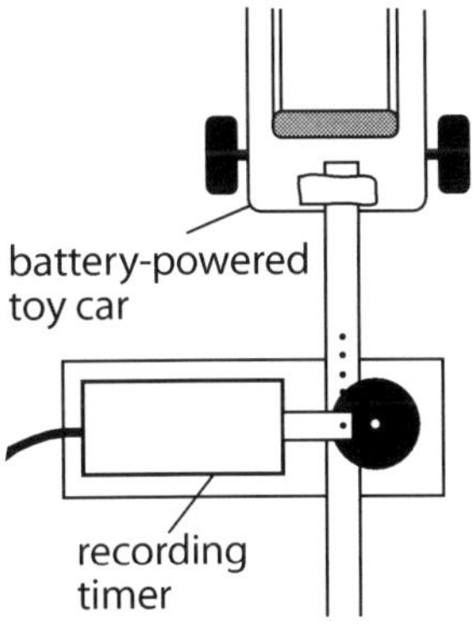


**Figure 1.1** *Step 1*

2. Turn on the timer and let the car travel at its full speed until all the tape has passed through the timer.
3. Every six dots is one-tenth of a second. Mark off the time intervals in one-tenth of a second on your tape
4. Measure the distance traveled in each tenth of a second. Record your data in a table similar to Table 2.1.

**Table 1.1** *Data Table for Investigation 1-1*

| Time (s) | 0.0 | 0.1 | 0.2 | 0.3 | 0.4 | 0.5 | 0.6 | 0.7 | 0.8 | 0.9 | 1.0 | 1.0 | 1.1 | ... |
|---|---|---|---|---|---|---|---|---|---|---|---|---|---|---|
| Distance per interval (cm) | | | | | | | | | | | | | | ... |
| Total distance (cm) | | | | | | | | | | | | | | ... |

5. Create a distance vs. time graph. On the *y*-axis, use total distance and on the *x*-axis, use time. Draw a best-fit line on your graph.
6. Find the slope of your graph and record it along with the appropriate units.

### Concluding Questions

1. What does the slope of a distance-time graph represent?
2. Find the average speed of the toy car over five 1 s intervals of the trip.
3. Compare your slope of the distance-time graph with your average speed over the five 1 s intervals.

# Investigation 1-2 Measuring Acceleration

## Purpose

To measure the uniform acceleration of an object

### *Part 1*

### Procedure

1. Figure 1.2.a shows one way to produce uniformly accelerated motion. (Your teacher may have a different method and will explain it to you.) Remove a 1-m piece of ticker tape from a roll. Pass the tape through a recording timer and tape it to a laboratory cart, as shown in the diagram. A 500 g mass is attached to the cart by a 1 m string that passes over a pulley. The force of gravity on the mass accelerates both the mass and the cart.
2. For best results in this experiment, there should be no slack in the ticker tape before the cart is released. One partner should place the hanging mass over the pulley, and hold onto the cart so that it does not accelerate prematurely. When all is ready, simultaneously turn on the timer and release the cart.

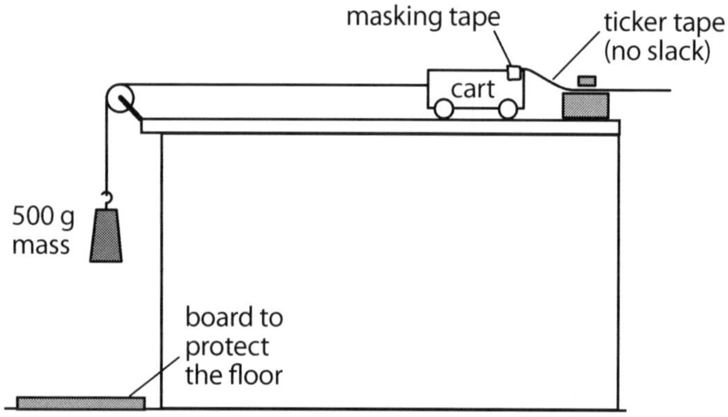


**Figure 1.2.a** *Apparatus setup for Part 1*

3. Your finished ticker tape record will look something like the one in Figure 1.2.b. Often there is a smudged grouping of dots at the start, so choose the first clear dot and label it the "0th" dot. On your tape, mark clearly the 0th dot, 6th dot, 12th dot, 18th dot, 24th dot, and so on until you have at least six time intervals. The timer has a frequency of 60 Hz. This means it makes 60 vibrations each second. The time interval between dots on your tape is 1/60 s. If you use a time interval of six dots, this is 6/60 s or 1/10 s. In other words, an interval of six dots is the same as 0.10 s.

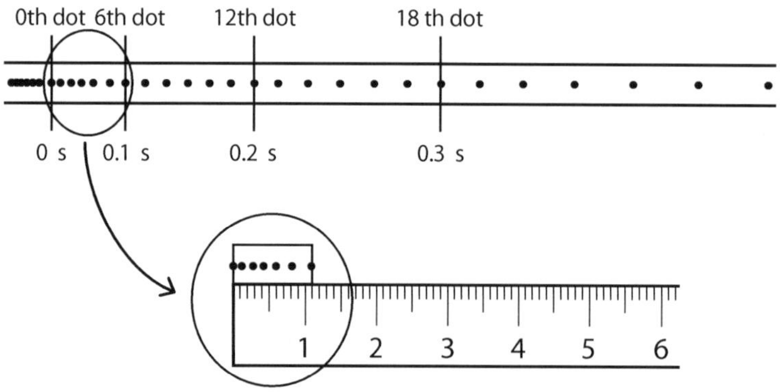


**Figure 1.2.b** *The beginning of the tape may have a smudged group of dots.*

4. Carefully measure the distance the cart travelled during each successive 0.10 s time interval. For example, in the sample tape in Figure 1.2.b, the distance travelled during the interval between 0 and 0.10 s was 1.1 cm. Figure 1.2.c shows how to measure the distance travelled during the second 0.10 s interval between 0.10 s and 0.20 s. In the sample tape, the distance is 2.8 cm. Prepare a table like Table 1.2. Record the distances travelled in each of the recorded intervals in your table.

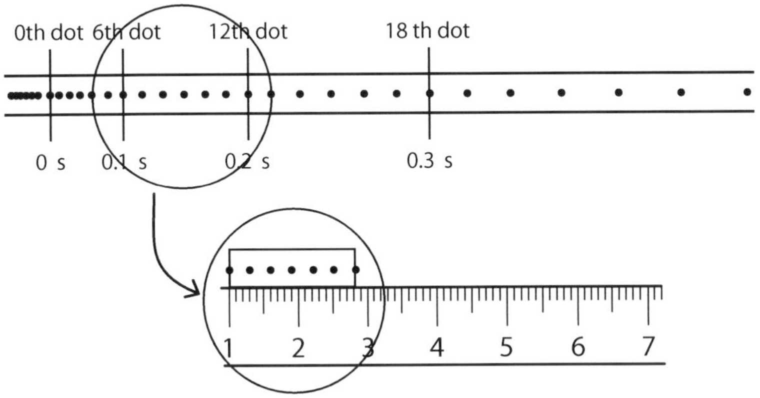


**Figure 1.2.c** *How to measure the distance between 0.10 s and 0.20 s*

**Table 1.2** *Data for an Accelerating Cart*

| Time Interval (s) | Distance Travelled (cm) | Average Speed for the Interval (cm/s) |
|---|---|---|
| 0 to 0.10 | | |
| 0.10 to 0.20 | | |
| 0.20 to 0.30 | | |
| 0.30 to 0.40 | | |
| 0.40 to 0.50 | | |
| 0.50 to 0.60 | | |

5. Your next task is to figure out the average speed of the cart during each of the 0.10 s time intervals. Since average speed is just the distance travelled during the time interval divided by the time interval, all you have to do is divide each measured distance by the time interval (0.10 s). During the first time interval on the sample tape, the cart moved a distance of 1.1 cm. The average speed of the cart during the first 0.10 s was therefore

$$\bar{v} = \frac{1.1\text{ cm}}{0.10\text{ s}} = 11\text{ cm/s}$$

During the second time interval (between 0.10 s and 0.20 s), the cart moved a distance of 1.8 cm. Its average speed during the second interval was therefore

$$\bar{v} = \frac{1.8\text{ cm}}{0.10\text{ s}} = 18\text{ cm/s}$$

6. Using your own tape data, calculate the average speed of the cart during each of the time intervals and complete Table 1.2.

## Concluding Questions

1. (a) What was the average speed of the cart during the first 0.10 s time interval?
   (b) What was the average speed of the cart during the second 0.10 s interval?
   (c) By how much did the average speed of the cart increase between the first interval and the second interval?
   (d) Calculate the acceleration of the cart between the first interval and the second interval by dividing the increase in average speed by the time interval, which was 0.10 s.

   Example**:** On the sample tape, the average speed increased from 11 cm/s to 18 cm/s between the first and second time intervals. Therefore, the acceleration was:

$$a = \frac{18\text{ cm/s} - 11\text{ cm/s}}{0.10\text{ s}} = \frac{7.0\text{ cm/s}}{0.10\text{ s}} = 70\text{ cm/s}^2$$

2. Calculate the acceleration of the cart between the second and third intervals, third and fourth intervals, fourth and fifth intervals, and fifth and sixth intervals. Allowing for slight variations due to experimental errors, is there any pattern to your results?

### *Part 2*

## Procedure

1. Using your data table from Investigation 1-2 (Table 1.2), plot a graph of speed vs. time for the accelerating cart, like the example shown below in Figure 1.2.d. Remember that the speeds in the table are average speeds for each interval and should be plotted midway through each time interval.

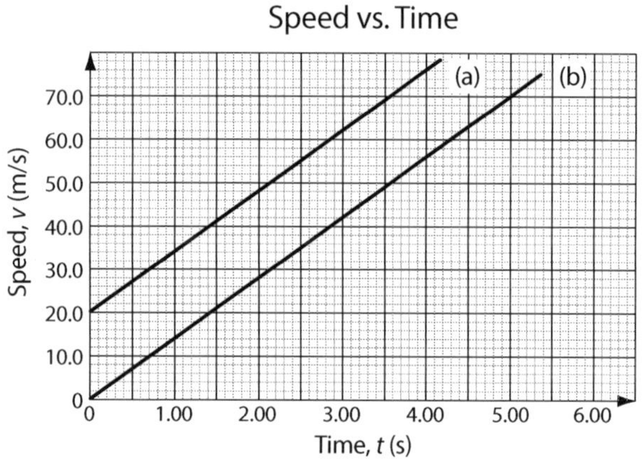


**Figure 1.2.d** *This is an example of a speed-time graph like the one you will draw.*

2. Draw a single straight line through all the plotted points. If there are stray points due to experimental error, try to draw a line that leaves as many strays on one side of it as on the other. If a point is an obvious gross error, ignore it when drawing your "best-fit line." If in doubt, ask your teacher for advice.
3. Determine the *y*-intercept of your line. Also, determine the slope of the line

## Concluding Questions

1. What was the acceleration of your cart according to the slope of your graph?
2. What is the equation for the speed-time graph you plotted for the cart?
3. In Investigation 1-2, you figured out the acceleration of your cart simply by comparing average speeds of the cart in successive time intervals. Compare the acceleration you calculated in Investigation 1-2 with the acceleration you just obtained using the slope of your speed-time graph. Which method of finding the acceleration "averages out" the experimental errors better? Explain.

# Investigation 1.3 Projectiles

## Purpose

To study the two-dimensional motion of a projectile

## Procedure

1. Set up the projectile apparatus in Figure 1.3.a. When the horizontal bar is released by a spring mechanism, ball A falls straight down and ball B is projected horizontally. Once "fired," both balls experience one force only (ignoring air resistance) — the force of gravity. Watch and listen as the two balls are projected simultaneously. Repeat the procedure several times.

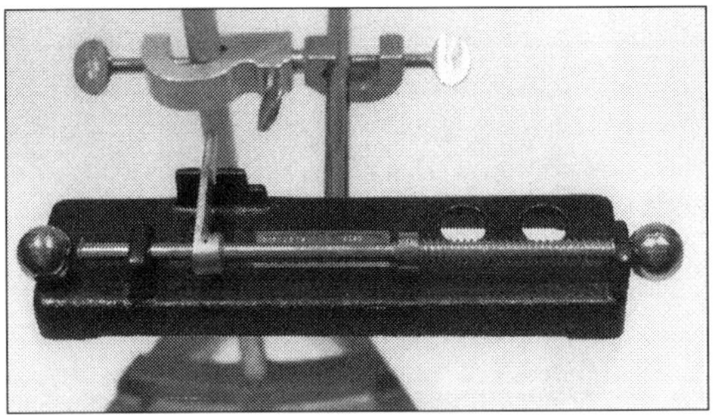

(a)

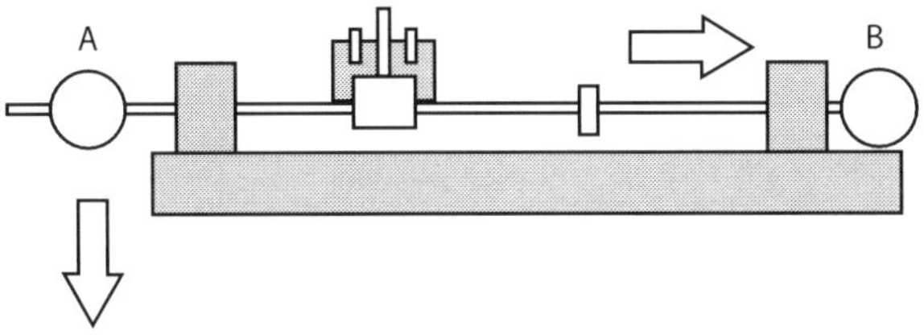


(b)

**Figure 1.3.a**

2. Figure 1.3.b(a) could be a tracing from a strobe photograph of two balls released simultaneously by a projectile apparatus similar to the one you just used. Make or obtain a copy of this tracing. Use a sharp, penciled dot to mark the position of the centre of each image of the balls. Figure 1.3.b(b) shows what to do.

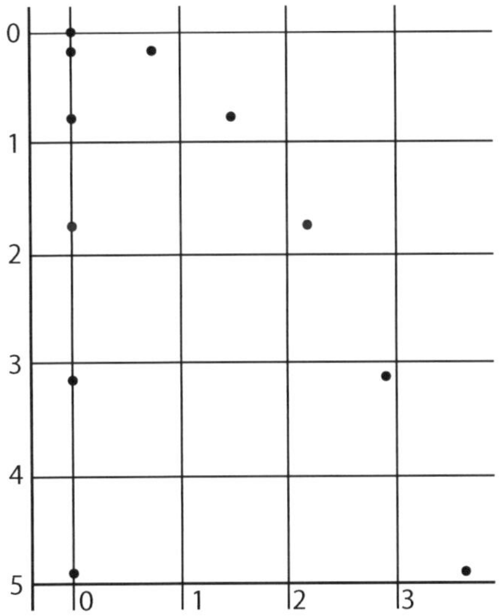


(a)

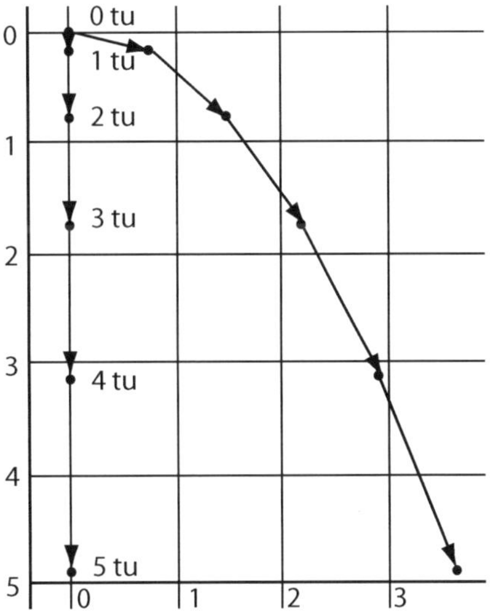


(b)

**Figure 1.3.b** *A tracing of a stroboscopic photograph made of a projected ball, falling simultaneously with a ball falling straight down, might look like this.*

3. Consider ball A first. (It is the one falling straight down.) Find out if its acceleration is uniform as follows: Call the time interval between images one "time unit" (tu). Measure the displacement of the ball during each successive tu. Since average velocity equals displacement divided by time, the average velocity during each successive time interval simply equals displacement divided by 1 tu.

4. Make a graph of the average vertical velocity $\bar{v}_y$ vs. time, $t$. Find out if the acceleration of falling ball A is uniform. Remember that, since this is average velocity, you should plot velocities *midway* through each time interval.
5. Now, consider ball B, which was projected horizontally. On your tracing, draw in successive velocity vectors as shown in Figure 1.3.b(b) above. These vectors are cute to look at, but they do not help you understand what is happening to ball B! Therefore, construct both horizontal and vertical components of each of the velocity vectors. See Figure 1.3.c.

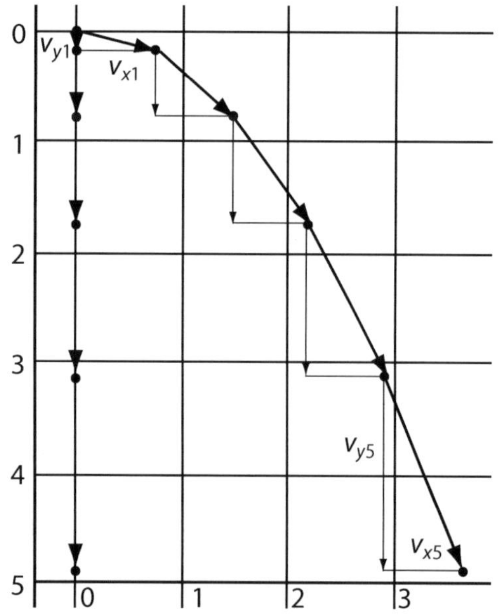


**Figure 1.3.c**

6. Compare successive vertical components of ball B's velocities with the corresponding vertical velocities of ball A. Plot a graph of $\bar{v}_y$ vs. $t$ for ball B.
7. Compare successive horizontal components ($\bar{v}_x$) with each other. Plot $\bar{v}_x$ vs. $t$.
8. (a) Plot total vertical displacement from rest ($d_y$) vs. time ($t$) for the vertical motion of either ball.
   (b) Plot $d_y$ vs. $t^2$.
9. Plot total horizontal displacement from rest ($d_x$) vs. time ($t$) for ball B.

### Concluding Questions

1. A rifle fires a bullet horizontally on level ground. Just as the bullet leaves the rifle, the rifle falls to the ground. Which will hit the ground first, the bullet or the rifle? Explain your answer.
2. When a ball is projected horizontally, what conclusions do you arrive at regarding
   (a) its horizontal velocity components?
   (b) its vertical velocity components?
3. Write a simple mathematical relationship (such as $d_x = \mathrm{k}\,t$, where k is the constant of proportionality) connecting the two variables in each of the following projectile situations:
   (a) $v_y$ vs. $t$
   (b) $v_x$ vs. $t$
   (c) $d_y$ vs. $t$

### Challenges

1. Build a "monkey gun" apparatus. See Figure 1.3.d. The projectile is a small marble, which is propelled by a "blow gun" made of a copper pipe, the diameter of which is just slightly larger than the marble. When the marble leaves the gun, it breaks a thin piece of aluminum foil, which opens an electric circuit. An electromagnet holding up a tin can target (the "monkey" in a tree?) is deactivated. Just as the marble leaves the gun, the "monkey" starts to fall to the ground. Will the marble hit the monkey or miss it? Explain your answer. Now test your prediction!

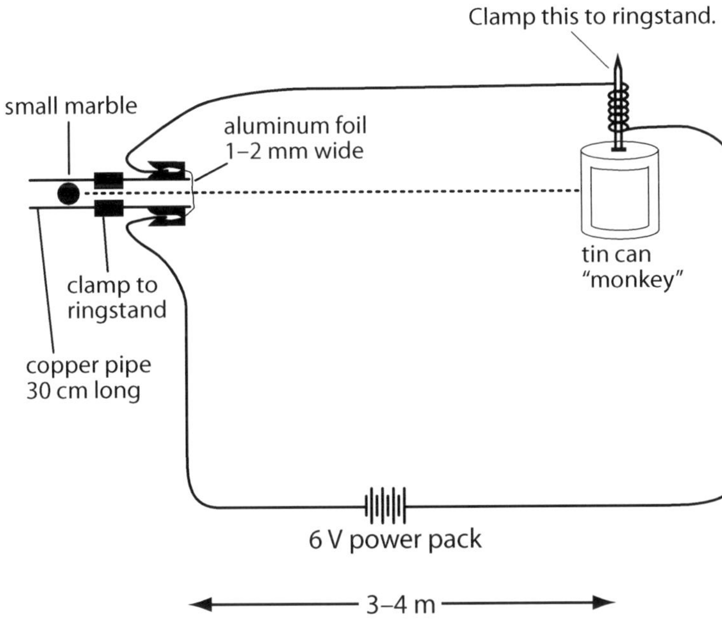


**Figure 1.10**

2. Imagine that the "blow gun" is aimed upward at some angle greater than zero relative to the horizontal. It is aimed at the "monkey" to begin with. Will it still hit the monkey if the monkey falls at the instant the marble leaves the gun? Explain your answer.

# 2 Dynamics

This chapter focuses on the following AP Physics 1 Big Ideas from the College Board:

**BIG IDEA 1:** Objects and systems have properties such as mass and charge. Systems may have internal structure.

**BIG IDEA 2:** Fields existing in space can be used to explain interactions.

**BIG IDEA 3:** The interactions of an object with other objects can be described by forces.

**BIG IDEA 4:** Interactions between systems can result in changes in those systems.

---

By the end of this chapter, you should know the meaning to these **key terms**:

- coefficient of friction
- force
- force due to gravity
- gravitational field strength
- gravity
- Hooke's law
- inverse square law
- kinetic friction
- mass
- Newton
- Newton's first law of motion
- Newton's second law of motion
- Newton's third law of motion
- Newton's law of universal gravitation
- normal force
- spring constant
- static friction
- universal gravitational constant
- weight

---

By the end of the chapter, you should be able to use and know when to use the following formulae:

$F_g = mg$

$F_g = G\frac{m_1 m_2}{r^2}$

$F_{fr} = \mu F_N$

$F = k\Delta x$

$F = ma$

*This bungee jumper experiences both the force of gravity and elastic force during her jump.*

# 2.1 Force of Gravity

## Warm Up

Take a sheet of paper and a book in each hand. Hold at shoulder level. If you release them at the same time, which will hit the ground first? Now place the sheet of paper on top of the book. The paper should not extend over the edges of the book. Will the paper fall at the same rate as the book, faster or slower? Test your prediction. Can you create a rule for falling objects that explains how different masses fall to Earth?

___

___

___

### Force

Every time you push, pull, twist or squeeze something you exert a force on it. Almost every time you exert a force on an object, you change something about that object: its speed, its direction, or its shape. A **force** is a push or a pull.

When a soccer player "heads" the ball the speed of the ball changes, and sometimes its direction does too. When a hockey player is given a solid body check, the force changes his direction and speed. When a golf ball is struck by a golf club, the force of the impact changes the ball's shape during the collision. The force due to air friction alters the shape of a raindrop, from a perfect sphere to something more like a teardrop.

Forces are measured in a unit called the **newton (N)**, named after Sir Isaac Newton.

### Gravitational Force

The force of gravity pulls on you all the time. The force of attraction between planet Earth and you keeps you from floating aimlessly off into space! Any two bodies in the universe exert a gravitational force on each other. The amount of force they exert depends upon how massive the bodies are and how far apart they are. Two unique facts about the force of gravity are: (1) it cannot be "shut off"; and (2) it is always an attractive force, never repulsive.

Gravitational force is an example of a force that acts on objects without touching them. This classifies gravity as an action-at-a-distance force. Gravitational force creates a gravitational field around a body. Think of a field as an area where a force is exerted. For example, magnets have a field around them created by the attraction and repulsion between magnetic poles. A gravitational field depends on the mass of an object. The bigger the mass, the bigger the gravitational field. For Earth, this means a small mass like a person is attracted to the centre of Earth because Earth is the larger mass. The gravitational force experienced by the person results mainly from the Earth's gravitational field. The force within the gravitational field is referred to as the gravitational field strength. It is measured as the gravitational force per unit mass or $g = \frac{F_g}{m}$. The symbol for gravitational field strength is $g$. At Earth's surface, $g$ is approximately 9.81 N/kg.

## Weight

Regardless of where you are on Earth, near the surface, objects will fall with the same acceleration regardless of their mass. Other forces such as air resistance may slow an object down, but the acceleration due to gravity remains constant. Gravitational force is equal to the product of an object's mass and the acceleration due to gravity.

$$F_g = mg$$

When we calculate the gravitational force acting on an object, we are calculating its **weight**. This is an example of a term that has a specific meaning in science, but has other everyday uses. Many times people use the term *weight* to refer to mass. For example, when someone asks you how much you weigh, they are actually asking you what your mass is. The difference between weight and mass is that weight in measured in newtons and mass is measured in metric units such as grams or kilograms.

### Quick Check

1. What is the force of gravity on a 90 kg person? What is the weight of this person?
2. If a person experiences a 637 N force of gravity on Earth's surface, what is the person's mass?
3. A 75 kg person would experience a force of gravity of 127.5 N on the Moon. What is the gravitational field strength on the Moon?

## Measuring the Force of Gravity

Gravity causes unsupported objects to fall toward Earth. The usual way to measure the force of gravity is to balance it with another force acting upward. For example, when you stand on a bathroom scale, gravity pulls you downward. A coiled spring inside the scale pushes upward and balances the force of gravity.

The common laboratory spring balance uses a spring that is stretched by the force of gravity acting on the object that is being "weighed" (Figure 2.1.1). If the spring is of good quality, the amount it stretches will depend directly on the force of gravity. That is, if the force of gravity doubles, the stretch will double. If the force of gravity triples, the stretch will triple. In other words, the amount of stretch is directly proportional to the force of gravity on the object.

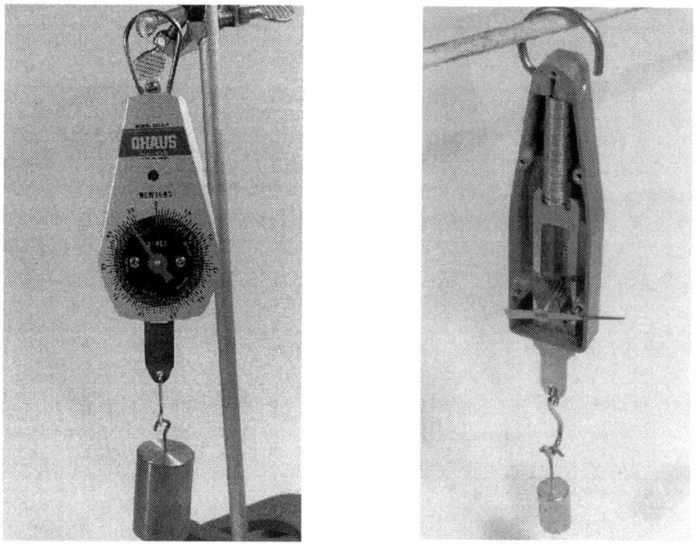


(a) (b)

**Figure 2.1.1** *An example of a laboratory spring balance showing the gauge (a) and the spring (b)*

## Newton's Law of Universal Gravitation

One of Sir Isaac Newton's many valuable contributions to science is his law of universal gravitation. Newton (1642–1727) realized that the force of gravity, which affects you and everything around you, is a universal force. Any two masses in the universe exert a gravitational force on each other. The force that keeps planets in orbit is the same force that makes an apple fall to the ground. How strong the force is depends on how massive the bodies are. It also depends on the distance between the two bodies.

Like all other forces, gravity is a mutual force. That is, the force with which the Earth pulls on a falling apple is equal to the force with which the apple pulls on the Earth, but in the opposite direction. The Earth pulls on your body with a force of gravity that is commonly referred to as your "weight." Simultaneously, your body exerts a force on planet Earth of the same magnitude but in the opposite direction.

Newton was able to use Kepler's laws of planetary motion as a starting point for developing his own ideas about gravity. Johannes Kepler (1571–1630) was a German astronomer who described the motion of the planets around the Sun now called Kepler's Laws. You will study these laws in future courses. Using Kepler's laws, Newton showed that the force of gravity between the Sun and the planets varied as the inverse of the square of the distance between the Sun and the planets. He was convinced that the inverse square relation would apply to everyday objects near Earth's surface as well. He produced arguments suggesting that the force would depend on the product of the masses of the two bodies attracted to one another. The result was his law of universal gravitation.

 

**Newton's law of universal gravitation** can be summarized as follows:

Every body in the universe attracts every other body with a force that (a) is directly proportional to the product of the masses of the two bodies, and (b) is inversely proportional to the square of the distance between the centres of mass of the two bodies.

The equation for Newton's law of universal gravitation is:

$$F_g = G\frac{m_1 m_2}{r^2}$$

where G is the **universal gravitation constant**, $m_1$ and $m_2$ are the masses of the bodies attracting each other, and $r$ is the distance between the centres of the two bodies.

Isaac Newton was unable to measure G, but Henry Cavendish (1731–1810) measured it later in experiments. The modern value for $G$ is $6.67 \times 10^{-11}$ $N{\bullet}m^2/kg^2$.

## Cavendish's Experiment to Measure *G*

You can imagine how difficult it is to measure the gravitational force between two ordinary objects. In 1797, Henry Cavendish performed a very sensitive experiment that was the first Earth-bound confirmation of the law of universal gravitation. Cavendish used two lead spheres mounted at the ends of a rod 2.0 m long. The rod was suspended horizontally from a wire that would *twist* an amount proportional to the gravitational force between the suspended masses and two larger fixed spherical masses placed near each of the suspended spheres. (See Figure 2.1.2.)

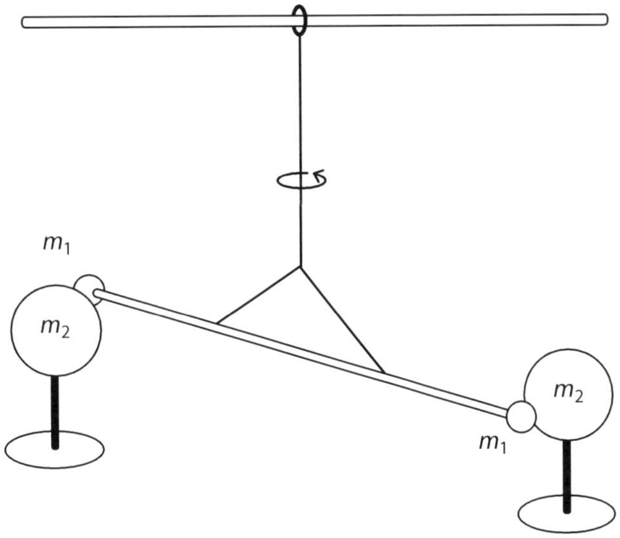


**Figure 2.1.2** *Cavendish's apparatus*

The forces involved in this experiment were extremely small (of the order $10^{-6}$ N), so great care had to be taken to eliminate errors due to air currents and static electricity. Cavendish did manage to provide confirmation of the law of universal gravitation, and he arrived at the first measured value of *G*.

## Earth's Gravitational Field Strength

To calculate the force of gravity on a mass *m*, you could simply multiply the mass by the gravitational field strength, *g* ($F = mg$). You could also use the law of universal gravitation:

$$F_g = G\frac{Mm}{r^2}, \text{ where } M \text{ is the mass of Earth.}$$

This means that $mg = G\frac{Mm}{r^2}$, and therefore,

$$g = G\frac{M}{r^2}$$

Thus, the gravitational field strength of Earth depends only on the mass of Earth and the distance, *r*, from the centre of Earth to the centre of mass of the object that has mass *m*.

### Quick Check

1. Given two small, chocolate-centred candies of masses *M* and *m*, what will happen to the force of gravity $F_g$ between them in the following situations?
   (a) *r* is doubled.

   (b) *r* is tripled.

   (c) *r* is reduced to 1/2 *r*.

   (d) *r* is reduced to 1/3 *r*.

2. The constant *G* in the law of universal gravitation has a value of $6.67 \times 10^{-11}$ N•m²/kg². Calculate the force of gravity between the following objects:
   (a) a 100.0 kg person and Earth. Earth's mass is $5.98 \times 10^{24}$ kg, and its radius is $6.38 \times 10^6$ m.

   (b) a 100.0 kg person and the Moon. The Moon's mass is $7.35 \times 10^{22}$ kg, and its radius is $1.74 \times 10^6$ m.

   (c) two 46 g golf balls whose centres of mass are 10 cm apart.

## 2.1 Review Questions

$G = 6.67 \times 10^{-11}$ N•m²/kg² — $g = 9.81$ N/kg

Earth's mass $= 5.98 \times 10^{24}$ kg — Earth's radius $= 6.38 \times 10^{6}$ m

1. What is the force of gravity on a 600 N person standing on Earth's surface?

2. How would the force of gravity between the Sun and Earth change if the mass of the Sun was three times greater than it is?

3. (a) What is the weight of an 80 kg person?

   (b) What is the weight of an 80 kg astronaut on the Moon where $g = 1.7$ m/s$^2$?

4. Given two candies with masses $M$ and $m$ a distance $d$ apart, what will the force of gravity $F_g$ between them become in the following situations?
   (a) Only $M$ is doubled.

   (b) Only $m$ is doubled.

   (c) Both $M$ and $m$ are doubled.

   (d) $M$, $m$, and $d$ are *all* doubled.

5. What is the force of gravity on a 70.0 kg man standing on Earth's surface, according to the law of universal gravitation? Check your answer using $F = mg$.

6. What is the force of gravitational attraction between a 75 kg boy and a 60.0 kg girl in the following situations?
   (a) when they are 2.0 m apart

   (b) when they are only 1.0 m apart

7. What is the force of gravity exerted on you when standing on the Moon, if your mass is 70.0 kg and the Moon's mass is $7.34 \times 10^{22}$ kg? The Moon's radius is $1.74 \times 10^{6}$ m.

8. What is the force of gravity exerted on you on Mars, if your mass is 70.0 kg and the mass of Mars is $6.37 \times 10^{23}$ kg? The radius of Mars is $3.43 \times 10^{6}$ m, and you are standing on its surface, searching for Mars bars.

9. What is the force of gravity exerted on a 70.0 kg person on Jupiter (assuming the person could find a place to stand)? Jupiter has a mass of $1.90 \times 10^{27}$ kg and a radius of $7.18 \times 10^{7}$ m.

# 2.2 Friction

## Warm Up

Fill a narrow-neck jar to the brim with rice. Poke a pencil into the jar and push the pencil until it can't go any farther. Repeat the poking until you can lift the jar with the pencil in the rice. Why does this happen?

______________________________________________

______________________________________________

______________________________________________

### Why We Need Friction

When a body moves, there is almost always a resisting force exerted on it by materials in contact with it. An aircraft moving through the air must overcome the resistance of the air. A submarine encounters resistance from the water. A car experiences resistance from the road surface and from the air. In all cases like this, the force opposing the motion of the body is called **friction**. Engineers attempt to design aircraft, ships, and automobiles so that friction is minimized.

Friction is not always a "bad" thing, of course. You need friction to bring your bike, car, or yourself to a stop. Walking on a frictionless floor would be a major challenge. Friction is desirable when you wish to strike a match or write with a pencil. If you ever have to use a parachute, you will appreciate the resisting force of the air on your parachute.

If you want to push a book along your bench, you know that you have to keep on pushing to keep it moving. This is true in many everyday situations. A skateboarder cannot coast along a level road indefinitely without some force being applied to counter the friction force. Friction is such a normal phenomenon, that for centuries it was believed impossible for an object to keep moving without a constant force being applied. About 400 years ago, Galileo Galilei (1546–1642) suggested that a body, once moving, would continue moving at the same speed and in the same direction indefinitely if friction were eliminated and no other unbalanced forces were present. It is difficult to verify this idea experimentally, and it seems to contradict everyday experiences. For some time, it was a hard concept for people to accept.

### Static and Kinetic Friction

Even the smoothest-looking piece of metal, if viewed under a microscope, will have irregular bumps and hollows. Where the bumps come in contact, the electrical attraction between the atoms of the two surfaces produces a small-scale "welding" of the materials at the points of contact (Figure 2.2.1). When one surface is moved over the other, the welded regions must be broken apart. Friction arises from the breaking of these welded regions and from the "plowing" effect as the harder surface moves through the softer one.

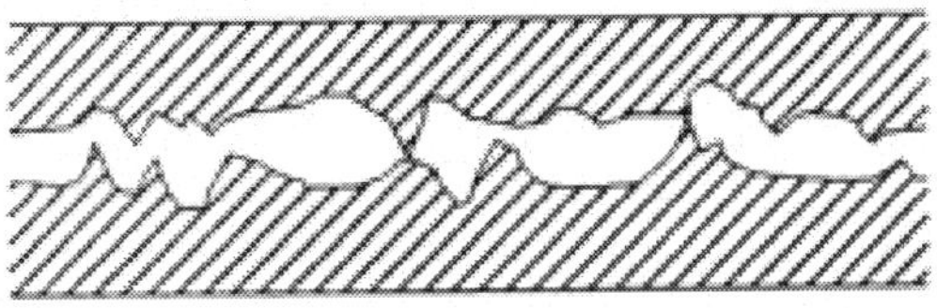

**Figure 2.2.1** *An artist's impression of two metal surfaces magnified*

**Static friction** acts when you have two objects at rest relative to one another. Static friction, for example, keeps a car with its parking brakes on from sliding down a hill. A block of wood will remain stationary on a sloped table until you increase the angle sufficiently that it begins to slide. The force required to overcome static friction is always greater than the force needed to balance **kinetic friction**. Kinetic friction is the friction force between two flat surfaces that exists when one surface slides over the other.

To overcome static friction, you have to break the "welds" before the objects can move relative to one another. When you push a a heavy object, you have probably noticed that the force needed to get the object moving was slightly greater than the force needed to keep it moving at steady speed.

The force of friction $F_{fr}$ is proportional to the force of gravity $F_g$ on the object sliding over a smooth surface. A more general fact about kinetic friction is that the force of friction is proportional to the **normal force** $F_N$, which is the force acting perpendicular to the surfaces.

If a block slides horizontally across a table as in Figure 2.2.2 (a), the force of gravity is equal in magnitude to the normal force, but if the surfaces are at an angle to the horizontal as in Figure 2.2.2 (b), the normal force does not equal the force of gravity. You will encounter situations like this in future physics courses.

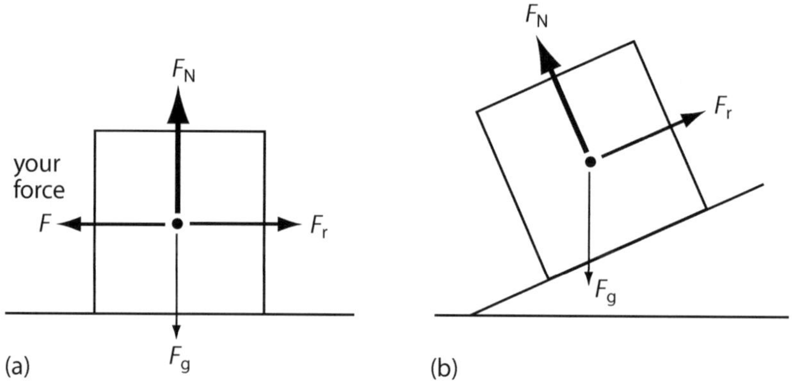


**Figure 2.2.2** **(a)** *For a block sliding horizontally, the force of gravity and the normal force are equal.* **(b)** *For block sliding on a slope, these two forces are not equal.*

## Coefficients of Friction

In general, for two objects with smooth flat surfaces sliding over one another, the force of friction is proportional to the normal force. The constant of proportionality is called the **coefficient of kinetic friction**. It is given the special symbol $\mu$, which is the Greek letter *mu*.

$$F_{fr} = \mu F_N$$

 

Table 2.2.1 lists some coefficients of kinetic friction.

**Table 2.2.1** *Coefficients of Kinetic Friction**

| Surfaces in Contact | Coefficient $\mu$* |
|---|---|
| wood on wood | 0.25 |
| steel on steel | 0.50 |
| steel on steel (lubricated) | 0.10 |
| rubber on dry asphalt | 0.40 |
| rubber on wet asphalt | 0.20 |
| rubber on ice | 0.005 |
| steel on ice | 0.01 |

* All values are approximate. Precise values vary with conditions such as degree of smoothness.

Surface area does not affect the force of friction appreciably. For example, it will require the same force to slide a building brick on its edge, as it will on its broad side. The two factors that have the greatest effect on friction are:

1. the normal force pushing the surfaces together, and
2. the nature of the surfaces.

### Sample Problem 2.2.1 — Kinetic Friction

The coefficient of kinetic friction between a wooden box and a concrete floor is 0.30. With what force must you push to slide the box across the floor at steady speed if the force of gravity on the box is 450 N?

| What to Think About | How to Do It |
|---|---|
| 1. If the box is moving at a constant speed, the forces acting on it are balanced. This means the force need top push the box is equal and opposite to the force of friction. Find the force of friction. | $F_{fr} = \mu F_N$ |
| 2. The box is on a flat surface. This means the force of gravity equals the normal force. Find the normal force | $F_N = F_g$<br>$F_N = 450\text{ N}$ |
| 3. Solve. | $F_{fr} = \mu F_g$<br>$= (0.30)(450\text{ N})$<br>$= 135\text{ N}$<br>$= 1.4 \times 10^2\text{ N}$<br><br>You have to push the box with a force of $1.4 \times 10^2$ N. |

## Practice Problems 2.2.1 — Kinetic Friction

1. What is the total force of friction on a wagon's wheels if it takes 30 N to move it at a constant speed across a bumpy path?

2. (a) A 10 kg box of candy rests on a floor with a coefficient of static friction of 0.30. What force is needed to move the box?

   (b) If the coefficient of kinetic friction is 0.25, what force is needed to keep the box moving at a constant speed?

3. What is the coefficient of kinetic friction between a rubber tire and the road if a 2000 kg car needs $1.57 \times 10^4$ N to keep the car moving at a constant speed?

## 2.2 Review Questions

1. (a) Where on a bicycle do you want to reduce friction? How is this done?

   (b) Where on a bicycle do you want friction?

2. (a) What is meant by the coefficient of kinetic friction?

   (b) Why are there no units attached to values of $\mu$?

3. A force of 120 N is needed to push a box along a level road at a steady speed. If the force of gravity on the box is 250 N, what is the coefficient of kinetic friction between the box and the road?

4. The coefficient of kinetic friction between a steel block and an ice rink surface is 0.0100. If a force of 24.5 N keeps the steel block moving at a steady speed, what is the force of gravity on the block?

5. A copper block has dimensions 1 cm × 2 cm × 4 cm. A force of 0.10 N will pull the block along a table surface at a steady speed if the 1 cm × 4 cm side is face down on the table. What force will be needed to pull the same block along when its 2 cm × 4 cm side is face down?

6. A 48 N cart is pulled across a concrete path at a constant speed. A 42 N force is required to keep the cart moving. What is the coefficient of kinetic friction between the path and the cart?

# 2.3 Hooke's Law

## Warm Up

Take three different known masses and a rubber band. Measure the length of the rubber band as it hangs from a hook. Add the smallest mass and measure the distance the rubber band stretches. Predict how far the rubber band will stretch with your other two masses. Test each one and record your predictions and results below.

______________________________________________

______________________________________________

______________________________________________

### Spring Constant

Figure 2.3.1 is a graph showing how the stretch of a certain spring varies with the force of gravity acting on it. This is not only a linear graph, but also a direct proportion. When the force of gravity on the spring is 1.0 N, the stretch is 0.75 cm. When the force is doubled to 2.0 N, the stretch doubles to 1.50 cm. If the force is tripled to 3.0 N, the stretch also triples to 2.25 cm.

If a force is exerted on an object, such as a spring or a block of metal, the object will be stretched or compressed. If the amount of stretching or compression, $x$, is small compared with the length of the object, then $x$ is proportional to the force, $F$, exerted on the object. Figure 2.3.1 illustrates this proportionality. In Figure 2.3.1, stretch is given the symbol $x$, and the straight-line graph through (0,0) suggests that $F_g \propto x$ or that $F_g = kx$. The slope of the graph is the **spring constant**, $k$.

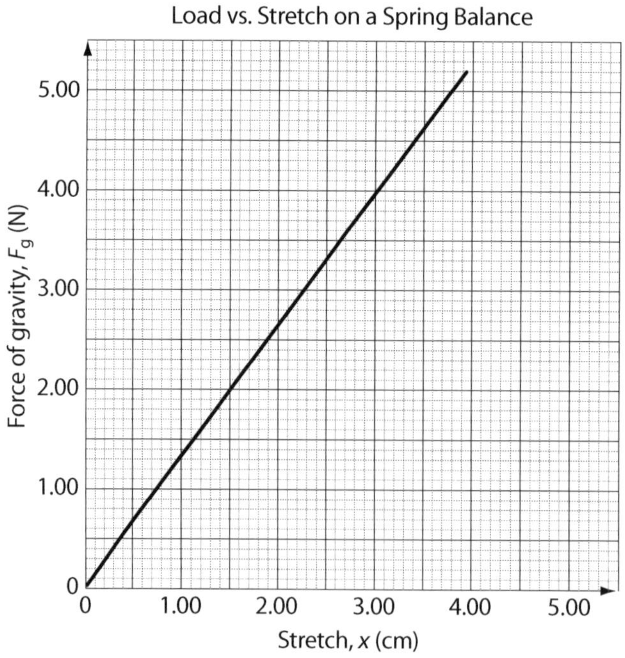


**Figure 2.3.1** *The amount of stretch in a spring is proportional to the amount of force exerted on the spring.*

The English scientist Robert Hooke (1635–1703) first noticed the direct proportion between the force exerted on a solid object and the change in length of the object caused by the force. If too much force is applied, and an object is stretched or compressed excessively, the direct proportion breaks down. In that case, the object may be permanently stretched or compressed. **Hooke's law** is written with force as the subject of the equation:

$$F = k\Delta x$$

where *F* is the applied force, *x* is the change in length, and *k* is the spring constant.

## Quick Check

1. What is the applied force on a spring when it is stretched 0.20 cm and the spring constant is 3.2 N/m?

2. On Figure 2.3.1, the slope of the line is the spring constant (*k*). What is *k* for the spring used in that example?

3. A 2.5 kg mass stretches a spring 10 cm. How far will the spring stretch when it supports 5.0 kg?

## 2.3 Review Questions

1. Why are the units for the spring constant?

2. Using symbols "x" for stretch and "F" for force of gravity, write a specific equation for the line in Figure 2.3.1.

3. (a) Use your equation to solve for the stretch of the spring when a force of gravity of 4.0 N acts on it. Check your solution by looking at the graph in Figure 2.3.1.

   (b) Use your equation to solve for the force of gravity needed to stretch the spring 2.0 cm. Check your solution by looking at the graph in Figure 2.3.1.

4. In a direct proportion graph, the slope of the graph is called the spring constant. At any point on the line, the ratio of the stretch to the force of gravity will equal the constant of proportionality. By looking at the graph, find the spring constant when $F = 5.0$ N.

5. A wooden beam was clamped horizontally, so that masses could be hung from its free end. The depression $x$ (in cm) caused by the force of gravity $F_g$ (in N) on the masses was measured for loads up to 100 N. The graph below summarizes all the data.

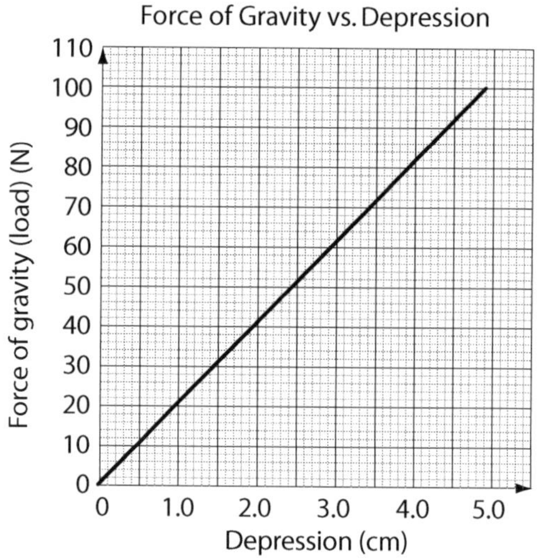


   a) What is the slope of the graph, expressed in appropriate units?

   (b) Write an equation specifically for this graph.

   (c) According to the above graph, how much will the beam be depressed by a load of 80.0 N?

   (d) According to the above graph, what load will cause the beam to be depressed by 3.0 cm?

# 2.4 Inertia and Newton's First Law

## Warm Up

You are attending a magic show and the magician stands beside a table set with fancy plates, cups, and silverware. Grabbing the edge of the tablecloth she quickly pulls the cloth out, and the plates, cups, and silverware stay in place. Is this magic or just physics in action? Explain your answer.

________________________________________________________________________

________________________________________________________________________

________________________________________________________________________

### Inertia

Imagine you are a passenger in a car, and the driver makes a sudden left turn. What sensation do you feel during the left turn? From your own experience, you might recall that you feel as if you are being pushed to the right. Contrary to what you feel, you are not being pushed to the right at all.

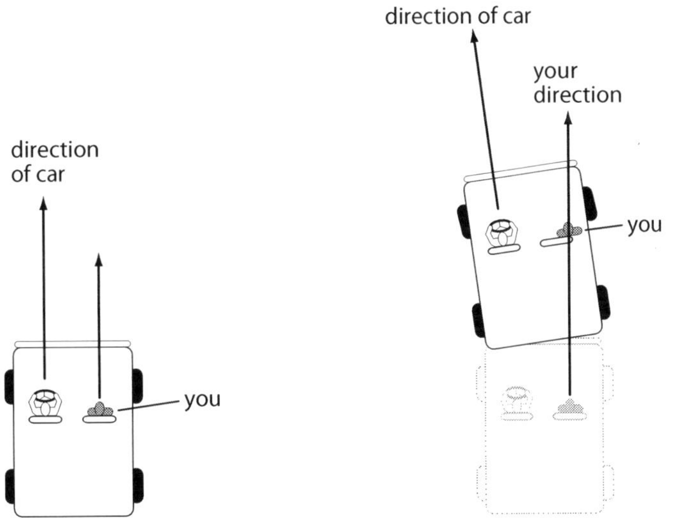


**Figure 2.4.1** *As the car turns, your body wants to keep moving straight ahead.*

Figure 2.4.1 illustrates what happens and explains why you feel the force acting on your body. The car starts out by going straight and then the driver steers the car to the left. The car is moving to the left but your body wants to carry on in a straight line. What's stopping you? The door of the car is moving left with the rest of the car so it is pushing you in the direction the car is going. You feel as if you are pushing against the door, but this feeling is not what is happening. What is happening is that your body is trying to continue along its original straight path while the car is turning left. The result is that you are being pulled along with the car rather than continuing in a straight line.

As a general rule, any object tends to continue moving with whatever speed and direction it already has. This can include zero speed. When a driver accelerates a car, a body in the car tends to keep doing what it was already doing. So if the car is stopped, you are stopped. As the car starts to move and speeds up, you feel as if you are being pushed back into your seat.

The tendency that all objects have to resist change in their states of motion is called **inertia**. Every object in the universe that has mass has this property of inertia. Galileo Galilei (1564–1642) was the first person to describe this property of nature, which is called the **law of inertia**.

Some objects have more inertia than others because they have more mass. A logging truck has much more inertia than a mountain bike. Because it has so much more inertia, the logging truck is

(a) more difficult to get moving,
(b) more difficult to stop,
(c) more difficult to turn at a corner.

## Measuring Inertia

Is there a way to measure inertia? You have measured it many times in science class. The way to measure inertia is to measure the object's mass. When you measure the mass of an object using a balance, that mass is equal to the object's **inertial mass**.

Strictly speaking, what the balance measures is called **gravitational mass**. This is because the unknown object is placed on one pan, and a standard mass is placed on the other pan. The masses are assumed to be equal when the force of gravity on the unknown mass balances the force of gravity on the standard mass. Gravitational mass is numerically equal to inertial mass, so a balance can be used to measure inertial mass as well.

### Quick Check

1. Why does it hurt more to kick a rock shaped like a soccer ball than a soccer ball?

______________________________

______________________________

2. When astronauts are living in the International Space Station (ISS) they are in orbit around Earth at a minimum altitude of 278 km. They live in an environment of apparent weightlessness. Compare the inertial mass of the astronauts when they live on the ISS to their inertial mass when they are on Earth.

______________________________

______________________________

## Newton's First Law

Isaac Newton (1642–1727) is considered one of the greatest scientists of all time. In any physics class you ever take, you will come across his name at some time. This is impressive, given that all his work was done more than 350 years ago. Newton is probably best known for his laws of motion. Newton's three laws describe motion as we experience it on Earth. They are also the foundation for helping to send humans to the Moon and deep-space vehicles out beyond our solar system.

**Newton's first law of motion** incorporated Galileo's law of inertia. The first law of motion, or law of inertia, can be stated this way:

> A body will continue to move at the same speed and in the same direction for as long as there are no unbalanced forces acting on it.

## Ideal Conditions

Put another way, an object wants to keep doing what it is already doing. This means if a basketball is placed on the floor, it will not move until another force acts on it. Someone picking up the ball is an example of a force acting on the ball.

Sometimes it appears that Newton's first law does not apply. For example, when coasting on your bicycle along a flat part of the road, you have probably noticed that you slow down even though it appears no forces are acting on the bicycle. In fact, the force of friction between the road and tires is responsible for slowing the bicycle. If there were no friction, the bicycle would continue at the same speed until another force acted on it. That is why in many physics problems about motion, you will see the assumption that there is no friction. A situation that is assumed to have no friction is called *ideal conditions*. Using ideal conditions, we can focus on the motion being observed. By specifying ideal conditions, we also show we know that friction would have to be considered under normal conditions.

### Quick Check

1. A car you are driving in encounters a patch of ice just as the car enters a corner turn. Using your knowledge of Newton's first law of motion, explain what will happen to the car.

2. You are a judge listening to an injury claim from a bus passenger. The passenger claims to have been hurt when the bus driver slammed on the brakes and a suitcase came flying from the front of the bus to hit the passenger. Do you believe the passenger's description of what happened? Explain your answer.

3. When you receive a drink for a take out order, usually there is a lid on the cup. Use Newton's first law to explain why the lid is necessary to prevent spills.

## 2.4 Review Questions

1. In the Warm Up of this section, you were asked to explain why the magician was able to pull the tablecloth out from the under the plates, cups and silverware. Using the concepts of inertia and Newton's first law, explain why this "magic act" succeeds.

2. Does 2 kg of apples have twice the inertia or half the inertia of 1 kg of apples? Explain your answer.

3. If the pen on your desk is at rest, can you say that no forces are acting on it? Explain your answer.

4. If the forces acting on the pen are balanced, is it correct to say that the pen is at rest? Explain your answer.

5. If you place a ball in the centre of a wagon and then quickly push the wagon forward, in what direction does the ball appear to go? Why?

6. Why do headrests in cars help protect a person from head and neck injury in a car accident?

7. A hockey puck moving a constant velocity across the ice eventually comes to a stop. Does this prove that Newton's first law does not apply to all situations?

8. You are travelling in a school bus on a field trip. The driver has to apply the brakes quickly to prevent an accident. Describe how your body would move in response to this rapid braking action.

9. While travelling in Africa you are chased by a very large elephant. Would it make more sense to run in a straight line to get away or in a zigzag motion? Explain your answer.

# 2.5 Newton's Second Law of Motion

## Warm Up

Take an empty spool of thread and wrap a string or thread around it three or four times, leaving the end loose so you can pull on it. Place the spool on the floor and pull on the thread horizontally to make the spool move to the right.

1. Based on your observations, what can you say about the direction of the force applied to the spool and the acceleration of the spool?

   ______________________________

   ______________________________

2. Would the direction of the force or the acceleration of the spool be affected if the thread were wrapped around the spool in the opposite direction? Explain your answer.

   ______________________________

   ______________________________

### Defining Newton's Second Law of Motion

In his second law of motion, Newton dealt with the problem of what happens when an unbalanced force acts on a body. **Newton's second law of motion** states: If an unbalanced force acts on a body, the body will accelerate. The rate at which it accelerates depends directly on the unbalanced force and inversely on the mass of the body.

$$\boldsymbol{a} = \frac{F}{m}$$

The direction in which the body accelerates will be the same direction as the unbalanced force. The measuring unit for force is the **newton (N)**. The measuring unit for mass is the kilogram (kg) and for acceleration is $m/s^2$. Therefore, using $F = ma$, one newton can be defined as the force needed to accelerate one kilogram at a rate of one metre per second per second.

Whenever Newton's second law is used, it is understood that the force $F$ in the equation $F = ma$ is the unbalanced force acting on the body. This unbalanced force is also called the net force. To calculate the unbalanced force acting on a 1.0 kg mass falling due to gravity, you use Newton's second law:

$$F = ma = 1.00\text{ kg} \times 9.81\text{ m/s}^2 = 9.81\text{ kg}\bullet\text{m/s}^2 = 9.81\text{ N}$$

To calculate the rate at which the mass accelerates, you rearrange Newton's second law to give:

$$a = \frac{F}{m} = \frac{9.81\text{ N}}{1.00\text{ kg}} = \frac{9.81\text{ kg}\bullet\text{m/s}^2}{1.00\text{ kg}} = 9.81\text{ m/s}^2$$

The acceleration of the mass is $g$ or $9.81\text{ m/s}^2$.

## Quick Check

1. A single engine plane has a mass of 1500 kg and acceleration of 0.400 m/s². What is the unbalanced force on the plane?

2. What is the mass of a rocket that accelerates at 2.0 m/s² and has a net force of 25 000 N?

3. Find the acceleration of a passenger jet that has a mass of 250 000 kg and provides an unbalanced force of 50 000 N.

### Multiple Forces

The example and problems in the Quick Check above involve only one unbalanced force. In other situations, like Sample Problem 2.5.1 below, there are more forces to consider.

Remember that, in these problems, it is important to identify the forces that create the unbalanced force. Figure 2.5.1 shows four different forces acting on a block. The two vertical forces are the force of gravity and the normal force (the force exerted by the floor on the block). The two horizontal forces are the applied force and the force of friction.

The two vertical forces balance each other because the force of gravity and the normal force equal each other in size and act in opposite directions. The unbalanced force is the difference between the applied force and the friction force opposing the applied force.

## Sample Problem 2.5.1 — Multiple Forces Acting on a Body

A 45.0 N block is being pushed along a floor, where the coefficient of kinetic friction is 0.333. If a force of 25.0 N is applied, at what rate will the block accelerate? The mass of the block is 4.60 kg.

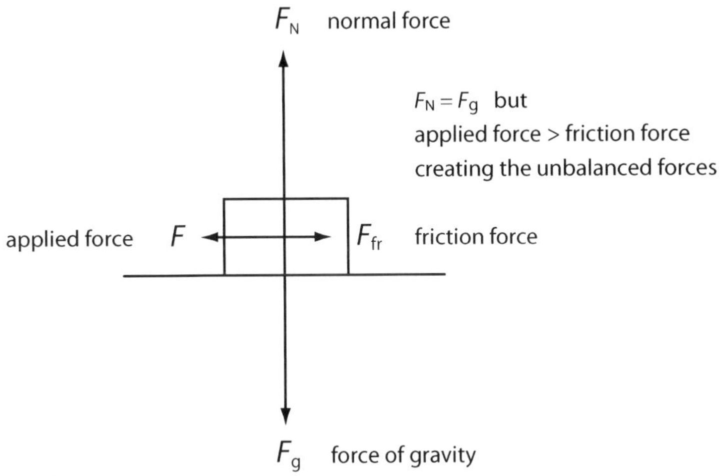


**Figure 2.5.1** *Forces acting on block*

| What to Think About | How to Do It |
|---|---|
| 1. Find the force of friction. | $F_{fr} = \mu F_N = \mu F_g = (0.333) \times (45.0\ N) = 15.0\ N$ |
| 2. Find the unbalanced force. | unbalanced force = applied force – friction force<br>$F = 25.0\ N - 15.0\ N = 10.0\ N$ |
| 3. Find the acceleration. | $a = \frac{F}{m} = \frac{10.0\ N}{4.60\ kg} = 2.17\ m/s^2$ |

## Practice Problems 2.5.1 — Multiple Forces Acting on a Body

1. A net force of 20 N is acting on a falling object. The object experiences air resistance of 6.0 N. If acceleration due to gravity is 9.8 $m/s^2$, what is the mass of the object?

2. A 900 N person stands on two scales so that one foot is on each scale. What will each scale register in Newtons?

3. What is the mass of a paratrooper who experiences an air resistance of 400 N and an acceleration of 4.5 $m/s^2$ during a parachute jump.

4. A force of 50 N accelerates a 5.0 kg block at 6.0 $m/s^2$ along a horizontal surface.
   (a) What is the frictional force acting on the block?

   (b) What is the coefficient of friction?

## 2.5 Review Questions

1. What unbalanced force is needed to accelerate a 5.0 kg cart at 5.0 m/s²?

2. A net force of $7.5 \times 10^4$ N acts on a spacecraft of mass $3.0 \times 10^4$ kg.
   (a) At what rate will the spacecraft accelerate?

   (b) Assuming constant acceleration is maintained, how fast will the spacecraft be moving after 25 s, if its initial speed was $5.0 \times 10^3$ m/s?

3. A model rocket has a mass of 0.12 kg. It accelerates vertically to 60.0 m/s in 1.2 s.
   (a) What is its average acceleration?

   (b) What is the unbalanced force on the rocket?

   (c) If the force of gravity on the rocket is 1.2 N, what is the total thrust of its engine?

4. What is the mass of a rock if a force of $2.4 \times 10^3$ N makes it accelerate at a rate of $4.0 \times 10^1$ m/s²?

5. A fully loaded military rocket has a mass of $3.0 \times 10^6$ kg, and the force of gravity on it at ground level is $2.9 \times 10^7$ N.
   (a) At what rate will the rocket accelerate during lift-off, if the engines provide a thrust of $3.3 \times 10^7$ N?

   (b) Why will this acceleration not remain constant?

6. A boy and his skateboard have a combined mass of 60.0 kg. After an initial shove, the boy starts coasting at 5.5 m/s along a level driveway. Friction brings him to rest in 5.0 s. The combined force of gravity on the boy and skateboard is $5.9 \times 10^2$ N. What is the average coefficient of rolling friction between the driveway and the skateboard wheels?

# 2.6 Newton's Third Law of Motion

## Warm Up

1. Consider the following situations. Draw a sketch of each situation and, on each diagram, indicate the forces being described. Share your results with the class.
   (a) If you wish to climb stairs, in which direction do *you* push? Which way to you move?
   (b) If you wish to swim forward, in which direction must your arms push? Which way do you move?
   (c) If you are rowing a boat, which way must your oars push if the boat is to move forward? Which way to do you move?
   (d) When a car is moving forward, in which direction do the *wheels* push on the road? Which way to do you move?

### Action and Reaction Forces

Isaac Newton observed that whenever forces exist between two bodies, the forces are mutual. If one body pushes on another, the other body exerts an equal force on the first body, but in the opposite direction. To do push-ups, for example, you push down on the floor. The floor exerts an equal force up on you. The floor lifts you up! Earth exerts a force of gravity on the Moon. What evidence is there that the Moon exerts an equal force on Earth?

Newton studied situations involving forces between pairs of bodies and he stated his conclusions about mutual forces between pairs of bodies as his third law. **Newton's third law of motion** is also called the **law of action and reaction**.

> If two bodies interact, the force the first body exerts on the second body will equal the force the second body exerts on the first body. The two forces will be opposite in direction and will act simultaneously over the same interval of time.

The first force is called the **action force**, and the second force is called the **reaction force**. If we call the first body A and the second body B, then the law of action and reaction can be expressed mathematically like this:

$$F_{\text{A on B}} = -F_{\text{B on A}}$$

where the minus sign indicates opposite direction.

It is important to remember that for both forces, each force is exerted on the other body. The forces do not cancel. This is a really important point. For example, imagine a horse pulling a cart. If we just consider the force the horse exerts on the cart, then Newton's third law tells us that the cart exerts an equal and opposite force on the horse. The two forces are illustrated in Figure 2.6.1.

You might look at the picture and say that the horse and cart do not move because the two forces seem to cancel each other out. They are equal and opposite. But remember that the horse is exerting an action force on the cart and the cart is exerting a reaction force on the horse. That is why the horse feels the heavy cart on its harness when it starts pulling.

When applying Newton's third law, always ask yourself what object or thing applies the force and what body or object receives the force. There must be two different bodies or objects.

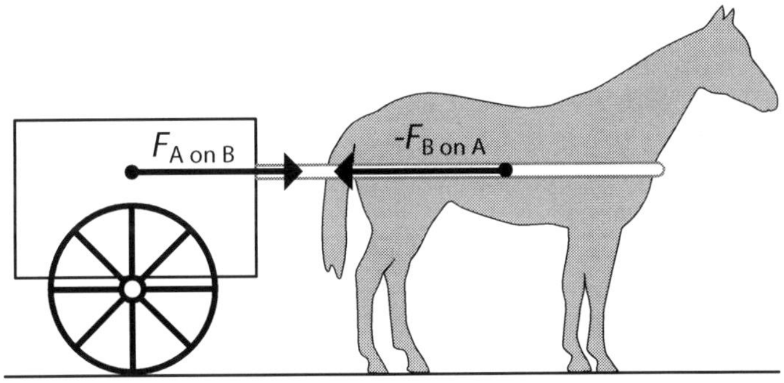


**Figure 2.6.1** *Movement occurs when the horse's feet exert a force on Earth's surface and Earth exerts an equal and opposite force back on the horse.*

## Quick Check

1. Review your diagrams from the Warm Up activity. In each diagram, label the action force and reaction force.
2. When you are walking, you are producing an action force toward the ground. Why do you move in the opposite direction?

 ______________________________________________

 ______________________________________________

3. You see a large dog running along a floating log. If the dog is running to your right, what, if anything, is happening to the log?

 ______________________________________________

 ______________________________________________

## 2.6 Review Questions

1. You are playing softball and your friend throws a ball to you. You catch the ball. The action force is the impact of the ball against your glove. What is the reaction force?

2. During a golf swing, is the club impacting on the ball the action force or the reaction force? Use a diagram to illustrate your answer.

3. If a soccer player kicks a ball with a force of 100 N, what is the magnitude of the reaction force?

4. Spiderman is having a tug of war with a grade 2 student. Both are pulling very hard from opposite ends. Who exerts a greater force on the rope? Explain your answer.

5. In a demolition derby a Hummer SUV collides head-on with a SMART car. Which car experiences a greater impact force? Explain your answer.

6. During a martial arts demonstration, a black belt uses a karate chop to break a large board with her hand by exerting a force of 2000 N. What force did the board exert on her hand?

7. A few years from now after much hard work, you are an astronaut and are completing a repair of some solar panels. To do this you have to take a space walk outside the International Space Station. By accident, you find yourself disconnected from the support rope and need to get back to the station. All you have is your tools with you. How can you propel yourself back to safety?

# 2.7 Dynamics

## Warm Up

The drawing shows an egg balanced on a spool of thread on a cookie sheet balanced on a cup of water. If a horizontal force is applied to the edge of the cookie sheet, what will happen to the egg? Explain your reasoning.

______________________________________________

______________________________________________

______________________________________________

### Review of Newton's Laws of Motion

While Galileo was chiefly responsible for establishing the science of **kinematics** which is concerned with describing motion, without reference to its cause, it was Isaac Newton (1642-1727) who laid the foundations for the science of **dynamics.** Newton was the first to clearly explain the relationship between motion and forces, which is the basis for dynamics.

**Newton's First Law of Motion**
If there is no net force acting on a body, it will continue to move with constant velocity.

This means that a body at rest will stay at rest; a body moving at a certain speed will continue to move at that speed and in the same direction unless and until an unbalanced (net) force acts on it. This property, possessed by all bodies having mass, is called **inertia**.

Your own experience tells you that if you want to push a book across your desk at constant velocity, you must exert a force on the book. Does this contradict the first law? No! To move the book along at steady velocity, your force just has to balance the friction force opposing its motion. When the force you apply equals the friction force, the *net* force is zero, because the vector sum of your applied force and the friction force is zero.

## Newton's Second Law of Motion

In an earlier course, you performed experiments to find out what happens when a net force acts on a body. These experiments showed you two facts about motion:

(1) A net force acting on a body causes it to accelerate in the direction of the net force. If the net force is doubled, the acceleration will double. If the net force is tripled, the acceleration will also triple. Experiments show that the acceleration is directly proportional to the net force on the object.

$$\text{acceleration} \propto \text{net force}$$

In symbols, $\vec{a} \propto \vec{F}$

(2) For a given net force, the acceleration of a body is inversely proportional to the mass of a body. For example, if a 10 N force will accelerate a 5 kg mass at a rate of 2 m/s$^2$, the same force will accelerate a 10 kg mass at 1 m/s$^2$, which is one-half the original acceleration.

$$\text{acceleration} \propto \frac{1}{\text{mass}}$$

In symbols, $\vec{a} \propto \frac{1}{\text{mass}}$

Newton's second law can be summarized as written below.

**Newton's Second Law**
The acceleration of a body is directly proportional to the net force acting on it and inversely proportional to its mass. Acceleration is in the same direction as the net *force.*

In symbols, $\vec{a} \propto \frac{\vec{F}}{\mathrm{m}}$ or $\vec{a} = \mathrm{k}\frac{\vec{F}}{m}$

If units for force and mass are chosen so that k = 1, then $\vec{a} = \frac{\vec{F}}{m}$.

Rearranging terms, the familiar form of Newton's second law is obtained as shown below.

$$\boldsymbol{\vec{F} = m\vec{a}}$$

In the Quick Check above only one unbalanced force was considered. In other

## Quick Check

1. What is the mass of a rocket that has an acceleration 20.0 $m/s^2$ at lift off and a thrust of 27 000 N?

2. A rising hot air balloon has a mass of 1000 kg and an acceleration of 3.50 $m/s^2$. What is the magnitude of the force lifting the balloon?

3. A 2.00 kg trout makes a sudden start to escape a predator. If the force generated to make this quick movement is 80.0 N, what is the brief acceleration of the trout?

situations, like Sample Problem 2.7.1 below, there are more forces to consider. Remember that in these problems it is important to identify the forces that create the unbalanced force. In a tug of war between two boys, each is pulling in the opposite direction. In the sample problem below, you need to find the net force that is causing boys to accelerate in the same direction.

### Sample Problem 2.7.1 — Multiple Forces Acting on a Body and Newton's Second Law

Gareth and Owen are pulling on a 1.45 kg rope in opposite directions. If Gareth pulls with a force of 20.0 N and the rope accelerates away from him at 1.15 $m/s^2$, what force is Owen pulling with?

| What to Think About | How to Do It |
| --- | --- |
| 1. Identify what you know and the positive direction. | Make $\vec{F}_{Owen}$ the positive direction.<br>$\vec{F}_{Gareth} = -20.0\ N$<br>$m = 1.45\ kg$<br>$\vec{a} = 1.15\ m/s^2$ |
| 2. Newton's second law applies so the net force is key. | $\vec{F}_{net} = \vec{F}_{Owen} - \vec{F}_{Gareth} = m\vec{a}$ |
| 3. Solve. | $\vec{F}_{Owen} = \vec{F}_{Gareth} + m\vec{a}$<br>$\vec{F}_{Owen} = 20\ N + (1.45\ kg)(1.15\ m/s^2)$<br>$\vec{F}_{Owen} = 21.7\ N$ |

### Practice Problems 2.7.1 — Multiple Forces Acting on a Body and Newton's Second Law

1. A model rocket engine can produce an acceleration of 30.0 m/s$^2$. If the total mass of the rocket is 0.350 kg at lift off, what is the thrust generated?

2. A 20.0 kg rock is held up by a cable that will break if the tension in the cable exceeds 200 N. At what upward acceleration will the string break?

## Types of Forces

While there are many different forces acting on objects in different situations, Table 2.7.1 lists a summary of common forces you have already encountered and will encounter in studying kinematics.

**Table 2.7.1** *Common Forces*

| Force | Symbol | Definition | Direction |
|---|---|---|---|
| Friction | $\vec{F}_{fr}$ | The force that acts to oppose sliding motion between surfaces. Static friction occurs when an object is not moving. Kinetic friction occurs when an object is moving. | Opposite to the direction of motion and parallel to the surface |
| Normal | $\vec{F}_N$ | The force exerted by the surface on an object | Perpendicular to and away from the surface |
| Tension | $\vec{F}_T$ | The pull exerted by a string or rope when attached to a body and pulled tight | Away from the object and parallel to the string or rope at the point of attachment |
| Thrust | $\vec{F}_{thrust}$ | A force for moving objects like rockets and planes | The same direction as the acceleration of the object, barring any opposing forces |
| Weight | $\vec{F}_g$ | The gravitational force Earth exerts on a body | Straight down toward the centre of Earth |

## Newton's Third Law of Motion

When you do push-ups, which way do you exert your force? If you think about it, you will realize that you cannot push yourself up! You exert a force downward on the floor. What raises your body is the force exerted on you by the floor. When you climb stairs, you push down. The stairs push you up. When you swim forward, you push backward; the water pushes you forward.

Isaac Newton realized that when a force is applied to a body, it has to be applied by another body. Imagine an axe striking a block of wood. That the axe exerts a force on the wood is obvious. The force exerted by the wood on the axe might be less apparent, but if you think about it, the axe is decelerated very quickly when the wood "hits back" at it!

> **Newton's Third Law**
> When one body exerts a force on a second body, the second body exerts an equal force on the first body, but in the opposite direction. The forces are exerted during the same interval of time.

In popular literature, the third law is sometimes called the **law of action and reaction**. The first force is the 'action' force and the second is the 'reaction' force. The action force equals the reaction force, but is opposite in direction. The two forces act on different bodies. If we call the first body A and the second body B, then Newton's third law can be written symbolically as:

$$\vec{F}_{\text{A on B}} = -\vec{F}_{\text{B on A}}$$

## Examples of Newton's Laws

Newton's laws are part of our everyday life. You are constantly part of examples where these laws are in action. Walking to class, driving a car, or taking the bus are all proof that Newton's laws are part of the world around you. To illustrate this point and to show you the interconnectedness of these laws, the following three sample problems combine different physics concepts you have already learned with Newton's three laws.

### Sample Problem 2.7.2 — Kinematics and Newton's Law

A 110 kg motorbike carrying a 50 kg rider coasts to a stop in a distance of 51 m. It was originally travelling 15 m/s. What was the stopping force exerted by the road on the motorbike and rider?

| What to Think About | How to Do It |
| --- | --- |
| 1. The stopping force is friction, which opposes the motion of the bike. Newton's second law will permit you to solve for $\vec{F}$, if first you calculate acceleration using the appropriate uniform acceleration equation. | $\vec{v}_f^2 = \vec{v}_o^2 + 2\vec{a}d$<br>$\vec{a} = \dfrac{\vec{v}_f^2 - \vec{v}_o^2}{2d}$ |
| 2. The acceleration is negative because its direction is opposite to the direction of the motion of the motorbike. (It is decelerating.) Newton's second law can now be used to solve for the net force, which is the stopping force due to friction. | $\vec{a} = \dfrac{0-(15\ \text{m/s})^2}{2(51\ \text{m})} = -2.2\ \text{m/s}^2$ |
| 3. The negative sign simply means that the stopping force is in a negative direction relative to the motion of the motorbike. | $\vec{F} = m\vec{a}$<br>$\vec{F} = (160\ \text{kg})(-2.2\ \text{m/s}^2)$<br>$\vec{F} = -3.5 \times 10^2\ \text{N}$ |

## Sample Problem 2.7.3 — Kinematics, Vectors, and Newton's Laws

A truck of mass $2.00 \times 10^3$ kg is towing a large boulder of mass $5.00 \times 10^2$ kg using a chain (of negligible mass). The tension in the chain is $3.00 \times 10^3$ N, and the force of friction on the boulder is $1.20 \times 10^3$ N (Figure 2.7.1).

(a) At what rate will the boulder accelerate?

(b) How far will the boulder move in 3.0 s, starting from rest?

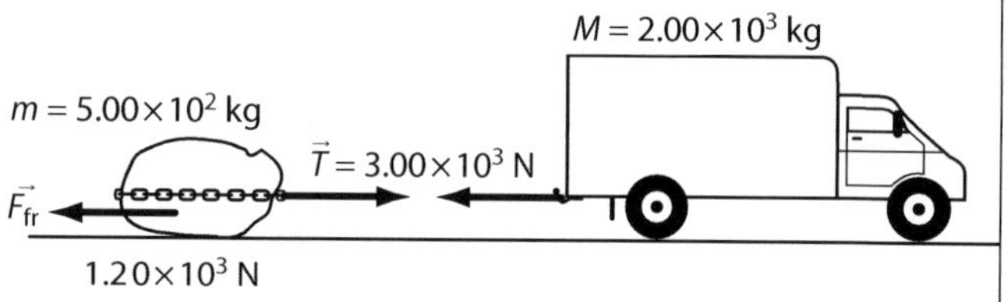


**Figure 2.7.1**

### What to Think About

1. Draw a free body diagram, showing the forces acting on the body in question, which is the boulder.

### How to Do It

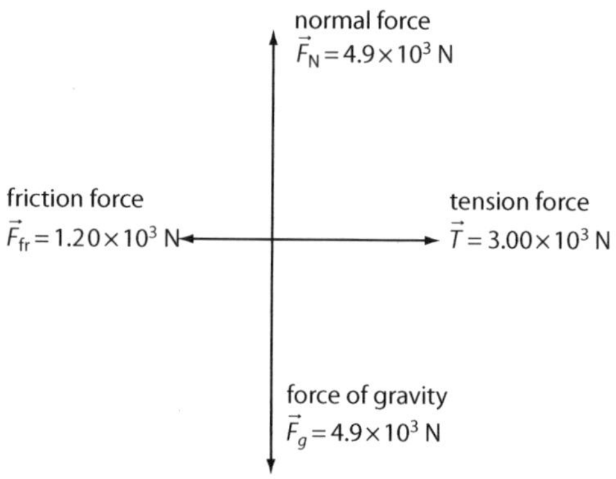


2. To solve for the acceleration of the boulder, you need to know the net force or resultant force acting on the boulder. Four forces are acting on the boulder:
   (1) the force of gravity ($m\vec{g}$)
   (2) the normal force ($\vec{F}_N$) exerted upward by the road (equal in magnitude but opposite in direction to $mg$)
   (3) the tension force ($\vec{T}$) exerted by the rope
   (4) the friction force ($\vec{F}_{fr}$) between the road and the boulder

The two $y$-components $m\vec{g}$ and $\vec{F}_N$ add up to zero.
The $x$-components $\vec{F}_{fr}$ and $\vec{T}$ have a resultant of:
$3.00 \times 10^3\ \text{N} - 1.20 \times 10^3\ \text{N} = 1.80 \times 10^3\ \text{N}$

3. Applying Newton's second law to the boulder, solve for its acceleration.

$$\vec{a} = \frac{\vec{F}}{m}$$

$$\vec{a} = \frac{1.80 \times 10^3\ \text{N}}{5.00 \times 10^2\ \text{kg}}$$

$$\vec{a} = 3.60\ \text{m/s}^2$$

4. To determine how far the boulder will move in 3.0 s, use the appropriate uniform acceleration equation. The boulder will move 16 m during the 3.0 s it is being pulled by the truck.

$$d = v_0 t + \frac{1}{2}at^2$$

$$d = 0 + \frac{1}{2}(3.6\ \text{m/s}^2)(3.0\ \text{s})^2$$

$$d = 16\ \text{m}$$

## Sample Problem 2.7.4 — Forces and Newton's Laws

In Figure 2.7.2, a 5.0 kg block is connected to another 5.0 kg block by a string of negligible mass. The inclined plane down which the second block slides makes an angle of 45° with the horizontal. Friction is negligible.

(a) At what rate will the masses accelerate?

(b) What is the tension in the string joining the two masses?

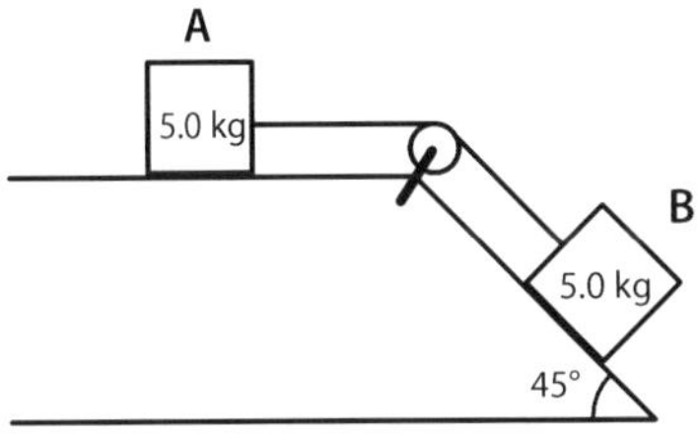


**Figure 2.7.2**

### What to Think About / How to Do It

1. Consider block A by itself. Draw a free body diagram showing the forces acting on block A. Forces $\vec{F}_N$ and $m_A\vec{g}$ are the *y*-component forces acting on mass A. Clearly, they are equal and opposite in direction, so their vector sum is zero.

$$\Sigma \vec{F}_y = 0$$

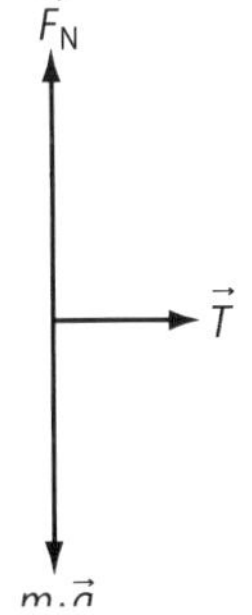


2. The resultant force on A will just equal the tension force $\vec{T}$ exerted on the rock by the rope. There is no friction force to oppose $\vec{T}$.

$\vec{T} = m_A\vec{a}$ (1)

$\vec{T} = (5.0\text{ kg})\vec{a}$

3. Consider block B by itself. Draw a free body diagram showing the forces acting on B. The direction along the plane is taken as the *x*-component direction. Again, the vector sum of the *y*-component forces $\vec{F}_N$ and $\vec{F}_y$ is zero.

$$\Sigma \vec{F}_y = 0$$

The resultant force causing acceleration is $\Sigma \vec{F}_x = \vec{F}_p - \vec{T}$, where $\vec{F}_p$ is the *x*-component of the force of gravity, $m_B\vec{g}$, on mass B.

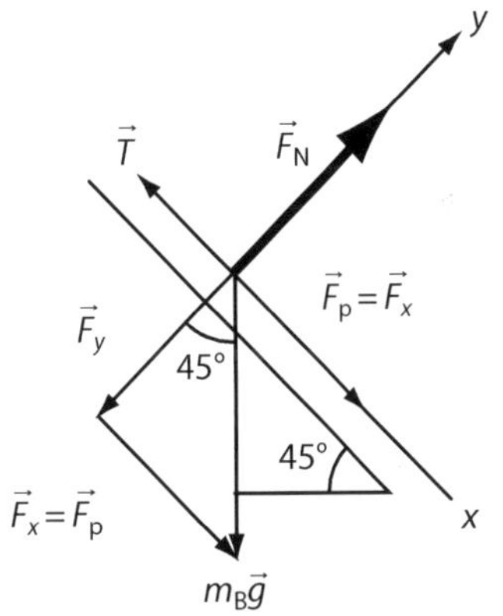


4. Since $\vec{F}_p = m_B\vec{g}\sin 45°$, calculate the net force causing acceleration.

$m_B\vec{g}\sin 45° - \vec{T} = m_B\vec{a}$

$(5.0\text{ kg})(9.8\text{ N/kg})(0.707) - \vec{T} = (5.0\text{ kg})\vec{a}$ (2)

$34.6\text{ N} - \vec{T} = (5.0\text{ kg})\vec{a}$

5. To solve for acceleration $\vec{a}$ add equations (1) and (2).

Then, $34.6\text{ N} = (10.0\text{ kg})\vec{a}$

Therefore, $\vec{a} = 3.46\text{ m/s}^2$

6. To solve for $\vec{T}$, use equation (1).

$\vec{T} = (5.0\text{ kg})(3.46\text{ m/s}^2) = 17.3\text{ N}$

## 2.7 Review Questions

1. At what rate, and in which direction, will the 10.0 kg mass accelerate when the masses in the diagram below are released? Assume friction in all parts of the system may be ignored.

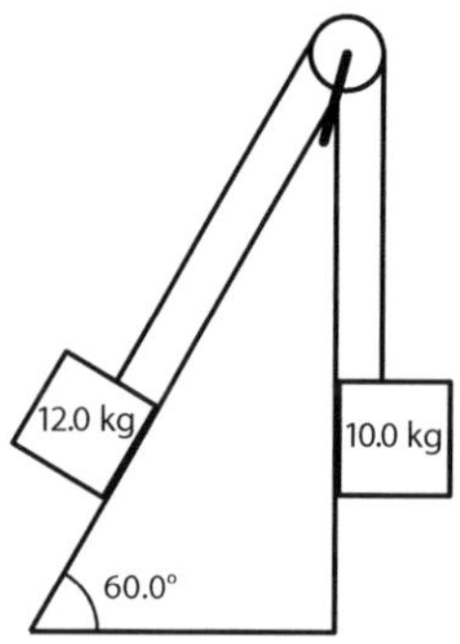


2. The two masses in the diagram below are connected by a rope of negligible mass. Friction is negligible. In what direction and at what rate will the 2.00 kg mass accelerate?

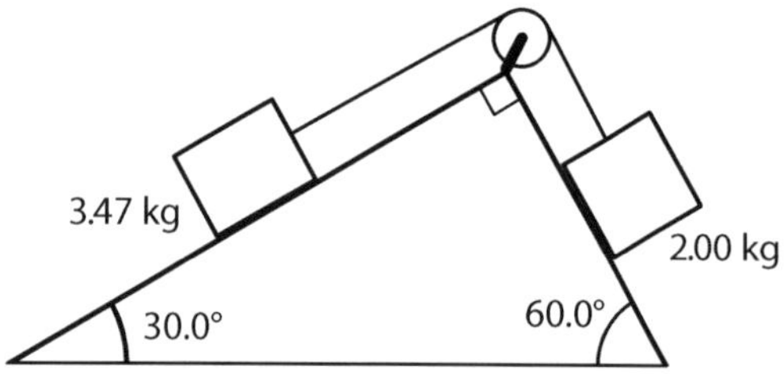


3. In the diagram below, a cord of negligible mass connects a 0.500 kg mass to a 1.00 kg mass. Friction in the system is negligible.
   (a) At what rate will the masses accelerate?
   (b) What is the tension in the cord while the masses are accelerating?

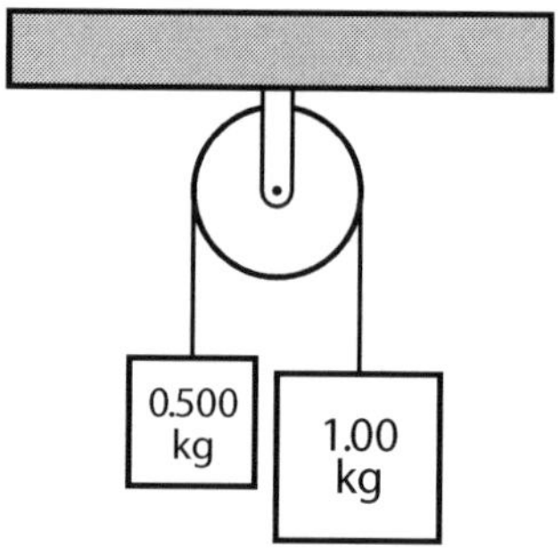


4. A criminal wants to escape from the third storey window of a jail, by going down a rope to the road below. Having taken high school physics, he thinks he can escape down the rope even though his mass is 75 kg and the rope can only support 65 kg without breaking. Explain how he can get down safely without breaking the rope.

5. The skier in the drawing below is descending a 35° slope on a surface where the coefficient of kinetic friction between his skis and the icy surface is 0.12.
   (a) If his mass (including his skis) is 72 kg, at what rate will he accelerate?
   (b) How fast is he moving after 8.0 s?

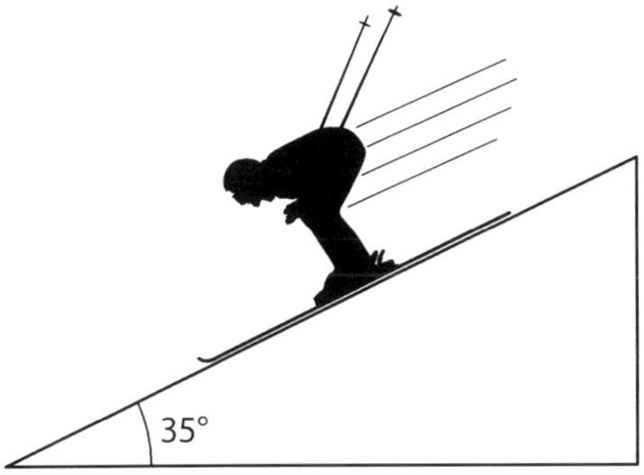


6. A 60.0 kg skydiver experiences air resistance during his jump. At one instant, the resistance is 320 N. At that instant, what is his acceleration? Describe his motion when the air resistance increases to the point where it equals the force of gravity on him.

# Chapter 2 Conceptual Review Questions

1. Propose a force standard different from the example of a stretched spring discussed in the text. Your standard must be capable of producing the same force repeatedly.

2. The glue on a piece of tape can exert forces. Can these forces be a type of simple friction? Explain, considering especially that tape can stick to vertical walls and even to ceilings.

3. When you learn to drive, you discover that you need to let up slightly on the brake pedal as you come to a stop or the car will stop with a jerk. Explain this in terms of the relationship between static and kinetic friction.

4. Which statement is correct? (a) Net force causes motion. (b) Net force causes change in motion. Explain your answer and give an example.

5. Describe a situation in which the net external force on a system is not zero, yet its speed remains constant.

6. A rock is thrown straight up. What is the net external force acting on the rock when it is at the top of its trajectory?

7. When you take off in a jet aircraft, there is a sensation of being pushed back into the seat. Explain why you move backward in the seat. Is there really a force backward on you?

# Chapter 2 Review Questions

1. What is the force of gravity on a 70.0 kg man standing on Earth's surface, according to the law of universal gravitation? Check your answer using $F = mg$.

2. The force of gravity on a black bear is 2500 N on Earth's surface. The animal becomes so "unbearable" that it is transported four Earth radii from the *surface* of Earth. What is the force of gravity on it now?

3. Both $G$ and $g$ are constants. Why is $G$ a *universal* constant and not $g$? Under what conditions is $g$ a constant?

4. (a) Calculate the value of $g$ at each of the locations shown in the table below. Express each answer as a multiple or a decimal fraction of Earth's $g$.

   (b) Would the force of gravity on you be greatest on the Moon, on Ganymede, or on Mercury?

5. What is the force of gravitational attraction between a 75 kg boy and a 60.0 kg girl
   (a) when they are 2.0 m apart?

   (b) when they are only 1.0 m apart?

6. Planet Mars has a mass of $6.4 \times 10^{23}$ kg, and you have a mass of $5.0 \times 10^{1}$ kg. What force of gravity is exerted between you and Mars, if you are standing on its surface? The radius of Mars is $3.4 \times 10^{6}$m.

| | Mass | Radius | Value of $g$ |
|---|---|---|---|
| On the Moon | $7.34 \times 10^{22}$ kg | $1.74 \times 10^{6}$ m | |
| On planet Mercury | $3.28 \times 10^{23}$ kg | $2.57 \times 10^{6}$ m | |
| On Ganymede* | $1.54 \times 10^{23}$ kg | $2.64 \times 10^{6}$ m | |
| On the Sun's surface | $1.98 \times 10^{30}$ kg | $6.95 \times 10^{8}$ m | |

* One of Jupiter's moons

7. To slide a metal puck across a greased sheet of metal at constant speed requires a force of 0.525 N. If the force of gravity on the puck is 5.00 N, what is the coefficient of friction between the puck and the greased metal?

8. (a) The force of gravity on a wooden crate is 560 N. It can be pushed along a certain floor at steady speed if a horizontal force of 224 N is applied to it. How much horizontal force will be needed to move a stack of two crates at the same steady speed?

   (b) What force will be needed if the two crates are not stacked but tied to one another side by side?

9. The coefficient of kinetic friction between a rubber disc and the ice is 0.0050. If the force of friction is 0.25 N, what is the force of gravity on the rubber disc?

10. A student added masses to the end of a hanging spring, then measured the amount of extension, or stretch, caused by the force of gravity on each mass. The following readings were obtained:

| | | | | | |
|---|---|---|---|---|---|
| Mass (kg) | 0.200 | 0.400 | 0.600 | 0.800 | 1.000 |
| Force of gravity (N) | 1.96 | 3.92 | 5.88 | 7.84 | 9.80 |
| Extension (cm) | 0.47 | 0.93 | 1.41 | 1.89 | 2.35 |

   (a) Plot a graph with force of gravity ($F_g$) on the *y*-axis and extension ($x$) on the *x*-axis. Determine the slope of the graph in appropriate units. Write an equation describing how the force of gravity varies with the extension.

   (b) Use both your graph and your equation to figure out the force of gravity that would stretch the spring 1.50 cm.

   (c) Use both your graph and your equation to figure out how much stretch would occur in the spring when the force of gravity is 6.50 N.

11. A person who does not wear a seatbelt may crash through the windshield if a car makes a sudden stop. Explain what happens to this person in terms of Newton's first law of motion. Explain why it is wise to wear a seatbelt.

12. In a frame of reference where there are no external, unbalanced forces, show that Newton's second law *includes* the law of inertia.

13. What unbalanced force is needed to accelerate a $2.0 \times 10^3$ kg vehicle at 1.5 $m/s^2$?

14. What is the acceleration of a $5.8 \times 10^3$ kg vehicle if an unbalanced force of $1.16 \times 10^2$ N acts on it?

15. What is the mass of a space satellite if a thrust of $2.0 \times 10^2$ N accelerates it at a rate of 0.40 $m/s^2$ during a small steering adjustment?

16. At what rate will a 5.0 kg object accelerate if a 12.8 N force is applied to it, and the friction force opposing its motion is 2.8 N?

17. A rope is strong enough to withstand a 750 N force without breaking. If two people pull on opposite ends of the rope, each with a force of 500 N, will it break? Explain.

18. State Newton's third law of motion. Describe an example of a situation involving the law of action and reaction that you have not already used.

19. Two tug-of-war teams are at opposite ends of a rope. Newton's third law says that the force exerted by team A will equal the force that team B exerts on team A. How can either team win the tug-of-war?

20. The following system is set up in your science lab.

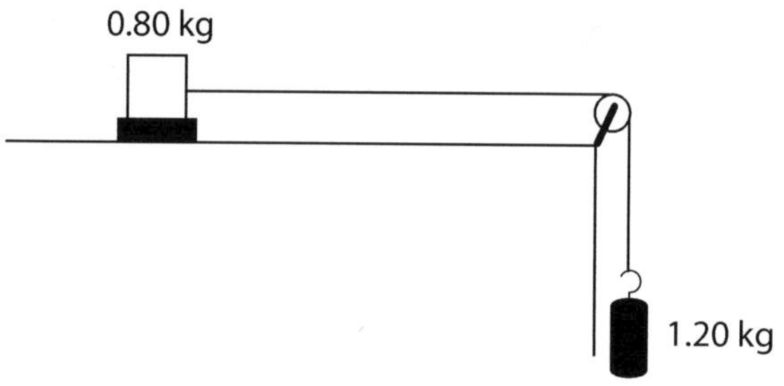


(a) At what rate will the system accelerate, assuming no friction?

(b) What is the tension in the string while the system accelerates?

21. A 9.6 kg box slides down a ramp inclined at 32° to the horizontal. At what rate will it accelerate if the coefficient of kinetic friction is 0.28?

22. Agatha Physics is travelling on a jet. As it accelerates down the runway, she holds a pendulum (consisting of a small washer on the end of a thread) in front of her and observes that the pendulum is displaced 10.0° from its usual vertical alignment. Help her by calculating the acceleration of the aircraft.

23. A block slides down a smooth inclined plane at steady speed when one end of the plane is raised to form an angle $\theta$ with the horizontal. Show that the coefficient of kinetic friction, $\mu$, can be calculated as follows:

$$\mu = \tan\theta$$

# Investigation 2-1 How Gravitational Force Depends on Distance

## Purpose

To use data to discover the nature of the relationship between gravitational force and distance

## Procedure

1. In an imaginary experiment, Superman was hired to measure the force of gravity on a 1 kg mass at different distances from the centre of Earth. He used a precise spring balance to obtain the data in Table 2.1. Make a graph with the force of gravity ($F_g$) on the $y$-axis and the distance from the centre of Earth ($r$) on the $x$-axis.
2. Your first graph will not be a straight line, because the relationship between $F_g$ and $r$ is not linear ($y \neq mx + b$) and is not a direct proportion ($y \neq mx$). The relationship is a **power law** ($y = m \cdot x^n$) where the power $n$ is neither 1 nor 0. How can you find out what the value of $n$ is? If you look at Figure 2.1.a, you will see the shapes of the graphs of several power law relationships. Which of these graphs does your graph most resemble?
   To find out if your graph is a particular type of relationship, plot force of gravity ($F_g$) on the $y$-axis, as before, and your chosen $r^n$ on the $x$-axis. Plot the following graphs and see which one gives a straight line: (a) $F_g$ vs. $r^{-1}$ (b) $F_g$ vs. $r^{-2}$

**Table 2.1** *The Force of Gravity on a Kilogram Mass*

| Force of Gravity (N) | Distance from Centre of Earth (Mm*) |
|---|---|
| 9.81 | 6.37 |
| 2.45 | 12.74 |
| 1.09 | 19.11 |
| 0.61 | 25.48 |
| 0.39 | 31.85 |

*1 Mm = 1 megametre = $10^6$ m

## Concluding Questions

1. (a) What variables must you plot to obtain a straight line (through the origin)?
   (b) What is the specific equation for your final straight line?
2. From your equation, calculate the following:
   (a) the distance at which the force of gravity on the kilogram mass is half of what it is at Earth's surface
   (b) the force of gravity on the 1 kg mass at a distance of 10 Earth radii (63.7 Mm)

Graphs of various power law relations

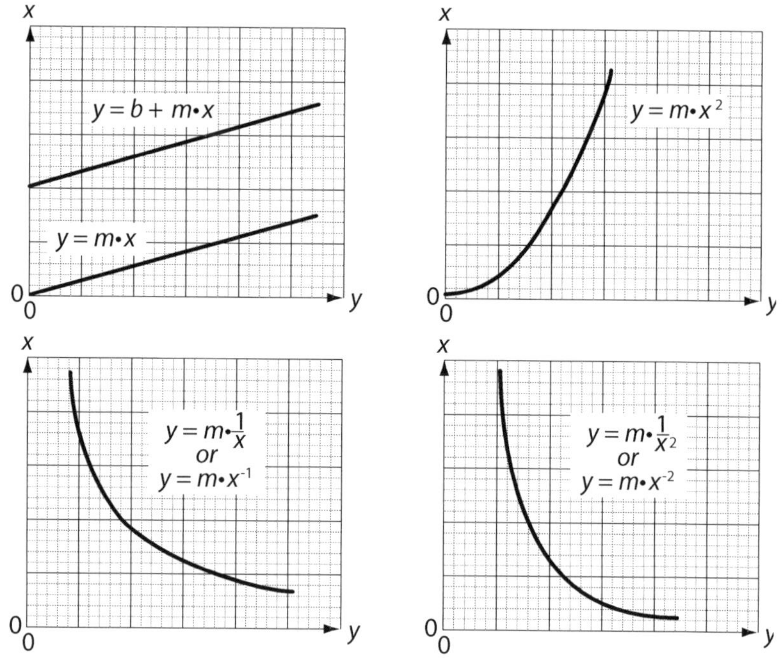


**Figure 2.1.a** *Power law graphs*

# Investigation 2-2 Friction Can Be a Real Drag!

### *Part 1*

### Purpose

To determine how does the force of friction ($F_{fr}$) depends on the force of gravity ($F_g$) on an object when the object slides over a "smooth" horizontal surface

### Procedure

1. Use a spring balance to measure the force of gravity on each of four nearly identical wood blocks provided. Write their weights, in N, in pencil on each block.
2. Prepare a data table like Table 2.2.

**Table 2.2** *Data For Investigation 2-2*

| Number of Blocks | Total Force of Gravity (N) | Force of Friction (N) |
|---|---|---|
| 1 | | |
| 2 | | |
| 3 | | |
| 4 | | |

3. Adjust your spring balance so that it reads 0 N when it is held in a horizontal position or parallel to the bench top. Attach it to the hook on one of the four blocks. See Figure 2.2.a. Set the wide side of the block on a smooth, clean bench top. To measure the force of sliding friction, measure the smallest force needed to keep the block sliding at a slow, steady speed along the bench top. You will have to give the block a small extra nudge to get it moving. Once it is moving, however, a steady force equal to the force of kinetic friction should keep it moving at a steady speed. Do several trials until you are satisfied you have a meaningful average friction force. Record the

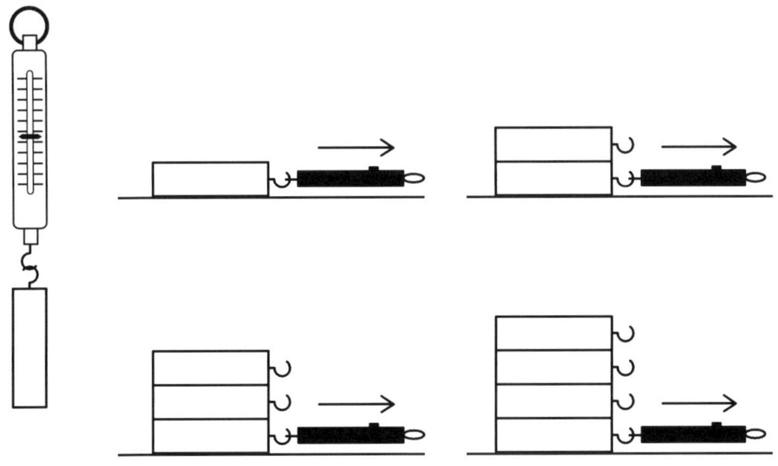

**Figure 2.2.a** *Friction — Part 1*

force of gravity and the force of sliding friction in your copy of Table 2.2.

4. Place a second block on top of the first. The total force of gravity will now be the sum of the weights of the two blocks. Measure the force of friction with two blocks.
5. Repeat with three, then four blocks. Record the total force of gravity and force of friction each time in Table 2.2.
6. Plot a graph with the force of kinetic friction $F_{fr}$ on the *y*-axis and force of gravity $F_g$ on the *x*-axis. Determine the slope of the graph and write a specific equation for your graph. Include the units for the slope, if any.

### Concluding Questions

1. When you doubled the force of gravity on the object sliding over your bench, what happened to the force of friction? What happened to the force of friction when the force of gravity was tripled? quadrupled?
2. What is the equation for your graph? (Remember to use the proper symbols and units.)
3. The slope of your graph is the coefficient of kinetic friction. What is the coefficient of kinetic friction between the block and the tabletop you used?
4. Name three situations where you need to have
   (a) a low coefficient of friction, and
   (b) a high coefficient of friction.

### Challenge

1. Measure the coefficient of kinetic friction between your blocks and a different horizontal surface.

***Part 2***

### Purpose

To determine how the force of kinetic friction varies with the area of contact between two smooth, flat surfaces, when all other factors are controlled

### Procedure

1. Make a prediction: If you double the area of contact between two smooth, flat objects, will the force of friction (a) stay the same, (b) double, (c) be cut in half, or (d) change in some other way?
2. Pile four blocks on top of one another as in Figure 2.2.b(a). Loop a string around the blocks, attach a spring balance, and measure the force of friction as in Part 1.

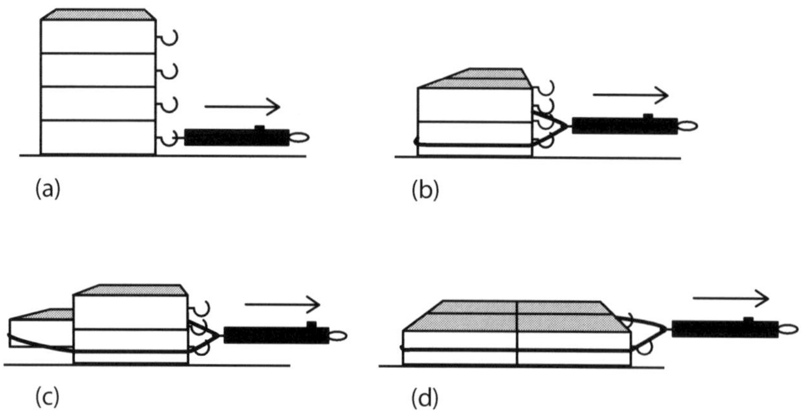


**Figure 2.2.b** *Friction — Part 2*

3. Prepare a table of data like Table 2.2.1. Record your results.

**Table 2.2.1** *Data for Investigation 2-2, Part 2*

| Number of Blocks | Area | Total Force of Gravity (N) | Force of Friction (N) |
|---|---|---|---|
| 4 | 1 × A | constant | |
| 4 | 2 × A | constant | |
| 4 | 3 × A | constant | |
| 4 | 4 × A | constant | |

4. Double the surface area by arranging the blocks as in Figure 2.2.b(b). Notice that the force of gravity is still the same; only the area has changed. Measure and record the force of friction. Measure it several times until you are satisfied that you have an acceptable average.
5. Arrange the blocks so that the surface area is tripled, then quadrupled without changing the force of gravity. See Figure 2.2.b. Measure and record the force of friction each time.

### Concluding Questions

1. After comparing your results for Part 2 with several other groups doing the same experiment, write a conclusion about the effect that varying the surface area has on the amount of friction between a smooth flat object of constant force of gravity and another smooth surface.
2. Discuss sources of error in this experiment.

# Investigation 2-3 Another Way to Weigh

### Purpose

To make a "gravity measurer" out of a metre stick

### Introduction

In an earlier course, you may have done an experiment where you added known masses to a spring and graphed the stretch of the spring against the force of gravity on the masses. In Investigation 2-3, you will learn how you can measure the force of gravity using a metre stick.

### Procedure

1. Set up the apparatus in Figure 2.3.a. Clamp a metre stick horizontally so that 80.0 cm overhangs the edge of your bench. (Use a piece of cardboard to protect the metre stick from damage by the clamp.) Tape a large paper clip to the end of the metre stick and bend the clip so that masses can be hung from it.

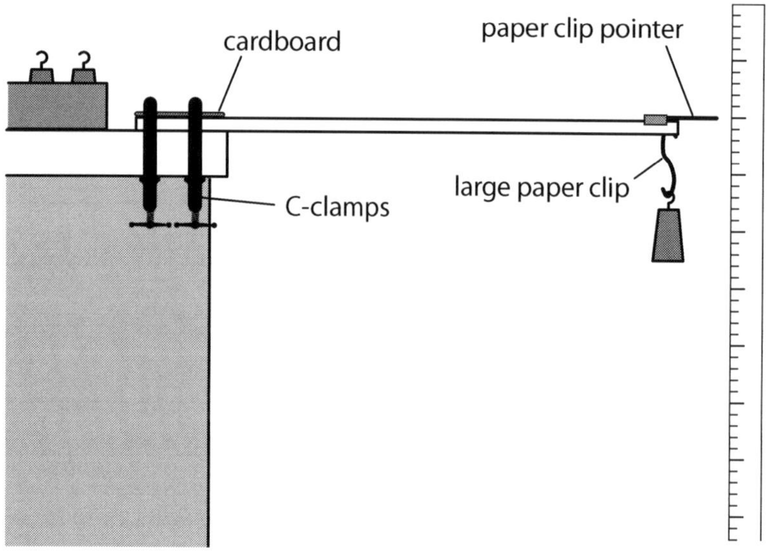


**Figure 2.3.a** *Step 1*

2. Mount another metre stick or ruler vertically so that the depression of the horizontal metre stick can be measured. Align the top edge of the horizontal metre stick with a convenient point on the vertical metre stick, such as 0.0 cm. Another paper clip could be used as a pointer.

3. Hang a 50.0 g mass on the paper clip and measure the depression or vertical drop of the end of the horizontal metre stick, estimating to the nearest one-tenth of a millimetre. The force of gravity on a 50.0 g mass is 0.490 N. Record the force of gravity and the depression in a table like Table 2.3.

4. Measure the depression caused by each of the forces of gravity listed in Table 2.3. When you finish reading the depression for 4.90 N, remove the masses and see whether the depression returns to 0.00 cm. If it does not, check that the metre stick is securely clamped. If it is not, tighten the clamps and repeat your measurements. Do not dismantle your set-up yet.

**Table 2.3** *Data for Investigation 2-3*

| Mass (g) | Depression ($y$) (cm) | Force of Gravity ($F_g$) (N) |
|---|---|---|
| 0 | | 0 |
| 50 | | 0.49 |
| 100 | | 0.98 |
| 150 | | 1.47 |
| 200 | | 1.96 |
| 250 | | 2.45 |
| 300 | | 2.94 |
| 350 | | 3.43 |
| 400 | | 3.92 |
| 450 | | 4.41 |
| 500 | | 4.90 |

5. Prepare a graph of force of gravity ($y$-axis) vs depression ($x$-axis). Find the slope, and write a specific equation for the line you obtain.
6. Hang an object with an unknown force of gravity (such as a small C-clamp) from the metre stick and measure the depression it causes. Find out what the force of gravity on it is (a) by direct reading of your graph and (b) by calculation using the equation for the line.
7. Measure the force of gravity on the object with the unknown force of gravity using a commercial laboratory spring balance.

### Concluding Questions

1. (a) What is the equation for the graph you prepared of $F$ vs. $x$? Remember to include the numerical value of your slope, with proper units.
   (b) Is the graph linear? Is the relationship between the two variables a direct proportion? Explain.
2. Calculate the percent difference between the unknown force of gravity as determined from the graph and as measured with a laboratory spring balance.

### Challenge

1. Make a "letter weigher" using a strip of hacksaw blade instead of a metre stick. Calibrate it in grams instead of newtons. (The gram is a mass unit, but most postal rate scales are based on mass instead of force of gravity.)

# Investigation 2-4 Investigating Inertia

### Purpose

To answer problems that will help you develop an understanding of inertia and Newton's first law of motion

### *Problem 1: How does a seatbelt work?*

**Figure 2.4.a** *Problem 1*

### Procedure

1. Place a small toy human figure on a toy car or truck as shown in Figure 2.4.a. Do not fasten the figure to the vehicle. Let the vehicle move toward an obstruction like another toy vehicle or a brick and collide with it. Observe what happens to the unattached passenger.
2. Repeat step 1, but this time give the toy human figure a "seatbelt" by taping it to the vehicle.

### Questions

1. How does this procedure illustrate inertia?
2. How does a seatbelt work?
3. Why are you more likely to survive a collision with a seatbelt than without one?

### *Problem 2: Does air have inertia?*

### Procedure

1. Fill a large garbage bag with air, and hold it as shown in Figure 2.4.b.
2. Quickly jerk the bag to one side. What happens to the air in the bag
   (a) when you start moving the bag?
   (b) when you stop moving the bag?

### Question

1. What evidence have you observed from this procedure that supports the claim that air has inertia?

**Figure 2.4.b** *Problem 2*

## *Problem 3: Inertia on an air track*

### Procedure

1. Place a glider on an air track as shown in Figure 2.4.c. Turn on the compressed air supply and check that the track is absolutely level. When the track is level the glider should have no tendency to move in one direction or the other. It should sit still.
2. Place the glider at one end of the track. Give it a slight nudge, and let it go.
3. Observe the motion of the glider.

### Questions

1. Are there any unbalanced forces on the glider?
2. Describe its motion.
3. How does this demonstration illustrate Newton's first law?

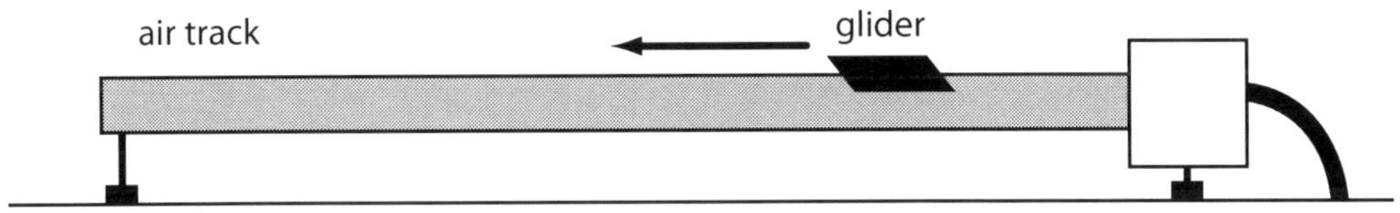


**Figure 2.4.c** *Problem 3*

## *Problem 4: Get on the right track.*

### Procedure

1. Place a battery-powered toy train on a circular track, and let it run a few full circles.
2. Predict which way the train will go if one of the sections of curved track is removed. Which one of the following will the train do? Explain your answer.
   (a) continue to move in a circle
   (b) move off along a radius of the circle
   (c) move off in a straight line tangent to the circle
   (d) follow some other path
3. Now test your prediction by setting up a section of track as shown in Figure 2.4.d.

### Question

1. What happens to the toy train when it leaves the track? Explain this in terms of inertia.

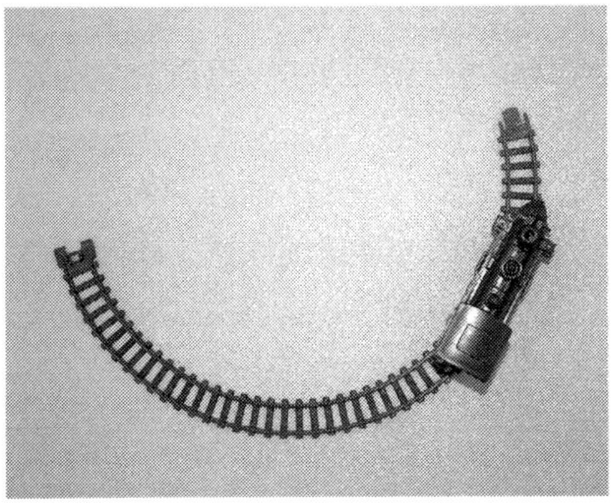

**Figure 2.4.d** *Problem 4*

## Problem 5: Where will the string break? Getting the "hang" of inertia

### Procedure

1. Attach two equal masses, either 500 g or 1 kg, to a supporting rod, as shown in Figure 2.4.e. Use string that is strong enough to support the hanging masses, but not so strong that you cannot break it with a moderate pull with your hand. Add a 50 cm length of the same kind of string to the bottom of each mass.
2. Predict where each string will break, above or below the mass, if you pull on the end of the string first gently and then abruptly. Test your predictions by experiment.

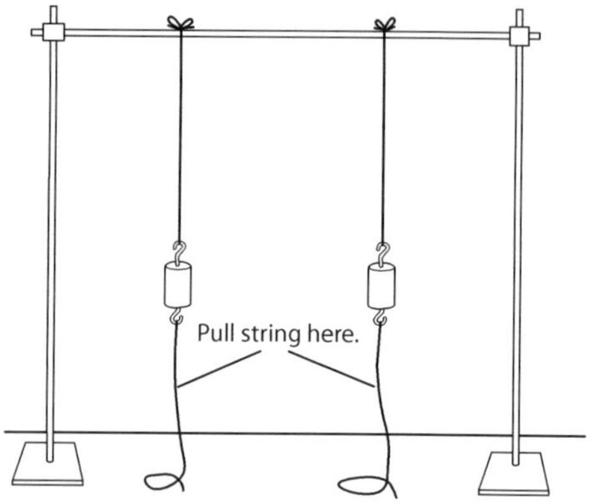

**Figure 2.4.e** *Problem 5*

### Questions

1. Explain what happened, in terms of inertia.
2. Which action illustrates the weight of the ball and which illustrates the mass of the ball?

## Problem 6: The pop-up coaster

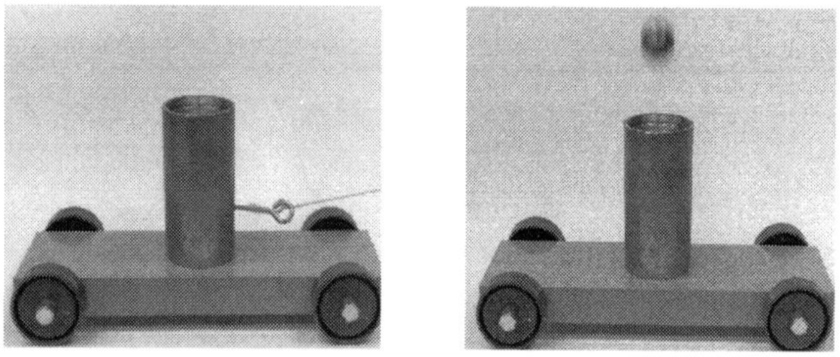
(a) (b)

**Figure 2.4.f** *Problem 6*

### Procedure

1. The cart in Figure 2.4.f contains a spring that can fire a steel ball straight up in the air. The cart is given a steady horizontal speed when pulled with a string. This also activates the trigger for the spring-loaded cannon. When the cart is moving with a steady speed, giving the string a sudden pull will release the spring and fire the ball up in the air.
2. Predict whether the ball will land ahead of the cannon, behind the cannon, or in the cannon. Explain your prediction.
3. Test your prediction.

### Questions

1. What forces are acting on the ball when it is in the air?
2. How does this procedure illustrate Newton's first law of motion?
3. Why does the ball sometimes miss the cart after it is released? Does this mean Newton's first law sometimes does not apply?

### Concluding Question

Use your understanding of inertia to explain the following situation: You are carrying a carton of milk with one hand and need to get a section of paper towel off the roll in your kitchen. You can only use one hand to tear off the paper towel. Why does a quick, jerking motion work better than a slow pulling motion when removing the paper towel section from the roll?

# Investigation 2-5 Newton's Second Law of Motion

## Purpose

To investigate how the change in speed of a cart is affected by
(a) the amount of unbalanced force, and (b) the amount of mass in the cart

## Procedure

### *Part 1: Setting up and moving the cart*

1. Set up the apparatus as shown in Figure 2.5.a(a). Start with three 200 g masses in the cart. Suspend a mass of 200 g from the end of a string, which passes over a pulley at the end of the bench. The force of gravity on this mass is 1.96 N or approximately 2.0 N.
2. Lift one end of your laboratory table so that the cart rolls toward the pulley at a steady speed. This can be checked with a ticker tape and your recording timer. If your bench cannot be lifted, do the experiment on a length of board, which can be raised at one end. What this lifting does is balance friction with a little help from gravity.
3. The class will now share the task of preparing and analyzing ticker-tape records of speed vs. time for each of the situations in Figure 2.5.a. Each lab group of two students will choose one of the eight set-ups and prepare two tapes or one for each partner. Note that the whole system of cart-plus-string-plus-hanging-mass moves as one unit. The mass of the whole system must be kept constant. This means that once you build your system you must not add any additional masses.

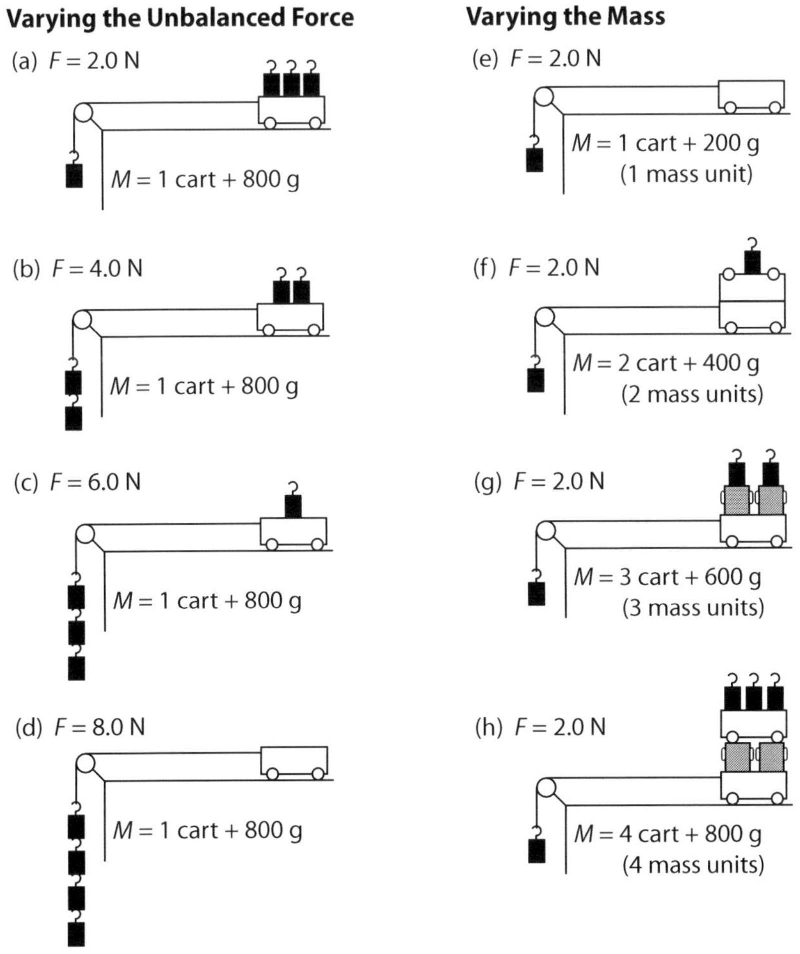


**Figure 2.5.a** *Cart and mass set-ups*

## *Part 2: Preparing Your Own Tape*

1. The class as a team will prepare and analyze tapes for each of the situations in Figure 2.5.a. If your class is large enough, compare duplicated data for any potential sources of error.
2. Use the technique you used to measure acceleration in an earlier chapter. Remember that a group of six dots represents 0.10 s and that the average speeds for each interval are plotted mid-way through each time interval and not at the end of the interval.
3. Prepare your graph. Label it carefully with the unbalanced force used (2.0 N, 4.0 N, 6.0 N, or 8.0 N) and the mass of the cart system.
4. The most important measurement you need is the acceleration of the cart. You get this from the slope of the graph. Express the acceleration in cm/s$^2$. You will share this information with the rest of the class.

## *Part 3: Analyzing Class Data*

1. Prepare the following tables of data, summarizing class results.

**Table 2.5.a** *Acceleration vs. Unbalanced Force (mass constant)*

| **Unbalanced Force** $F$ (N) | **Acceleration** $a$ (cm/s$^2$) |
|---|---|
| 0 | 0 |
| 2.0 | |
| 4.0 | |
| 6.0 | |
| 8.0 | |

**Table 2.5.b** *Acceleration vs Mass (unbalanced force constant)*

| **Mass,** $m$ (mass units) | **Acceleration,** $a$ (cm/s$^2$) | $\frac{1}{\text{mass}}, \frac{1}{m}$ (mass units$^{-1}$) |
|---|---|---|
| 1.0 | | 1.0 |
| 2.0 | | 0.50 |
| 3.0 | | 0.33 |
| 4.0 | | 0.25 |

2. Plot a graph of acceleration ($y$-axis) against unbalanced force ($x$-axis).
3. Plot a graph of acceleration against mass.
4. Plot a graph of acceleration against the reciprocal of mass ($1/m$).

### Concluding Questions

1. Describe how the speed of a cart changes when a constant unbalanced force pulls it.
2. According to your first graph ($a$ vs. $F$), how does acceleration depend on unbalanced force? Does your graph suggest that acceleration is directly proportional to unbalanced force? Support your answer with your data.
3 According to your second and third graphs, how does the acceleration of the cart vary when the mass is doubled, tripled, and quadrupled?
4 Write an equation for the third graph, complete with the numerical value and units for the slope.
5 What were some of the experimental difficulties you encountered in this investigation, which would make it difficult to obtain ideal results?

# Investigation 2-6 Newton's Third Law

## Purpose

To observe demonstrations of Newton's third law and identify the action and reaction forces

## Procedure

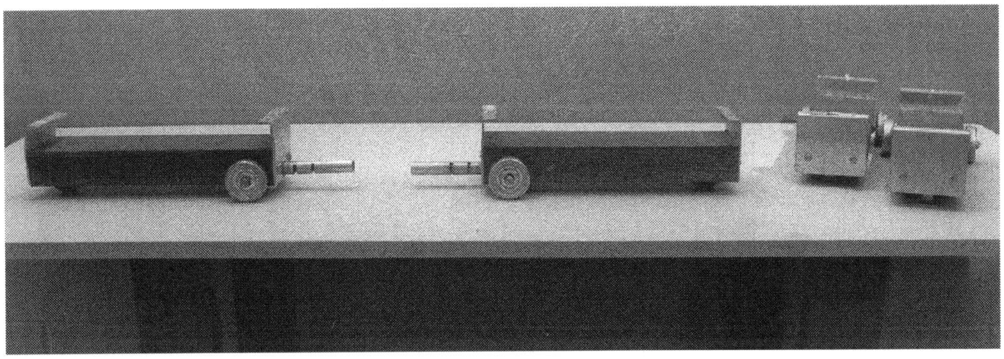

### *Part 1: Exploding Carts*

**Figure 2.6.a** *Laboratory carts*

1. Push two identical laboratory carts together so that their spring bumpers are compressed. Release the carts on a flat table or floor. Observe as they accelerate away from each other.
   (a) What force makes the carts accelerate?
   (b) Why do the two carts, of identical mass, accelerate at the same rate?
   (c) How does this demonstration illustrate Newton's third law?
2. Predict what will happen if you double the mass of one of the carts by placing an extra cart on top of it. Test your prediction.
   (a) Has the force repelling the carts changed?
   (b) What has changed?
3. Try making the mass of one of the carts much greater than the mass of the other.
   (a) Is the force changed?
   (b) What has changed?

## *Part 2: Motion from Rest*

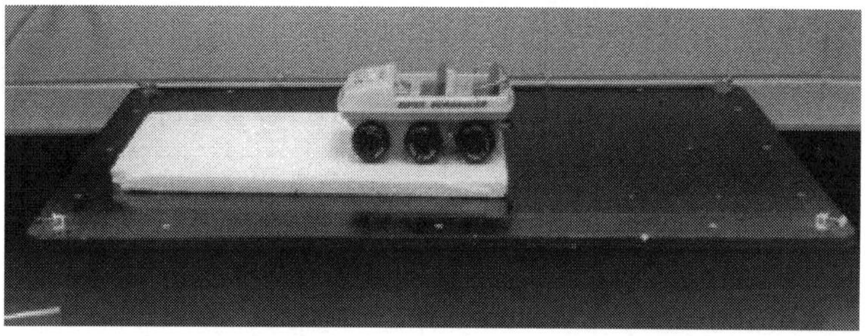

**Figure 2.6.b** Set-up for part 2

1. Place a piece of light plastic insulating Styrofoam board (50 cm × 25 cm × 2.5 cm) at one end of an air table as shown in Figure 2.6.b. Place a wind-up toy car or a radio-controlled car at one end of the board. Turn on the air table and start the car moving. Observe and describe what happens:
   (a) to the car
   (b) to the "road" under the car
2. How does this demonstration illustrate Newton's Third Law?

## *Part 3: Tug of War*

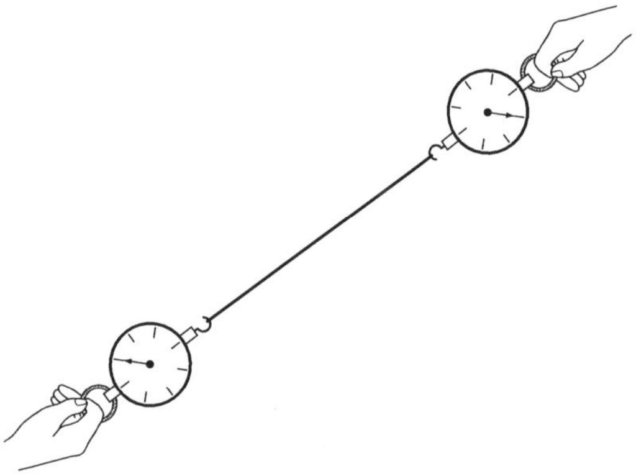

**Figure 2.6.c** *Students stretching the string*

1. Tie a string between two 20 N spring balances. Have two students stretch the string between them as shown in Figure 2.6.c. What do the two spring balances read?
2. Try pulling with different forces. Compare the forces on each spring balance each time you pull on the string with a different force. Does it matter who does the pulling?
3. Try adding a third spring balance in the middle of the string. How does this demonstration illustrate Newton's third law?

### Concluding Questions

1. When a car moves forward, in which direction do the wheels of the car push on the road? What force actually makes the car move forward?
2. List and discuss three examples of situations from your own everyday experience, that involve Newton's third law.

# 3 Circular Motion and Gravitation

This chapter focuses on the following AP Physics 1 Big Ideas from the College Board:

**BIG IDEA 1:** Objects and systems have properties such as mass and charge. Systems may have internal structure.

**BIG IDEA 2:** Fields existing in space can be used to explain interactions.

**BIG IDEA 3:** The interactions of an object with other objects can be described by forces.

**BIG IDEA 4:** Interactions between systems can result in changes in those systems.

---

By the end of this chapter, you should know the meaning of these **key terms**:

- centripetal acceleration
- centripetal force
- free fall
- Newton's law of universal gravitation
- uniform circular motion

---

By the end of this chapter, you should be able to use and know when to use the following formulae:

$T = \frac{1}{f}$ $a_c = \frac{v^2}{r} = \frac{4\ {}^{2}r}{T^2}$ $F_c = ma_c$ $F_g = G\frac{m_1m_2}{r^2}$

*This stamp commemorates the first American, Colonel John Glen, to orbit the Earth on February 20, 1962. The stamp was released to the public at the same time he arrived safely back to Earth. The space craft featured in the image was the Mercury Friendship 7 and is now housed at the National Air and Space Museum in Washington, D.C.*

# 3.1 Motion in a Circle

## Warm Up

Imagine you are swinging a tin can on a string in a circle above your head as shown in the diagram. Suddenly, the string breaks! Draw on the diagram the direction in which the can will move.

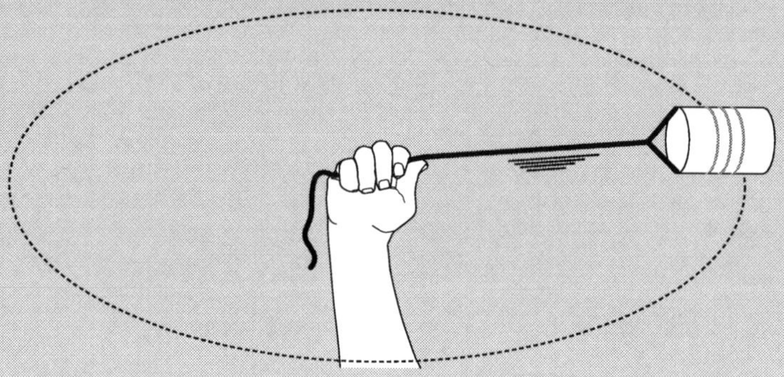

### Gravity and Motion

In a previous course, you may have solved problems involving the force of gravity and the acceleration due to gravity ($\vec{g}$). You assumed $g$ remains constant as a body falls from a height, and you considered many situations, most of which happened on or near the surface of Earth. Here are some questions you should be able to answer after you study this chapter:

- Is $\vec{g}$ the same for a satellite orbiting Earth several hundred kilometres above the surface as it is at Earth's surface?
- Does Earth exert a force of gravity on the Moon?
- Why does the Moon not "fall down" to Earth?

The force that keeps you firmly attached to this planet is the type of force that keeps Earth in orbit around the Sun. The force of gravity exists between any two masses in the universe.

All the planets orbit the Sun in elliptical orbits. Satellites (both artificial and our Moon) orbit Earth in elliptical paths. The ellipses are usually very close to being circular, however, so we begin our study of gravity by learning about objects moving in circular paths.

### Uniform Circular Motion

Imagine you are driving a car around a circular track, maintaining the same speed all the way around the track. Any object that moves in a circle at steady speed is said to be in **uniform circular motion.** Is such an object accelerating? It may seem to have zero acceleration, but in fact an object moving in a circle has a constant acceleration — not because of a change in speed, but because of its constantly changing direction. Remember: acceleration is defined as change in velocity divided by change in time, and velocity is a vector quantity.

$$\vec{a} = \frac{\Delta\vec{v}}{\Delta t}$$

## Identifying Centripetal Acceleration

If a body is moving in a circular path, in what direction does it accelerate? Figure 3.1.1 shows two consecutive positions of a body moving in a circle. Velocity vectors are labelled $\vec{v}_0$ and $\vec{v}_1$. To find out the direction of the acceleration, we need the direction of $\Delta\vec{v}$. Since $\Delta\vec{v}$ is the vector difference between $\vec{v}_1$ and $\vec{v}_0$, we use the rules for vector subtraction.

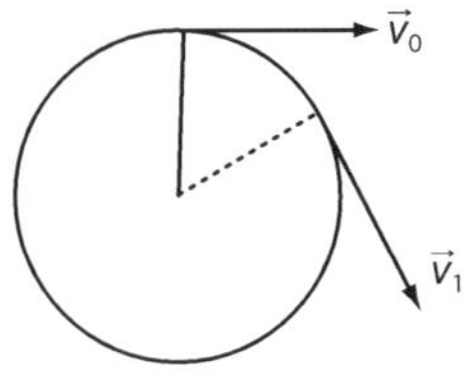


**Figure 3.1.1** *Two consecutive positions of a body moving in a circle*

Figure 3.1.2 shows how to find the vector difference, $\Delta\vec{v}$, between $\vec{v}_1$ and $\vec{v}_0$.

$$\Delta\vec{v} = \vec{v}_1 - \vec{v}_0$$

$$\Delta\vec{v} = \vec{v}_1 + (-\vec{v}_0)$$

Vector $\Delta\vec{v}$ is the resultant of $\vec{v}_1$ and ($-\vec{v}_0$).

In Figure 3.1.2, the velocity vectors chosen represent the velocity of the body at two different times. The time interval between the occurrences of the velocities is relatively long.

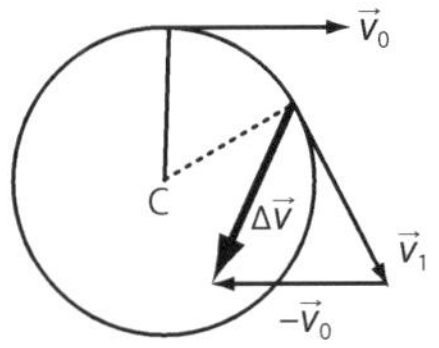


**Figure 3.1.2** *The vector difference, $\Delta\vec{v}$, between $\vec{v}_1$ and $\vec{v}_0$*

If this time interval ($\Delta t$) is shortened, the direction of $\Delta\vec{v}$ becomes closer and closer to being toward the centre of the circle as in Figure 3.1.3.

In fact, as $\Delta t \rightarrow 0$, the direction of $\Delta\vec{v}$ and therefore the direction of the acceleration $\vec{a}$ for all practical purposes, is toward the centre of the circle.

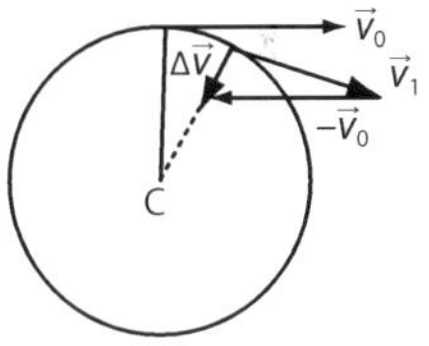


**Figure 3.1.3** *As $\Delta t$ is shortened, the direction of $\Delta\vec{v}$ becomes closer and closer to being toward the centre of the circle.*

## Direction of Centripetal Acceleration

Since the direction of the acceleration of a body moving at uniform speed in a circle is toward the centre of the circle, the acceleration is called **centripetal acceleration**. **Centripetal** means directed toward a centre.

A device called an **accelerometer** can be used to show that a body moving in a circle accelerates toward the centre of the circle (Figure 3.1.4). If the accelerometer is attached to a lab cart accelerating in a straight line, the colored water inside the cart forms a wedge pointing in the direction of the acceleration. If the same accelerometer is attached to a toy train travelling at constant speed on a circular track, the accelerometer shows no acceleration in the direction of travel, but a definite acceleration perpendicular to the direction of travel (Figure 3.1.5). In other words, the train on the circular track accelerates toward the centre of the track.

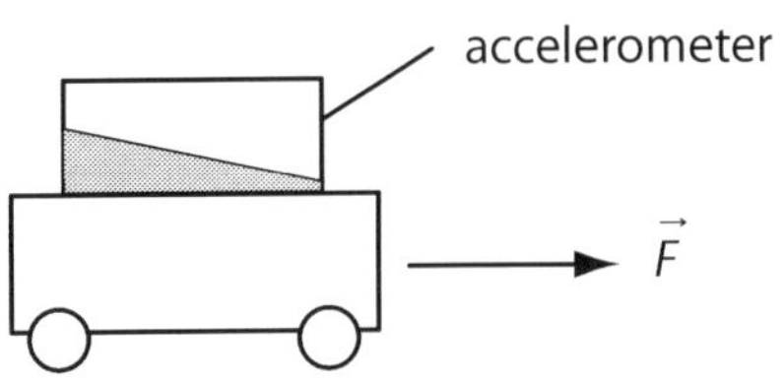


**Figure 3.1.4** *An accelerometer on a lab cart*

**Figure 3.1.5** *An accelerometer on a train going around a curve. Note the direction of the force is pointed inward to the centre of the circle.*

In Figure 3.1.6, a body is moving in a circle of radius $\vec{R}_0$. The radius is a displacement vector. The velocity of the body is $\vec{v}_0$. Following a very short time interval $\Delta t$, the body has moved through a small angle $\theta$, and the body has a new velocity $\vec{v}_1$, the same magnitude as $\vec{v}_0$, but in a new direction.

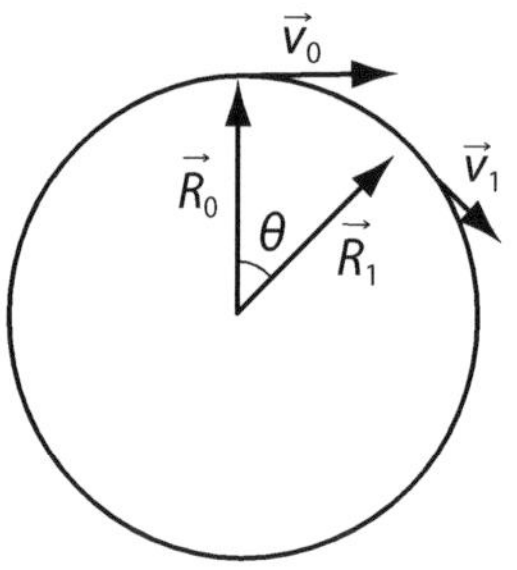


**Figure 3.1.6** *A body moving at $\vec{v}_0$ in a circle of radius $\vec{R}_0$*

## Defining Centripetal Acceleration

In Figure 3.1.7(a), $\Delta\vec{R}$ is the vector difference between $\vec{R}_1$ and $\vec{R}_0$.

$$\vec{R}_1 + (-\vec{R}_0) = \Delta\vec{R}$$

or

$$\vec{R}_0 + \Delta\vec{R} = \vec{R}_1$$

Figure 3.1.7(b) shows vector subtraction of the velocity vectors. Vector $\vec{v}$ is the vector difference between $\vec{v}_1$ and $\vec{v}_0$.

$$\vec{v}_1 + (-\vec{v}_0) = \Delta\vec{v}$$

or

$$\vec{v}_0 + \Delta\vec{v} = \vec{v}_1$$

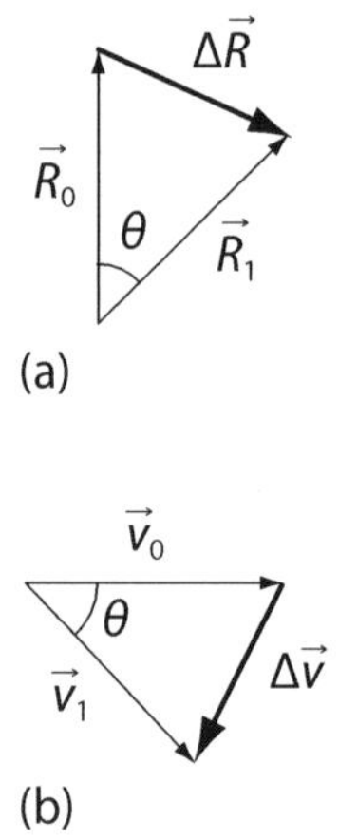


**Figure 3.1.7** *Radius vectors (a) and velocity vectors (b) in circular motion*

Now, consider the triangles formed by the radius vectors in Figure 3.1.7(a) and the velocity vectors in Figure 3.1.7(b). Both are isosceles triangles with a common angle $\theta$, so they are similar triangles. Corresponding sides of similar triangles are proportional; therefore,

$$\frac{\Delta v}{\Delta R} = \frac{v}{R}$$

(The subscripts have been dropped because the magnitudes of the speeds and the radii do not change.)

$$\Delta v = \frac{v}{R}\Delta R$$

During a time interval $\Delta t$, the average acceleration is $\dfrac{\Delta v}{\Delta t}$, so

$$\vec{a} = \frac{\Delta v}{\Delta t} = \frac{v}{R} \bullet \frac{\Delta R}{\Delta t}$$

Consider what happens during the motion of one complete circle of the body in Figures 3.1.6 and 3.1.7.

If the time interval $\Delta t$ is chosen to be very small ($\Delta t \to 0$), Figure 3.1.8 shows that each $\Delta\vec{R}$ becomes closer to being equal to the section of corresponding arc $\Delta s$ on the circumference of the circle. If $\Delta s$ is the arc in question, then $\Delta\vec{R} \to \Delta s$ as $\Delta t \to 0$.

The speed $v$ of the body as it moves around the circle is $v = \frac{\Delta s}{\Delta t}$, and if $\Delta t \to 0$,

$$v = \frac{\Delta R}{\Delta t}$$

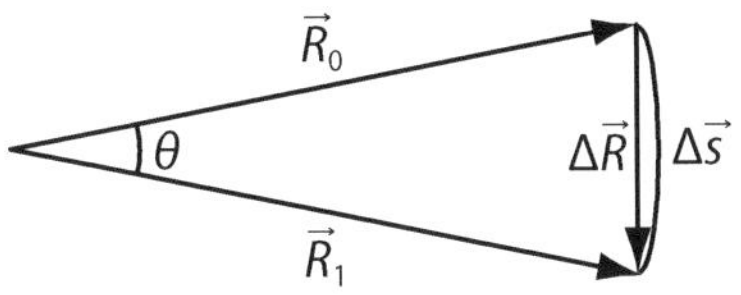


**Figure 3.1.8** *If $\Delta t \to 0$, $\Delta\vec{R} \to \Delta s$.*

It can therefore be said that the average acceleration during time $\Delta t$ is

$$\vec{a} = \frac{\Delta v}{\Delta t} = \frac{v}{R} \bullet \frac{\Delta R}{\Delta t} = \frac{v}{R} \bullet v = \frac{v^2}{R}$$

If $\Delta t \to 0$, the magnitude of the average acceleration approaches the instantaneous centripetal acceleration, $\vec{a}_c$. The magnitude of the **centripetal acceleration** is, therefore,

$$a_c = \frac{v^2}{R}$$

To summarize: when a body moves in a circle with uniform speed, it accelerates toward the centre of the circle, and the acceleration has a magnitude of $\frac{v^2}{R}$.

## Another Way to Calculate Centripetal Acceleration

Newton's second law suggests that since the acceleration is toward the centre of the circle, the net force causing it should also be a centripetal force**.** If the centripetal force causing the centripetal acceleration is "turned off," the body will travel off in a direction that is along a tangent to the circle.

Another useful equation for calculating centripetal acceleration can be derived from $a_c = \frac{v^2}{R}$. If one full revolution of the body is considered, its speed will equal the circumference of the circle divided by the period of the revolution; that is, $v = \frac{2\pi R}{T}$, where $R$ is the radius of the circle, and $T$ is the period of one revolution.

Since $a_c = \frac{v^2}{R}$, then $a_c = \left(\frac{2\pi R}{T}\right)^2 \frac{1}{R}$, therefore,

$$a_c = \frac{4\pi^2 R}{T^2}$$

Both equations for centripetal acceleration are useful in many situations. You will use them when studying the motion of planets around the Sun, satellites around Earth, electrons in a magnetic field, and any kind of circular motion.

## Quick Check

1. What is the centripetal acceleration of the Moon toward Earth?
   Given: $R = 3.84 \times 10^8$ m and $T = 2.36 \times 10^6$ s

2. A skater travels at 2.0 m/s in a circle of radius 4.0 m. What is her centripetal acceleration?

3. A 20.0 g rubber stopper is attached to a 0.855 m string. The stopper is spun in a horizontal circle making one revolution in 1.36 s. What is the acceleration of the stopper?

## Centripetal Force

The net force that causes centripetal acceleration is called centripetal force. Acceleration and net force are related by Newton's second law, which says that $F = ma$. So the magnitude of the centripetal force can be calculated by:

$$\text{centripetal force} \qquad F_c = ma_c$$

Therefore, $$F_c = m\frac{v^2}{R} \text{ or } F_c = m\frac{4\pi^2 R}{T^2}$$

### Sample Problem 3.1.1 — Centripetal Force

In a local playground a merry-go-round is turning at 4.50 m/s. If a 50.0 kg person is standing on the platforms edge, which is 5.80 m from the centre, what force of friction is necessary to keep her from falling off the platform?

| What to Think About | How to Do It |
|---|---|
| 1. This is a circular motion question and the force of friction between the person and the platform is the centripetal force. | $a_c = \frac{v^2}{R}$ |
| 2. Find the centripetal acceleration. | $a_c = \frac{(4.50 \text{ m/s})^2}{5.80 \text{ m}}$<br>$a_c = 3.49 \text{ m/s}^2$ |
| 3. Find the centripetal force, which is the frictional force keeping her on the platform as it spins. | $F_{fr} = F_c = ma_c$<br>$F_{fr} = (50.0 \text{ kg})(3.49 \text{ m/s}^2)$<br>$F_{fr} = 175 \text{N}$ |

## Practice Problems 3.1.1 — Centripetal Force

1. A 61 kg skater cuts a circle of radius 4.0 m on the ice. If her speed is 4.00 m/s, what is the centripetal force? What exerts this force?

2. What centripetal force is needed to keep a 12 kg object revolving with a frequency of 5.0 Hz in an orbit of radius 6.0 m?

3. A $1.2 \times 10^3$ kg car rounds a curve of radius 50.0 m at a speed of 80.0 km/h (22 m/s).
   (a) What is the centripetal acceleration of the car?

   (b) How much centripetal force is needed to cause this acceleration?

   (c) If the coefficient of kinetic friction $\mu$ is 0.25 on a slippery road, will the force of friction between the road and the wheels of the car be enough to keep the car from skidding?

# 3.1 Review Questions

Use $g = 9.80$ m/s$^2$

1. A 1.00 kg rock is swung in a horizontal circle of radius 1.50 m, at the end of a rope. One complete revolution takes 0.80 s.
   (a) What is the speed of the rock?

   (b) What is the centripetal acceleration of the rock?

   (c) What is the centripetal force exerted on the rock?

   (d) What exerts the centripetal force?

   (e) The circle traced out by the rock was described as being horizontal. Would the rope, as it swings, be horizontal too? Explain.

2. A spider that could not find its web site (because its computer crashed?) is on the outside edge of an old phonograph record. It holds on for dear life, as the record rotates at 78 rpm. The radius of the record is 15 cm.
   (a) What is the linear speed $v$ of the record at its outside edge?

   (b) What is the centripetal acceleration of the spider?

   (c) How much frictional force must there be to keep the spider from flying off the spinning record, if its mass is 1.0 g?

3. A satellite is orbiting Earth at a distance of $6.70 \times 10^6$ m from the Earth's centre. If its period of revolution around Earth is $5.45 \times 10^3$ s, what is the value of $g$ at this distance?

 

4. A pendulum 1.00 m long and with a 1.20 kg bob is swinging with a maximum speed of 2.50 m/s. Calculate the total force exerted by the string on the swinging mass when the mass is at the bottom of its swing.

5. A motocross rider at the peak of his jump has a speed such that his centripetal acceleration is equal to $g$. As a result, he does not feel any supporting force from the seat of his bike, which is also accelerating at rate $g$. Therefore, he feels as if there is no force of gravity on him, a condition described as apparent weightlessness. If the radius of the approximately circular jump is 75.0 m, what was the speed of the bike?

6. Planet Earth has a period of rotation of 24 h and a radius of $6.4 \times 10^6$ m.
   (a) What is the centripetal acceleration toward Earth's centre of a person standing on the equator?

   (b) With what frequency $f$, in hertz, would Earth have to spin to make the centripetal acceleration $a_c$ equal in magnitude to $g$? Compare this with Earth's normal frequency of rotation. (1 rotation in 24 h = $1.16 \times 10^{-5}$ Hz)

   (c) If Earth could be made to spin so fast that $a_c = g$, how would this affect the apparent force of gravity on you? Explain.

7. A 25 kg child is on a swing, which has a radius of 2.00 m. If the child is moving 4.0 m/s at the bottom of one swing, what is the centripetal force exerted by the ropes of the swing on the child? What is the total force exerted by the ropes when the swing is at its lowest point?

8. At the bottom of a power dive, a plane is travelling in a circle of radius 1.00 km at a speed of $2.50 \times 10^2$ m/s. What is the total force exerted upward on the 90.0 kg pilot by his seat?

9. Tarzan is swinging through the jungle on a vine that will break if the force exceeds $2.0 \times 10^3$ N. If the length of the vine is 5.0 m and Tarzan's mass is $1.00 \times 10^2$ kg, what is the highest speed he can safely travel while swinging on the vine? **Hint:** At what point in the swing will the tension in the vine be greatest?

10. Earth orbits the Sun at a distance of $1.5 \times 10^{11}$ m.
    (a) What is its centripetal acceleration toward the Sun?

    (b) If the mass of Earth is $6.0 \times 10^{24}$ kg, what is the centripetal force exerted by the Sun on Earth? What provides this force?

11. A roller coaster loop has a radius of 12 m. To prevent the passengers in a car from not falling out at the top of the loop, what is the minimum speed the car must have at the top?

12. A highway curve is designed to handle vehicles travelling 50 km/h safely.
    (a) Assuming the coefficient of kinetic friction between the rubber tires and the road is 0.60, what is the minimum radius of curvature allowable for the section of road?

    (b) For added safety, the road might be built with "banking." In what direction should the road be banked? Why does this help?

# 3.2 Gravity and Kepler's Solar System

## Warm Up

If you drop a piece of paper and a book from the same height, which object will hit the ground first? If you put the piece of paper on top of the book and drop them together, why does the paper fall at the same rate as the book? What can you conclude about the rate at which objects fall?

___

___

___

### Falling Objects

If gravity is the only force acting on a body, the body is in **free fall**. If there is no friction, each of the bodies in Figure 3.2.1 is in free fall. Each is accelerating downward at rate $\vec{g}$, which is independent of the mass of the body and has a magnitude of 9.80 m/s$^2$ near Earth's surface.

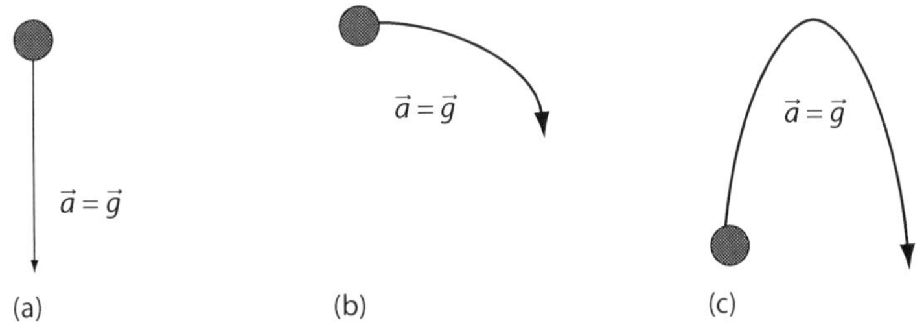


**Figure 3.2.1** *In all three situations, the only force causing the acceleration of the free-falling body is gravity.*

"What goes up must come down." This simple truth has been known for centuries. Any unsupported object will fall to the ground. According to legend, Isaac Newton (1642–1727) was sitting under an apple tree when he saw an apple fall to the ground. He looked up at the Moon and wondered, "Why should the Moon not fall down, as well?"

### The Moon in Free Fall

Might the Moon be in "free fall"? If it is, then why does it not fall to Earth like other unsupported bodies? Newton created a diagram like the one in Figure 3.2.2 to explain why the Moon circles Earth without "falling down" in the usual sense.

Imagine you are at the top of a mountain that is high enough so that there is essentially no air to offer resistance to the motion of a body projected horizontally from the top of the mountain. If a cannon is loaded with a small amount of gunpowder, a cannonball will be projected horizontally at low speed and follow a curved path until it strikes the ground at A. If more gunpowder is used, a greater initial speed will produce a curved path ending at B.

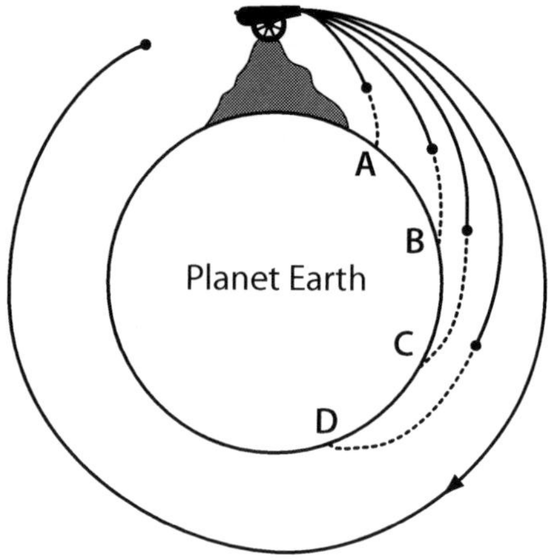


**Figure 3.2.2** *Newton's diagram explaining why the Moon doesn't fall to Earth.*

With increasing initial speeds, paths ending at C and D will be achieved. If the initial speed is just high enough, the path will have a curvature parallel with Earth's curvature, and the cannonball will circle Earth for an indefinite period. The cannonball will orbit Earth, just like the Moon.

Isaac Newton actually anticipated artificial Earth satellites. Of course, the technology for sending a satellite into orbit was not available 300 years ago. To place an artificial satellite in orbit 500 km above Earth's surface requires a horizontal speed of approximately 7.6 km/s. It will take such a satellite approximately 90 minutes to complete one orbit.

The Moon was our first satellite. No one knows how or why it attained its orbit, but it is in a nearly circular path around this planet. The Moon is, indeed, in free fall. It does "fall toward Earth." Its horizontal speed is great enough that it completes its orbit with no danger of colliding with Earth's surface — just like the cannonball in Figure 3.2.2 but at a much greater altitude. The Moon's mean distance from Earth is $3.84 \times 10^5$ km. The orbit is actually slightly elliptical; hence mean (average) distance.

## Gravitational Force, Earth, and the Moon

Could the centripetal force needed to keep the Moon in a near-circular orbit around Earth be the same force that makes an apple fall from a tree? What would exert this force of gravity on the Moon?

Since every known thing on Earth experiences the pull of gravity, Newton was certain that Earth itself exerted a gravitational force on objects near its surface. At Earth's surface, gravity makes objects accelerate at a rate of 9.8 m/s$^2$. What would the acceleration due to gravity be at a distance as far away as the Moon?

Treating the Moon as a body in circular orbit, the acceleration due to gravity is just the centripetal acceleration of the Moon. Therefore,

$$a_c = \frac{4\pi^2 R}{T^2} = \frac{4\pi^2(3.84 \times 10^8 \text{ m})}{[(27.3 \text{ d})(24 \text{ h/d})(3600 \text{ s/h})]^2} = 2.7 \times 10^{-3} \text{ m/s}^2$$

If this value of $a_c$ was really the magnitude of $g$ at the Moon's distance from Earth, it is much smaller than the value of $g$ at Earth's surface. Newton was convinced that, since $F = ma$, the force of gravity causing this acceleration must decrease rapidly with distance from Earth.

In Investigation 3.2, you will be provided with data about most of the planets in the solar system. Given their orbital radii and their periods of revolution, you will calculate their centripetal accelerations toward the Sun. You will then use graphical analysis to determine the nature of the relationship between $a_c$, caused by the force of gravity of the Sun on the planet, and distance $R$ from the Sun.

## Johannes Kepler

Johannes Kepler (1571–1630) was a German mathematician who had worked in the astronomical laboratory of Danish astronomer Tycho Brahe (1546–1601). Brahe is famous for his precise observations of the positions of almost 800 stars and his accurate records of the positions of planets over a period of two decades. Brahe did all his work without a telescope! The telescope had not yet been invented.

Kepler was fascinated with planetary motions, and devoted his life to a search for mathematical patterns in their motions. To find these patterns he relied completely on the observations of Tycho Brahe. Kepler formulated three laws describing the orbits of the planets around the Sun.

## Kepler's Three Laws of Planetary Motion

1. Each planet orbits the Sun in an elliptical path, with the Sun at one of the two foci of the ellipse.
2. A line joining the centre of the Sun and the centre of any planet will trace out equal areas in equal intervals of time (Figure 3.2.3). If time intervals $T_2$–$T_1$ and $T_4$–$T_3$ are equal, the areas traced out by the orbital radius of a planet during these intervals will be equal. (The diagram is not to scale.)

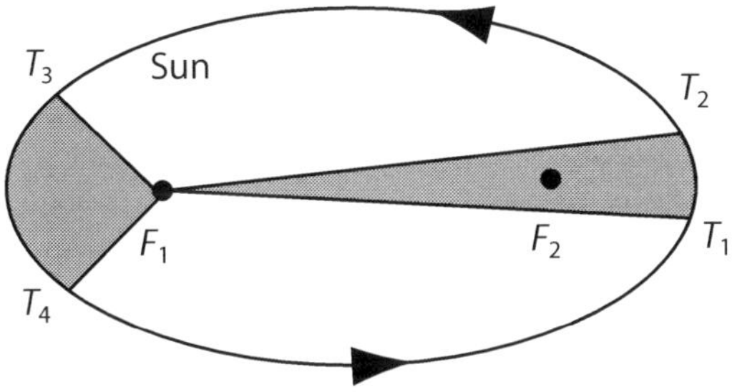


**Figure 3.2.3** *Kepler's second law*

3. For any planet in the solar system, the cube of its mean orbital radius divided by the square of its period of revolution is a constant.

$$\frac{\overline{R}^3}{T^2} = K$$

Kepler's three laws can be neatly summarized in half a page of this text, but remember that to arrive at these laws required many years of work by this dedicated mathematician, not to mention the 20 years spent by Tycho Brahe making his painstaking observations of the heavenly wanderers, the planets.

In Investigation 3.3, you will calculate Kepler's constant K for the solar system.

### Sample Problem 3.2.1 — Kepler's Laws

Planet Xerox (a close copy of planet Earth) was discovered by Superman on one of his excursions to the far extremes of the solar system. Its distance from the Sun is $1.50 \times 10^{13}$ m. How long will this planet take to orbit the Sun?

| What to Think About | How to Do It |
|---|---|
| 1. Collect data needed to answer the question. | Earth's orbital radius, $R_e = 1.5 \times 10^{11}$ m<br>Earth's period of revolution, $T_e = 1.0$ a<br>Xerox's orbital radius, $R_X = 1.50 \times 10^{13}$ m |
| 2. You could solve the problem using Kepler's constant derived in Investigation 4.2.2. Using Kepler's third law, you would simply solve for $T_X$. Another way to solve the problem is to use data for Earth (above) and the fact that $$\frac{R_X^3}{T_X^2} = \frac{R_e^3}{T_e^2} = K_{Sun}$$ | $T_x^2 = \frac{R_x^3}{R_e^3} \cdot T_e^2$<br>$T_x^2 = \frac{[1.5 \times 10^{13} m]^3}{[1.5 \times 10^{11} m]^3} \cdot [1.0a]^2$<br>$T_x^2 = 1.0 \times 10^6 a^2$<br>$T_x = 1.0 \times 10^3 a$ |
| 3. The planet Xerox has a period of revolution around the Sun of $1.0 \times 10^3$ a. | |

### Practice Problems 3.2.1 — Kepler's Laws

1. A certain asteroid has a mean orbital radius of $5.0 \times 10^{11}$ m. What is its period of revolution around the Sun?

2. A satellite is placed in orbit around Earth with an orbital radius of $2.0 \times 10^7$ m. What is its period of revolution? Use the facts that the Moon's period of revolution is $2.36 \times 10^6$ s and its orbital radius is $3.84 \times 10^8$ m.

# 3.2 Review Questions

1. What is the period of revolution of a planet that is 5.2 times as far away from the Sun as Earth?

2. The diagram below shows the orbit of a comet around the Sun. Mark on the diagram where the comet will be moving fastest. Explain in terms of Kepler's second law.

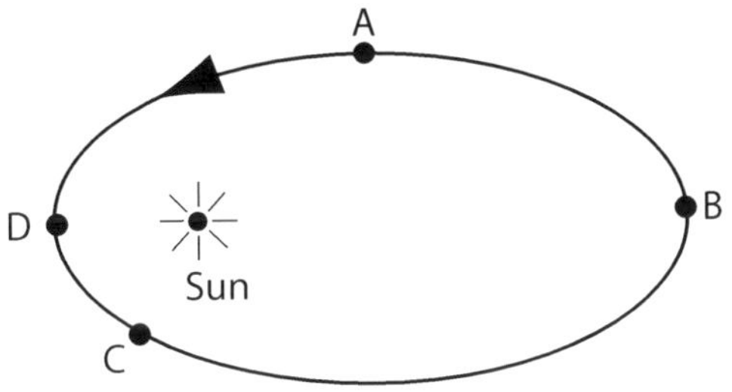


3. A satellite has period $T$ and orbital radius $R$. To increase the period to $8T$, what must the new orbital radius be?

4. The Earth orbits the Sun once a year, so its period of revolution is 1.0 a. If a space probe orbits the Sun with an orbital radius nine times that of Earth, what is the space probe's period of revolution?

5. For satellites of Earth, Kepler's law applies, but a different constant K must be used. Calculate what K would be for Earth's satellites, using only the fact that the Moon has a mean orbital radius of $3.84 \times 10^8$ m and a period of revolution of $2.36 \times 10^6$ s.

6. Using K for Earth's satellites, calculate the mean orbital radius of an Earth satellite that is in geosynchronous orbit. (A communications satellite in geosynchronous orbit orbits Earth in the plane of the equator in a period of 24 h, and therefore stays above one point on Earth's surface as Earth completes its daily rotation).

7. Halley's comet is a satellite of the Sun. It passed Earth in 1910 on its way around the Sun, and passed it again in 1986.
   (a) What is the period of revolution of Halley's comet, in years (a)?

   (b) What is the mean orbital radius of Halley's comet?

   (c) The mean orbital radius equals the average of the orbiting comet's closest and farthest distances from the Sun. If the closest Halley's comet gets to the Sun is $8.9 \times 10^{10}$ m, what is its farthest distance from the Sun?

   (d) When Halley's comet is at its farthest distance from the Sun, where is it located in relation to the orbits of the outer planets?

8. The Earth is $1.49 \times 10^8$ km from the Sun, and its period of revolution is 1.0 a. Venus is $1.08 \times 10^8$ km from the Sun, on average. Use Kepler's third law to calculate the length of a Venus year in Earth years (a).

# 3.3 Newton's Law of Universal Gravitation

## Warm Up

The Moon orbits Earth about once every 28 days. Why doesn't the Moon crash into Earth?

______________________________________________

______________________________________________

______________________________________________

### From Kepler to Newton

Kepler's three laws describe the orbits of the planets around the Sun. Newton used Kepler's laws to derive a law describing the nature of the gravitational forces that cause the planets to move in these orbits.

Newton concluded that the force that keeps planets in orbit is the same force that makes an apple fall to the ground. He stated that there is a gravitational force between any two bodies in the universe. Like all other forces, gravity is a mutual force. That is, the force with which Earth pulls on a falling apple is equal to the force with which the apple pulls on Earth, but in the opposite direction. Earth pulls on your body with a force of gravity that is commonly referred to as your "weight." Simultaneously, your body exerts a force on planet Earth of the same magnitude but in the opposite direction. Relative to each other, Earth "weighs" the same as your body!

Newton was able to use Kepler's laws as a starting point for showing that the force of gravity between the Sun and the planets varied as the inverse of the square of the distance between the Sun and the planets. He was convinced that the inverse square relation would apply to everyday objects near the surface of Earth as well. He produced arguments suggesting that the force should depend on the product of the masses of the two bodies being attracted to one another. The mathematical details of how Newton arrived at his famous **law of universal gravitation** can be found in many references, but are too lengthy to reproduce here.

**Newton's Law of Universal Gravitation**

Every body in the universe attracts every other body with a force that is (a) directly proportional to the product of the masses of the two bodies and (b) inversely proportional to the square of the distance between the centres of mass of the two bodies.

The equation for Newton's law of universal gravitation is:

$$F = G\frac{Mm}{R^2}$$

The constant of proportionality G is called the universal gravitation constant. Isaac Newton was unable to measure G, but it was measured later in experiments by Henry Cavendish (1731–1810).

The modern value for G is $6.67 \times 10^{-11}$ $Nm^2/kg^2$.

## Cavendish's Experiment to Measure G

You can imagine how difficult it is to measure the gravitational force between two ordinary objects. In 1797, Henry Cavendish performed a very sensitive experiment, which was the first "Earthbound" confirmation of the law of universal gravitation. Cavendish used two lead spheres mounted at the ends of a rod 2.0 m long. The rod was suspended horizontally from a wire that would twist an amount proportional to the gravitational force between the suspended masses and two larger fixed spherical masses placed near each of the suspended spheres (Figure 3.3.1).

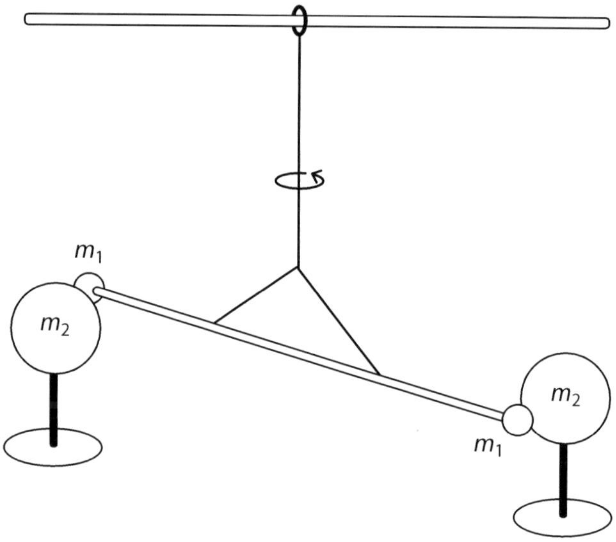


**Figure 3.3.1** *Cavendish's apparatus for confirming Newton's law of universal gravitation*

The forces involved in this experiment were extremely small (in the order of $10^{-6}$ N), so great care had to be taken to eliminate errors from air currents and static electricity. Cavendish did manage to provide confirmation of the law of universal gravitation, and he arrived at the first measured value of G.

## Gravitational Field Strength of the Earth

To calculate the force of gravity on a mass *m*, you simply multiply the mass by the gravitational field strength *g* ($F = mg$.) You could also use the law of universal gravitation:

$$F = G\frac{Mm}{R^2}, \text{ where } M \text{ is the mass of Earth.}$$

This means that $mg = G\frac{Mm}{R^2}$ and, therefore,

$$g = G\frac{M}{R^2}$$

Thus, the gravitational field strength of Earth depends only on the mass of Earth and the distance, *R*, from the centre of Earth to the centre of mass of the object that has mass *m*.

**Sample Problem 3.3.1 — Newton's Law of Universal Gravitation**

What is the force of gravity on a 70.0 kg man standing on Earth's surface, according to the law of universal gravitation? Check your answer using $F = mg$.

| What to Think About | How to Do It |
|---|---|
| 1. What data do you need? | $G = 6.67 \times 10^{-11}\ Nm^2/kg^2$<br>$g = 9.80\ N/kg$<br>Earth's mass $= 5.98 \times 10^{24}$ kg<br>Earth's radius $= 6.38 \times 10^6$ m |
| 2. Find the force of gravity using the law of universal gravitation. | $F_g = G\frac{m_1 m_2}{r^2}$<br>$F_g = (6.67 \times 10^{-11}\ Nm^2/kg^2)\left(\frac{(70.0\ kg)(5.98 \times 10^{24}\ kg)}{(6.38 \times 10^6\ m)^2}\right)$<br>$F_g = 686\ N$ |
| 3. Calculate the force of gravity using $F = mg$. | $F_g = mg$<br>$F_g = (70.\ kg)(9.80\ m/s^2)$<br>$F_g = 686\ N$ |

**Practice Problems 3.3.1 — Newton's Law of Universal Gravitation**

1. What is the force of gravitational attraction between a 75 kg boy and a 60.0 kg girl
   (a) when they are 2.0 m apart?

   (b) when they are only 1.0 m apart?

*Practice Problems continued*

### Practice Problems 3.3.1 — Newton's Law of Universal Gravitation (Continued)

2. What is the force of gravity exerted on you if your mass is 70.0 kg and you are standing on the Moon? The Moon's mass is $7.34 \times 10^{22}$ kg and its radius is $1.74 \times 10^{6}$ m.

3. What is the force of gravity exerted on you by Mars, if your mass is 70.0 kg and the mass of Mars is $6.37 \times 10^{23}$ kg? The radius of Mars is $3.43 \times 10^{6}$ m, and you are standing on its surface, searching for Mars bars.

## Weightlessness

According to Newton's law of universal gravitation, the force of gravity between any two bodies varies *inversely* as the square of the distance between the centres of mass of the two bodies.

Figure 3.3.2 is a graph showing how the force of gravity (commonly called "weight") changes with distance measured from Earth's centre. To be truly "weightless" (experience no force of gravity) an object would have to be an infinite distance from any other mass. According to the law of universal gravitation, as $R \rightarrow \infty$, $F \rightarrow 0$.

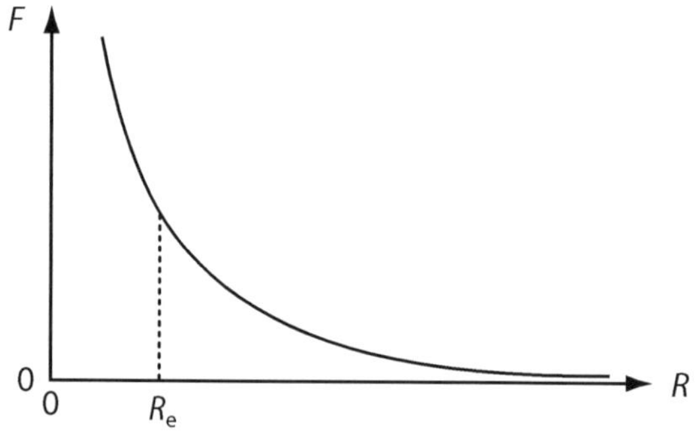


**Figure 3.3.2** *The force of gravity decreases dramatically with distance from Earth.*

Obviously, true weightlessness is not likely to be achieved! When people talk about "weightlessness," they usually are referring to *apparent* weightlessness. Apparent weightlessness is experienced when you feel zero force from supporting structures like your seat, the floor, or Earth's surface. This will happen when your supporting structure has the same acceleration as you have. Of course, if there is no supporting structure as when you jump off a cliff or a ladder or when you are in the middle of a jump you will also experience apparent weightlessness.

## Examples of Apparent Weightlessness

### 1. A Falling Elevator

Imagine a person standing on a scale in an elevator (Figure 3.3.3(a)). When the elevator is standing still, the scale will give the true weight of the person, which is the force of gravity exerted by Earth on the person ($F = mg$). In the illustration, this is shown as the pair of forces of the person's weight ($w = mg$) and the normal force ($N$) from the scale exerting a force back on the person. With no acceleration, the scale reads the true weight: $w = N = mg$.

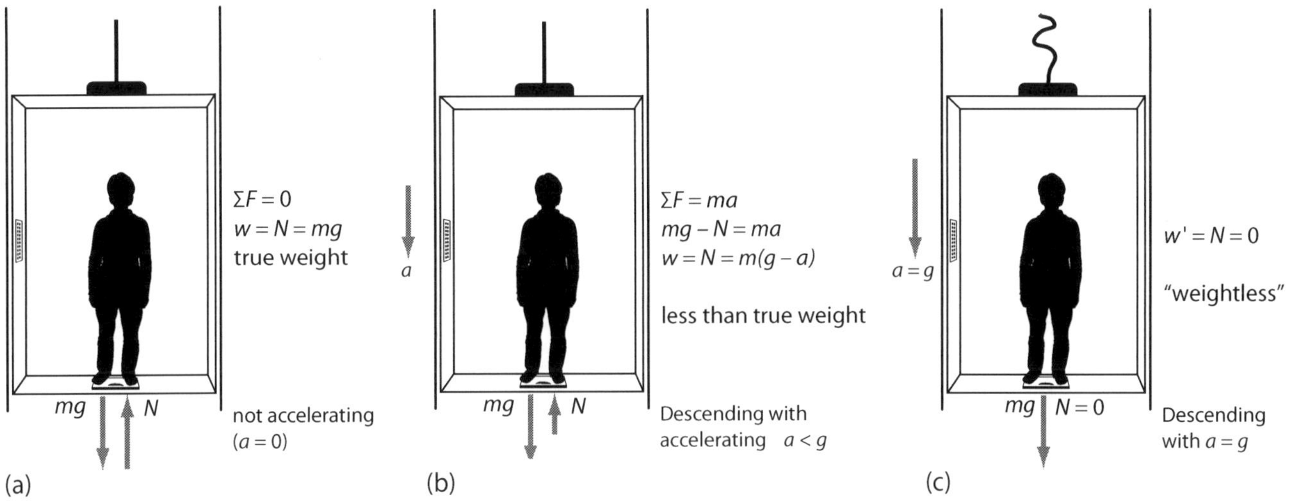


**Figure 3.3.3** *A person in an elevator can experience apparent weightlessness.*

In Figure 3.3.3(b) the elevator is accelerating down at a rate less than gravity. Now the person's weight is greater than the normal force being exerted back, so the person appears to be lighter than their true weight based on the reading on the weigh scale.

Imagine now that the cable breaks, as in Figure 3.3.3(c). The elevator will accelerate down at rate $a = g$. The person in the elevator will also fall, accelerating at rate $a = g$. The scale, placed in the elevator by the person, will read the apparent weight of the person, which is zero. In this situation, $w = N = 0$. At this moment, the person experiences true weightlessness. You get a similar feeling when you go over a large bump while driving in a car or take a quick drop on an amusement park ride.

### 2. Orbiting Astronauts

Astronauts in an orbiting space vehicle feel weightless for the same reason as a person in a falling elevator. Both the astronauts and the vehicle they occupy are in free fall. The astronauts feel no resistance from any supporting structure, so they feel weightless.

### 3. Momentary Weightlessness

You experience brief sensations of weightlessness during everyday activities. If you are running, you will experience apparent "weightlessness" during those intervals when both feet are off the ground, because you are in a momentary free fall situation. Jumping off a diving board or riding your bike swiftly over a bump, you will experience brief moments of apparent weightlessness.

## Quick Check

1. Why would a BMX rider feel momentarily "weightless" during a jump?

2. A 70.0 kg man is in an elevator that is accelerating downward at a rate of 1.0 m/s$^2$. What is the man's *apparent weight?*

3. How fast would Earth have to move at the equator before a person standing on the equator felt "weightless"? Earth's radius is $6.37 \times 10^6$ m.

4. Earth is in free fall toward the Sun. Why do you not feel "weightless" when you are an occupant of this satellite of the Sun?

### Satellites in Circular Orbits — Orbital Velocity

What orbital (tangential) speed must a space vehicle have to achieve a circular orbit at a given altitude (Figure 3.3.4)? Since the centripetal force ($mv^2/R$) is provided by gravity, we can write:

$$\frac{mv^2}{R} = \frac{GMm}{R^2}$$

Therefore, $$v^2 = \frac{GM}{R}, \text{ and}$$

$$v_{\text{orbital}} = \sqrt{\frac{GM}{R}}$$

where $M$ is the mass of Earth, $R$ is the distance from Earth's centre to the space vehicle, and G is the universal gravitation constant.

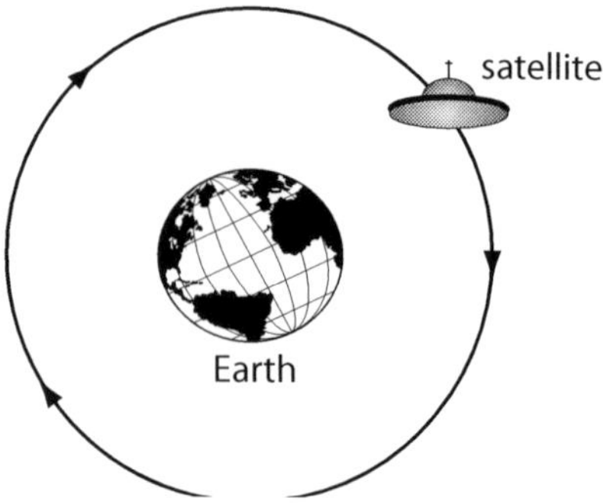


**Figure 3.3.4** *A space vehicle must achieve and maintain a minimum speed to remain in orbit.*

 

### Quick Check

1. What orbital speed is required by an Earth satellite in orbit $1.0 \times 10^3$ km above Earth's surface? Does it make a difference what the mass of the satellite is? Explain your answer. Earth's mass = $5.98 \times 10^{24}$ kg — Earth's radius = $6.37 \times 10^6$ m

2. What is the speed of a satellite orbiting Earth at a distance of $9.0 \times 10^5$ m above Earth's surface?

## Gravitational Potential Energy

Newton's law of universal gravitation tells us the force between a space vehicle and planet Earth at any distance $R$ from the centre of mass of Earth:

$$F = G\frac{Mm}{R^2}$$

where $M$ is the mass of Earth, $m$ is the mass of the space vehicle, and $R$ is the distance from Earth's centre to the space vehicle.

If a space vehicle is to travel to other parts of the solar system, it must first escape the grasp of Earth's gravitational field. How much energy must be supplied to the vehicle to take it *from Earth's surface* (where $R = R_e$) to a distance where the gravitational force due to Earth is "zero" ($R \rightarrow \infty$)?

The force on the space vehicle is continually changing. Figure 3.3.5 shows how the force changes with distance. To get the vehicle out of Earth's gravitational field, enough energy must be supplied to the space vehicle to equal the amount of work done against the force of gravity over a distance between Earth's surface and infinity where the force approaches zero.

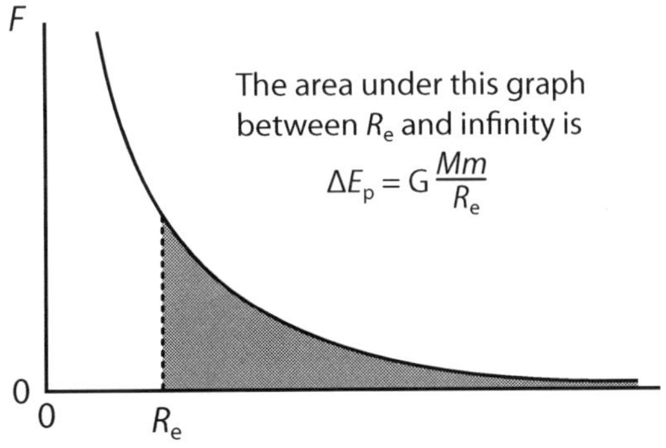


**Figure 3.3.5** *A large force is needed at first to move the space vehicle out of Earth's gravitational field.*

The amount of work that must be done to escape Earth's gravitational field is equal to the area underneath the force vs. distance graph, between $R = R_e$ and $R \to \infty$ (Figure 3.3.5). Using calculus, it can be shown that the area under the graph (shaded portion) is equal to $GMm/R_e$. This area represents the change in gravitational potential energy of the vehicle as it moves from distance $R_e$ out to infinity.

$$E_p = G\frac{Mm}{R_e}$$

In routine, Earthbound problems involving gravitational potential energy, we often arbitrarily take the "zero" level of potential energy to be at Earth's surface. In situations involving space travel, it is conventional and convenient to the let the "zero" of $E_p$ be at infinity.

Since the change in $E_p$ between $R = R_e$ and $R \to \infty$ is $+G\frac{Mm}{R_e}$, the $E_p$ at Earth's surface is negative.

$$E_p\ (at\ R = R_e) = -G\frac{Mm}{R_e}$$

## Escape Velocity

How fast must a spaceship travel to escape the gravitational bond of the planet Earth? In order to escape Earth's gravitational pull, the space vehicle must start with enough kinetic energy to do the work needed to bring its potential energy to zero. Sitting on the launch pad, the total energy of the space vehicle is

$$E_p = -G\frac{Mm}{R_e}$$

If the space vehicle is to escape Earth's field, it must be given sufficient kinetic energy so that:

$$-G\frac{Mm}{R_e} + E_k = 0$$

$$-G\frac{Mm}{R_e} + \frac{1}{2}mv^2 = 0$$

$$\frac{1}{2}mv^2 = G\frac{Mm}{R_e}$$

$$v^2 = 2G\frac{M}{R_e}$$

$$v = \sqrt{\frac{2GM}{R_e}}$$

This means that $v_{escape} = \sqrt{\frac{2GM}{R_e}}$ is the minimum speed the space vehicle must be given in order to escape Earth's gravitational pull.

This minimum speed for escape is called the escape velocity for planet Earth. It depends only on Earth's mass and Earth's radius. Obviously different planets or moons would have different escape velocities, as questions in the rest of the chapter will show.

## Quick Check

1. A $2.0 \times 10^4$ kg satellite orbits a planet in a circle of radius $2.2 \times 10^6$ m. Relative to zero at infinity, the gravitational potential energy of the satellite is $-6.0 \times 10^9$ J. What is the mass of the planet?

2. Ganymede, one of Jupiter's moons, is larger than the planet Mercury. Its mass is $1.54 \times 10^{23}$ kg, and its radius is $2.64 \times 10^6$ m.
   (a) What is the gravitational field strength, $g$, on Ganymede?

   (b) What is the escape velocity for a space vehicle trying to leave Ganymede?

# 3.3 Review Questions

$G = 6.67 \times 10^{-11}$ Nm²/kg²
$M_e = 5.98 \times 10^{24}$ kg
$R_e = 6.37 \times 10^{6}$ m

1. What is the force of gravity exerted on a 70.0 kg person on Jupiter (assuming the person could find a place to stand)? Jupiter has a mass of $1.90 \times 10^{27}$ kg and a radius of $7.18 \times 10^{7}$ m.

2. What is the gravitational field strength of Earth at a distance equal to the Moon's orbital radius of $3.84 \times 10^{8}$ m? Compare this with the centripetal acceleration of the Moon, calculated earlier in the chapter.

3. Calculate the orbital speed of the Moon around Earth, using the Moon's orbital radius and the value of Earth's gravitational field strength at that distance.

4. Both G and $g$ are constants. Why is G a universal constant and not $g$? Under what conditions is $g$ a constant?

5. Calculate the value of $g$ at each of the locations in the table below. Express each answer as a multiple or a decimal fraction of Earth's $g$. Would the force of gravity on you be greatest on the Moon, on Ganymede (*one of Jupiter's Moons), or on Mercury?

| | **Mass** | **Radius** |
|---|---|---|
| (a) On the Moon | $7.34 \times 10^{22}$ kg | $1.74 \times 10^{6}$ m |
| (b) On planet Mercury | $3.28 \times 10^{23}$ kg | $2.57 \times 10^{6}$ m |
| (c) On Ganymede* | $1.54 \times 10^{23}$ kg | $2.64 \times 10^{6}$ m |
| (d) On the surface of the Sun | $1.98 \times 10^{30}$ kg | $6.95 \times 10^{8}$ m |

6. Use Newton's law of universal gravitation and the formula for centripetal force to show that you can calculate the mass of Earth knowing only the orbital radius and the period of an Earth satellite. Then calculate Earth's mass using the Moon's period ($2.36 \times 10^{6}$ s) and orbital radius ($3.84 \times 10^{8}$ m).

7. Calculate the gravitational force between the Sun and the planetoid Pluto. The mass of the Sun is $2 \times 10^{30}$ kg, and the mass of Pluto is $6 \times 10^{23}$ kg. Pluto is $6 \times 10^{12}$ m away from the Sun.

8. An acrobat does a complete loop at the end of a rope attached to a horizontal bar. The distance from the support to the acrobat's centre of gravity is 3.0 m. How fast must she move at the top of her loop to feel "weightless" at that point?

9. A motocross rider travelling 20.0 m/s feels "weightless" as his bike rides over the peak of a mound. What is the radius of curvature of the mound?

10. Substitute values for G, $M_e$, and $R_e$ in the formula for escape velocity and calculate the escape velocity for planet Earth. Does the mass of the space vehicle make a difference? Explain.

11. Calculate escape velocities for the Sun, the Moon, and Mars, given the following information.

| | **Mass** | **Radius** |
|---|---|---|
| Sun | $2.0 \times 10^{30}$ kg | $7.0 \times 10^{8}$ m |
| Moon | $7.4 \times 10^{22}$ kg | $1.7 \times 10^{6}$ m |
| Mars | $6.4 \times 10^{23}$ kg | $3.4 \times 10^{6}$ m |

12. Travelling to other planets involves not only Earth's gravitational field but also that of the Sun and the other planets. Would it be easier to travel to Venus or to Mars? (Which would require the lower escape speed?)

# Chapter 3 Conceptual Review Questions

1. Can centripetal acceleration change the speed of circular motion? Explain.

2. If centripetal force is directed toward the center, why do you feel that you are 'thrown' away from the center as a car goes around a curve? Explain.

3. Is there a real force that throws water from clothes during the spin cycle of a washing machine? Explain how the water is removed from the clothes.

4. Two friends are having a conversation. Cassidy says a satellite in orbit is in freefall because the satellite keeps falling toward Earth. Gareth says a satellite in orbit is not in freefall because the acceleration due to gravity is not $9.8 m/s^2$. Who do you agree with and why?

# Chapter 3 Review Questions

$G = 6.67 \times 10^{-11}\ Nm^2/kg^2$

1. How much centripetal force is needed to keep a 43 kg object revolving with a frequency of 0.20 Hz in an orbit of radius 4.8 m?

2. What centripetal force must be exerted by the ice on a hockey player of mass 72 kg who cuts a curve of radius 3.0 m while travelling 5.0 m/s?

3. A 1.25 kg steel puck is swung in a circle of radius 3.6 m at the end of a cord of negligible mass, on a frictionless ice surface. The period of one revolution is 1.6 s. Calculate:
   (a) the speed of the puck.

   (b) the centripetal acceleration of the puck.

   (c) the centripetal force on the puck.

4. A satellite is orbiting Earth $1.00 \times 10^2$ km above the surface. At this altitude, $g = 9.5\ m/s^2$. If Earth's radius is $6.4 \times 10^3$ km, what is the period of revolution of the satellite?

5. How much centripetal force is needed to keep a 10.0 kg object revolving with a frequency of 1.5 Hz in an orbit of radius 2.0 m?

6. A 45 kg ape swings through the bottom of his arc on a swinging vine, with a speed of 3.0 m/s. If the distance from the supporting tree branch to his centre of gravity is 4.0 m, calculate the total tension in the vine.

7. A 1440 N football player, who missed a tackle in a very important high school game, is sent by his coach on a spaceship to a distance of four Earth radii from the centre of Earth. What will the force of gravity on him be at that altitude?

8. Earth's elliptical orbit around the Sun brings it closest to the Sun in January of each year and farthest in July. During what month would Earth's (a) speed and (b) centripetal acceleration be greatest?

9. What is the force of gravity on a 70.0 kg woman (a) here on Earth? (b) on an asteroid of mass $1.0 \times 10^9$ kg and radius $4.5 \times 10^4$ m?

10. What is the force of gravity on a 52 kg astronaut orbiting Earth 25 600 km above Earth's surface?

11. What is the altitude above Earth's surface of a satellite with an orbital speed of 6.5 km/s?

12. How far must you travel from Earth's surface before $g$ is reduced to one-half its value at Earth's surface?

13. (a) At what speed must a satellite be travelling to complete a circular orbit just grazing Earth's surface?

(b) How does Earth's escape velocity compare with the speed needed to simply orbit Earth at the lowest possible altitude?

14. The "bump" on a motocross track is part of a circle with a radius of 50.0 m. What is the maximum speed at which a motorbike can travel over the highest point of the bump without leaving the ground?

15. At what distance from Earth, on a line between Earth's centre and the Moon's centre, will a spacecraft experience zero net gravitational force? (Earth's mass = $6.0 \times 10^{24}$ kg; Moon's mass = $7.4 \times 10^{22}$ kg; distance from Earth's centre to Moon's centre = $3.8 \times 10^{8}$ m)

16. The acceleration due to gravity at the surface of a planet of radius $3.5 \times 10^{6}$ m is $3.2\ \text{m/s}^2$. What is the mass of the planet?

17. A Snowbird jet travelling 600.0 km/h pulls out of a dive. If the centripetal acceleration of the plane is 6 *g's*, what is the radius of the arc in which the plane is moving?

18. Draw a vector diagram showing the forces acting on a car rounding a curve on a frictionless road that is banked at angle $\theta$. Prove that the correct angle of banking ($\theta$) that is appropriate for speed $v$ and radius $R$ is given by: $\tan = \frac{v^2}{gR}$.

19. For a spherical planet of uniform density, show that $g = \frac{4}{3} r\rho G R$, where $\rho$ is the density of the planet and $R$ is the radius of the planet.

# Investigation 3.1 Circular Orbits

## Purpose

To investigate factors involved in the uniform circular motion of a mass revolving at the end of a string

## Introduction

Some aspects of circular motion can be studied using the simple equipment shown in Figure 3.1.a. A small mass $m$ (a bundle of three washers) "orbits" on the end of a string. A large mass $M$ experiences a force of gravity $Mg$. In this investigation, $M$ is chosen to be a bundle of nine identical washers, so that $M = 3m$.

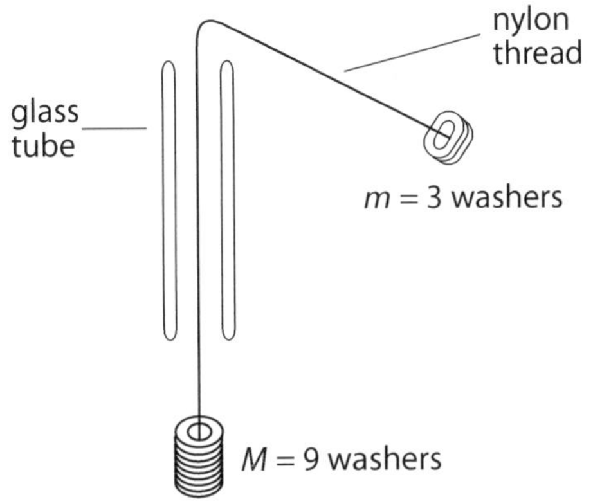


**Figure 3.1.a**

The glass tube is smoothly polished at the top, and strong, smooth nylon thread joins the two masses. In effect, the edge of the tube acts like a pulley, changing the direction of the tension force in the string without changing its magnitude.

When the small mass $m$ is made to "orbit" around the top end of the glass tube, mass $M$ remains static, so the tension in the string along its length $L$ is equal to the downward force of gravity on $M$, which is $Mg$.

The radius of the orbit is not $L$, however, but $R$ (the horizontal distance from $m$ to the vertical glass tube). See Figure 3.1.b.

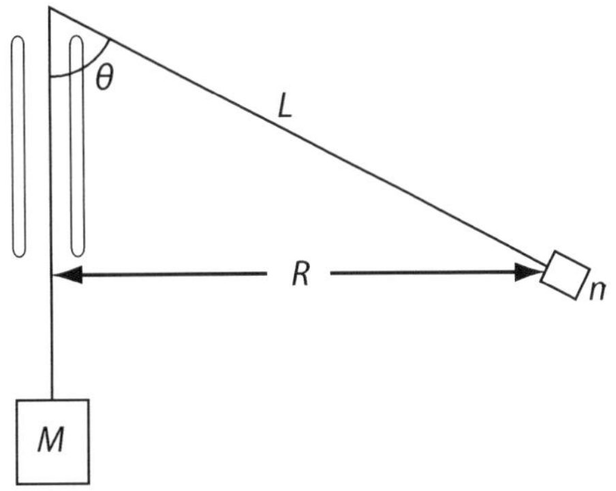


**Figure 3.1.b**

When the small mass $m$ is made to "orbit" the top of the glass tube, we will assume the upward force on the stationary mass $M$ has a magnitude of $Mg$. The reaction force exerted on $m$ through the string has the same magnitude ($Mg$), but is exerted in the opposite direction. In Figure 3.1.c, this tension force is labelled $T = Mg$.

Consider the two components of $\vec{T}$. The vertical component $\vec{F}_y$ balances the downward force of gravity on *m*, so $\vec{F}_y = mg$. The horizontal component of $\vec{T}$ is the centripetal force, so $\vec{F}_x = \vec{F}_c$.

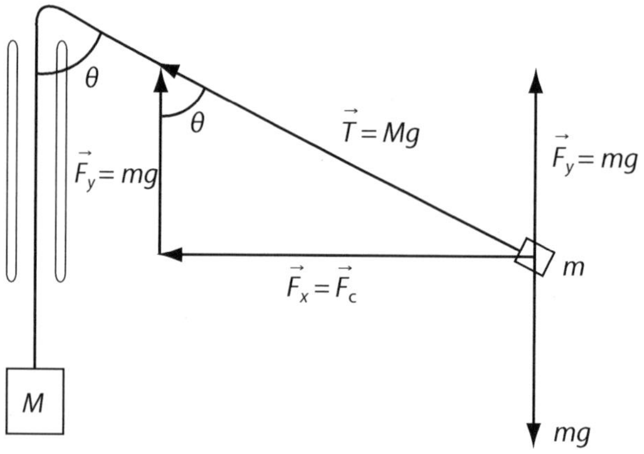


**Figure 3.1.c**

### Procedure

1. Prepare the apparatus, using three identical washers for the orbiting mass and nine washers for the large mass. Predict what the angle $\theta$ between the thread and the vertical glass tube will be, using the fact that

$$\cos = \frac{F_y}{T} = \frac{mg}{Mg} = \frac{m}{M}$$

2. In this investigation, you will vary *L* and measure the period of revolution *T* for each length *L*. Measure from the centre of gravity of the mass *m* along the string, and mark off distances of 20 cm, 40 cm, 60 cm, 80 cm, and 100 cm with chalk or a small dab of correction fluid.
3. Hold the glass tube vertically in your hand, and swing mass *m* until it achieves a stable orbit such that length *L* is 20.0 cm. While you keep the orbiting mass revolving, have your partner make the following measurements (as best they can, for it will be difficult!):
   (a) The radius of the orbit *R:* Your partner will have to hold a metre stick as near to the orbiting mass as they dare (to avoid decapitation) and estimate *R* as closely as possible;
   (b) The period of revolution *T:* Your partner will time how long the mass takes to make 10 revolutions; then divide the total time by 10.
4. Repeat step 3 for lengths of 40.0 cm, 60.0 cm, 80.0 cm, and 100.0 cm. Record all your measurements in a table like Table 3.1.1.
5. Calculate the ratio of *R/L*. From Figure 3.1.10 you can see that this ratio equals sin $\theta$. Calculate $\theta$ knowing sin $\theta$.

**Table 3.1.1** *Data for Investigation 3.1*

| Length of String, *L* [cm] | Radius of Orbit, *R* [cm] | Period of Revolution, *T* [s] | sin $\theta$ $= \frac{R}{L}$ | $\theta$ [°] | cos $\theta$ $= \frac{m}{M}$ | $\theta$ [°] |
|---|---|---|---|---|---|---|
| 20.0 | | | | | | |
| 40.0 | | | | | | |
| 60.0 | | | | | | |
| 80.0 | | | | | | |
| 100.0 | | | | | | |

6. Plot a graph with $T$ on the $y$-axis (since it is the dependent variable) and $L$ on the $x$-axis (since it is the independent variable).
7. Examine the shape of your graph of $T$ vs. $L$, and make an educated guess at what the power law might be. For example, if you think the power law is most likely $T^n = k \cdot L$, then plot a graph of $T^n$ vs. $L$. If you choose the correct value of $n$, your graph should be a straight line passing through (0,0).
8. Determine the slope of your final, straight-line graph, and express it in appropriate units. Then write an equation for your straight line, incorporating the slope.

9. You can use the results of your experiment to do a check on the formula for centripetal force.

$$\text{Since } F_c = \frac{m4\pi^2 R}{T^2}\text{, therefore } T^2 = \frac{m4\pi^2 R}{F_c}.$$

Figure 3.1.b shows you that $R = L\sin\theta$, and Figure 3.1.c makes it clear that

$F_c = F_x = Mg\sin\theta$. Therefore, we can write

$$T^2 = \frac{m4\pi^2 L\sin\theta}{Mg\sin\theta} = \frac{m4\pi^2}{Mg}L$$

Thus, the theoretical slope of a graph of $T^2$ vs. $L$ should be $\frac{m4\pi^2}{Mg}$.

## Concluding Questions

1. Compare the average value of angle $\theta$ calculated from $\sin\theta = R/L$ with the value of $\theta$ predicted using $\cos\theta = m/M$. What is the percent difference between the two results?
2. According to your results, how does the period $T$ of the orbiting mass vary with the length $L$? Write a specific equation for your graphical result.
3. What is the theoretical value of your slope for the graph in Concluding Question 2? What is the percent difference between your graph's actual slope and the theoretical slope?
4. Discuss sources of error in this experiment and how you might be able to reduce their effects.

## Challenges

1. Discuss how the results of your experiment would be affected if the ratio of the masses used was 1:2 instead of 1:3. How would this affect
   (a) the angle $\theta$ made by the string with the vertical glass tube?
   (b) the relationship between the period of revolution and the length of the string?
2. Design a way of testing out the centripetal force formula using an air puck on an air table. See if you can design a way of showing that Newton's second law really does apply to centripetal acceleration.

# Investigation 3.2 Centripetal Acceleration of Planets

### Purpose

To use planetary data to determine how the centripetal acceleration of planets varies with their distances from the Sun

### Procedure

1. Prepare a table similar to Table 3.2.1. Calculate values of $a_c$ for each of the planets listed, using $a_c = \frac{4\pi^2 R}{T^2}$.
   **Note:** The orbits of the planets are actually elliptical, but they are close to being circular. The radii given in Table 3.2.1 are mean orbital radii.
2. Plot a graph of $a_c$ (on the *y*-axis) vs. $R$ (on the *x*-axis). Label your graph using appropriate units.
3. Make an educated guess at the power law involved. Plot $a_c$ vs. $R^n$, where $n$ is your reasoned best choice. Repeat this procedure if necessary until you obtain a straight line.

**Table 3.2.1** *Planetary Data: Mean Orbital Radii and Periods*

| Planet | Mean Orbital Radius, $R$ | Period of Revolution, $T$ | Centripetal Acceleration, $a_c$ |
|---|---|---|---|
| | [m] | [s] | [m/s$^2$] |
| Mercury | $0.58 \times 10^{11}$ | $7.60 \times 10^{6}$ | |
| Venus | $1.08 \times 10^{11}$ | $1.94 \times 10^{7}$ | |
| Earth | $1.49 \times 10^{11}$ | $3.16 \times 10^{7}$ | |
| Mars | $2.28 \times 10^{11}$ | $5.94 \times 10^{7}$ | |
| Jupiter | $7.78 \times 10^{11}$ | $3.74 \times 10^{8}$ | |
| Saturn | $14.3 \times 10^{11}$ | $9.30 \times 10^{8}$ | |
| Uranus | $28.7 \times 10^{11}$ | $2.66 \times 10^{9}$ | |

### Concluding Question

1. Write an equation for your final, straight-line graph, complete with a numerical value for the slope in appropriate units. Describe the nature of the relationship between centripetal acceleration and distance in words.

# Investigation 3.3 Determining Kepler's Constant for the Solar System

### Purpose

To use astronomical data for the planets in the solar system to calculate the value of K, Kepler's constant

### Procedure

1. Table 3.2.1 in Investigation 3.2.1 lists the mean orbital radii and periods for seven planets. Use this information to prepare a data table and calculate $K = \frac{R^3}{T^2}$ for each planet. Express K in appropriate units.
2. In Investigation 3.2, you obtained a straight-line graph when you plotted $a_c$ vs. $\frac{1}{R^2}$. Therefore, $a_c = k \cdot \frac{1}{R^2}$, where $k$ is the slope of your graph.

   As you know, $a_c = \frac{4\pi^2 R}{T^2}$. The slope of your graph was:

$$k = \frac{\Delta a_c}{\Delta \frac{1}{R^2}} = \frac{a_c - 0}{\frac{1}{R^2 - 0}} = a_c R^2 = \frac{4\pi^2 R}{T^2} \cdot R^2 = 4\pi^2 \cdot \frac{R^3}{T^2} = 4\pi^2 \text{K}$$

   where K is Kepler's constant.

   Slope $k = 4\pi^2$K, where K is Kepler's constant for the solar system. Calculate K using the slope $k$ of your graph from Investigation 4.2.1. $\text{K} = \left(\frac{k}{4\pi^2}\right)$

### Concluding Questions

1. What is the mean value of K, according to Procedure step 1? Procedure step 2?
2. Planet Neptune has a mean orbital radius of $4.50 \times 10^{12}$ m. What is its period of revolution according to Kepler's third law? How many Earth years is this?
3. Pluto has a period of revolution of $7.82 \times 10^9$ s. What is its mean orbital radius?

# 4 Energy

This chapter focuses on the following AP Physics 1 Big Ideas from the College Board:

**BIG IDEA 3:** The interactions of an object with other objects can be described by forces.

**BIG IDEA 4**: Interactions between systems can result in changes in those systems.

**BIG IDEA 5:** Changes that occur as a result of interactions are constrained by conservation laws.

---

By the end of this chapter, you should know the meaning to these **key terms**:

- conduction
- convection
- efficiency
- energy
- gravitational potential energy
- heat
- kinetic energy
- law of conservation of energy
- power
- radiation
- specific heat capacity
- temperature
- thermal energy
- watt
- work

---

By the end of the chapter, you should be able to use and know when to use the following formulae:

$W = Fd$

$W = \Delta E$

$E_p = mgh$

$E_k = \frac{1}{2} mv^2$

$P = \frac{W}{\Delta t} = \frac{\Delta E}{\Delta t}$

$efficiency = \frac{W_{out}}{W_{in}} = \frac{P_{out}}{P_{in}}$

*An explosion is an example of chemical, sound, light, and thermal energy being released all at the same time.*

# 4.1 Do You Know the Meaning of Work?

## Warm Up

Bounce a rubber or tennis ball up and down several times. List all the different forms of energy you observe.

__________________________________________________________________

__________________________________________________________________

__________________________________________________________________

### What is Energy?

Energy appears in a variety of forms. Some forms you are familiar with include light, sound, thermal energy, electrical energy, elastic potential energy, gravitational potential energy, chemical potential energy, nuclear energy, and mechanical energy. What is energy? Your experience tells you it is associated with movement or with the potential for motion. Energy is what makes things move. The usual definition of energy says that energy is the capacity to do work.

In physics, **work** has a specific meaning. If work is to be done on an object, two things must happen: (1) a force must act on the object and (2) the object must move through a distance in the direction of the force. The amount of work done is equal to the product of the force exerted and the distance the force causes the object to move, measured in the direction of the force.

$$\textbf{work} = \textbf{force} \times \textbf{distance}$$

$$W = Fd$$

Since force is measured in newtons (N) and distance in metres (m), work can be measured in newton-metres. One newton-metre (N·m) is called a **joule (J)** after James Joule (1818–1889), an English physicist.

$$1\ \text{J} = 1\ \text{N·m}$$

### Sample Problem 4.1.1 — Calculating Work

How much work does a golfer do lifting a 46 g golf ball out of the hole and up to his pocket (0.95 m above the ground)?

| What to Think About | How to Do It |
| --- | --- |
| 1. Find the correct formula. | $W = Fd$ |
| 2. Find the force in newtons. | $F = mg = (0.046\text{kg})(9.81\text{ m/s}^2)$<br>$F = 0.45\text{ N}$ |
| 3. Find work done. | $W = Fd = (0.45\text{ N})(0.95\text{ m})$<br>$= 0.43\text{ J}$<br>The golfer does 0.43 J of work lifting the golf ball from the hole to his pocket. |

## Practice Problems 4.1.1 — Calculating Work

1. How much work will you do if you push a block of concrete 4.3 m along a floor, with a steady force of 25 N?

2. If your mass is 70.0 kg, how much work will you do climbing a flight of stairs 25.0 m high, moving at a steady pace? ($g$ = 9.81 N/kg)

3. Your car is stuck in the mud. You push on it with a force of 300.0 N for 10.0 s, but it will not move. How much work have you done in the 10.0 s?

## Power

A machine is powerful if it can do a lot of work in a short time. **Power** is the measure of the amount of work a machine can do in one second.

$$\text{power} = \frac{\text{work}}{\text{time}}$$

$$\boldsymbol{P = \frac{W}{\Delta t}}$$

Power could be measured in joules per second (J/s), but one joule per second is called one **watt (W)**, after James Watt (1736–1819), a Scottish engineer.

1 W = 1 J/s

Power can be measured in kilowatts (kW) or megawatts (MW).

1 kW = 1000 W ($10^3$ W)
1 MW = 1 000 000 W ($10^6$ W)

## Sample Problem 4.1.2 — Calculating Power

The power of a small motor in a toy can be calculated by the amount of work it does in a period of time. What is the power rating of a toy motor that does 4200 J of work in 70.0 s?

| What to Think About | How to Do It |
| --- | --- |
| 1. Find the correct formula. | $P = \frac{\Delta W}{\Delta t}$ |
| 2. Calculate the power. | $P = \frac{4200\ \text{J}}{70.0\ \text{s}} = 60\ \text{W}$<br>The power rating of the toy motor is 60 W. |

## Practice Problems 4.1.2 — Calculating Power

1. An airport baggage handler lifts 42 pieces of luggage, averaging 24 kg each, through a height of 1.6 m onto a baggage cart, in a time of 3.6 min. In this situation, what is the power of the baggage handler?

2. How much work or energy (in J) does a 150 W light bulb convert to heat and light in 1.0 h?

3. A mechanical lifting system is approximately 25% efficient. This means that only 25% of the energy used to lift a mass is converted into useable energy. The rest is mostly lost as heat. If $1.5 \times 10^8$ W is used for 2.0 h, how much energy (in J) of useable work is produced? How much heat is produced?

### What's Watt?

Power is commonly measured in **horsepower**. Eventually, horsepower may be replaced by the **kilowatt**, which is a metric unit, but the horsepower (non-metric) will persist for some time because it is firmly entrenched in our vocabulary.

The Scottish engineer James Watt is famous for his improved design of a steam engine, invented earlier by Thomas Newcomen. Watt's new engine was used at first for pumping water out of coal mines, work that previously had been done by horses. Customers wanted to know how many horses Watt's new engines would replace. So that he could answer their questions, Watt did the following:

1. He measured the force, in pounds, exerted by the average horse over a distance, measured in feet.
2. He calculated the amount of work the horse did, in a unit he called foot-pounds.
3. He measured the time it took the horse to do the work.
4. He calculated how much work the horse would do in one second, which is the average power of the horse. He found this to be 550 foot-pounds per second. This was taken to be the average power of one horse equal to one horsepower.

$$1 \text{ horsepower} = 550 \frac{\text{foot-pounds}}{\text{second}}$$

The modern unit for power is the watt (W). One horsepower is equivalent to 746 W, which is almost 3/4 kW. The following example finds the power in an electric motor and them shows how to convert watts to horsepower.

**Sample Problem 4.1.3 — Calculating Horsepower**

An electric motor is used, with a pulley and a rope, to lift a 650 N load from the road up to a height of 12 m. This job is done in a time of 11 s. What is the power output of the motor?

| What to Think About | How to Do It |
|---|---|
| 1. Find the correct formula. | $P = \frac{\text{work}}{\text{time}} = \frac{W}{\Delta t}$ |
| 2. Calculate the power in watts. | $P = \frac{Fd}{\Delta t} = \frac{(650\ \text{N})(12\ \text{m})}{11\ \text{s}}$<br>$= 7.1\ 10^2\ \text{W}$ |
| 3. Calculate the horsepower. | The often-used unit of power, 1 horsepower, is equivalent to $7.5 \times 10^2$ W.<br>The motor in this question would have a horsepower of<br>$\frac{7.1 \times 10^2\ \text{W}}{7.5 \times 10^2\ \text{W/HP}} = 0.95\ \text{HP}$ |

## 4.1 Review Questions

1. How much work is done on a 10.0 kg mass by Earth's gravitational field when the mass drops a distance of 5.0 m?

2. A girl uses a 3.0 m long ramp to push her 110 kg motorbike up to a trailer. The floor of the trailer is 1.2 m above the ground. How much work is done on the motorbike?

3. The force of gravity on a box of apples is 98.0 N. How much work will you do
   (a) if you lift the box from the floor to a height of 1.2 m?

   (b if you carry the box horizontally a distance of 2.0 m?

4. A hiker carries a 25 kg load up a hill at a steady speed through a vertical height of 350 m. How much work does she do on the load?

5. The force of gravity on a box is 100.0 N. The coefficient of friction between the floor and the box is 0.250. How much work is done when the box is pushed along the floor, at a steady speed, for a distance of 15.0 m?

6. Which of the variables below would improve in your favour if you used a pulley system of MA = 8 to lift a load, compared with a pulley system of MA = 2? Explain your answer.
   (a) effort distance
   (b) effort force
   (c) work done by you
   (d) your power
   (e) work done by the machine

7. Draw a pulley system that has a mechanical advantage of 1/2. For what purpose might you use such a system?

8. How powerful is a motor that can lift a 500.0 kg load through a height of 12.0 m in a time of 12 s?

9. A motor does 25 MJ (megajoules) of work in one hour.
   (a) What is the power rating of the motor?

   (b) How many horsepower is this motor, if 1 HP = 746 W?

10. How much energy is consumed by a 100.0 W light bulb, if it is left on for 12.0 h?

11. An appliance that consumes electrical energy at the rate of 1500 J/s, accomplishes 1200 J/s of useful work. How efficient is the appliance?

# 4.2 Mechanical Energy

## Warm Up

Fill a coffee can with three or four handfuls of dry sand. Measure the temperature of the sand. Now shake the can vigorously for three minutes. Take the temperature of the sand. Describe what happened to the temperature and explain why you think it occurred.

______________________________________________

______________________________________________

______________________________________________

### Kinetic Energy

A moving object can do work. A falling axe does work to split a log. A moving baseball bat does work to stop a baseball, momentarily compress the ball out of its normal shape, then reverse its direction, and send it off at high speed.

Since a moving object has the ability to do work, it must have energy. We call the energy of a moving object its **kinetic energy.** A body that is at rest can gain kinetic energy if work is done on it by an external force. To get such a body moving at speed $v$, a net force must be exerted on it to accelerate it from rest up to speed $v$. The amount of work, $W$, which must be done can be calculated as follows:

$$W = Fd = (ma)d = m(ad)$$

Remember that for an object accelerating from rest at a uniform rate, $v_f^2 = 2ad$.

Therefore,
$$(ad) = \frac{v_f^2}{2}$$

and

$$W = m(ad) = m\left(\frac{v_f^2}{2}\right) = \frac{1}{2}mv^2$$

The work done on the object to accelerate it up to a speed $v$ results in an amount of energy being transferred to the object, which is equal in magnitude to $\frac{1}{2}mv^2$. This is the object's kinetic energy, $E_k$.

$$E_k = \frac{1}{2}mv^2$$

Once an object has kinetic energy, it can do work on other objects.

## Quick Check

1. A golfer wishes to improve his driving distance. Which would have more effect? Explain your answer.
   (a) doubling the mass of his golf club
   *OR*
   (b) doubling the speed with which the clubhead strikes the ball

2. How much work must be done to accelerate a 110 kg motorbike and its 60.0 kg rider from 0 to 80 km/h?

3. How much work is needed to slow down a 1200 kg vehicle from 80 km/h to 50 km/h? What does this work?

4. How much work is needed to accelerate a 1.0 g insect from rest up to 12 m/s?

## Gravitational Potential Energy

Figure 4.2.1 shows an extremely simple mechanical system. A basketball player lifts a basketball straight up to a height *h*. The ball has mass *m*, so the force of gravity on the ball is *mg*. In lifting the ball, the basketball player has done work equal to *mgh* on the ball. He has transferred energy to the ball. Chemical energy in his cell molecules has been changed into **gravitational potential energy** because of the work he did.

Work Is always a measure of energy transferred to a body. When the basketball is held up at height *h*, it has gravitational potential energy ($E_p$) equal to *mgh*.

$$E_p = mgh$$

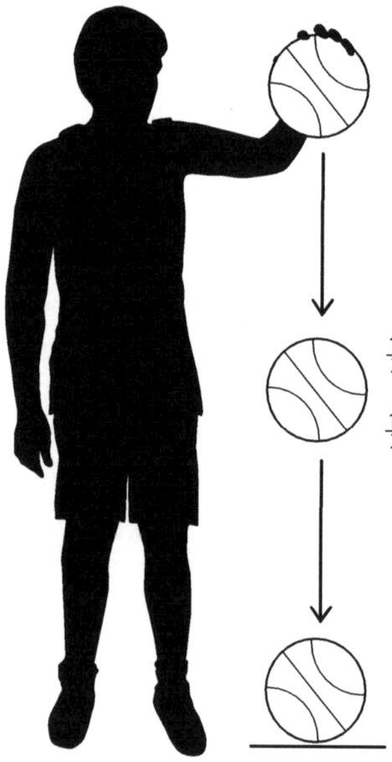


**Figure 4.2.1** *At its highest point, the ball has only gravitational potential energy. Once it starts dropping, it has kinetic energy as well.*

## Reference Point

When calculating gravitational potential energy, the height an object moves is always measured from the starting point of the movement. This is called the **reference point**. This is important because it means, the amount of potential energy in an object is relative to where the measurement occurs. For example, a table 1.0 m high has a 1.0 kg book on it. If the book is lifted 0.5 m above the table, how much gravitational potential energy does the book have? If $h$ is measured from the table, it has 4.5 J of potential energy because $h = 0.5$ m or $E_p = (91.0\text{ kg})(9.8\text{ m/s}^2)(0.5\text{ m})$. If $h$ is measured from the ground, the book has 14.7 J of potential energy because $h = 1.5$ m or $E_p = (91.0\text{ kg})(9.8\text{ m/s}^2)(1.5\text{ m})$.

Both answers are correct. What is important that the reference point is identified and only the vertical height is measured when determining the amount of gravitational potential energy in an object.

### Quick Check

1. A box of bananas is lifted 5 m and gains a certain amount of potential energy. If the box is lifted another 5 m, describe how the potential energy changes.

2. What is the mass of a television if it takes 620 J to lift it 2.5 m.

3. If it takes 240 J to lift a 4 kg object, how high is the object lifted?

## Work Energy Theorem

If a force is applied to an object over a distance, the amount of kinetic energy in the object changes. For example, a car speeds up because the force of the engine turns the wheels faster over a distance. The increased speed of the car represents the increase in the car's kinetic energy. You may have noticed that when the formula for kinetic energy was derived, work equaled the amount of kinetic energy:

$$W = \frac{1}{2}mv^2$$

The work-energy theorem states that the work done on a system the energy changes or:

$$\boldsymbol{W = \Delta E}$$

## Law of Conservation of Energy

Now consider what happens when the basketball you saw in Figure 4.2.1 is allowed to fall under the influence of the force of gravity. The unbalanced force, ignoring air friction, is equal to the force of gravity on the ball. For any situation where an object of mass $m$ is pulled by an unbalanced force $F$, there will be an acceleration, $a$. Newton's second law of motion tells us that $F = ma$.

In our example, the basketball is a free-falling body, and $a = g$. As the ball falls through height $h$, its speed increases from 0 to $v_f$. For uniform acceleration,

$$v_f^2 = 2ad$$

For this situation, $v_f^2 = 2gh$. Since the unbalanced force pulling the ball down is $mg$, the work done on the ball by Earth's gravitational field is $mgh$.

$$\text{If } v_f^2 = 2gh, \text{ then } gh = \frac{v_f^2}{2}$$

$$\text{Therefore, } mgh = m\left(\frac{v_f^2}{2}\right) = \frac{1}{2}mv_f^2$$

When the ball is at the top of its path, all its energy is gravitational potential energy. The ball is not moving. It has energy only because of its position above the floor from which it was lifted. As the ball falls, it loses its potential energy and gains energy of motion, kinetic energy. Just before it collides with the floor, all the energy of the ball is kinetic energy, and the potential energy is zero. The amount of kinetic energy ($E_k$) at the bottom of its fall is given by:

$$E_k = \frac{1}{2}mv_f^2$$

On the way down, the kinetic energy of the ball at any time depends on the speed the ball has reached. For any speed $v$, kinetic energy $E_k = mv_f^2$. As the ball gains kinetic energy, it loses gravitational potential energy. At all times the sum of the gravitational potential energy and the kinetic energy is constant.

$$E_p + E_k = \text{constant}$$

This is an example of the **law of conservation of energy**, which states:

> The total energy of a mechanical system is constant. Energy can be transformed from one form into another, but the total amount of energy is unchanged.

As the ball falls through positions 1, 2, 3, etc., the sum of the potential energy and the kinetic energy remains constant:

$$mgh_1 + \frac{1}{2}mv_1^2 = mgh_2 + \frac{1}{2}mv_2^2 = mgh_3 + \frac{1}{2}mv_3^2 = \ldots$$

Notice that mechanical energy can be either potential or kinetic. For a mechanical system, the total mechanical energy is constant.

### Sample Problem 4.2.1 — The Law of Conservation of Energy

The pendulum bob in Figure 4.2.2 is pulled back far enough that it is raised 0.36 m above its original level. When it is released, how fast will it be moving at the bottom of its swing?

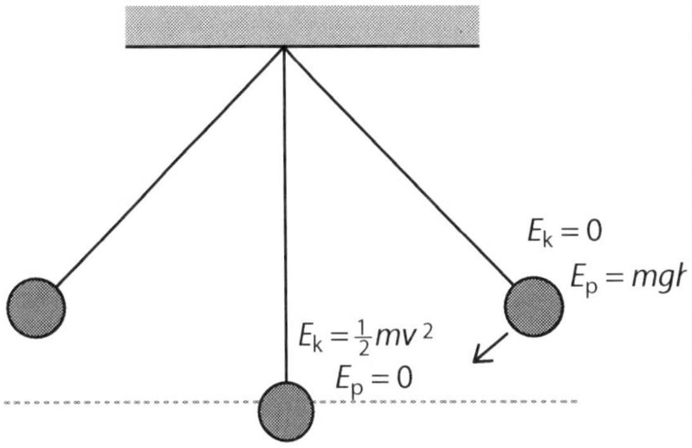


**Figure 4.2.2** *Moving pendulum*

| What to Think About | How to Do It |
| --- | --- |
| 1. When the pendulum is pulled back, it is also lifted through a height *h*, and work *mgh* is done in lifting the bob against the force of gravity. The bob gains gravitational potential energy equal to the work done on it, so $E_p = mgh$. When the bob is released, its gravitational potential energy is transformed into kinetic energy. At the bottom of the swing, $E_p = 0$, and, $E_k = \frac{1}{2}mv^2$ but the kinetic energy at the bottom of the swing must equal the gravitational potential energy at the top according to the law of conservation of energy. | $E_p = mgh = \frac{1}{2} mv^2$ |
| 2. Rearrange to find speed. | Therefore, $v^2 = 2gh$<br>and $v \sqrt{2gh}$ |
| 3. Solve to find the speed of the bob at the bottom of the swing. | $v = \sqrt{2gh}$<br>$= \sqrt{2(9.8\ m/s^2)(0.36\ m)}$<br>$= 2.7\ m/s$<br><br>The pendulum bob will be moving 2.7 m/s at the bottom of its swing. |

## Practice Problems 4.2.1 — The Law of Conservation of Energy

1. Spiderman shoots a web line 9 m long and swings on the end of it, like a pendulum. His starting point is 3.0 m above the lowest point in his swing. How fast is Spiderman moving as he passes through the bottom of the swing?

2. A vehicle moving with a speed of 90 km/h (25 m/s) loses its brakes but sees a runaway hill near the highway. If the driver steers his vehicle into the runaway hill, how far up the hill (vertically) will the vehicle travel before it comes to a stop? (Ignore friction.)

3. A 500 kg roller coaster car is going 10 m/s at the bottom of its run. How high can you build the next hill on the track so that it can get over without any additional work being done on the car? (Ignore friction.) Is your answer reasonable?

Once an object has kinetic energy, the object itself can do work on other objects. This is called the work-energy theorem and is written:

$$W = \Delta E_k$$

**Quick Check**

1. A golfer wishes to improve his driving distance. Which would have more effect, (a) doubling the mass of his golf club or (b) doubling the speed with which the club head strikes the ball? Explain your answer.

2. How much work must be done to accelerate a 110 kg motorbike and its 60.0 kg rider from 0 to 80 km/h?

3. How much work is needed to slow down a 1200 kg vehicle from 80 km/h to 50 km/h? What does this work?

## Potential Energy

**Potential energy** is sometimes referred to as *stored* energy. A skier has potential energy at the top of a hill, because work has been done (by the skier or by a ski tow) to raise the skier from the bottom of the hill to the top. If the skier has been lifted a height $h$ from the bottom of the hill, and the force of gravity on the skier is $mg$, then the amount of *work* done on the skier is $W = mgh$.

The energy transferred to the skier because of this amount of work done on the skier is now potentially available to do work. In this situation, it can be said that the skier has **gravitational potential energy**.

$$\text{gravitational } E_p = mgh$$

A stretched spring or a compressed spring has potential energy. Work must be done to stretch or compress a spring. In the example of Figure 4.3.6 the work done to stretch the spring a distance $x$ is $\frac{1}{2}F \cdot x$. For this particular spring, force is directly proportional to extension (stretch), so $F = kx$.

The work done to stretch the spring is, therefore, $W = \frac{1}{2}(kx)x = \frac{1}{2}kx^2$.

The amount of energy transferred to the spring because of the work done on it is potentially available to do work. In this case, the stored energy is called **elastic potential energy**.

$$\text{elastic } E_p = \frac{1}{2}kx^2$$

An object has kinetic energy because of its motion. It has potential energy because of its position (in the case of gravitational potential energy) or its shape (elastic potential energy).

## Quick Check

1. How much gravitational energy is gained by a 45 kg girl if she climbs 6.0 m up a flight of stairs?

2. (a) A spring in a toy gun requires an average force of 1.2 N to compress it a distance of 3.0 cm. How much elastic potential energy is stored in the spring when it is fully compressed?

   (b) If all the elastic potential energy is transferred to a 10.0 g "bullet" (a plastic rod with a suction cup on the end), how fast will the "bullet" move as it leaves the gun?

3. Discuss the forms of energy involved when a basketball is dropped from your hand, bounces on the floor, and moves back up into your hand.

## Power

The word **power** is used in a variety of ways in everyday language, but in physics it has a specific meaning. Power is the rate at which work is done or the rate at which energy is transformed from one form to another.

$$\text{power} = \frac{\text{work done}}{\text{time}} = \frac{\text{energy transformed}}{\text{time}}$$

Power is measured in watts (W), where $1\text{ W} = 1\frac{\text{J}}{\text{s}}$.

A typical household light bulb transforms energy at the rate of 60 W. Most of the electrical energy, unfortunately, is transformed into heat instead of light. Approximately 57 W of heat and 3 W of light are produced by the bulb. An incandescent light bulb is only about 5 percent efficient. A kettle might transform electrical energy into heat at the rate of 1500 W. The power rating of an electrical appliance is usually printed somewhere on the appliance.

A commonly used unit for power is the **horsepower (hp)**. In the metric system, the hp is defined as 750 W. (The electrical kettle just described is 2 hp.) The hp was originally defined by James Watt, who was looking for a way to describe the power of his newly invented steam engines, in terms that people accustomed to using horses to do their work could understand.

### Quick Check

1. How much work can a 5.00 hp motor do in 10.0 min?

2. A 60.0 kg boy runs up a flight of stairs 3.32 m high in 2.60 s.
   What is his power output (a) in watts? (b) in hp?

3. How long would it take a 5.0 hp motor to lift a 500.0 kg safe up to a window 30.0 m above the ground?

# 4.3 Review Questions

1. A worker does 100 J of work in moving a 20 kg box over a 10 m distance. What is the minimum force required to do this?

2. Another worker moves another 20 kg box over a 10 m distance. If the coefficient of friction between the box and the floor is 0.25, what is the work done by the frictional force.

3. In a baseball game, the pitcher throws a ball and the catcher catches the ball in her mitt. With reference to the catchers mitt, was positive work done, was negative work done, or was the net work zero?

4. In the drawing below, how much work is done by the person mowing the lawn if the force pushing the lawn mower is 100 N at an angle of 30° below the horizontal and moves the mower 40.0 m?

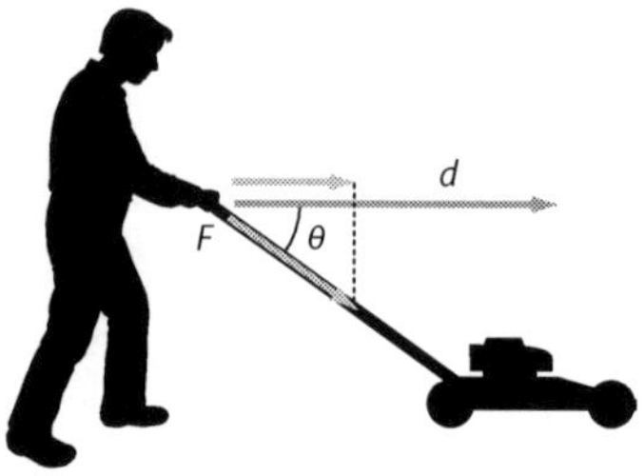


5. Find the work done for the first 5.00 s by the variable force in the graph below.

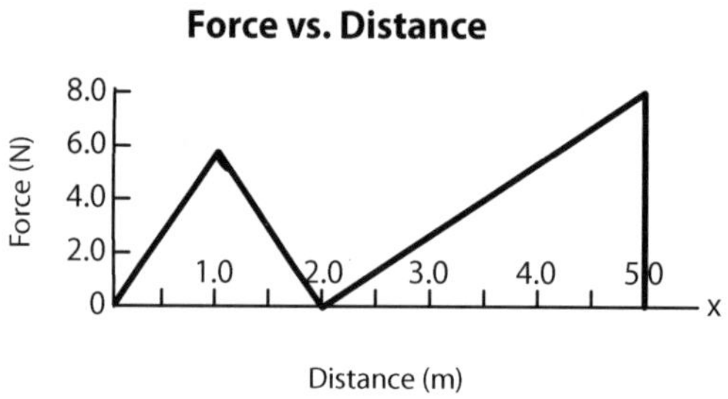


6. Truck A is traveling twice as fast as truck B, but truck B has four times the mass of truck A. Which truck has more kinetic energy?

7. How much work is needed to accelerate a 1.0 g insect from rest up to 12 m/s?

8. If the speed of a proton is tripled by a particle accelerator, by how much will its kinetic energy increase? (Ignore relativistic effects.)

9. A 1500 kg car travels at 80 km/h. What is the kinetic energy of the car? What net work would it take to stop the car?

10. A car travelling at 50 km/h stops in 70.0 m. What is the stopping distance if the car's speed is 90 km/h?

11. You and your friend are sitting at the table looking at your physics book. Your friend says the book has 0 J of potential energy. You say because the book weighs 1 kg and is 1 m off the ground, it has 9.8 J. Who is correct?

12. How much more gravitational potential energy does a 4.0 kg box have when it is on a shelf 1.5 m high than when it is on a shelf that is 75 cm high?

13. Five books of mass 0.750 kg and 5 cm thick are placed separately on a table. How much work must be done to stack the books one on top of the other?

14. A man slides a 100.0 kg box along the floor for a distance of 4.0 m. If the coefficient of kinetic friction is 0.250, and the man does the job in 3.6 s, what is his power output (a) in watts? and (b) in hp?

15. A certain automobile engine is rated at 350 hp. What is its power (a) in watts? (b) in kilowatts (1 kW = 1000 W)?

# 4.4 The Law of Conservation of Mechanical Energy

## Warm Up

Your teacher sets up a pendulum in the classroom with a 5 kg bob on the end and stands to one side of it so the bob is next to his or her nose. If the bob is released, will it swing back and touch your teacher's nose? Explain your thinking.

_______________________________________________

_______________________________________________

_______________________________________________

### Conservation of Mechanical Energy

Consider a frictionless pendulum as it makes a swing from one side to the other. If we decide to assign the bob zero potential energy at the bottom of its swing, as we did in Investigation 3.4.1, then it gains potential energy equal to *mgh* when it reaches the highest point in its swing. When it swings through the lowest part of its swing, its potential energy returns to zero, but it still has the same total energy. At the bottom of the swing, all the potential energy the bob had at the top of its swing has been transformed into kinetic energy. Ignoring energy lost because of friction in the system,

$$E_k \text{ (bottom of swing)} = E_p \text{ (top of swing)}$$

At any point in the swing, ignoring energy losses because of work done overcoming friction, the *total mechanical energy* $(E_k + E_p)$ is constant.

$$\text{total mechanical energy} = E_k + E_p = \text{constant}$$

If the subscripts 1 and 2 are used to represent any two positions of the pendulum, the **law of conservation of mechanical energy** for this situation can be written:

$$\frac{1}{2}mv_1^2 + mgh_1 = \frac{1}{2}mv_2^2 + mgh_2$$

This description would also apply to a body falling under the influence of the force of gravity, from an initial height *h*.

Although we have looked at only a single example of a mechanical situation (the pendulum), the law of conservation of energy applies in a very general way to all similar energy transformations. Taking all forms of energy into account, a broader statement can be made about energy in general.

Energy can be transformed from one form to another, but it is never created and it is never destroyed. Total energy remains constant.

**Sample Problem 4.4.1 — Conservation of Mechanical Energy**

A 45.93 g golf ball is struck by a golf club, and it leaves the face of the club with a speed of 75.0 m/s.

(a) How much kinetic energy does the golf ball have as it leaves the face of the club?

(b) If air friction is ignored, from what height would the same golf ball have to be dropped to gain this much kinetic energy?

| What to Think About | How to Do It |
| --- | --- |
| **(a)**<br>1. When the ball is struck, all the energy in the ball is kinetic. Find the total kinetic energy. | $E_k = \frac{1}{2}mv^2$<br>$E_k = \frac{1}{2}(0.04593\ kg)(75.0\ m/s)^2$<br>$E_k = 129\ J$ |
| **(b)**<br>1. The question is really asking how high the ball will go when kinetic energy is zero and all the kinetic energy has been converted to potential energy. We know at top of ball's flight, $E_k = E_p$. Find $h$ from $E_p$. | $E_k = E_p = mgh$<br>$h = \dfrac{E_p}{mg}$<br>$h = \dfrac{129\ J}{(0.04593\ kg)(75.0\ m/s)}$<br>$h = 37.4\ m$ |

**Practice Problems 4.4.1 — Conservation of Mechanical Energy**

1. A 1.00 kg pendulum bob is released from a height of 0.200 m. Its speed at the bottom of its swing is 1.95 m/s on the first pass. How much energy is lost due to friction during one complete swing of the pendulum?

2. A rope is hanging from the roof of the gymnasium. You are going to run at the rope, grab it, and see how high you are carried off the floor by the swinging rope. How fast must you run if you want to swing to a height of 1.5 m off the floor? Does your mass matter? Does the length of the rope matter? Discuss your answers.

*Practice Problems continued*

**Practice Problems 4.4.1 — Conservation of Mechanical Energy (Continued)**

3. A skier slides down a frictionless 25° slope from a height of 12 m. How fast is she moving at the bottom of the hill? Does the slope of the hill matter? Explain.

## Categorizing Forces in a System

Using the law of conservation of energy can be a powerful tool in your problem solving tool kit. Before examining a specific problem, you need to consider two additional concepts. First, you should consider the type of system based on the two categories of forces that may act within or on it: conservative and nonconservative forces. Second, if there is a collision, you need to know if the collision was elastic or inelastic.

A force is **conservative** if the work done by it in moving an object is independent of the object's path. This means only the initial and final positions of an object are used when determining the amount of work done on the object. For example, gravity is a conservative force. In calculations of gravitational potential energy, an object gains from work being done on it. You only need to know the starting and finishing positions of the object. A force is **nonconservative** if the work done by it in moving an object depends on the object's path. For example, friction is a nonconservative force. The longer an object is pushed, the longer the frictional force is acting on that object.

## Types of Collisions in a System

Whenever two or more objects interact in a way that energy and/or momentum are exchanged, a collision has occurred. In an **elastic collision**, the total kinetic energy is conserved. In an **inelastic collision**, the total kinetic energy in not conserved. Some of the kinetic energy is lost. In everyday collisions, this is the common type that occurs. Another form of an inelastic collision is when a moving object hits and sticks to another object. This is called a **completely inelastic collision**.

Regardless of the type of collision, for isolated systems, the momentum is always conserved. Remember that momentum is a vector quantity. This difference between momentum and energy, a scalar quantity, is an example of the difference between vector and scalar quantities.

## Applying the Law of Conservation of Energy

A ballistic pendulum, used to measure the speed of a bullet indirectly, is a good illustration of the use of both the law of conservation of momentum and the law of conservation of mechanical energy.

A bullet of mass $m$ is fired at an unknown speed $v$ into a sand-filled pendulum bob of mass $M$, causing the bob to swing to the right and rise to a height $h$ (Figure 4.4.1). How can the speed $v$ be calculated?

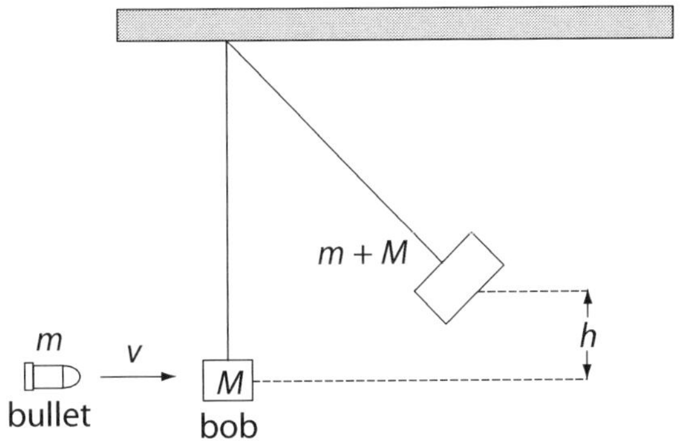


**Figure 4.4.1** *A ballistic pendulum*

The bullet entering the bob transfers its momentum to the bob, and the combined masses continue on at initial speed $v'$. Since momentum is conserved,

$$mv = (m + M)v' \qquad \text{(I)}$$

The bob and bullet together now have kinetic energy due to their motion.

$$E_k = ½(m + M)v'^2 \qquad \text{(II)}$$

The bob and bullet rise and momentarily come to rest at height $h$, where all the mechanical energy is in the form of gravitational potential energy.

$$E_p = (m + M)gh \qquad \text{(III)}$$

If we assume that mechanical energy is conserved (energy loss due to friction is negligible), then

$$½(m + M)v'^2 = (m + M)gh$$

Therefore, $$v'^2 = 2gh$$

According to equation I, $$v' = \frac{m}{m + M} \cdot v'$$

However, $$v' = \sqrt{2gh}$$

Therefore, $$\frac{m}{m + M} \cdot v = \sqrt{2gh}$$

and $$v = \frac{m + M}{m} \cdot \sqrt{2gh}$$

## Quick Check

1. A 5.0 g bullet is fired into the ballistic pendulum described in Figure 4.5.1. If the bob has a mass of 2.0 kg and the bob rises a vertical distance of 8.0 cm, how fast was the bullet moving? (Use $g = 9.80\ m/s^2$.)

2. In designing a ballistic pendulum, you want a bullet of mass 6.0 g and speed $6.0 \times 10^2$ m/s to make the pendulum bob rise 3.0 cm. What mass must the bob have?

3. A 56 kg boy jumps down from a 2.0 m high ladder. Using only the law of conservation of mechanical energy, determine his kinetic energy and his speed when he is half-way down.

## 4.4 Review Questions

1. Which best describes an *elastic collision* between two objects?

| | total energy | total momentum | kinetic energy |
|---|---|---|---|
| **A** | conserved | conserved | conserved |
| **B** | conserved | conserved | not conserved |
| **C** | conserved | not conserved | not conserved |
| **D** | not conserved | not conserved | not conserved |

2. A 50 g golf ball is thrown upward with an initial velocity of 12 m/s. Assume the initial potential energy is zero. Find the potential energy, kinetic energy and total energy of the system at each of the following:
   (a) the initial position

   (b) at a point 2.75 m above the initial position

   (c) at the maximum height the ball reaches

3. A new roller coaster has come to the local amusement park as shown in the diagram below. The speed of the roller coaster at point A is 4.0 m/s.

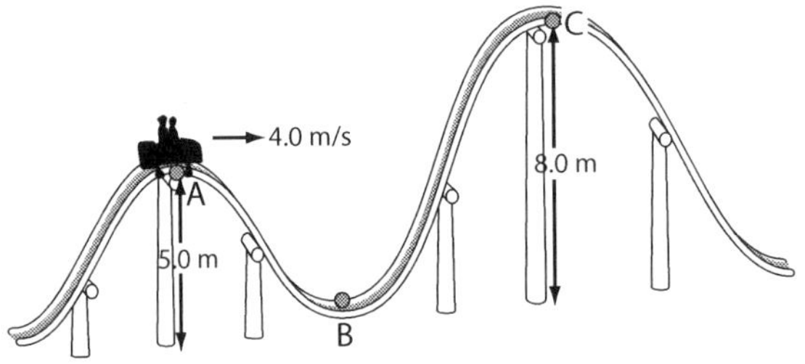


   (a) What is its speed at point B?

   (b) Is the roller coaster going fast enough to get to the top of the second hill (point C)?

   (c) How fast does the roller coaster have to be going at point B to make it to the top of the second hill?

   (d) Why don't you need to know the mass of the roller coaster car?

4. A 45 kg youngster slides down a homemade snowslide, which is 3.0 m high. At the bottom of the slide she is moving 7.0 m/s. How much energy was lost during the trip down the slide? What would account for this loss?

5. A skier slides down the ice-covered hill on the left, passing P, and coasts up the hill on the right to a vertical height *h* of 12 m. How fast was the skier moving when passing point P? Assume that frictional effects are negligible.

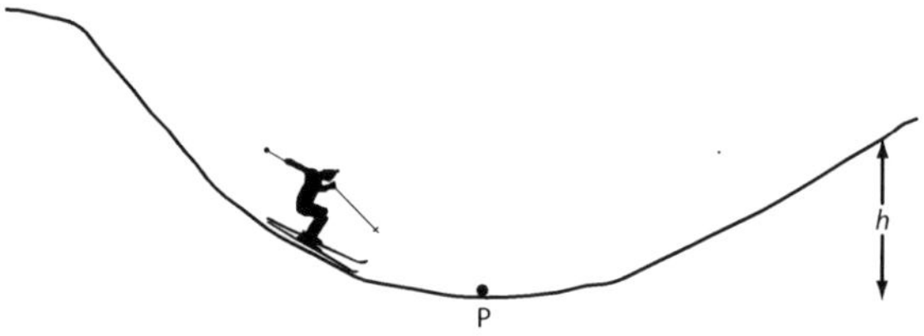


6. The pendulum bob in the diagram below has a mass of 0.500 kg. The pendulum is 1.20 m long. The bob is raised up a vertical distance of 0.150 m relative to its starting height. If friction is ignored, how fast will the bob be moving as it swings through A?

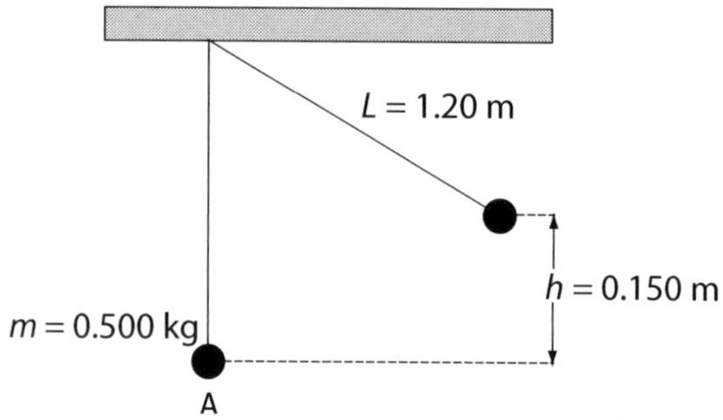

# Chapter 4 Conceptual Review Questions

1. Give an example of a situation in which there is a force and a displacement, but the force does no work. Explain why it does no work.

2. Describe a situation in which a force is exerted for a long time but does no work. Explain.

3. Most electrical appliances are rated in watts. Does this rating depend on how long the appliance is on? (When off, it is a zero-watt device.) Explain in terms of the definition of power.

4. Work done on a system puts energy into it. Work done by a system removes energy from it. Give an example for each statement.

5. Do devices with efficiencies of less than one violate the law of conservation of energy? Explain.

# Chapter 4 Review Questions

1. (a) How much work will you do if you lift a 0.67 kg book from a table top up a distance of 1.5 m to a shelf?

   (b) How much work will be done on the book if you lift it and move it 1.5 m sideways to a spot on the same shelf?

2. If you push a 75 N block along a floor a distance of 4.2 m at a steady speed, and the coefficient of kinetic friction is 0.40, how much work will you do on the block?

3. Discuss the scientific accuracy of this statement: *I used a ramp to get my motorbike up on my truck, and the ramp saved me a lot of work!*

4. One watt is equivalent to 1 J/s, so a joule is the same as a watt·second. How many joules are there in 1 kW·h?

5. A skier has 60 kJ of gravitational potential energy when at the top of the hill. Assuming no friction, how much kinetic energy does she have when she is one-third of the way down the hill?

6. The head of a golf club transfers a certain amount of kinetic energy to the ball upon impact. Let this be $E_k$. If the golfer lightens the mass of the club head by 1/3, and increases the club head speed so that it is 3 times it previous speed, how much kinetic energy will be transferred to the ball now?

7. A pendulum bob is moving 1.8 m/s at the bottom of its swing. To what height above the bottom of the swing will the bob travel?

8. The pendulum bob shown here must circle the rod, and the string must remain taut at the top of the swing. How far up must the bob be raised before releasing it to accomplish these goals?

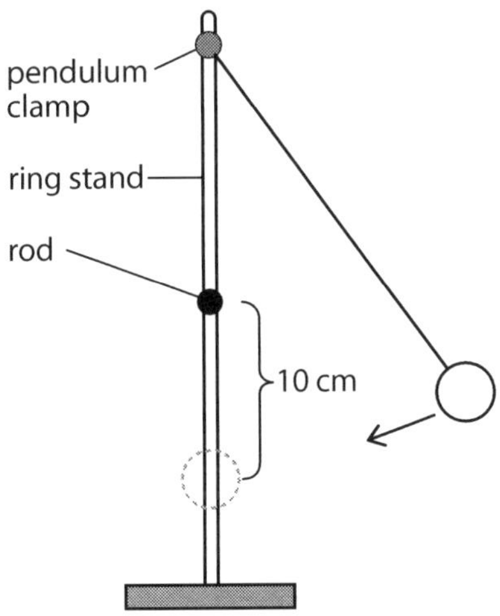


9. Tarzan grabs a vine 12 m long and swings on the end of it, like a pendulum. His starting point is 5.0 m above the lowest point in his swing. How fast is Tarzan moving as he passes through the bottom of the swing?

10. A child pulls a toy wagon along the road for a distance of 250 m. The force he exerts along the handle is 32 N. The handle makes an angle of 30° with the horizontal road. How much work does the child do on the wagon? Express your answer in kJ.

11. How much kinetic energy does a $1.0 \times 10^3$ kg car, travelling at 90 km/h, have?

12. How much gravitational potential energy does a 75 kg skier have when at the top of a hill $2.0 \times 10^3$ m high?

13. A large ball of modelling clay is dropped from a height of 2 m to the floor. The ball does not bounce back up in the air. Explain this in terms of the conservation laws discussed in this chapter.

14. A girl lifts a 30. kg box from the ground up to a table 1.0 m high in a time of 1.5 s. A weightlifter friend carries a 100. kg load across the gym in 5.0 s, without dropping it or lifting it higher. Who has the greater power output? Explain.

15. How much work can a 6.0 hp motor do in an 8.0 h working day? Express your answer in megajoules. (1 MJ = $10^6$ J)

16. A 5.00 g bullet is fired into a 6.00 kg block, which is suspended from a string 1.00 m long. The string deflects through an angle of 12.0°. How fast was the bullet moving?

# Investigation 4-1 Measuring the Power of a Small Motor

### Purpose

To measure the rate at which a small electric motor does work and thus determine its power output

### Procedure

1. Use a small electric motor equipped with a special shaft on which a 2.0 m length of string can be wound. Clamp the motor to a ring stand (Figure 4.1.a).

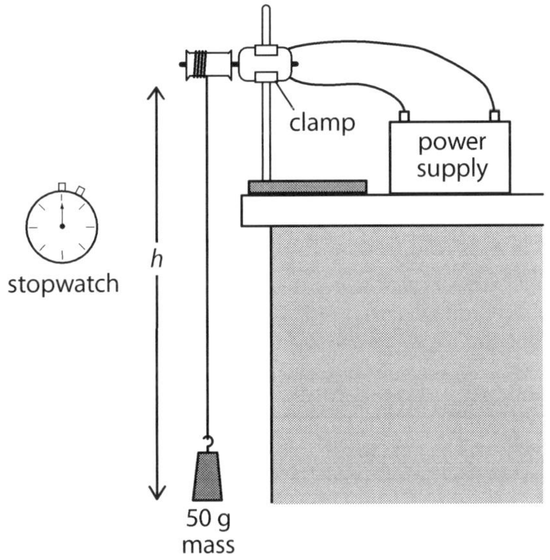


**Figure 4.1.a** *Power Step 1*

2. Try different source voltages with the motor to see what you need so that the motor will lift a mass of 50.0 g up from the floor in a time of approximately 2.0–3.0 s.
3. To measure the useful power of the motor, you will need to know the force of gravity on the mass, the height through which the mass will be raised, and the time it takes to lift the mass through that height. (Remember that 1 kg of mass has a force of gravity on it of 9.8 N.)
4. Calculate the power of the motor for at least three different sets of conditions, using

   $\text{power} = \dfrac{\text{work}}{\text{time}}$. Try different loads and/or different source voltages to vary the conditions.

### Concluding Questions

1. What is the maximum power output you measured for your motor?
2. What was the maximum power a member of your class achieved with the motor?

# Investigation 4.2 Energy Changes of a Swinging Pendulum

### Purpose

To predict the maximum speed reached by a pendulum swinging from a known height above its rest position, and to check the prediction by measurement

### Procedure

1. Attach a massive pendulum bob (1 kg) by a sturdy cable to a support on the ceiling of your classroom.
2. Design a system so that you can raise the bob to the same height *h* repeatedly. Measure *h* from the lowest position the bob reaches during each swing (Figure 4.2.a).

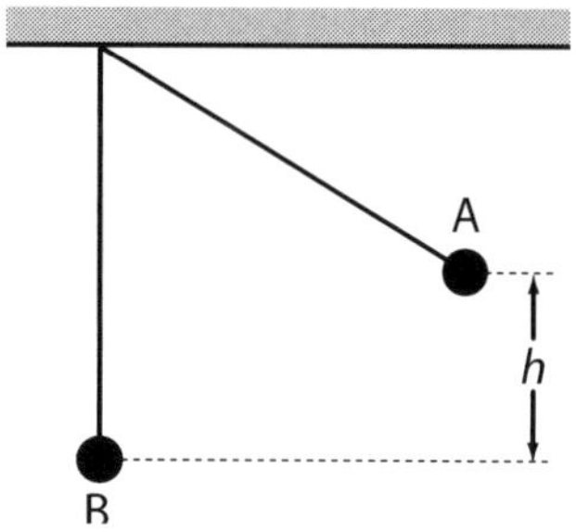


**Figure 4.2.a**

3. Choose the value of *h* you are going to use, then calculate how much gravitational potential energy ($E_p$) the bob will have at height *h*.
4. Let the bob swing once, and record the height *h′* reached by the bob on its *return swing.* Repeat this measurement four more times and average your five measurements of *h′*. Calculate the loss of $E_p$ during one full swing (*mgh* – *mgh′*).
5. The loss of energy during one complete swing can be accounted for by assuming work is done by the bob and string to overcome the force of friction due to the air. As the bob moves from its starting position A to the bottom of its swing at B, it will lose an amount of energy equal to one-quarter of the loss for one full swing, which you calculated in procedure step 4. What happens to the rest of the potential energy the bob has when it is at A?

   Let us assume that all the remaining potential energy is changed into kinetic energy. At the bottom of the swing, all the bob's energy is kinetic energy, $E_k = \frac{1}{2}mv^2$. This energy was initially the potential energy of the bob at A. If there was no air friction (or other forms of friction), we could predict that

$$E_k \text{ (bottom of swing)} = E_p \text{ (top of swing)}$$

   Since there *is* a loss of potential energy due to friction, this loss must be taken into account. The loss of energy during the swing from A to B is $\frac{1}{4}(mgh - mgh')$.

   To predict the speed of the bob at B, calculate *v* using the following equation:

$$\frac{1}{2}mv^2 = mgh - \frac{1}{4}(mgh - mgh')$$

6. Attach a short length of ticker tape (no longer than needed) to the 1 kg mass, and use a recording timer to measure the maximum speed reached by the swinging mass. (If your timer vibrates with a frequency of 60 Hz, the time between dots is 1/60 s.) When several groups have duplicated the same measurement using the same starting height, average the values of *v*.

### Concluding Questions

1. What is the percent difference between your predicted speed and your measured speed?
2. What are some sources of error in this experiment?
3. If you had used a bob with a different mass, how would that affect the predicted speed? Explain your answer.
4. Do your results suggest that the total energy of the bob (potential and kinetic) remains constant during a full swing? Discuss your answer.

### Challenge

1. Predict what these graphs would look like, for one-half swing of the pendulum:
   (a) $v$ vs. $x$
   (b) $E_p$ vs. $x$
   (c) $E_k$ vs. $x$
   (d) total $E$ vs. $x$
2. Design and carry out an experiment to test your predictions in question 1.

# 5 Momentum

This chapter focuses on the following AP Physics 1 Big Ideas from the College Board:

**BIG IDEA 3:** The interactions of an object with other objects can be described by forces.

**BIG IDEA 4**: Interactions between systems can result in changes in those systems.

**BIG IDEA 5:** Changes that occur as a result of interactions are constrained by conservation laws.

---

By the end of this chapter, you should know the meaning of these **key terms**:

- conservative forces
- elastic collisions
- energy
- force of friction
- force of gravity (weight)
- gravitational potential energy
- horsepower
- impulse
- inelastic collisions
- inertia
- kinetic energy
- law of conservation of energy
- law of conservation of momentum
- momentum
- Newton's three laws of motion
- net force
- nonconservative forces
- power
- work
- work-energy theorem

---

By the end of this chapter, you should be able to use and know when to use the following formulae:

$$\vec{p} = m\vec{v} \qquad \vec{p} = F_{\text{net}}\ t$$

*The movement of a cheetah, sports car, and runner all involve force, distance, mass, velocity, and acceleration. These factors form the foundation for the study of momentum and energy in this chapter.*

# 5.1 Momentum

## Warm Up

Consider the following objects and motion in the two columns below:

| | |
|---|---|
| feather | fast (10 m/s) |
| marble | average (5 m/s) |
| softball | slow (2 m/s) |

1. Connect an object in the first column with a motion in the second column for the following situations.
   (a) The combination that will cause the most pain if the object hits your leg

   ______________________ + ______________________

   (b) The combination that will cause the least pain if the object hits your leg

   ______________________ + ______________________

2. Explain your reasoning for each answer.

   (a) ____________________________________________________________

   ____________________________________________________________

   (b) ____________________________________________________________

   ____________________________________________________________

### Mass × Velocity = Momentum

One of the most important concepts in physics is that of momentum**.** Isaac Newton first used the idea when he wrote his second law of motion. In his original version, the second law looks like this:

$$F = \frac{m\Delta v}{\Delta t}$$

Newton called the product of mass and velocity (*mv*) a quantity of motion. Thus, his second law stated that the unbalanced force on an object is equal to the rate of change of a quantity of motion with respect to time. We now call the product of mass × velocity **momentum** and we give it the symbol *p*. The unit of measurement for momentum is kg•m/s.

$$p = m\Delta v$$

Newton's second law can be written this way:

$$F = ma = \frac{m\Delta v}{\Delta t} = \frac{\Delta p}{\Delta t}$$

Thus, the unbalanced force equals the rate of change of momentum with respect to time.

 

## Quick Check

1. What is the momentum of a 100 kg motorbike travelling at 10 m/s?

2. What is the mass of plane that is travelling at 200 km/h and has a momentum of $1.1 \times 10^6$ kg•m/s?

3. How fast does a 0.01 kg bug have to fly to have a momentum of 0.25 kg•m/s? Is this possible?

## Impulse

According to Newton's second law, in its original form $F = \frac{m\Delta v}{\Delta t} = \frac{\Delta p}{\Delta t}$. This can be rearranged to:

$$\mathbf{\Delta p = F\Delta t = m\Delta v = impulse}$$

The product of the force and the time interval during which it acts is called the **impulse**. The last equation shows that the impulse is equal to the change in momentum it produces.

This is an important relationship when considering an object that is undergoing a change in momentum. An object's momentum changes because an impulse has been placed on the object. For example, if you are driving down a road at a constant velocity, you and your vehicle have a momentum. When you press on the gas pedal, the velocity of the vehicle increases. The momentum has also increased. This increased momentum was caused by a force being exerted on the vehicle over a period of time. Or put another way, the vehicle experienced an impulse. The amount of impulse equals the change in momentum in the vehicle.

### Units for Momentum and Impulse

Momentum is measured in kg•m/s because these units have the dimensions of mass and velocity. Impulse is measured in N•s because these units have the dimensions of force and time. Since impulse is equal to change in momentum, these units must be equivalent. It can easily be shown that this is true:

$$(\text{N}\cdot\text{s}) = (\text{kg}\cdot\text{m/s}^2)\cdot(\text{s}) = (\text{kg}\cdot\text{m/s})$$

Momentum and impulse may be expressed in either unit.

**Quick Check**

1. (a) What is the momentum of a 112 kg football player running with a velocity of 3.6 m/s?

   (b) What impulse must a tackler impart to the football player to bring him to a stop?

   (c) If the tackle was completed in 0.80 s, what average force did the tackler exert on the other player?

   (d) Why is the force negative in question 1(c)?

   ______________________________________________

   ______________________________________________

## Law of Conservation of Momentum

Any moving body has momentum equal to the product of the body's mass and its velocity. What makes momentum such an important quantity in nature is the fact that in a closed system, momentum is **c**onserved. A closed system is one where no outside forces act on the system. This is the **law of conservation of momentum**. In other words, the total change in momentum within the closed, two-body system is zero. This means that the total momentum is constant, or that momentum is conserved.

Scientists have done many, many experiments with momentum and are convinced that momentum truly is a conserved quantity in nature. At the subatomic level in experiments done with high-energy particle accelerators, physicists rely heavily on the law of conservation of momentum in interpreting the results of collisions of particles.

### Conservation of Momentum and Newton's Third Law

Newton's third law is a special case of the law of conservation of momentum. This can be shown by using a proof. A proof is a mathematical solution that logically demonstrates something to be true. The following is a proof showing that Newton's third law is a special case of the law of conservation of momentum.

Consider two bodies interacting such that body A exerts a force on body B, and body B exerts an equal force on body A, but in the opposite direction.

$$F_{\text{A on B}} = -F_{\text{B on A}}$$

$$\text{action force} = -\text{ reaction force}$$

The minus sign indicates that the direction of the reaction force is opposite to that of the action force. Using Newton's second law, written in terms of momentum:

$$\frac{m_B v_B}{t} = -\frac{m_A v_A}{t}$$

 

The time intervals on both sides of the equation are the same because both forces act over the same interval of time. So the equation can be simplified to:

$$m_B v_B = -m_A v_A$$

Therefore, $m_A v_A + m_B v_B = 0$

or $p_A + p_B = 0$

## Other Examples of the Law of Conservation of Momentum

If you have ever played pool or billiards you will be familiar with the law of conservation of momentum. When the cue ball, or white ball, hits another ball, momentum is conserved. For example, if all the momentum is transferred from the cue ball to the billiard ball, the cue ball will stop and the billiard ball will move.

### Sample Problem 5.1.1 — Conservation of Momentum

A railway car of mass $6.0 \times 10^3$ kg is coasting along a track with a velocity of 5.5 m/s when suddenly a $3.0 \times 10^3$ kg load of sulphur is dumped into the car. What is its new velocity?

| What to Think About | How to Do It |
|---|---|
| 1. What do I know about the problem? | The momentum of the railway car will not change because of the law of conservation of momentum.<br><br>Let initial mass be $m_1$ and initial velocity be $v_1$. The final mass of the railway car will be $m_2$ and the final velocity $v_2$. |
| 2. What am I trying to solve? | Solve for the final velocity $v_2$. |
| 3. What formula applies to this situation? | $m_1 v_1 = m_2 v_2$ |
| 4. Find the final velocity $v_2$. | $(6.0 \times 10^3 \text{ kg})(5.5 \text{ m/s}) = (6.0 \times 10^3 \text{ kg} + 3.0 \times 10^3 \text{ kg})(v_2)$<br><br>$33 \times 10^3 \text{ kg•m/s} = (9.0 \times 10^3 \text{ kg})(v_2)$<br><br>$v_2 = \frac{33\ 10^3 \text{ kg•m/s}}{9.0\ 10^3 \text{ kg}}$<br><br>$= 3.7 \text{ m/s}$<br><br>The rail car's new velocity is 3.7 m/s |

## Practice Problems 5.1.1 — Conservation of Momentum

1. Two identical air track gliders each have a mass of 100 g and are sitting on an air track. One glider is at rest and the other glider is moving toward it at a velocity. When they collide they stick together and move off at 2.0 m/s. What was the initial velocity of the moving glider?

2. A 1.0 kg ball of putty is rolling towards a resting 4.5 kg bowling ball at 1.5 m/s. When they collide and stick together, what is the resulting momentum of the two objects stuck together?

3. A ball rolls at a velocity of 3.5 m/s toward a 5.0 kg ball at rest. They collide and move off at a velocity of 2.5 m/s. What was the mass of the moving ball?

# 5.1 Review Questions

1. What is the momentum of a 75 g mouse running across the floor with a velocity of 2.6 m/s?

2. What is the impulse of a 55 N force exerted over a time interval of 1.0 ms?

3. A 0.060 kg rifle bullet leaves the muzzle with a velocity of $6.0 \times 10^2$ m/s. If the 3.0 kg rifle is held very loosely, with what velocity will it recoil?

4. A 53 kg skateboarder on a 2.0 kg skateboard is coasting along at 1.6 m/s. He collides with a stationary skateboarder of mass 43 kg, also on a 2.0 kg skateboard, and the two skateboarders coast off in the same direction that the first skateboarder was travelling.What velocity will the combined skateboarders now have?

5. What impulse is needed to change the velocity of a 10.0 kg object from 12.6 m/s to 25.5 m/s in a time of 5.00 s? How much force is needed?

6. A $1.5 \times 10^3$ kg car travelling at 44 m/s collides head-on with a $1.0 \times 10^3$ kg car travelling at 22 m/s in the opposite direction. If the cars stick together on impact, what is the velocity of the wreckage immediately after impact? (Hint: Let the velocity of the second car be −22 m/s, since it is moving in a direction opposite to the first car.)

7. (a) What impulse must be imparted by a baseball bat to a 145 g ball to change its velocity from 40.0 m/s to −50.0 m/s?

   (b) If the collision between the baseball and the bat lasts 1.00 ms, what force was exerted on the ball? (1 ms = $10^{-3}$ s)

# 5.2 Momentum and Impulse

## Warm Up

A golf ball is placed on top of a basketball. Both are dropped from a 1.0 m height. What will happen to the golf ball after the basketball hits the ground?

______________________________________________________________________

______________________________________________________________________

______________________________________________________________________

### Newton's Second Law in Terms of Momentum

One of the most important concepts in physics is the idea of **momentum.** Newton first used the concept when he formulated his second law of motion. He called the product of mass and velocity "quantity of motion" but this product has come to be known as momentum.

What makes momentum so important is that it is a conserved quantity. In an isolated system (a system in which no external forces interfere), the total momentum of the objects in the system will remain constant. This is the **law of conservation of momentum.**

Any moving object has momentum. Momentum ($\vec{p}$) is calculated by multiplying the mass of the body by its velocity.

momentum = mass × velocity

$$\vec{p} = m\vec{v}$$

Momentum is a vector quantity, and the direction of the momentum vector is the same as the direction of the velocity vector. When you add momenta (the plural of momentum), you must use vector addition.

Newton's second law can be rewritten in terms of momentum:

$$\vec{F} = m\vec{a} = m\frac{\Delta\vec{v}}{\Delta t} = m\frac{[\vec{v}_f - \vec{v}_0]}{\Delta t} = \frac{[m\vec{v}_f - m\vec{v}_0]}{\Delta t} = \frac{\Delta[m\vec{v}]}{\Delta t} = \frac{\Delta\vec{p}}{\Delta t}$$

Newton's second law can be stated in words, in terms of momentum, as given below.

An unbalanced net force acting on a body changes its motion so that the rate of change of momentum is equal to the unbalanced force.

## Impulse

If the equation for net force just derived is rearranged by multiplying both sides of the equation by $\Delta t$, then

$$\vec{F}\Delta t = \Delta(m\vec{v})$$

The product of the net force and the time interval during which it acts is called the **impulse** of the force. The impulse of the force equals the change in momentum it causes. A given change in momentum can be produced by a large force acting for a short time *or* by a small force acting for a long time!

## Units for Momentum and Impulse

Momentum has measuring units that have the dimensions of [mass] x [velocity], which are kg·m/s. Impulse has units with the dimensions of [force] × [time], which are N·s.

$$1\text{ N}\cdot\text{s} = 1\text{ kg}\cdot\frac{\text{m}}{\text{s}^2}\cdot\text{s}$$

$$1\text{ N}\cdot\text{s} = 1\text{ kg}\cdot\frac{\text{m}}{\text{s}}$$

Therefore, N·s is equivalent to kg·m/s. Momentum can be expressed in either units, and so can impulse.

## Conservation of Momentum

Consider an isolated system consisting of two laboratory carts with a compressed spring between them. Before the spring is released by a triggering mechanism, the carts are stationary. The carts have masses $m_A$ and $m_B$ respectively. The total momentum is zero, since neither cart is moving.

The spring is now released. Cart A pushes on cart B and, according to Newton's third law, cart B exerts the same force on cart A, but in the opposite direction.

$$\vec{F}_{\text{A on B}} = -\vec{F}_{\text{B on A}}$$

$$\frac{\Delta[m_B\vec{v}_B]}{\Delta t} = -\frac{\Delta[m_A\vec{v}_A]}{\Delta t}$$

Since the time intervals are the same for both forces, $\Delta t$ can be eliminated.

Therefore $\quad \Delta[m_B\vec{v}_B] = -\Delta[m_A\vec{v}_A]$

Or $\quad \Delta\vec{p}_B = -\Delta\vec{p}_A$

This means that $\quad \Delta\vec{p}_A + \Delta\vec{p}_B = 0$

The total change of momentum of the isolated system is zero. Since the momentum of the two-cart system was zero to begin with, it must be still zero. Both carts are moving after the spring pushes them apart, and both have momentum, but the directions are opposite. The vector sum of the momenta is still zero.

Similar arguments can be used for interacting bodies that have momentum to begin with — the change in momentum will still be zero, and the total momentum will remain constant.

The law of conservation of momentum applies to any isolated system.

The total momentum of an isolated system of objects will remain constant.

## Sample Problem 5.2.1 — Law of Conservation of Momentum

A rifle bullet of mass 0.060 kg leaves the muzzle with a velocity $6.0 \times 10^2$ m/s. If the 3.0 kg rifle is held very loosely, with what velocity will it recoil when the bullet is fired?

| What to Think About | How to Do It |
|---|---|
| 1. Momentum is conserved. Since before the rifle is fired the momentum of the isolated rifle-bullet system is zero, the total momentum after the bullet is fired is still zero! The subscript "r" denotes "rifle" and "b" denotes "bullet." | $\Delta\vec{p}_r + \Delta\vec{p}_b = 0$ |
| 2. Remember that momentum is the product of an object's mass and velocity. | $m_r\vec{v}_r + m_b\vec{v}_b = 0$<br>$(3.0\text{ kg})(\vec{v}_r) + (0.060\text{ kg})(6.00 \times 10^2\text{ m/s}) = 0$ |
| 3. The rifle will recoil with a velocity of 12 m/s in the opposite direction to the velocity of the bullet. | $\vec{v}_r = \dfrac{-(0.060\text{ kg})(6.00 \times 10^2\text{ m/s})}{3.0\text{ kg}}$<br>$\vec{v}_r = -12\text{ m/s}$ |

## Practice Problems 5.2.1 — Law of Conservation of Momentum

1. A $6.0 \times 10^3$ kg railway car is coasting along the track at 7.0 m/s. Suddenly a $2.0 \times 10^3$ kg load of coal is dumped into the car. What is its new velocity?

2. A $1.2 \times 10^3$ kg car travelling 33 m/s collides head-on with a $1.8 \times 10^3$ kg car travelling 22 m/s in the opposite direction. If the cars stick together, what is the velocity of the wreckage immediately after impact?

3. A 0.060 kg rifle bullet leaves the muzzle with a velocity of $6.0 \times 10^2$ m/s. The 3.0 kg rifle is held firmly by a 60.0 kg man. With what initial velocity will the man and rifle recoil? Compare your answer with the answer to Sample Problem 3.2.1.

## 5.2 Review Questions

1. What is the momentum of a 0.25 g bug flying with a speed of 12 m/s?

2. (a) What is the momentum of a 112 kg football player running at 4.8 m/s?

   (b) What impulse must a tackler impart to the football player in (a) to stop him?

   (c) If the tackle is completed in 1.2 s, what average force must the tackler have exerted on the other player?

3. You are doing a space walk outside the International Space Station (ISS), with no cable between you and the ISS. Your small maneuvering rocket pack suddenly quits on you, and you are stranded in space with nothing but a $50 000 camera in your hands. What will you do to get back to the space station?

4. A rocket expels $1.2 \times 10^3$ kg of gas each second, and the gas leaves the rocket with a speed of $5.0 \times 10^4$ m/s. Will the thrust produced by the rocket be sufficient to lift it, if the force of gravity on the rocket is $5.8 \times 10^7$ N?

5. A 3.2 kg cart travelling 1.2 m/s collides with a stationary 1.8 kg cart, and the two carts stick together. What is their common velocity after the collision?

6. A bullet of mass *m* is fired into a steel wall with velocity $\vec{v}$, then rebounds with velocity $-1/2\,\vec{v}$. A second bullet of the same mass *m* is fired into a wall covered with modelling clay, and it does not rebound. Which bullet exerts a greater force on the wall: the one that rebounds or the one that does not? Show your reasoning.

7. (a) What impulse must be imparted to a 145 g baseball to change its velocity from 40.0 m/s south to 50.0 m/s north?

(b) If the collision between the baseball and the bat lasted 1.00 ms (milliseconds), what force did the bat exert on the baseball?

8. To measure the speed of a bullet, a physicist fired a 45.0 g bullet into a large block of modelling clay that rested on a metal disk floating on a large air table. The combined mass of the modelling clay and disk was 18.0 kg. By using strobe photography, the speed of the disk was measured to be 0.900 m/s immediately after the impact of the bullet. What was the speed of the bullet?

9. A $2.0 \times 10^3$ kg car travelling 15 m/s rear-ends another car of mass $1.0 \times 10^3$ kg. The second car was initially moving 6.0 m/s in the same direction. What is their common velocity after the collision if the cars lock together during the impact?

10. What impulse is needed to change the speed of a 10.0 kg body from 20.0 m/s to 12.0 m/s in a time of 5.0 s? What force is needed to do this?

# 5.3 Momentum in Two-Dimensional Situations

## Warm Up

A firecracker bursts, sending four equal-size fragments in different directions along the compass points north, east, south, and west. Draw a vector diagram of the four momentum vectors. Explain the momentum concepts you used in creating this diagram.

### Conservation of Momentum in Two Dimensions

All the examples and exercises with momentum have so far dealt with motion in a straight line. The principles involved all apply, however, to two- or three- dimensional situations as well.

When considering a collision between two or more objects, it is important to remember that momentum is a vector and that momentum is conserved. This means you always account for the direction along with the magnitude of each object's momentum. From the law of conservation of momentum, it also means that the total momentum before the collision equals the total momentum after the collision.

Three sample questions involving momentum in two dimensions will help show how useful the law of conservation of momentum can be in solving problems.

**Sample Problem 5.3.1 — Collision Between Two Objects: Right Angles**

A 60.0 kg hockey player travelling 2.0 m/s toward the north collides with a 50.0 kg player travelling 1.0 m/s toward the west. The two become tangled together. With what velocity will they move after the collision?

| What to Think About | How to Do It |
|---|---|
| 1. Momentum is a vector quantity, so you must follow the rules for vector addition. | Before the collision, the momentum of the first player is: $\vec{p}_1 = (60.0\ \text{kg})(2.0\ \text{m/s}) = 120\ \text{kg·m/s (north)}$ Before the collision, the momentum of the second player is: $\vec{p}_2 = (50.0\ \text{kg})(1.0\ \text{m/s}) = 50.0\ \text{kg·m/s (west)}$ |

*Sample Problem continued*

## Sample Problem 5.3.1 — Collision Between Two Objects: Right Angles (Continued)

**What to Think About**

2. After the collision, the tangled players have a momentum equal to the vector sum of $\vec{p}_1$ and $\vec{p}_2$. Figure 5.3.1 shows how to find the vector sum. Since the vector triangle has a right angle, the Pythagorean theorem can be used to solve for $\vec{p}_R$.

**How to Do It**

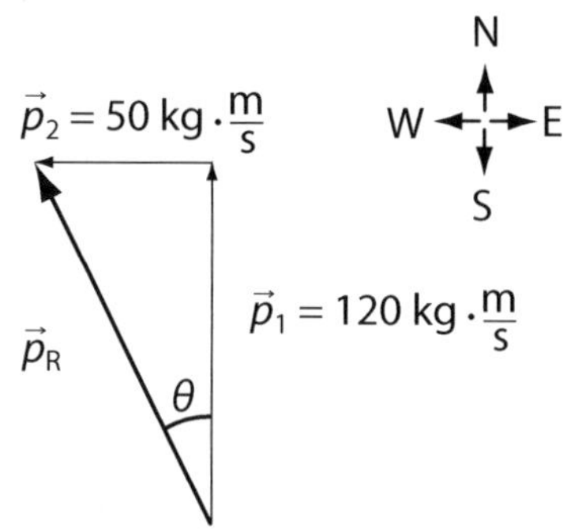


Figure 5.3.1

$$\vec{p}_R^{\,2} = \vec{p}_1^{\,2} + \vec{p}_2^{\,2}$$

$$\vec{p}_R^{\,2} = (120 \text{ kg}\cdot\text{m/s})^2 + (50 \text{ kg}\cdot\text{m/s})^2$$

$$\vec{p} = 130 \text{ kg}\cdot\text{m/s}$$

3. Since $\vec{p}_R = (m_1 + m_2) = \vec{v}_R$, the velocity of the tangled players will have magnitude.

$$\vec{v}_R = \frac{\vec{p}_R}{m_1 + m_2} = \frac{1.3 \times 10^2 \text{ kg}\cdot\text{m/s}}{1.1 \times 10^2 \text{ kg}} = 1.2 \text{ m/s}$$

4. The answer is not yet complete, since velocities have specific directions. From the momentum vector diagram, calculate the angle.

$$\tan = \frac{50 \text{ kg}\cdot\text{m/s}}{120 \text{ kg}\cdot\text{m/s}} = 0.4167$$

5. The resultant velocity of the hockey players is 1.2 m/s, directed 23° W of N.

$\theta = 22.6°$ to the west of north

## Sample Problem 5.3.2 — Collision Between Two Objects: Vector Components

A 0.050 kg air puck moving with a velocity of 2.0 m/s collides with an identical but stationary air puck. The direction of the incident puck is changed by 60° from its original path, and the angle between the two pucks after the collision is 90°. What are the speeds of the two pucks after they collide?

**What to Think About**

1. Momentum is conserved, so the resultant momentum after the collision must equal the momentum of the incident puck. The directions of the momenta of the two pucks are known. The resultant momentum must equal $\vec{p}_{io}$

**How to Do It**

$$\vec{p}_{io} = (0.050 \text{ kg})(2.0 \text{ m/s}) = 0.10 \text{ kg}\cdot\text{m/s}$$

*Sample Problem continued*

## Sample Problem 5.3.2 — Collision Between Two Objects: Vector Components (Continued)

### What to Think About

2. In Figure 5.3.2, the resultant momentum ($\vec{p}_R = \vec{p}_{io}$) was drawn first. Then the directions of $\vec{p}_{if}$ and $\vec{p}_{sf}$ were constructed. As you can see, it is then a simple task to complete the momentum vector triangle.

3. After the collision, $\vec{p}_R = \vec{p}_{io} = 0.10$ kg·m/s in the direction shown. Use trigonometry to solve for the magnitudes of $\vec{p}_{if}$ and $\vec{p}_{sf}$.

**Challenge:** Can you see a shorter way to solve this particular problem?

### How to Do It

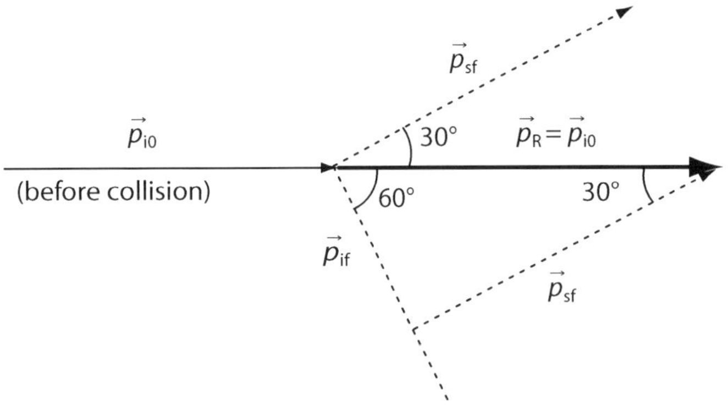


Figure 5.3.2

$\vec{p}_{if} = \vec{p}_R \cos 60^\circ$

$\vec{p}_{if} = (0.10 \text{ kg·m/s})(0.500)$

$\vec{p}_{if} = 0.050 \text{ kg·m/s}$

$$\vec{v}_{if} = \frac{\vec{p}_{if}}{m_i} = \frac{0.050 \text{ kg·m/s}}{0.050 \text{ kg}} = 1.0 \text{ m/s}$$

Similarly,

$\vec{p}_{sf} = \vec{p}_R \sin 60^\circ$

$\vec{p}_{sf} = (0.10 \text{ kg·m/s})(0.866)$

$\vec{p}_{sf} = 0.087 \text{ kg·m/s}$

$$\vec{v}_{sf} = \frac{\vec{p}_{sf}}{m_s} = \frac{0.087 \text{ kg·m/s}}{0.050 \text{ kg}} = 1.7 \text{ m/s}$$

## Sample Problem 5.3.3 — Collision Between Two Objects: Vector Addition

A metal disk explodes into three pieces, which fly off in the same geometric plane. The first piece has a mass of 2.4 kg, and it flies off north at 10.0 m/s. The second piece has a mass of 2.0 kg and it flies east at 12.5 m/s. What is the speed and direction of the third piece, which has a mass of 1.4 kg?

### What to Think About

1. Before the explosion, total momentum was zero. After the explosion, the vector sum of the three momenta must be zero, as well, since momentum is conserved. Begin by drawing momentum vectors for the two fragments for which you have full information. The momentum of the third fragment must be such that the three momenta have a vector sum of zero. They must form a closed triangle (Figure 5.3. 3).

### How to Do It

The momentum of the first fragment,
$\vec{p}_1 = (2.4\text{ kg})(10.0\text{ m/s}) = 24\text{ kg·m/s (north)}$

The momentum of the second fragment,
$\vec{p}_2 = (2.0\text{ kg})(12.5\text{ m/s}) = 25\text{ kg·m/s (east)}$

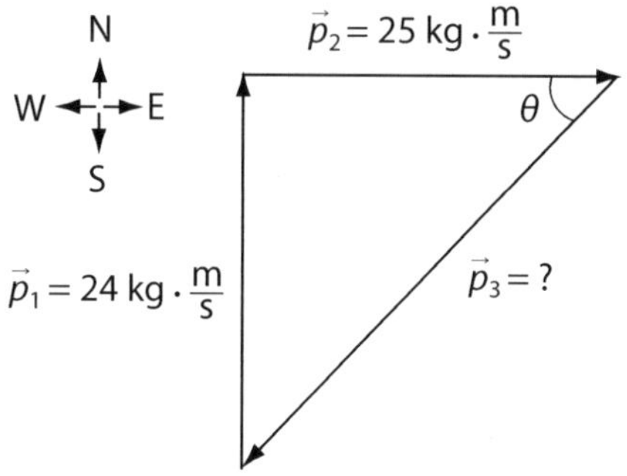


Figure 5.3.3

### What to Think About

2. Since these momentum vectors form a right-angled triangle, use the Pythagorean theorem to solve for the magnitude of $\vec{p}_3$.

### How to Do It

$$\vec{p}_1 = \sqrt{(24\text{ kg·m/s})^2 + (25\text{ kg·m/s})^2} = 35\text{ kg·m/s}$$

$$\vec{v}_3 = \frac{\vec{p}_3}{m_3} = \frac{35\text{ kg·m/s}}{1.4\text{ kg}} = 25\text{ m/s}$$

### What to Think About

3. Therefore, the velocity of the third fragment is 25 m/s in a direction 44° south of west.

### How to Do It

$$\tan\theta = \frac{24\text{ kg·m/s}}{25\text{ kg·m/s}}$$

$$\tan\theta = 0.9600$$

$$\theta = 44^\circ$$

**Special Note:** In each of the three examples, the angle between vectors has been a right angle. If there is no right angle, the problem may be solved using a scale diagram or by using sine law or cosine law. Another method is to use *x*- and *y*-components of velocities or momenta.

## 5.3 Review Questions

1. A hockey player of mass 82 kg is travelling north with a velocity of 4.1 m/s. He collides with a 76 kg player travelling east at 3.4 m/s. If the two players lock together momentarily, in what direction will they be going immediately after the collision? How fast will they be moving?

2. A $2.5 \times 10^3$ kg car travelling west at 6.0 m/s is hit by a $6.0 \times 10^3$ kg truck going south at 4.0 m/s. The two vehicles lock together on impact. What is the speed and direction of the wreckage immediately after impact?

3. A frustrated physics student blew up her physics textbook, using a small amount of an explosive. It broke into three pieces, which miraculously flew off in directions that were all in the same geometric plane. A 0.200 kg piece flew off at 20.0 m/s, and a 0.100 kg piece went off at 90° to the first piece at 30.0 m/s.
   (a) What was the momentum of the third piece?

   (b) If the mass of the third piece was 0.150 kg, what was its velocity right after the explosion?

4. A proton of mass m collides obliquely with another proton. The first proton is moving with a speed of $6.0 \times 10^6$ m/s before it hits the second, stationary proton. Assuming the collision is perfectly elastic (no kinetic energy is lost), and using the fact that the first proton is moved 30° from its initial path after the collision, figure out the speed and direction of each proton after the collision.

5. A 0.40 kg model airplane is travelling 20 km/h toward the south. A 0.50 kg model airplane, travelling 25 km/h in a direction 20° east of south, collides with the first model airplane. The two planes stick together on impact. What is the direction and magnitude of the velocity of the combined wreckage immediately after the collision?

6. What impulse is needed to change the velocity of a 90.0 kg football player from 3.6 m/s toward the north and make it 1.2 m/s toward the northeast? In what direction must the force be exerted?

# Chapter 5 Conceptual Review Questions

1. An object that has a small mass and an object that has a large mass have the same momentum. Which object has the largest kinetic energy?

2. How can a small force impart the same momentum to an object as a large force?

3. Explain in terms of impulse how padding reduces forces in a collision. State this in terms of a real example, such as the advantages of a carpeted vs. tile floor for a day care center.

4. Under what circumstances is momentum conserved?

5. Explain in terms of momentum and Newton's laws how a car's air resistance is due in part to the fact that it pushes air in its direction of motion.

# Chapter 5 Review Questions

1. How much momentum does a 0.500 kg rock have when thrown at 25.0 m/s?

2. What impulse must be imparted toa 100.0 g ball to get it moving at 40.0 m/s?

3. A 2.4 kg cart moving 0.64 m/s collides with a stationary 1.8 kg cart. The carts lock together. What is their combined velocity after the collision?

4. A $1.5 \times 10^3$ kg car collides head-on with a $1.2 \times 10^3$ kg car. Both cars were travelling at the same speed, 20.0 m/s, but in opposite directions. What will the velocity of the combined wreckage be immediately after the collision?

5. An 80 kg rider on a 120 kg motorbike, travelling 25 m/s in a direction 12° west of north, enters a highway without properly checking that the road is clear. He collides with a 1200 kg car travelling north at 20 m/s. The two vehicles and rider become entangled. In what direction and at what speed will the wreckage move immediately after the collision? (Assume the car's mass includes its occupants.)

6. A 52 kg girl is coasting along the floor on a large 2.0 kg skateboard. If she is moving 1.8 m/s when a 46 kg boy jumps on to the same skateboard, what is the speed of the skateboard immediately after the boy jumps on it?

7. A 30.0 kg hockey player travelling 1.0 m/s toward the south collides with a 25.0 kg hockey player moving 0.50 m/s toward the west. They become tangled and they move off together. With what speed and in what direction will the two players move immediately after the collision?

8. A $5.00 \times 10^{-3}$ kg steel ball moving 1.20 m/s collides elastically (i.e., with no loss of kinetic energy) with an identical, stationary steel ball. The incident ball is deflected 30° from its original path.
   (a) Draw a vector diagram showing the paths of both balls after the perfectly elastic collision.
   (b) What is the velocity of the incident ball after the collision?
   (c) What is the velocity of the struck ball after the collision?

# Investigation 5.1 Momentum in Explosions and Collisions

## Purpose

To measure and compare momentum before and after "explosions" and "collisions"

### *Part 1 An "Explosion" of Two Carts (Demonstration)*

## Procedure

1. Two laboratory carts of equal mass are equipped with spring bumpers (Figure 5.1.a). Predict how the speeds of the carts will compare when the springs are compressed, and the two carts are allowed to "explode" apart. Design a way to compare speeds using only a metre stick. Test your prediction.

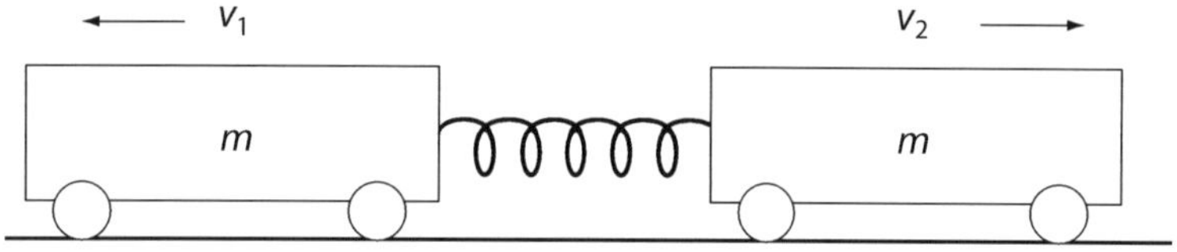


**Figure 5.1.a**

2. Place an extra laboratory cart on top of one of the identical carts, so that you double the mass of the bottom cart. Again, predict how the speeds will compare after the carts "explode" apart. Test your prediction.

## Concluding Question

1. On what basis did you make your predictions? Were they correct? If not, explain why they were not.

### *Part 2 Straight-Line Collisions of Carts of Equal Mass (Demonstration)*

## Procedure

1. (a) Predict what will happen if a spring-bumpered cart moving with a speed *v* is made to collide head-on with a second cart of equal mass, which is initially at rest. Test your prediction.
   (b) Repeat the procedure in (a), but this time attach a strip of Velcro to two identical carts so that when they collide they will stick together when they collide. Predict what the speed of the combined carts will be after the collision, if the incoming cart has speed *v*.
2. (a) Predict what will happen if two identical spring-loaded carts, travelling toward each other at speed *v*, collide head-on. Test your prediction.
   (b) Predict what will happen if two identical carts, equipped with Velcro bumpers, approach each other, both at speed *v*, and stick together following the collision. Test your prediction.

## Concluding Question

1. On what basis did you make your predictions in procedure steps 1 and 2? Were they correct? If not, explain why they did not work out.

### *Part 3 Oblique Collisions of Pucks on an Air Table (Demonstration)*

#### Procedure

1. Place two pucks of identical mass on an air table (Figure 5.1.b). Observe what happens when a moving puck collides with a stationary puck (a) head-on and (b) at an oblique angle. Pay particular attention to the angle between the incident puck and the struck puck.

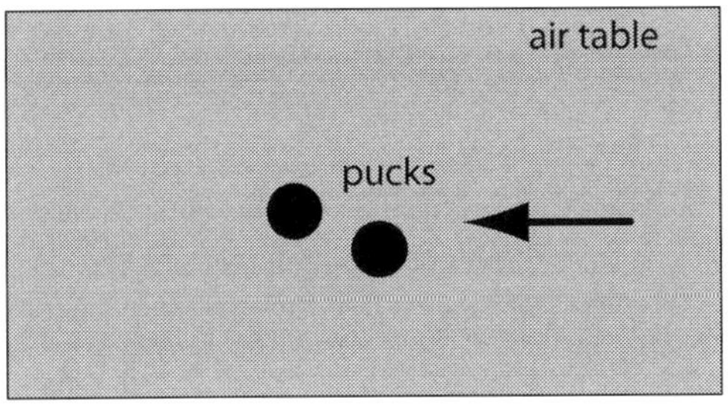


**Figure 5.1.b**

> If you have the equipment, take a strobe photograph of these two types of collision and measure the angles from the photograph.

2. Try varying the masses of the pucks. Observe whether the angle between the incident puck and the struck puck is the same as it was when the pucks had identical mass.

#### Concluding Questions

1. What do you conclude about the angle between the incident puck and the struck puck after they collided (a) head-on and (b) obliquely, when their masses are identical?
2. Does this conclusion hold true when the masses are different?

# 6 Simple Harmonic Motion

This chapter focuses on the following AP Physics 1 Big Ideas from the College Board:

**BIG IDEA 3:** The interactions of an object with other objects can be described by forces.

**BIG IDEA 5:** Changes that occur as a result of interactions are constrained by conservation laws.

---

By the end of this chapter, you should know the meaning of these **key terms**:

- deformation
- elastic potential energy
- force constant
- frequency
- period
- restoring force
- simple harmonic motion

---

By the end of this chapter, you should be able to use and know when to use the following formulae:

$$F = -kx$$

$$PE_{el} = ½ Kx^2$$

$$T = 2\pi\sqrt{\frac{L}{g}}$$

$$x = A \cos(2\pi ft)$$

*This clock uses a pendulum for keeping time. The swinging mass of the pendulum is a harmonic oscillator; it swings back and forth in a precise time interval.*

# 6.1 Stress and Strain: Hooke's Law Revisited

## Warm Up

Suspend a 500 g mass from a vertical spring and let the mass settle to the equilibrium position. This position will be where the mass is not moving and we call it EQ. What forces act upon the mass when it is at the EQ positon?

Pull the mass slightly below the EQ position and release, causing the system to oscillate above and below the EQ position with period (*T*) and frequency (*f*). What factors affect the period of oscillation?

Try different masses to see the effect that mass has on period *T*. Try a stiffer spring to see the effect that the spring stiffness constant has on the period *T*.

### Restoring Force

Newton's first law implies that an object oscillating back and forth is experiencing forces. Without force, the object would move in a straight line at a constant speed rather than oscillate. Consider, for example, plucking a plastic ruler to the left as shown in Figure 6.1.1. The deformation of the ruler creates a force in the opposite direction, known as a **restoring force**. Once released, the restoring force causes the ruler to move back toward its stable equilibrium position, where the net force on it is zero. However, by the time the ruler gets there, it gains momentum and continues to move to the right, producing the opposite deformation. It is then forced to the left, back through equilibrium, and the process is repeated until dissipative forces dampen the motion. These forces remove mechanical energy from the system, gradually reducing the motion until the ruler comes to rest.

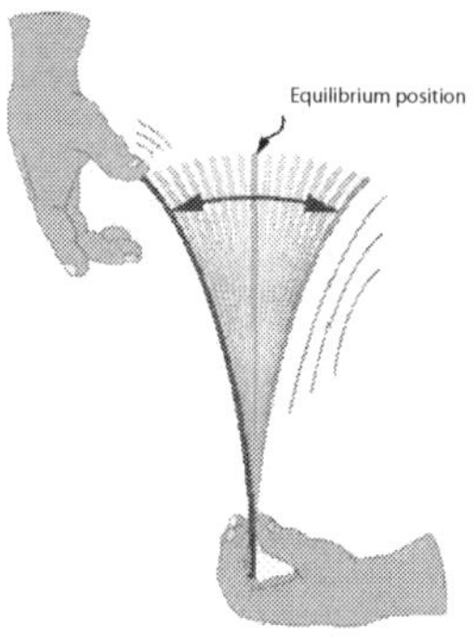


**Figure 6.1.1** *When displaced from its vertical equilibrium position, this plastic ruler oscillates back and forth because of the restoring force opposing displacement. When the ruler is on the left, there is a force to the right, and vice versa.*

The simplest oscillations occur when the restoring force is directly proportional to displacement. When stress and strain were covered in Newton's Third Law of Motion, the name was given to this relationship between force and displacement was Hooke's law:

$$F = -kx$$

Here, $F$ is the restoring force, $x$ is the displacement from equilibrium or **deformation**, and $k$ is a constant related to the difficulty in deforming the system. The minus sign indicates the restoring force is in the direction opposite to the displacement.

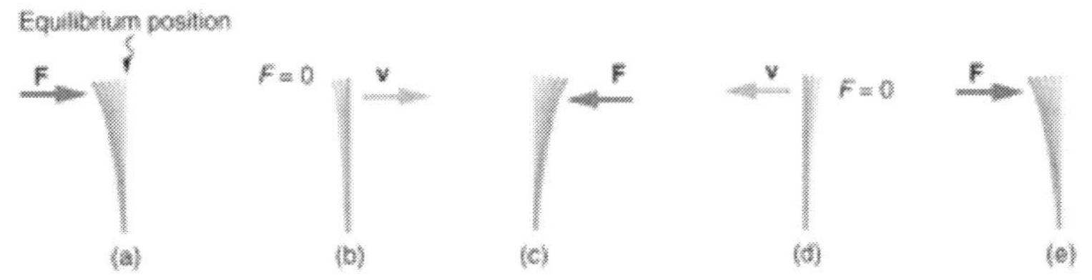


**Figure 6.1.2** *(a) The plastic ruler has been released, and the restoring force is returning the ruler to its equilibrium position. (b) The net force is zero at the equilibrium position, but the ruler has momentum and continues to move to the right. (c) The restoring force is in the opposite direction. It stops the ruler and moves it back toward equilibrium again. (d) Now the ruler has momentum to the left. (e) In the absence of damping (caused by frictional forces), the ruler reaches its original position. From there, the motion will repeat itself.*

## Force Constant

The **force constant** $k$ is related to the rigidity (or stiffness) of a system — the larger the force constant, the greater the restoring force, and the stiffer the system. The units of $k$ are newtons per meter (N/m). For example, $k$ is directly related to Young's modulus when we stretch a string. Figure 6.1.3 shows a graph of the absolute value of the restoring force versus the displacement for a system that can be described by Hooke's law — a simple spring in this case. The slope of the graph equals the force constant $k$ in newtons per meter. In a previous lab you measured restoring forces created by springs, determined if they follow Hooke's law, and calculated their force constants if they do.

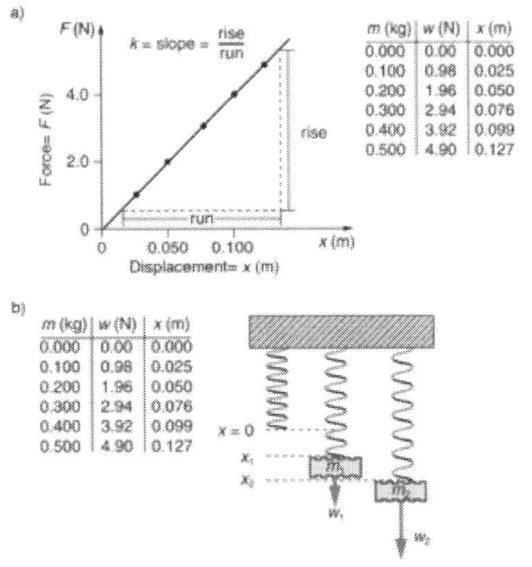


**Figure 6.1.3** *(a) A graph of absolute value of the restoring force versus displacement is displayed. The fact that the graph is a straight line means that the system obeys Hooke's law. The slope of the graph is the force constant k. (b) The data in the graph were generated by measuring the displacement of a spring from equilibrium while supporting various weights. The restoring force equals the weight supported, if the mass is stationary.*

### Sample Problem 6.1.1 — How Stiff are Car Springs?

What is the force constant for the suspension system of a car that settles 1.20 cm when an 80.0-kg person gets in?

| What to Think About | How to Do It |
|---|---|
| 1. Consider the car to be in its equilibrium position $x = 0$ before the person gets in. The car then settles down 1.20 cm, which means it is displaced to a position $x$. | $x = -1.20 \times 10^{-2}$ m |
| 2. At that point, the springs supply a restoring force $F$ equal to the person's weight | $F = mg = (80.0 \text{ kg})(9.80 \text{ m/s}^2) = 784 \text{ N}$<br>$F = -kx$ |
| 3. Solve for $k$. | $k = -\dfrac{F}{x}$ |
| 4. $F$ and $x$ have opposite signs because they are in opposite directions—the restoring force is up, and the displacement is down. Also, a car would oscillate up and down when a person got in if it were not for damping due to frictional forces provided by shock absorbers. Bouncing cars are a sure sign of bad shock absorbers. | $k = \dfrac{784 \text{N}}{-1.20 \times 10^{-2} \text{ m}}$<br>$k = 6.53 \times 10^4 \text{ N/m}$ |

### Practice Problems 6.1.1 — Hooke's Law

1. A garage door spring has a spring constant of 800 N/m. How much will it stretch if a 200 N force is applied to it?

2. Two identical springs each have a spring constant of 40 N/m. The springs are joined together in series. Determine the effective spring constant of the "springs in series" system, and how much force is required to stretch the spring system a total of 10 cm?

## Energy in Hooke's Law of Deformation

In order to produce a deformation, work must be done. That is, a force must be exerted through a distance, whether you pluck a guitar string or compress a car spring. If the only result is deformation, and no work goes into thermal, sound, or kinetic energy, then all the work is initially stored in the deformed object as some form of potential energy. The potential energy stored in a spring is $PE_{el} = ½\, Kx^2$. Here, we generalize the idea to elastic potential energy for a deformation of any system that can be described by Hooke's law.

$$PE_{el} = ½\, Kx^2$$

where $PE_{el}$ is the **elastic potential energy** stored in any deformed system that obeys Hooke's law and has a displacement x from equilibrium and a force constant *k*. It is possible to find the work done in deforming a system in order to find the energy stored. This work is performed by an applied force $F_{app}$. The applied force is exactly opposite to the restoring force (action-reaction), and so $F_{app} = kx$. Figure 6.1.4 shows a graph of the applied force versus deformation x for a system that can be described by Hooke's law. Work done on the system is force multiplied by distance, which equals the area under the curve or $½\, Kx^2$. This is method A in Figure 6.1.4. Another way to determine the work is to note that the force increases linearly from 0 to *kx*, so that the average force is $½\, Kx$, the distance moved is *x*, and thus $W = F_{app}d = [(½\, Kx](x) = ½\, Kx^2$. This is method B in Figure 6.1.4.

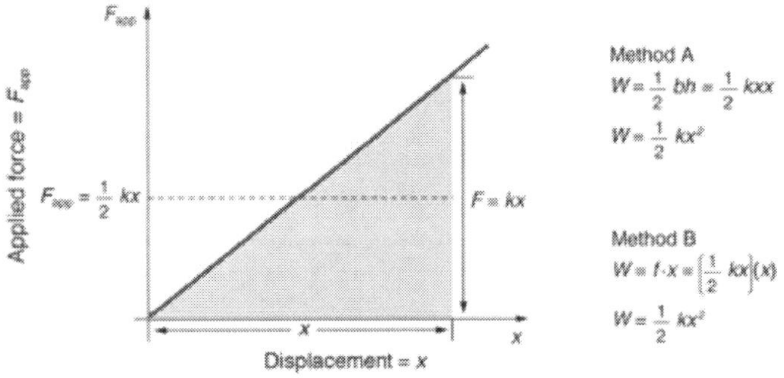


**Figure 6.1.4** *A graph of applied force versus distance for the deformation of a system that can be described by Hooke's law is displayed. The work done on the system equals the area under the graph or the area of the triangle, which is half its base multiplied by its height, or* $W = ½\, Kx^2$

## Sample Problem 6.1.2 — – Calculating Stored Energy: A Tranquilizer Gun Spring

A tranquilizer gun has a spring mechanism to launch the dart containing medicine needed to calm an animal:

a. How much energy is stored in the spring of a tranquilizer gun that has a force constant of 50.0 N/m and is compressed 0.150 m?

b. If you neglect friction and the mass of the spring, at what speed will a 2.00-g projectile dart be when ejected from the gun?

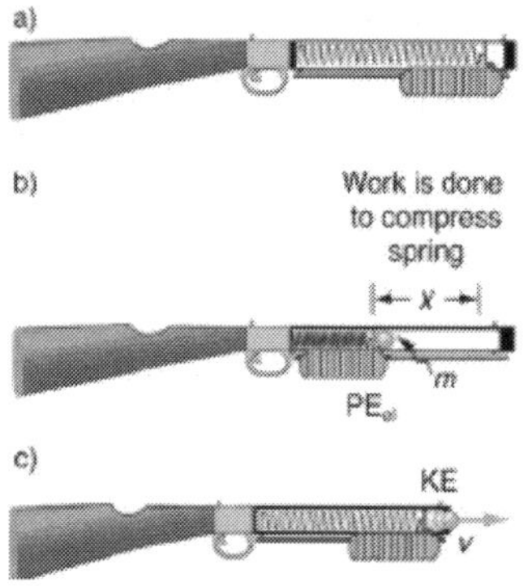


**Figure 6.1.5.** *(a) In this image of the gun, the spring is uncompressed before being cocked. (b) The spring has been compressed a distance x, and the projectile is in place. (c) When released, the spring converts elastic potential energy PEel into kinetic energy.*

| What to Think About | How to Do It |
|---|---|
| **Part (a)** | |
| 1. Enter the given values for *k* and *x*. | $PE_{el} = 1/2\ Kx^2 = 1/2(50\ N/m)(0.150\ m)^2$<br>$PE_{el} = 0.563\ N \cdot m$ |
| **Part (b)** | |
| 1. Find $PE_{el}$ | $KE_f = PE_{el}$ or $1/2\ mv^2 = 1/2\ Kx^2$ |
| 2. Solve for *v* | $v = \sqrt{\frac{2PE_{el}}{m}} = \sqrt{\frac{2(0.563\ J)}{0.003\ kg}} = 23.7\ J/kg$ |
| 3. Convert units | $v = 23.7\ m/s$ |

## Practice Problems 6.1.2 — Energy Stored in a Spring

1. A spring with a spring constant of 35 N/m is stretched by 4.0 m. How much energy is stored in the spring?

2. A spring with a spring constant of 80 N/m is compressed such that it has 200 J of elastic potential energy. What distance was the spring compressed?

3. A block of mass 0.400 kg slides across a horizontal frictionless surface with a speed of 0.50 m/s. The block runs into and compresses a spring of spring constant 750 N/m and compresses it a certain distance before coming to a complete stop. What distance was the spring compressed assuming that all of the original kinetic energy of the block is converted to elastic potential energy in the spring?

## 6.1 Review Questions

1. A red spring is positioned vertically and a 600 gram mass attached to the spring causes it to displace 30 cm. A green spring is also positioned vertically and has a spring constant 1.3 times that of the red spring. If the 600 gram mass is attached to the green spring what would be its extension?

2. A 50 gram mass is hung from a vertical spring with a spring constant of 20 N/m. Determine the amount of elastic potential energy stored in the spring.

3. A person of mass m is attached to a bungee elastic cord of length L when in its natural state, and the bungee cord is attached to a high platform. The man falls off the platform and reaches a maximum distance 2L beneath the platform. Determine the bungee cord spring constant in terms of m, g, L.

4. A 420 gram block is attached to the end of a horizontal ideal spring and rests on a frictionless surface. The block is pulled and stretched 2.1 cm beyond its natural length. Then the block is released its initial acceleration is 8.0 $m/s^2$. Determine the spring constant.

5. A spring is compressed 25.0 cm by an applied force F. As a result of the compression the elastic potential energy stored in the spring is 100 J. Determine the magnitude of the force F.

# 6.2 Simple Harmonic Motion: A Special Periodic Motion

## Warm Up

Find a bowl or basin that is shaped like a hemisphere on the inside. Place a marble inside the bowl and tilt the bowl periodically so the marble rolls from the bottom of the bowl to equally high points on the sides of the bowl. Get a feel for the force required to maintain this periodic motion. What is the restoring force and what role does the force play in moving the marble?

___

___

___

### Periodic Motion

When you pluck a guitar string, the resulting sound has a steady tone and lasts a long time. Each successive vibration of the string takes the same time as the previous one. We define periodic motion to be a motion that repeats itself at regular time intervals, such as exhibited by the guitar string or by an object on a spring moving up and down. The time to complete one oscillation remains constant and is called the period ($T$). Its units are usually seconds, but may be any convenient unit of time. The word period refers to the time for some event whether repetitive or not; but we shall be primarily interested in periodic motion, which is by definition repetitive. A concept closely related to period is the frequency of an event. For example, if you get a paycheck twice a month, the frequency of payment is two per month and the period between checks is half a month. Frequency ($f$) is defined to be the number of events per unit time. For periodic motion, frequency is the number of oscillations per unit time.

The relationship between frequency and period is:

$$f = 1/T$$

The SI unit for frequency is the cycle per second, which is defined to be a hertz (Hz):

$$1\text{ Hz} = 1\text{cycle/sec or } 1\text{ Hz} = 1/\text{s}$$

A cycle is one complete oscillation. Note that a vibration can be a single or multiple event, whereas oscillations are usually repetitive for a significant number of cycles.

**Sample Problem 6.2.1 — Determining Period and Frequency**

A medical imaging device produces ultrasound by oscillating with a period of 0.400 μs. What is the frequency of this oscillation?

| What to Think About | How to Do It |
|---|---|
| | $f = 1/T$ |
| Substitute 0.400 μs for T in f = 1/T | $f = 1/0.400 \times 10^{-6}$ |
| Solve | $f = 2.50 \times 10^{6}$ Hz |

**Practice Problems 6.2.1 — Frequency and Period of Oscillations**

1. The frequency of middle C on a typical musical instrument is 264 Hz. What is the time for one complete oscillation?

2. A stroboscope is set to flash every $8.00 \times 10^{-5}$ s. What is the frequency of flashes?

3. Each piston of an engine makes a sharp sound every other revolution of the engine. (a) How fast is a race car going if its eight-cylinder engine emits a sound of frequency 750 Hz, given that the engine makes 2000 revolutions per kilometer? (b) At how many revolutions per minute is the engine rotating

## Simple Harmonic Motion

The oscillations of a system in which the net force can be described by Hooke's law are of special importance, because they are very common. They are also the simplest oscillatory systems. **Simple Harmonic Motion** (SHM) is the name given to oscillatory motion for a system where the net force can be described by Hooke's law, and such a system is called a simple harmonic oscillator. If the net force can be described by Hooke's law and there is no damping by friction or other non-conservative forces, then a simple harmonic oscillator will oscillate with equal displacement on either side of the equilibrium position, as shown for an object on a spring in Figure 6.2.1. The maximum displacement from equilibrium is called the **amplitude** (***X*** or sometimes ***A***). The units for amplitude and displacement are the same, but depend on the type of oscillation. For the object on the spring, the units of amplitude and displacement are meters; whereas for sound oscillations, they have units of pressure (and other types of oscillations have yet other units). Because amplitude is the maximum displacement, it is related to the energy in the oscillation.

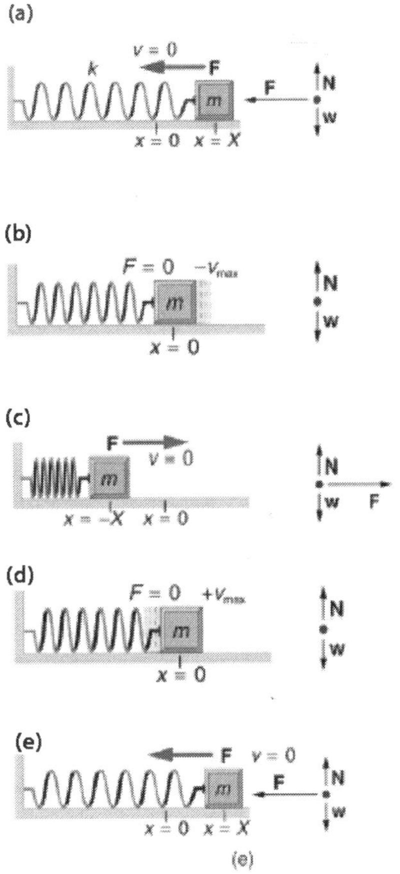


**Figure 6.2.1** *An object attached to a spring sliding on a frictionless surface is an uncomplicated simple harmonic oscillator. When displaced from equilibrium, the object performs simple harmonic motion that has an amplitude X and a period T. The object's maximum speed occurs as it passes through equilibrium. The stiffer the spring is, the smaller the period T. The greater the mass of the object is, the greater the period T.*

What is so significant about simple harmonic motion? One special thing is that the period T and frequency f of a simple harmonic oscillator are independent of amplitude. The string of a guitar, for example, will oscillate with the same frequency whether plucked gently or hard. Because the period is constant, a simple harmonic oscillator can be used as a clock.

Two important factors do affect the period of a simple harmonic oscillator. The period is related to how stiff the system is. A very stiff object has a large force constant k, which causes the system to have a smaller period. For example, you can adjust a diving board's stiffness—the stiffer it is, the faster it vibrates, and the shorter its period. Period also depends on the mass of the oscillating system. The more massive the system is, the longer the period. For example, a heavy person on a diving board bounces up and down more slowly than a light one.

In fact, the mass m and the force constant k are the only factors that affect the period and frequency of simple harmonic motion.

The period of a simple harmonic oscillator is given by

$$T = 2\pi\sqrt{\frac{m}{k}}$$

and, because $f = 1/T$, the frequency of a simple harmonic oscillator is

$$f = \frac{1}{2\pi}\sqrt{\frac{m}{k}}$$

**Sample Problem 6.2.2 — Calculate the Frequency and Period of Oscillations: Bad Shock Absorbers in a Car**

If the shock absorbers in a car go bad, then the car will oscillate at the least provocation, such as when going over bumps in the road and after stopping (See Figure 6.3.2). Calculate the frequency and period of these oscillations for such a car if the car's mass (including its load) is 900 kg and the force constant (k) of the suspension system is $6.53 \times 10^4$ N/m.

| What to Think About | How to Do It |
|---|---|
| 1. Enter the known values of *k* and *m*. | $f = \frac{1}{2\pi}\sqrt{\frac{m}{k}} = \frac{1}{2\pi}\sqrt{\frac{6.53 \times 10^4\ N/m}{900 kg}}$ |
| 2. Calculate the frequency | $f = \frac{1}{2\pi}\sqrt{72.6/s^2} = 1.3656/s = 1.36 Hz$ |
| 3. You could use $T = 2\pi\sqrt{\frac{m}{k}}$ to calculate the period, but it is simpler to use the relationship T = 1 / f and substitute the value just found for f. | $T = \frac{1}{f} = \frac{1}{1.356 Hz} = 0.738\ sec$ |

## Practice Problems 6.2.2 — Frequency and Period of Oscillations

1. A 200 gram mass is suspended from a vertical spring with spring constant 10.0 N/m. Determine the amount of extension when the mass-spring system settles at its equilibrium position; and if the mass if pulled down and released what will be the period of oscillation of the system.

2. A 10 kg block attached to the end of a spring that is hung from the ceiling and causes the spring to extend 20 cm. The block is then pulled down slightly and released causing the mass-spring system to oscillate up and down. What is the block's period and frequency of oscillation?

3. A 500 gram mass is attached to a vertical spring. The mass is pulled down slightly and released which caused the mass-spring system to oscillate with a frequency of 0.500 Hz. Determine the spring constant $k$.

## Simple Harmonic Motion and Waves

If a time-exposure photograph of the bouncing car were taken as it drove by, the headlight would make a wavelike streak, as shown in Figure 6.2.2. Similarly, Figure 9.2.3 shows an object bouncing on a spring as it leaves a wavelike "trace of its position on a moving strip of paper. Both waves are sine functions. All simple harmonic motion is intimately related to sine and cosine waves.

**Figure 6.2.2** *The bouncing car makes a wavelike motion. If the restoring force in the suspension system can be described only by Hooke's law, then the wave is a sine function. The wave is the trace produced by the headlight as the car moves to the right.*

A sinusoid is a mathematical curve that describes a smooth repetitive oscillation. When an object moves in simple harmonic motion, a graph of its position as a function of time has a sinusoidal shape with an amplitude A. The graphs of the sine and cosine functions are sinusoids of different phases. They have the same general shape but are out of phase with each other by 90° or ¼ of a cycle.

### Sine Graph

The sine graph or sine function has an up-down curve that resembles a wave. Notice the curve repeats every 2π radians or 360°. The curve starts at 0 and moves to 1 by π/2 radians at 90° and then moves down to –1.

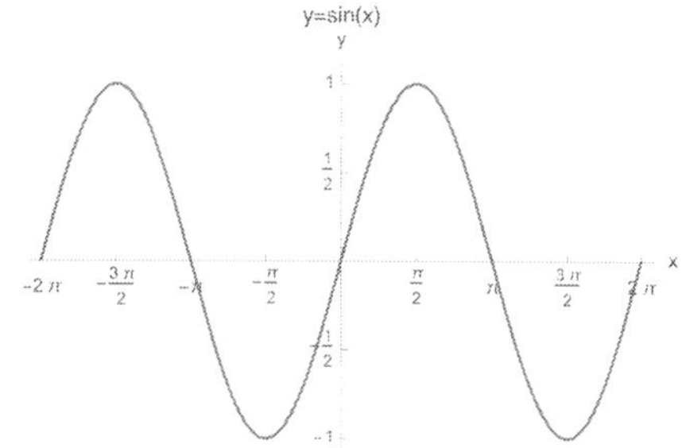


### Cosine Graph

The cosine graph or cosine function is similar to the sine function, but it starts at 1 and heads down until π radians at 180°. The curve then moves back up towards 1.

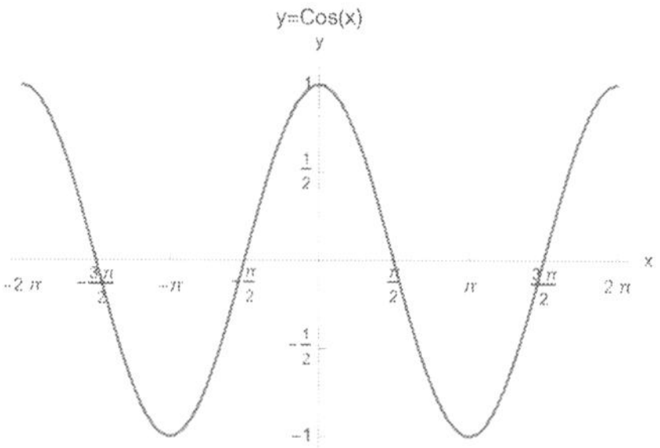


### Cosine and Sine Graph

Notice that both functions follow each other except they are π/2 radians or 90° apart.

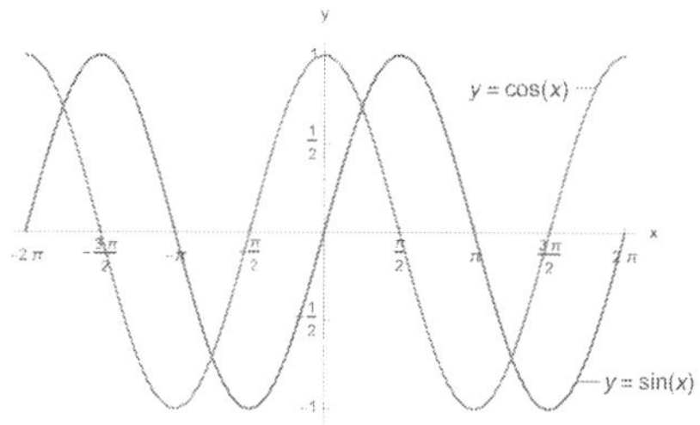

## Mass-Spring System

In the mass-spring system shown below, the equilibrium position (x=0) is the position of the mass where the upward spring force equals the downward gravitational force.

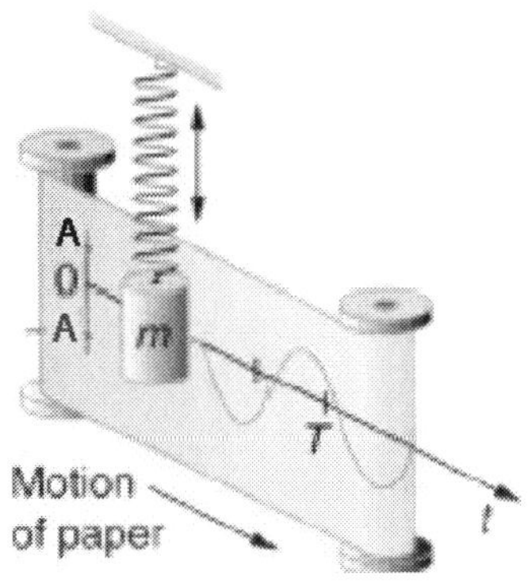


**Figure 6.2.3** *The vertical position of an object bouncing on a spring is recorded on a strip of moving paper, leaving a wave form pattern.*

If the mass is displaced a distance A from the equilibrium position and released, it will oscillate in SHM with period $T$ and frequency $f$, and with maximum amplitude $A$. The instantaneous position can be determined using the cosine function or sine function. Both equations can be used to find the instantaneous position of the mass, but the equation to use depends upon the initial position of the mass when $t = 0$. In other words, we need to know the position of the mass when timing begins. There are two conditions to consider.

**Condition 1**

Use the Cosine function when $x = A$ when $t = 0$

*Cosine function*
$x = A\cos(2\pi ft)$

**Condition 2**

Use the Sine function when at $x = 0$ when $t = 0$.

*Sine function*
$x = A\sin(2\pi ft)$

Remember the following when using these functions.

- Instantaneous position($x$) is a function of time ($t$), and the variables in the equations are expressed using these symbols and units.
- Equilibrium position (EQ) is where $x = 0$
- Instantaneous position ($x$) above or below the EQ position or baseline.
- Maximum Amplitude ($A$) is the initial displacement above or below the EQ position.
- Frequency of oscillation ($f$) is in Hz or $s^{-1}$
- Period of oscillation ($T$) is in seconds.
- Time ($t$) is the specific time for which we are calculating instantaneous position.
- Calculator must be set to **Radians Mode** when using the sine or cosine equations.

The equation on the AP Physics 1 formula sheet corresponds with the plot of the cosine.

## Postion, Velocity and Acceleration during SHM

Understanding sine and cosine graphs allows you to identify locations or specific times on a position-time graph where the velocity and acceleration are maximum or zero. For example, Figure 6.2.4 shows an object undergoing simple harmonic motion. Note that the initial position has the vertical displacement at its maximum value X ; v is initially zero and then negative as the object moves down; and the initial acceleration is negative, back toward the equilibrium position and becomes zero at that point. It a characteristic of all SHM that the object's position versus time graph is a sine or cosine graph, and that the restoring force is proportional to its displacement from equilibrium.

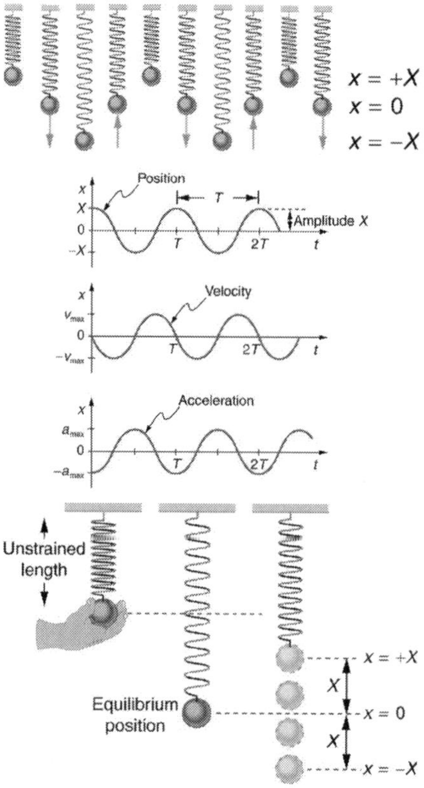


**Figure 6.2.4** *Graphs of position, velocity, and acceleration versus t for the motion of an object on a spring.*

## Quick Check

1. At t = 0 s the spring-mass system shown below has an initial positive displacement of +A. Label axes and show ONE complete oscillation on each graph (position, velocity, and acceleration).

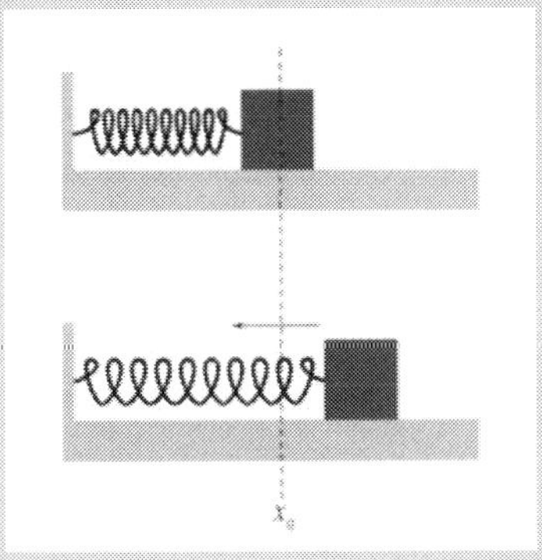

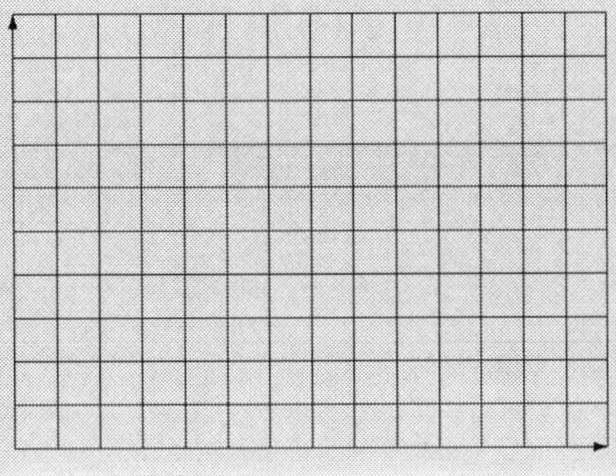

## 6.2 Review Questions

1. An unknown mass is attached to a vertical spring and causes it to stretch 10 cm. If the mass-spring system is set into oscillation, determine the period and frequency.

2. A 0.100 kg mass is suspended from a vertical spring whose spring constant is 50.0 N/m. If the mass-spring system is set into oscillation determine the period and frequency of oscillation.

3. A horizontal mass-spring system is oscillating on a frictionless surface with a frequency of 0.50 Hz. The mass attached to the spring is 100 grams. Determine the period of oscillation and the spring force constant.

4. An object of mass 500 grams oscillates on the end of a vertical spring. What mass would cause the frequency of the harmonic oscillator to double?

5. An object is hung from a vertical spring with a force constant of 12 N/m. The mass-spring system is set into oscillation and has a frequency of 0.40 Hz. What is the mass of the object?

6. A 100 g mass is suspended from a vertical spring with spring constant $k = 20$ N/m.

(a) Determine the displacement of the spring when the mass has settled at the EQ position.

(b) The mass is displaced 1.5 cm from the equilibrium position and released causing the mass-spring system to oscillate in SHM. Calculate the period $T$ of the mass-spring system.

(c) Sketch the position-time graph showing position of the mass as a function of time. Note that at t = 0, x = 1.5 cm.

(d) Calculate the instantaneous position when $t = \frac{1}{4}T$.

(e) Calculate the instantaneous position when $t = \frac{1}{2}T$.

(f) Calculate the instantaneous position when $t = \frac{3}{2}T$.

# 6.3 The Simple Pendulum

## Warm Up

Build a simple pendulum by cutting a piece of a string or dental floss so that it is about 1 m long. Attach a small object of high density to the end of the string (for example, a metal nut or a car key). The period of a pendulum is the time for one swing complete swing. Starting at an angle of less than 15º determine what factors change the period of your pendulum.

____________________________________________________________

____________________________________________________________

____________________________________________________________

### Simple Pendulum

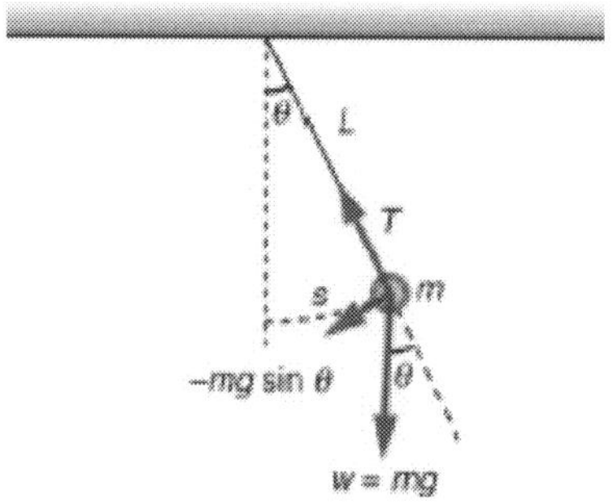


**Figure 6.3.1** *A simple pendulum has a small-diameter bob and a string that has a very small mass but is strong enough not to stretch appreciably. The linear displacement from equilibrium is s, the length of the arc. Also shown are the forces on the bob, which result in a net force of −mgsinθ toward the equilibrium position that is, a restoring force.*

Pendulums are in common usage. Some have crucial uses, such as in clocks; some are for fun, such as a child's swing; and some are just there, such as the sinker on a fishing line. For small displacements, a pendulum is a simple harmonic oscillator. A simple pendulum is defined to have an object that has a small mass, also known as the pendulum bob, which is suspended from a light wire or string, such as shown in Figure 6.3.1. Exploring the simple pendulum a bit further, we can discover the conditions under which it performs simple harmonic motion, and we can derive an interesting expression for its period.

We begin by defining the displacement to be the arc length $s$. We see from Figure 6.3.1 that the net force on the bob is tangent to the arc and equals $-mg \sin \theta$. The weight $mg$ has components $mg \cos \theta$ along the string and $mg \sin \theta$ tangent to the arc. Tension in the string exactly cancels the component $mg \cos \theta$ parallel to the string. This leaves a net restoring force back toward the equilibrium position at $\theta = 0$.

Now, if we can show that the restoring force is directly proportional to the displacement, then we have a simple harmonic oscillator. In trying to determine if we have a simple harmonic oscillator, we should note that for small angles less than about 15°, $\sin\theta \approx \theta$. This is because for smaller angles $\sin\theta$ and $\theta$ differ by about 1%. Thus for angles less than about 15°, the restoring force F is:

$$F \approx -mg\theta$$

The displacement s is directly proportional to $\theta$. When $\theta$ is expressed in radians, the arc length in a circle is related to its radius ( L in this instance) by:

$$s = L\theta$$

so that

$$\theta = \frac{s}{L}$$

For small angles, then, the expression for the restoring force is:

$$F \approx -\frac{mg}{L}s$$

This expression is of the form:

$$F = -kx,$$

where the force constant is given by $k = mg/L$ and the displacement is given by $x = s$. For angles less than about 15°, the restoring force is directly proportional to the displacement, and the simple pendulum is a simple harmonic oscillator. Using this equation, we can find the period of a pendulum for amplitudes less than about 15°. For the simple pendulum:

$$T = 2\pi\sqrt{\frac{m}{k}} = 2\pi\sqrt{\frac{m}{\frac{mg}{L}}}$$

Thus,

$$T = 2\pi\sqrt{\frac{L}{g}}$$

for the period of a simple pendulum. This result is interesting because of its simplicity. The only things that affect the period of a simple pendulum are its length and the acceleration due to gravity. The period is completely independent of other factors, such as mass. As with simple harmonic oscillators, the period $T$ for a pendulum is nearly independent of amplitude, especially if $\theta$ is less than about $15^0$. Even simple pendulum clocks can be finely adjusted and accurate. Note the dependence of $T$ on $g$. If the length of a pendulum is precisely known, it can actually be used to measure the acceleration due to gravity.

**Sample Problem 6.3.1 — Measuring *g* with a Pendulum**

What is the acceleration due to gravity in a region where a simple pendulum having a length 75.000 cm has a period of 1.7357 s?

| What to Think About | How to Do It |
|---|---|
| 1. Assume angle of deflection is less than 15°. | |
| 2. Square $T = 2\pi\sqrt{\frac{L}{g}}$ and solve for *g*. | $g = 4\pi^2 \frac{L}{T^2}$ |
| 3. Substitute known values into the new equation. | $g = 4\pi^2 \frac{0.75000 m}{(1.7357 s)^2}$ |
| 4. Calculate to find *g*. | |
| **Final Thoughts**<br>This method for determining *g* can be very accurate. This is why length and period are given to five digits in this example. For the precision of the approximation $\sin\theta \approx \theta$ to be better than the precision of the pendulum length and period, the maximum displacement angle should be kept below about 0.50°. | $g = 9.8281 \, m/s^2$ |

**Practice Problems 6.3.1 — Simple Pendulum and Frequency**

1. Determine the frequency of oscillation for a string pendulum of length 10 cm.

## 6.3 Review Questions

1. What is the length in centimeters of a simple pendulum whose period is 1.0 s?

2. Find the frequency of a simple pendulum 20 cm long.

3. A string pendulum of length 90 cm has a 50 gram mass attached to the end of the string. Determine the period of the pendulum, and if the 50 gram mass is replaced with a 100 gram mass will the period of the pendulum increase, decrease or remain the same. Explain.

4. A pendulum 100 cm long oscillates 30 times per minute in a certain location. What is the value of g at this location?

5. A string pendulum clock on Earth swings back and forth with a period of 1 s. If the same pendulum clock is onboard the International Space Station which is free-falling towards the Earth, will the pendulum clock have a period which is greater, less, the same, or none of the above? Explain.

6. A simple pendulum has a period of oscillation of 1.2 seconds on Earth. The same pendulum is taken to the moon where the gravity is one-sixth that of the Earth's gravity. Qualitatively Explain how the diminished gravity affects the period and frequency of the pendulum. Quantitatively determine the period and frequency of the pendulum on the moon.

# 6.4 Energy and the Simple Harmonic Oscillator

## Warm Up

Observe the spring-pulley-mass system as shown below. When a mass M is at rest what forces act upon it? Sketch the free body diagram. What types of energy are stored in "the system"?

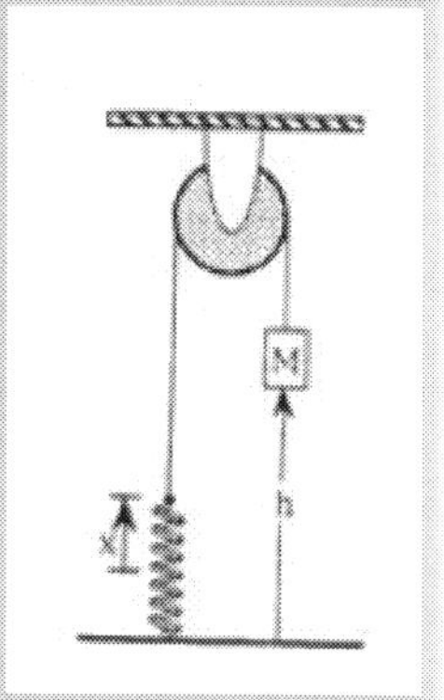


---

If you were to slightly raise the mass M and release it, causing the system to oscillate in SHM, what types of energy are present when the system oscillates? Qualitatively explain how mechanical energy is the system is conserved as energy is transformed from one form to another.

---

---

### Simple Harmonic Oscillator

To study the energy of a simple harmonic oscillator, we first consider all the forms of energy it can have. We know from section 6.1, Hooke's Law:Stress and Strain Revisited, the energy stored in the deformation of a simple harmonic oscillator is a form of potential energy given by:

$$PE_{el} = \tfrac{1}{2} kx^2$$

Because a simple harmonic oscillator has no dissipative forces, the other important form of energy is kinetic energy KE. Conservation of energy for these two forms is

$$KE + PE_{el} = \text{constant}$$

Or

$$\tfrac{1}{2} mv^2 + \tfrac{1}{2} kx^2 = \text{constant}$$

This statement of conservation of energy is valid for all simple harmonic oscillators, including ones where the gravitational force plays a role. Namely, for a simple pendulum we replace the velocity with $v = L\omega$, the spring constant with $k = mg/L$, and the displacement term with $x = L\theta$. Thus

$$\tfrac{1}{2} mL^2 \omega^2 + \tfrac{1}{2} mgL\theta^2 = \text{constant}$$

In the case of undamped simple harmonic motion, the energy oscillates back and forth between kinetic and potential, going completely from one to the other as the system oscillates. So for the simple example of an object on a frictionless surface attached to a spring, as shown again in Figure 6.4.1, the motion starts with all of the energy stored in the spring. As the object starts to move, the elastic potential energy is converted to kinetic energy, becoming entirely kinetic energy at the equilibrium position. It is then converted back into elastic potential energy by the spring, the velocity becomes zero when the kinetic energy is completely converted, and so on. This concept provides extra insight here and in later applications of simple harmonic motion, such as alternating current circuits.

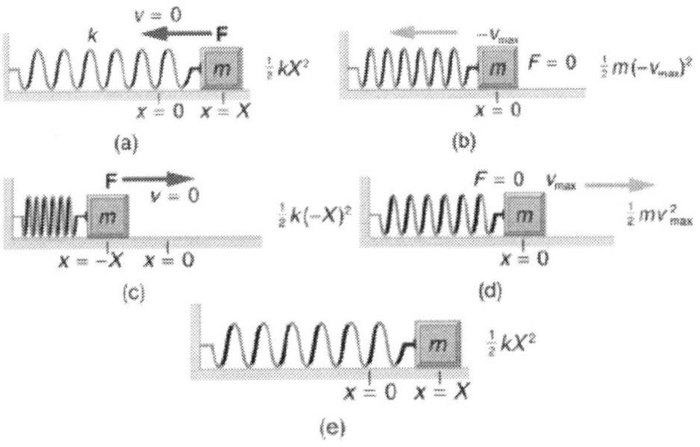


**Figure 6.4.1** *The transformation of energy in simple harmonic motion is illustrated for an object attached to a spring on a frictionless surface.*

The conservation of energy principle can be used to derive an expression for velocity $v$. If we start our simple harmonic motion with zero velocity and maximum displacement ( $x = X$ ), then the total energy is

$$\frac{1}{2} kX^2$$

This total energy is constant and is shifted back and forth between kinetic energy and potential energy, at most times being shared by each. The conservation of energy for this system in equation form is thus:

$$\frac{1}{2} mv^2 + \frac{1}{2} kx^2 = \frac{1}{2} kX^2$$

Solving this equation for v yields:

$$v = \pm\sqrt{\frac{k}{m}(X^2 - x^2)}$$

Manipulating this expression algebraically gives:

$$v = \pm\sqrt{\frac{k}{m}}X\sqrt{1-\frac{x^2}{X^2}}$$

and so

$$v = \pm v_{\max}\sqrt{1-\frac{x^2}{X^2}}$$

where

$$v_{\max} = \sqrt{\frac{k}{m}}X$$

From this expression, we see that the velocity is a maximum ($v_{max}$) at $x = 0$, as stated earlier in $v(t) = -v_{max}\sin\frac{2\pi t}{T}$

Notice that the maximum velocity depends on three factors. Maximum velocity is directly proportional to amplitude. As you might guess, the greater the maximum displacement the greater the maximum velocity. Maximum velocity is also greater for stiffer systems, because they exert greater force for the same displacement. This observation is seen in the expression for $v_{max}$; it is proportional to the square root of the force constant *k*. Finally, the maximum velocity is smaller for objects that have larger masses, because the maximum velocity is inversely proportional to the square root of *m*. For a given force, objects that have large masses accelerate more slowly.

A similar calculation for the simple pendulum produces a similar result, namely:

$$\omega_{max} = \sqrt{\frac{g}{L}}\theta_{max}$$

**Sample Problem 6.4.1 — Determine the Maximum Speed of an Oscillating System: A Bumpy Road**

Suppose that a car is 900 kg and has a suspension system that has a force constant $k = 6.53 \times 10^4$ N/m. The car hits a bump and bounces with an amplitude of 0.100 m. What is its maximum vertical velocity if you assume no damping occurs?

| What to Think About | How to Do It |
|---|---|
| 1. We can use the expression for $v_{max}$ given in $v_{max} = \sqrt{\frac{k}{m}}X$ to determine the maximum vertical velocity | $v_{max} = \sqrt{\frac{k}{m}}X$ <br> $v_{max} = \sqrt{\frac{6.53 \times 10^4 \text{ N/m}}{900 \text{ kg}}}(0.100 \text{ m})$ |
| 2. Find $v_{max}$ | $v_{max} = 0.852 \text{ m/s}$ |

## Practice Problems 6.4.1 — Maximum Speed of an Oscillating System

1. A 10 kg block attached to the end of a spring that is hung from the ceiling and causes the spring to stretch 20 cm. The block is then pulled down an extra 5.0 cm and released causing the mass-spring system to oscillate up and down. What is the maximum speed of the block as it passes through the equilibrium position?

2. A long rope with a heavy ball tied to its end is attached to the ceiling. The ball-pendulum is pulled back 10 degrees from vertical and released. When the ball reaches its lowest point it has a speed of 2.0 m/s. Determine the length of the rope and the period of oscillation for this ball-pendulum system? For an extra challenge choose another angle (less than 15 degrees) and show that the period remains the same even though the height *h* and velocity *v* differ.

3. Consider the mass-pulley-spring system shown below:

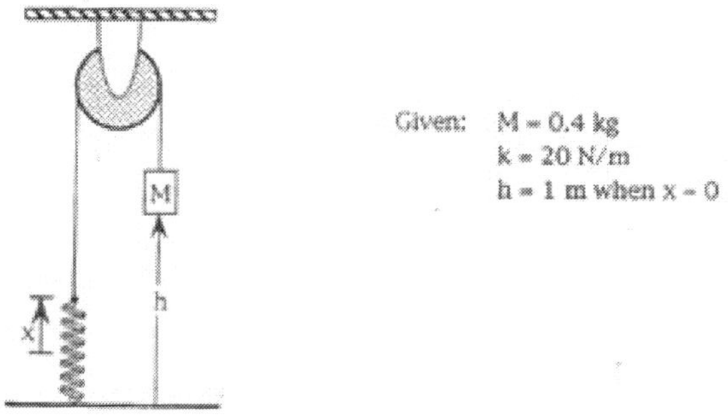


(a) What are the values of "*x*" and "*h*" when the system is in equilibrium?

(b) *M* is lifted to a height of 1 m and then dropped. Find its speed as it passes through the equilibrium point.

(c) As *M* oscillates (vibrates) about the EQ position find the maximum value of *x*.

## Mass Attached to Spring

Consider a mass *m* attached to a spring, with spring constant *k*, fixed to a wall. When the mass is displaced from its equilibrium position and released, the mass undergoes simple harmonic motion. The spring exerts a force $F = -kv$ on the mass. The potential energy of the system is stored in the spring. It will be zero when the spring is in the equilibrium position. All the internal energy exists in the form of kinetic energy, given by $KE = ½mv^2$. As the system oscillates, which means that the spring compresses and expands, there is a change in the structure of the system and a corresponding change in its internal energy. Its kinetic energy is converted to potential energy and vice versa. This occurs at an equal rate, which means that a loss of kinetic energy yields a gain in potential energy, thus preserving the work-energy theorem and the law of conservation of energy.

### Quick Check

1. Why does it hurt more if your hand is snapped with a ruler than with a loose spring, even if the displacement of each system is equal?

2. You are observing a simple harmonic oscillator. Identify one way you could decrease the maximum velocity of the system.

## 6.4 Review Questions

1. A toy pistol uses a spring of force constant 100 N/m to propel an 8.00 gram rubber dart. If the spring is compressed by 5.00 cm, what is the rubber dart's maximum velocity?

2. A toy pistol uses a spring of force constant 100 N/m to propel an 8.00 gram rubber dart. If the spring is compressed by 10.0 cm and the dart is fired straight up into the air, how high will the dart go?

3. A spring with a force constant *K* is compressed by 8 cm. A 50 gram ball is placed against the end of the spring, which is then released and fires the ball horizontally at a speed of 12 m/s. Determine the spring constant.

4. A 500 gram mass falls directly onto a vertical spring from a height of 2.00 m, causing the spring to compress 10.0 cm. Determine the spring constant.

5. A spring is compressed 25 cm and stores 50 J of elastic potential energy. What compression would result in an elastic potential energy of 100 J?

6. A 60 kg bungee jumper jumps from a bridge. She is tied to a bungee cord that is 12 m long when unstretched, and she falls a total of 31 m relative to the bridge. (a) Calculate the spring constant of the bungee cord. (b) Assume that Hooke's law applies and calculate the maximum upward acceleration experienced by the jumper when she is at maximum displacement.

# Chapter 6 Conceptual Review Questions

1. Pendulum clocks are made to run at the correct rate by adjusting the pendulum's length. Suppose you move from one city to another where the acceleration due to gravity is slightly greater, taking your pendulum clock with you, will you have to lengthen or shorten the pendulum to keep the correct time, other factors remaining constant? Explain your answer.

2. An object of mass $M$ oscillates on the end of a vertical spring. What change in mass would cause the frequency of the harmonic oscillator to double? Express your answer in terms of $M$.

3. A pendulum clock on Earth swings back and forth with a period of $T$. If the pendulum clock is ascending in an elevator at a constant speed, will the period be larger, smaller, or stay the same. Explain.

4. A ball of mass m is attached to a string of length $L$ forming a simple pendulum. The pendulum ball is raised to a height of 50 cm above its lowest point and released. It oscillated with a period $T$ and maximum velocity $v$ at the lowest point in its swing. How would the period and maximum velocity be affected if the pendulum balls initial height was doubled? Express your answers in terms of $T$ and $v$.

5. An object of mass $m$ is attached to a horizontal spring, and stretched a distance $x$ from equilibrium and release, causing the mass-spring system to oscillate on a frictionless surface with period $T$. The experiment is repeated with a mass of 4 m. What is the new period of oscillation in terms of $T$?

# Chapter 6 Review Questions

1. A lamp is suspended from a high ceiling with a cable that is 4 m long. Find its period and frequency of oscillation when it is set into motion as a simple. pendulum.

2. A 100 gram mass is suspended from a vertical spring whose spring constant is 50 N/m. Calculate how much the spring stretches as it settles to an equilibrium position.

3. A 200 gram mass is attached to a vertical spring with spring constant 12 N/m and the system is in oscillation. What length of pendulum would have the same frequency as the mass-spring system?

4. Two identical springs, each with spring constant 20 N/m, are joined together in parallel. determine the effective spring constant, and the period of oscillation when a 500 gram mass is attached to both springs and the system is oscillating.

5. A pendulum of length 50.0 cm has the same period of oscillation as a nearby mass-spring system. The mass attached to the spring is 0.500 kg. Determine the spring constant.

6. Two identical springs, each with a spring constant 10.0 N/m are joined together in series and attached to the ceiling. A 200 gram mass is attached to the springs. Determine the effective spring constant of the two-spring system, and the frequency of oscillation when a 100 gram mass is attached to the springs and the system is in oscillation.

7. A 4 kg mass attached to a spring is observed to oscillate with a period of 2 seconds. What is the period of oscillation if a 6 kg mass is attached to the spring?

8. A small ball is floating in a swimming pool. A student gently pushes the ball 2.00 cm below its equilibrium position and releases it, causing the ball to bob up and down with a period 0f 0.750 s.

(a) Sketch the position-time graph for the ball which oscillates in SHM. (When t = 0, x = -2.00 cm). Show one complete oscillation.

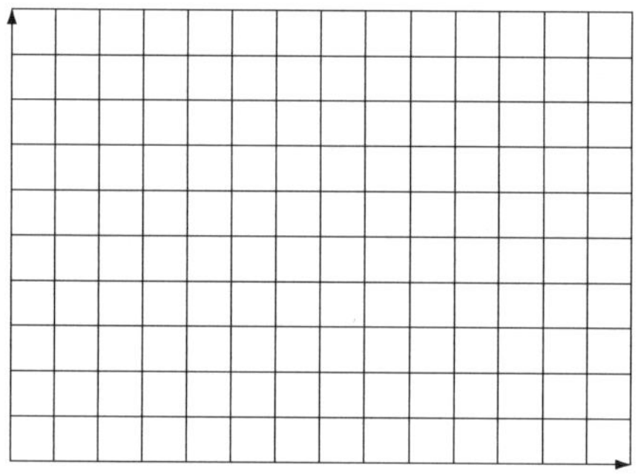

(b) Calculate the position of the ball when t = ¼ T

(c) Calculate the position of the ball when t = ½ T

(d) Calculate the position of the ball when t = ¾ T

9. A 800 gram mass is attached to a horizontal spring. The mass-spring system is set into simple harmonic motion. The displacement *x* of the object as a function of time is shown graphically.

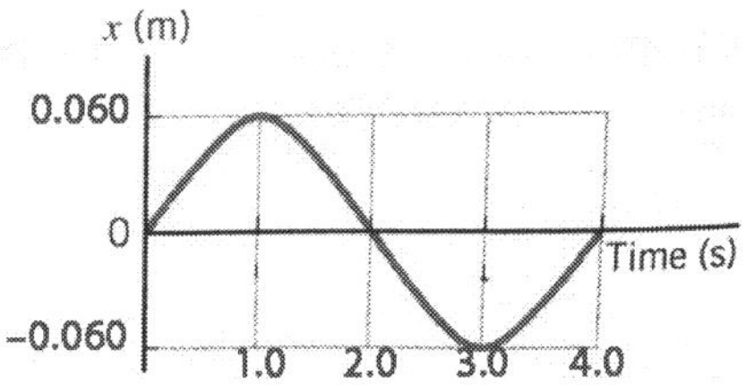


(a) Determine the amplitude of oscillation

(b) Angular frequency (angular velocity)

(c) The spring constant

(d) The speed of the block when $t = 1.0$ s

(e) The acceleration of the block when $t = 1.0$ s

10. A simple pendulum as a period of 5 seconds on Earth. It is brought to Mars where the gravity is 38% of the Earth's gravity. What will be the pendulum's period on Mars?

11. Describe an experiment that uses a simple pendulum to determine the acceleration due to gravity *g* in your own locale. Cut a piece of a string or dental floss so that it is about 1 m long. Attach a small object of high density to the end of the string (for example, a metal nut or a car key). Starting at an angle of less than $15^0$, allow the pendulum to swing and measure the pendulum's period for 10 oscillations using a stopwatch. Calculate *g*. How accurate is this measurement? How might it be improved?

# 7 Torque and Rotational Motion

This chapter focuses on the following AP Physics 1 Big Ideas from the College Board:

**BIG IDEA 3:** The interactions of an object with other objects can be described by forces.

**BIG IDEA 4:** Interactions between systems can result in changes in those systems.

**BIG IDEA 5:** Changes that occur as a result of interactions are constrained by conservation laws.

---

By the end of this chapter, you should know the meaning of these **key terms**:

- angular acceleration
- angular momentum
- angular velocity
- change in angular rotation
- change in angular velocity
- change in angular momentum
- moment of inertia
- rotational kinetic energy
- tangential acceleration

---

By the end of this chapter, you should be able to use and know when to use the following formulae:

$$\theta = \frac{x}{r} \qquad \omega = \frac{v}{r}$$

$$\alpha = \frac{a_t}{r} \qquad \theta = \omega t$$

$$\omega = \omega_o + \alpha t \qquad \theta = \omega_0 + \tfrac{1}{2}\alpha t^2$$

$$\omega^2 = \omega_0 + 2\alpha\theta \qquad \alpha = \frac{(\text{net } \tau)}{I}$$

$$KE_{rot} = \frac{1}{2} I\omega^2 \qquad \text{net } \tau = \frac{\Delta L}{\Delta t}$$

*Thinking of a tornado conjures up images of raw destructive power. Tornadoes blow houses away as if they were made of paper and have been known to pierce tree trunks with pieces of straw. They descend from clouds in funnel-like shapes that spin violently, particularly at the bottom where they are most narrow, producing winds as high as 500 km/h*

# 7.1 Torque

## Warm Up

Of the three pictures hanging on a wall, which one has the greatest tension force in the two wires? Explain your reasoning.

______________________________________________

______________________________________________

______________________________________________

### First Condition for Static Equilibrium

You have already observed many situations where several forces acted on a body, yet the body did not move. If a body is at rest, and there are two or more forces acting on it, then the forces acting on the object must have a resultant of zero. Another way of saying this is that the *net force is zero*.

A trivial example of an object having two forces acting on it but a net force of zero is a pen sitting on a flat desk. The force of gravity pulls down on the pen, but it does not accelerate. The table exerts an equal force upward on the pen, so that the net force on the pen is zero.

If the net force on a body is zero, and the body is not moving, it is said to be in a state of **static equilibrium.** In physics, the subject of **statics** deals with the calculation of forces acting on bodies that are in static equilibrium.

**First Condition for Static Equilibrium or Translational Equilibrium**
For a body to be in static equilibrium, the vector sum of all the forces on it must be zero.

$$\vec{F} = 0$$

The sum of the components of *F* must also be zero.

For forces acting in two dimensions,

$$\vec{F}_x = 0 \text{ and } \vec{F}_y = 0$$

## Applications of Static Equilibrium

When you work with force vectors in static equilibrium the masses do not move. By measuring the angles between the masses, you constructed a vector diagram that looks something like the one in Figure 7.1.1(a). In the Figure, $\vec{F}_1 = 4.0$ N, $\vec{F}_2 = 5.0$ N, and $\vec{F}_3 = 3.0$ N. By adding the force vectors together, you can form a triangle that confirms the structure was in static equilibrium like in Figure 7.1.1(b).

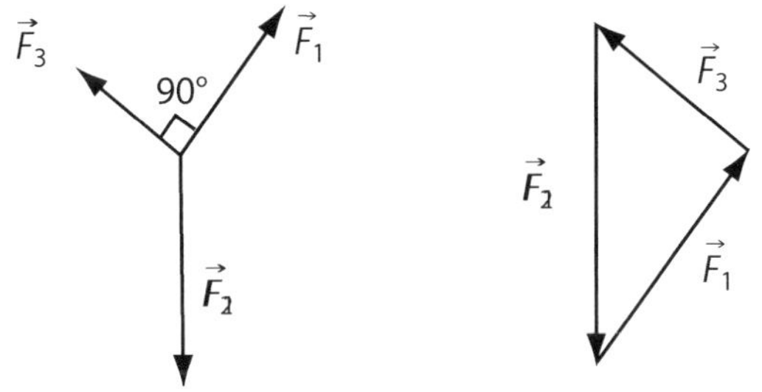


$$\Sigma\vec{F} = 0$$
$$\text{or } \vec{F}_1 + \vec{F}_2 + \vec{F}_3 = 0$$

(a) (b)

**Figure 7.1.1** *Adding the force vectors confirmed that the structure was in static equilibrium.*

Another way to solve this problem is to find the *x* component and *y* component of each vector and the sum the *x* and *y* components. For the structure to be in equilibrium, both sets of components sum to zero.

First, resolve each vector into its *x* and *y* components as shown in Table 7.1.1. Using our knowledge of trigonometric ratios and geometry, we find the angle of $\vec{F}_1$ and $\vec{F}_3$ to the horizontal to be 53° and 37°. Now each vector can be resolved into *x* and *y* components. Remember to keep track of the sign of each vector. In this problem, the right direction and up are to be taken as positive.

**Table 7.1.1** *Force Vector Components*

| | ***x* component** | ***y* component** | |
|---|---|---|---|
| $\vec{F}_1$ | $F_{1x} = F_1 \cos 53°$ | $F_{1y} = F_1 \sin 53°$ | 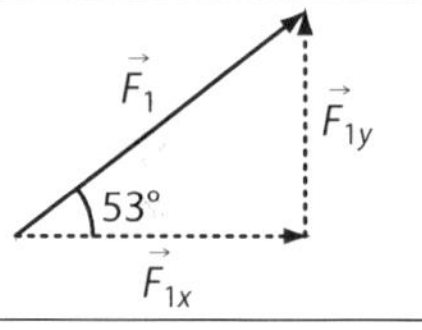  |
| $\vec{F}_2$ | No *x component* | $-F_{2y} = -mg$ | 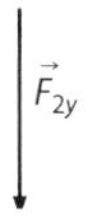  |
| $\vec{F}_3$ | $-F_{3x} = -F_3 \cos 37°$ | $F_{3y} = F_3 \sin 37°$ | 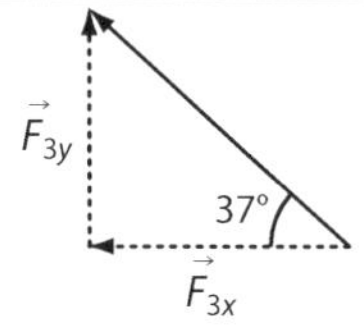  |
| Sum | $F_x = F_{1x} + F_{3x} = 0$<br>$F_x = F_1 \cos 53° + (-F_3 \cos 37°)$<br>$F_x = 4.0 \cos 53° + (-3.0 \cos 37°)$<br>$F_x = 0$ | $F_y = F_{1y} + F_{2y} + F_{3y} = 0$<br>$F_y = F_1 \sin 53° + (-mg) + F_3 \sin 37°$<br>$F_y = 4.0 \sin 53° + (-5.0) + 3.0 \sin 37°$<br>$F_y = 0$ | |

Based on the sum of each component, we can conclude that the first condition of static equilibrium has been met. The structure is said to be in *translational static equilibrium*, which means no acceleration or motion is occurring.

### Sample Problem 7.1.1 — Static Equilibrium

A picture with a mass of 4.00 kg hangs on a wall (Figure 10.1.2). What are the magnitudes of the tension forces in the wires?

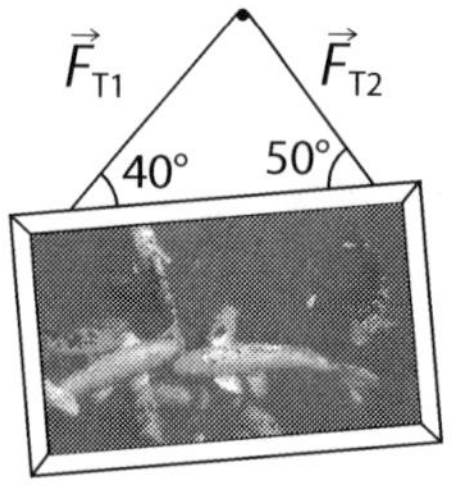


**Figure 10.1.2**

**What to Think About**

1. Represent the problem with a diagram to show forces (Figure 7.1.3).
2. All the forces are acting on one point, so this is a translational static equilibrium problem.
3. Find the *x* and *y* components of each vector.
4. Remember that the *x* and y components must sum to zero. Solve to find $F_T$.

NOTE: There are two variables so you will need two equations and then solve both using the substitution method you learned in Math class.

**How to Do It**

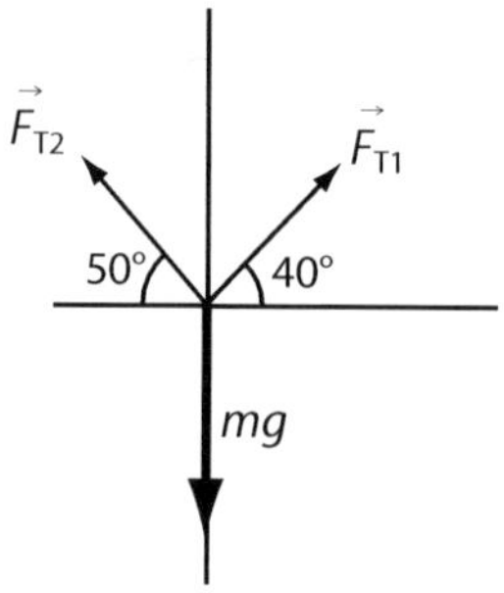


**Figure 7.1.3**

| | *x* | *y* |
|---|---|---|
| $F_{T1}$ | $\cos 40° = \frac{F_{1x}}{F_{T1}}$ | $\sin 40° = \frac{F_{1y}}{F_{T1}}$ |
| $F_{T2}$ | $-\cos 50° = \frac{F_{2x}}{F_{T2}}$ | $\sin 50° = \frac{F_{2y}}{F_{T2}}$ |
| $F_{T3}$ | | $F_3 = -mg$ |

$F = 0$

$F_{T1x} = F_{T2x}$

$F_{T2}\cos 50° = F_{T1}\cos 40°$

$0.643F_{T2} = 0.766F_{T1}$

$F_{T1} = \dfrac{0.643F_{T2}}{0.766}$

$F = 0$

$F_{T1y} + F_{T2y} = F_{T3}$

$F_{T1}\sin 40° + F_{T2}\sin 50° = mg$

$0.643F_{T1} + 0.766F_{T2} = mg$

$(0.643)\dfrac{0.643F_{T2}}{0.766} + 0.766F_{T2} = mg$

$F_{T2} = 30.0 \text{ N}$

Use this answer to solve for $F_{T1}$:

$F_{T1} = 25.2 \text{ N}$

## Practice Problems 7.1.1 — Static Equilibrium

1. Two rugby players pull on a ball in the directions shown in Figure 10.1.4. What is the *magnitude* of the force that must be exerted by a third player, to achieve translational static equilibrium of the ball?

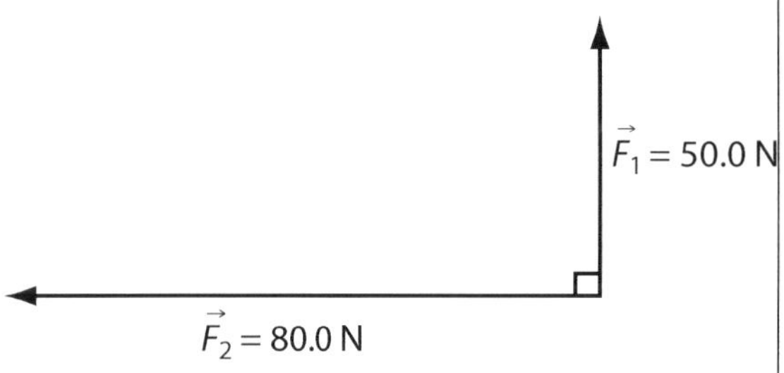


**Figure 7.1.4**

2. A 50.0 kg mass is supported by a rope. When a horizontal force is used to hold the mass at an angle $\theta$ with the vertical, the tension in the rope is 850.0 N. What is angle $\theta$?

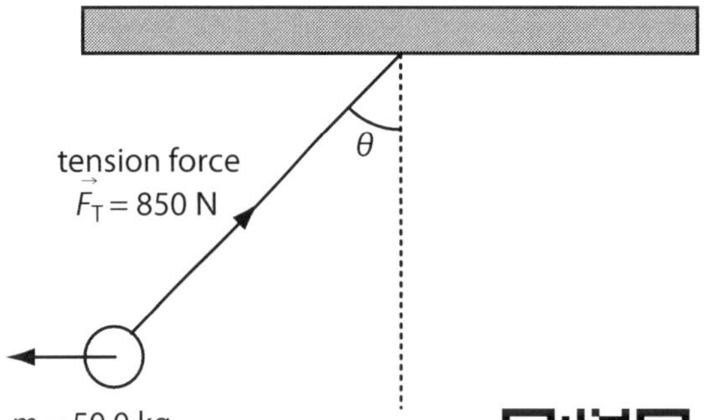


**Figure 7.1.5**

3. (a) A traffic light is suspended midway between two supports, as shown in Figure 7.1.6. If the mass of the traffic light is 60.0 kg, what is the tension in the cord between A and B?

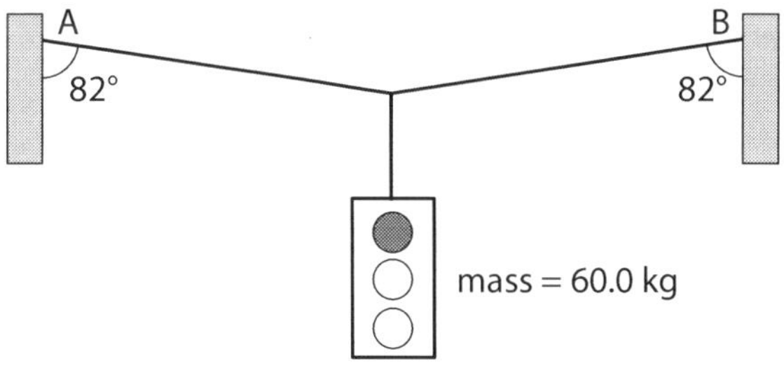


**Figure 7.1.6**

(b) Explain why it is not possible to have the cord absolutely straight between the two supports in this static equilibrium situation.

## Second Condition for Static Equilibrium or Rotational Equilibrium

In this chapter, you have encountered situations where static equilibrium exists because the net force was zero. In these situations, all the forces acted through one point. What if the forces do NOT act through the same point?

## Torque

In Figure 7.1.7, there are two forces, equal in magnitude, acting on a uniform bar. The forces act in opposite directions, and they act at *different* points on the bar. The net force is zero because the forces are equal but opposite in direction, *but the bar is not in static equilibrium.* Obviously, the bar would rotate about its mid-point. When forces on the same body do not act through the same point, there must be another condition required for static equilibrium. Investigation 7.1 looks at this "extra" requirement. First, here are some necessary definitions.

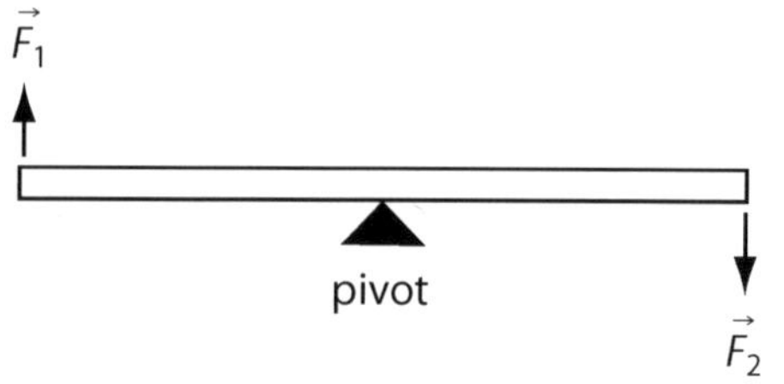


**Figure 7.1.7** *The two forces acting on the bar are equal in magnitude but acting in opposite directions.*

In Figure 7.1.8, a force $\vec{F}$ is exerted at a distance $\ell$ from the **pivot** or **fulcrum**. The product of a force $\vec{F}$ and its distance $\ell$ from the fulcrum, measured perpendicular to the direction of the force vector, is called the **torque** ($\tau$) of that force about the pivot. The distance $\ell$ is called the **lever arm**.

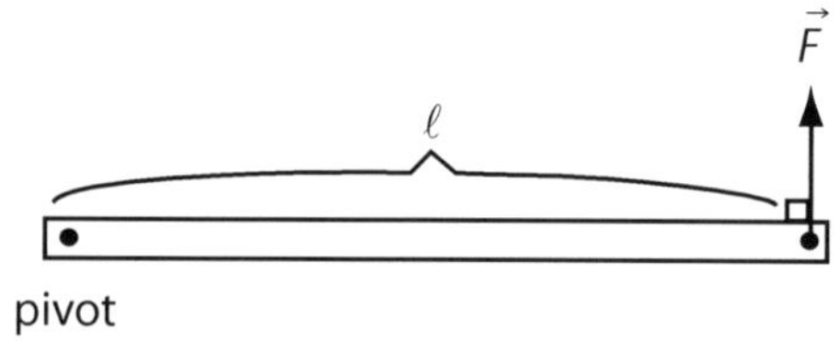


**Figure 7.1.8** *The torque is calculated by multiplying a force $\vec{F}$ by its distance $\ell$ from the pivot.*

The force causing a torque is not always perpendicular to the line joining the pivot to the point where the force is applied. Figure 7.3.9 shows an example of this. Here, the line along which the force acts is at an angle $\theta$ to the rod. The force is applied at a distance $\ell$ from the pivot, but the distance you must use to calculate torque ($\tau$) is the *perpendicular* distance from the pivot to the line of action of the force. This distance is labeled $\ell_\perp$ in Figure 7.1.9.

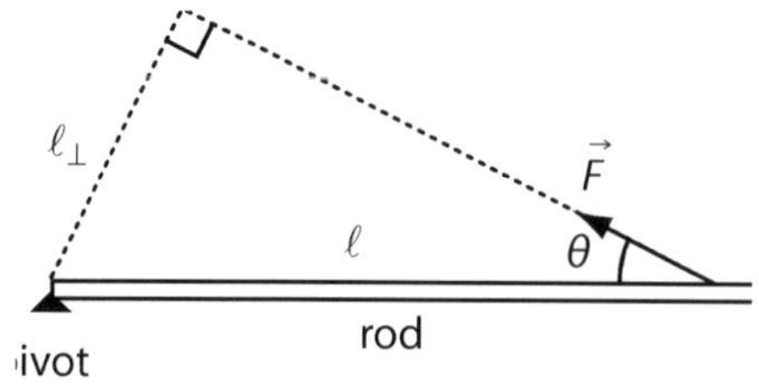


The torque due to force $\vec{F}$ is $\tau = \vec{F} \cdot \ell_\perp$ or $\tau = \vec{F} \cdot \ell \cdot \sin\theta$

**Figure 7.1.9** *The force causing a torque is not always perpendicular.*

Another way of working out the same problem is to use the lever arm $\ell$ "as is," but use the component of $\vec{F}$ *in a direction perpendicular to the rod*, as shown in Figure 7.1.10. This component is labeled $\vec{F}_{\perp}$.

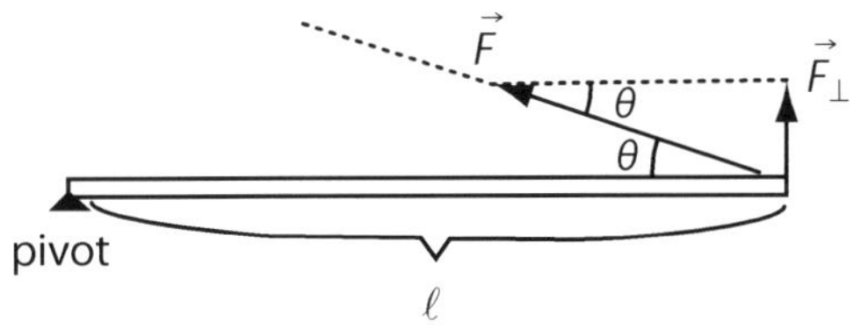


**Figure 7.1.10** *A component of $\vec{F}$ perpendicular to the rod can be used to calculate torque.*

In Figure 7.1.10, the torque can be calculated as shown below.

$$\tau = \vec{F}_{\perp} \cdot \ell = [\vec{F} \cdot \sin\theta] \cdot \ell = \vec{F} \cdot \ell \cdot \sin\theta$$

As you can see, this approach gives the same answer as the first method, used in Figure 7.1.10.

## Quick Check

1. What is the length of a beam that has a pivot at one end and a 10.0 N force pulling the beam in a clockwise direction so that a torque of 50.0 Nm is produced?

2. A brother and sister are on a teeter-totter at a local park. The brother is twice the weight of his sister. Where should he sit relative to the pivot so that the teeter-totter balances?

3. The rod in Figure 7.1.9 has a length of 2.5 m. A 60.0 N force is exerted at an angle of 30° to the rod, which tends to rotate in an *counterclockwise* direction. Calculate the torque produced by the force.

## Centre of Gravity

Every molecule of wood in the metre stick in Figure 7.1.11 has mass and therefore experiences a force due to gravity. The figure shows a few sample vectors that represent the force of gravity on individual molecules making up the wood. The resultant of all these force vectors would be the total force of gravity on the metre stick. Where would the resultant force appear to act?

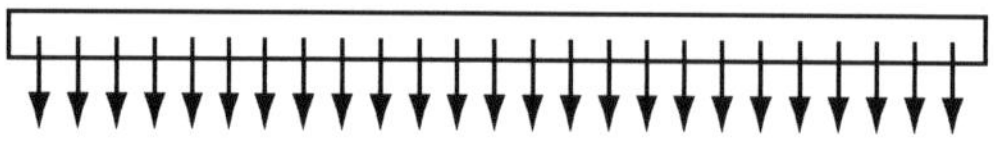


**Figure 7.1.11** *The force of gravity acts on every part of the metre stick.*

You know from experience that there is a point within any rigid body where a single upward force can be used to balance the force of gravity on the body without causing any rotation of the body. For example, if you hold a metre stick with the tip of your finger at the mid-point of the uniform stick, the metre stick will remain in static equilibrium. (It will not move up, down, or sideways, and it will have no tendency to rotate.)

There is a single point in a body where the force of gravity may be considered to act. This point is called the **centre of gravity** of the body. A body supported at its centre of gravity by a force equal to the force of gravity on the body (but in the opposite direction) will experience no translational or rotational motion as a result of the supporting force.

Figure 7.1.12 shows four objects with differing shapes. The label "CG" indicates the probable location of the centre of gravity. Notice that the CG may be *outside* the solid part of the object, as is the case with the drinking glass.

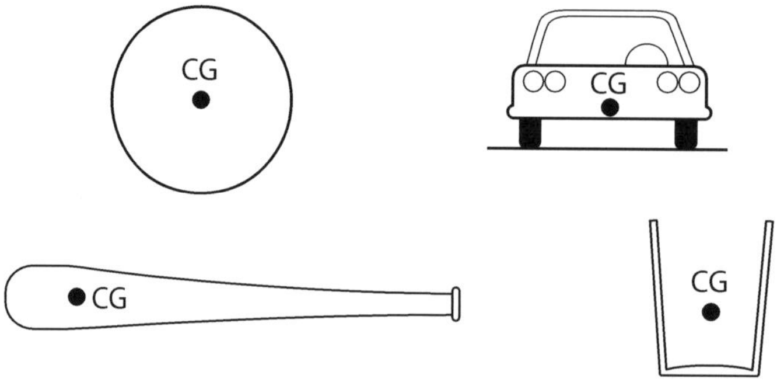


**Figure 7.1.12** *Examples of the location of the centre of gravity (CG) in different objects.*

## Centre of Mass

The **centre of mass** of an object is the point where the mass of the object might be considered to be concentrated for the purpose of calculation. For most situations, the centre of mass is in the same place as the centre of gravity. An exception would be when the gravitational field over the object being considered is non-uniform. This would have to be a very large object! The centre of mass of a large spherical planet would be at the centre of the planet, if its mass is uniformly distributed. Where would you expect the centre of mass of the Earth-Moon system to be located?

Earlier in this chapter, it was shown that for a body to be in translational static equilibrium, the vector sum of all the forces on it must be zero. This means that the sum of all the forces acting up must equal the sum of all the forces acting down. The sum of all the forces acting to the left must equal the sum of all the forces acting to the right. No matter how you look at it, the first condition for static equilibrium is:

$$\Sigma \vec{F} = 0$$

If you completed Investigation 7.1, you found that for rotational equilibrium, a second requirement must be met. Not only must the vector sum of the forces on a body be zero, but also the sum of all the clockwise torques must equal the sum of all the counterclockwise torques.

**Second Condition for Static Equilibrium**

$$\Sigma \tau_{\text{clockwise}} = \Sigma \tau_{\text{counterclockwise}}$$

If a torque which tends to make an object rotate counterclockwise is assigned a positive (+) value, and a clockwise torque is assigned a negative (–) value, then the second condition for static equilibrium can be written this way:

$$\Sigma \tau = 0$$

# 7.1 Review Questions

1. What force $\vec{F}_1$ is needed to balance the beam in the diagram below?

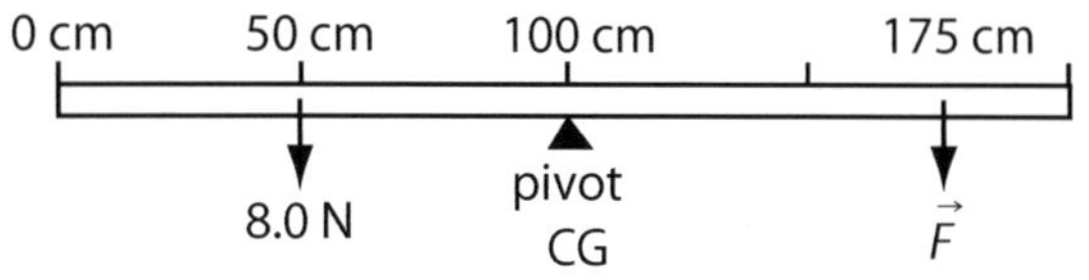


2. How far from the pivot must the 64 N object be placed to balance the beam in the diagram below?

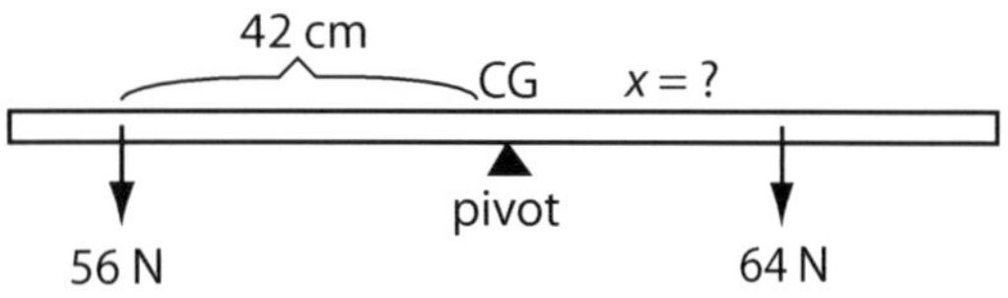


3. What upward force $\vec{F}_1$ is needed to achieve rotational equilibrium in the diagram below?

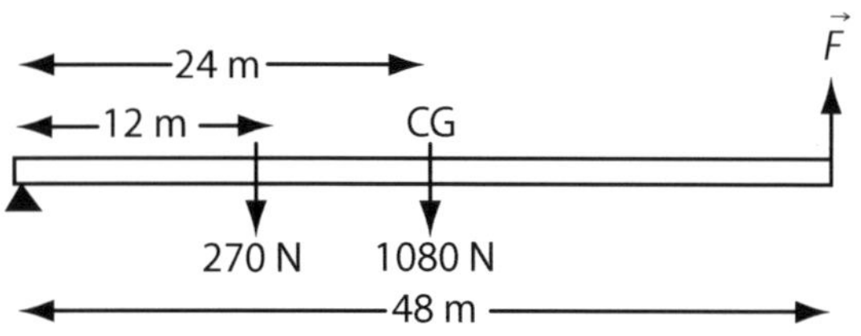


4. The force of gravity on the bridge in the diagram below is $9.60 \times 10^5$ N. What upward force must be exerted at end Q to support the bridge and the truck, if the force of gravity on the truck is $4.80 \times 10^4$ N? **Hint:** Treat the bridge as if it were a lever with an imaginary pivot at P. What torques tend to rotate the "lever" about pivot P?

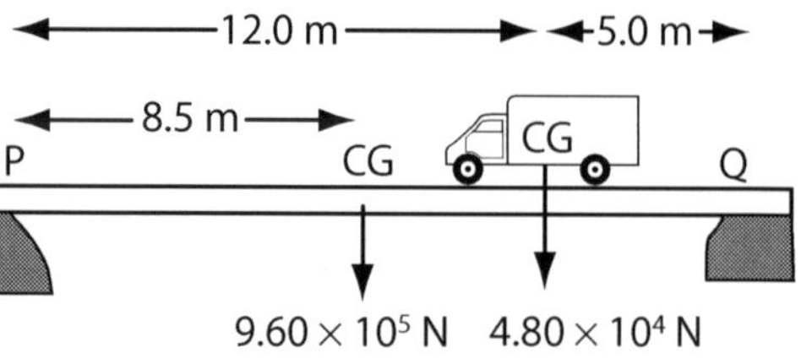


5. A small 42.0 N sign is suspended from the end of a hinged rod, which is 2.40 m long and uniform in shape as shown in the diagram below. What tension force exists in the rope holding up both the rod and the sign? The rope makes an angle of 60° with the 36.0 N rod.

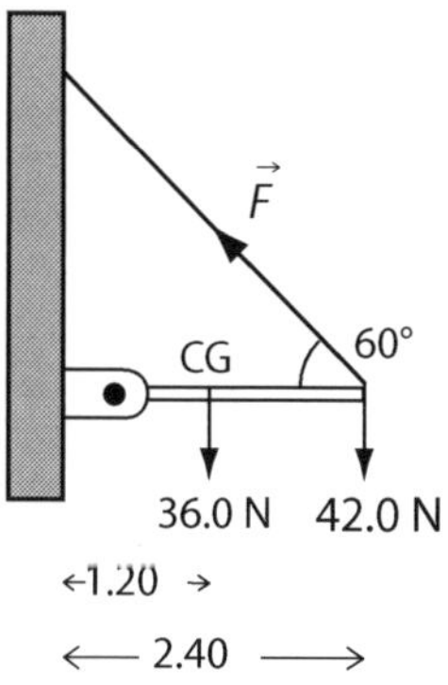

# 7.2 Rotational Motion

## Warm Up

Find a circular object like a vinyl record or cut a small piece of string of length (r) and use it to trace out a circle of radius r. Then take the cut piece of string and lay it on the outer edge of the circle. Approximately how many pieces string would it take to cover the entire circumference of the circle? What is the formula for the circumference of a circle?

________________________________________

________________________________________

________________________________________

Why do tornados spin? And why do tornados spin so rapidly? The answer is related to the idea of rotation. The air masses that produce tornados are themselves rotating, and when the radii of the air masses decrease, their rate of rotation increases. An ice skater increases her spin in an exactly analogous manner, as seen in Figure 7.2.1. The skater starts her rotation with outstretched limbs and increases her rate of spin by pulling them in toward her body. The same physics describes the exhilarating spin of a skater and the wrenching force of a tornado. They both involve a rotating motion.

**Figure 7.2.1** *This figure skater increases her rate of spin by pulling her arms and her extended leg closer to her axis of rotation. (credit: Luu, Wikimedia Commons)*

### Radians

In Kinematics, we studied motion along a straight line and introduced such concepts as displacement, velocity, and acceleration. We begin the study the motion of rotating objects by defining three angular quantities needed to describe rotational motion: rotational angle, arc length and radius of curvature. The three quantities will give the unit radians which is used to measure rotation angle.

When objects rotate about some axis—for example, when the DVD in Figure 7.2.2 rotates about its center—each point in the object follows a circular arc. Consider a line from the center of the DVD to its edge. Each pit used to record sound along this line moves through the same angle in the same amount of time. The rotation angle is the amount of rotation and is analogous to linear distance. We define the rotation angle $\Delta\theta$ to be the ratio of the arc length to the radius of curvature:

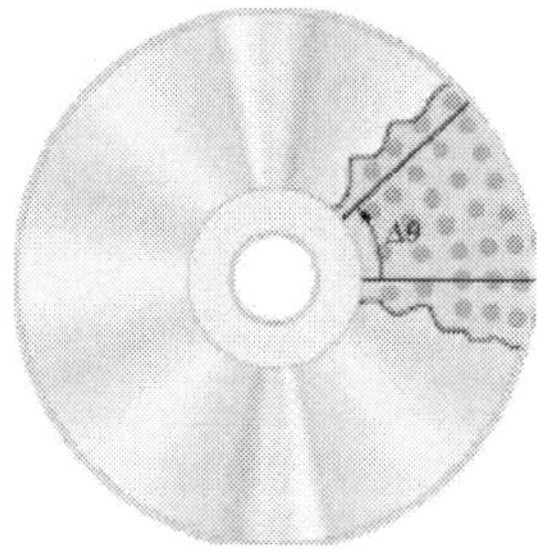


**Figure 7.2.2** *All points on a DVD travel in circular arcs. The pits along a line from the center to the edge all move through the same angle $\Delta\theta$ in a time $\Delta t$.*

The arc length $\Delta s$ is the distance traveled along a circular path as shown in Figure 7.2.3 Note that $r$ is the radius of curvature of the circular path. We know that for one complete revolution, the arc length is the circumference of a circle of radius $r$. The circumference of a circle is $2\pi r$. Thus for one complete revolution the rotation angle is

$$\Delta\theta = \frac{2\pi r}{r} = 2\pi$$

This result is the basis for defining the units used to measure rotation angles, $\Delta\theta$ to be radians (rad), defined so that

$$2\pi \text{ rad} = 1 \text{ revolution.}$$

A comparison of some useful angles expressed in both degrees and radians is shown in Table 7.2.1.

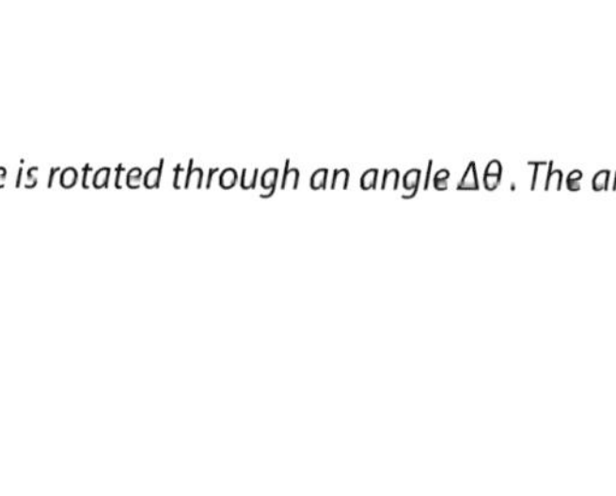


**Figure 7.2.3** *The radius of a circle is rotated through an angle $\Delta\theta$. The arc length $\Delta s$ is described on the circumference.*

**Table 7.2.1** *Comparison of Angular Units*

| Degree Measure | Radian Measure |
|---|---|
| 30° | π/6 |
| 60° | π/3 |
| 90° | π/2 |
| 120° | 2π/3 |
| 135° | 3π/4 |
| 180° | π |

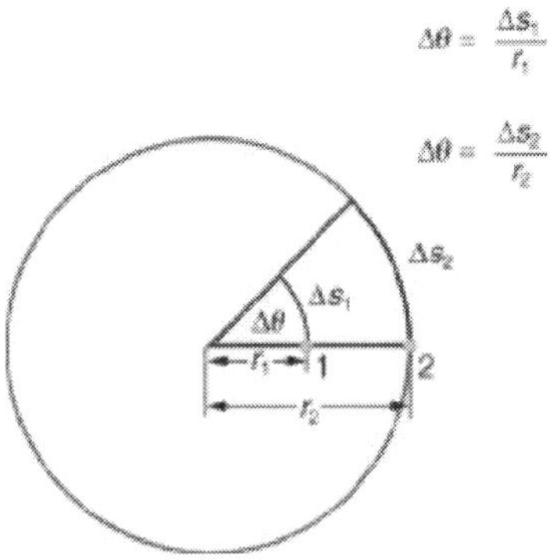


**Figure 7.2.4** Points 1 and 2 rotate through the same angle ( Δθ ), but point 2 moves through a greater arc length (Δs) because it is at a greater distance from the center of rotation (r) .

If $\Delta\theta = 2\pi$ rad, then the DVD has made one complete revolution, and every point on the DVD is back at its original position. Because there are 360º in a circle or one revolution, the relationship between radians and degrees is thus

$$2\pi \text{ rad} = 360°$$

so that

$$1 \text{ rad} = \frac{360°}{2\pi} \approx 57.3°$$

### Quick Check

1. Convert the following angles from degrees to radians
a) 15°
b) 45 °
c) 270 °
d) – 520 °

2. Convert the following angles from radians to degrees
a) $\frac{10\pi}{9}$ b) $\frac{11\pi}{4}$

c) $-\frac{13\pi}{12}$ d) $-\frac{11\pi}{3}$

## Angular Velocity

In the chapter Circular Motion and Gravitation, you examined uniform circular motion, which is motion in a circle at constant speed and can also be called constant **angular velocity**. Angular velocity is given the symbol $\omega$ and is defined as the rate of **change in angle of rotation** ($\theta$) over the change in time (Figure 7.2.5). According to the sign convention, the counter clockwise direction is considered as positive direction and clockwise direction as negative

$$\omega = \frac{\Delta\theta}{\Delta t}$$

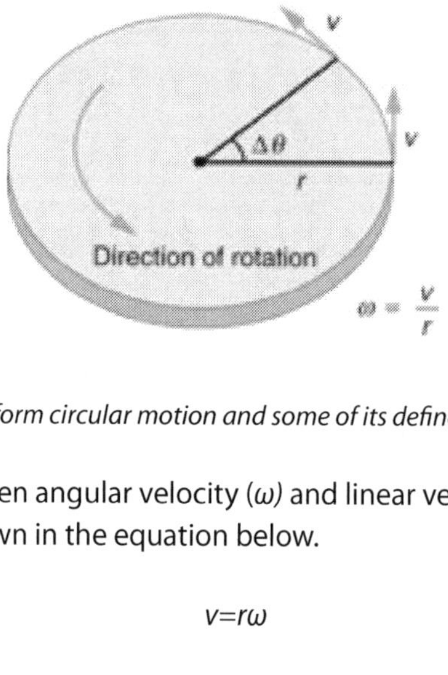


**Figure 7.2.5** *Uniform circular motion and some of its defined quantities.*

The relationship between angular velocity ($\omega$) and linear velocity ($v$) depends on the radius of curvature ($r$) as shown in the equation below.

$$v = r\omega$$

or

$$\omega = \frac{v}{r}$$

## Sample Problem 7.2.1 — How Fast Does a Car Tire Spin?

Calculate the angular velocity of a 0.300 m radius car tire as shown below when the car travels at 15.0 m/s.

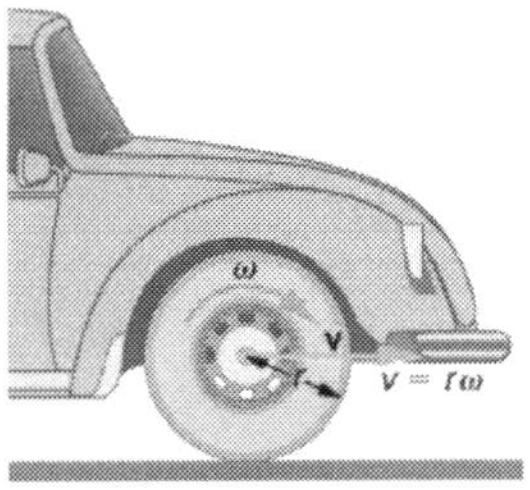


| What to Think About | How to Do It |
| --- | --- |
| 1. Because the linear speed of the tire rim is the same as the speed of the car, we have v = 15.0 m/s. | Start with following relationship: $\omega = \frac{v}{r}$ |
| 2. The radius of the tire is given to be r = 0.300 m. | Substitute the knowns |
| 3. Knowing v and r, we can use the second relationship in v = rω, ω = v/r to calculate the angular velocity. | $\omega = \frac{15.0m/s}{0.300m} = 50.0rad/s$ |

## Practice Problems 7.2.1 — Angular Velocity

1. A truck tire has radius of 0.50 m and rotates at 3.0 Hz. Find the angular velocity of the tire and tangential velocity of the truck, and the angular velocity.

2. A computer hard drive has radius of 6.000 cm and rotates at 7200 rpm. Find the angular velocity, and tangential velocity at the outer edge of the disk.

3. The tire of a large truck has a diameter of 100 cm, and is rolling along a level road. A point P located on the perimeter of the tire has an angular speed of 6.00 rad/s. What is the tangential velocity of the truck expressed in m/s?

## Angular Acceleration

Angular velocity is not constant when a skater pulls in her arms, when a child starts up a merry-go-round from rest, or when a computer's hard disk slows to a halt when switched off. In all these cases, there is an **angular acceleration,** in which ω changes. The faster the change occurs, the great the angular acceleration. Angular acceleration, , is defined as the rate of change of angular velocity over a period of time and is expressed as:

$$\alpha = \frac{\Delta\omega}{\Delta t}$$

Where Δω is the **change in angular velocity** and $\Delta t$ is the change in time. The units of angular acceleration are (rad/s)/s or rad/s$^2$. If $\omega$ increases, then $\alpha$ is positive. If $\omega$ decreases, then $\alpha$ is negative.

### Sample Problem 7.2.2 — Calculating the Angular Acceleration and Deceleration of a Bike Wheel

Suppose a teenager puts her bicycle on its back and starts the rear wheel spinning from rest to a final angular velocity of 250 rpm in 5.00 s.

(a) Calculate the angular acceleration in rad/s$^2$.

(b) If she now slams on the brakes, causing an angular acceleration of – 87.3 rad/s$^2$ , how long does it take the wheel to stop?

| What to Think About | How to Do It |
|---|---|
| **Part (a)** | |
| 1. The angular acceleration can be found directly from its definition in α = Δω/Δt because the final angular velocity and time are given. | $\alpha = \frac{\Delta\omega}{\Delta t}$ |
| 2. Because Δω is in revolutions per minute (rpm) and we want the standard units of rad/s$^2$ for angular acceleration, convert Δω from rpm to rad/s. | $\alpha = \frac{250\ \text{rpm}}{5.00\ \text{s}}$<br>$\Delta\omega = 250\frac{\text{rev}}{\text{min}} \cdot \frac{2\pi\ \text{rad}}{\text{rev}} \cdot \frac{1\ \text{min}}{60\ \text{sec}} = 26.2\frac{\text{rad}}{\text{s}}$ |
| 3. Entering this quantity into the expression for α. | $\alpha = \frac{\Delta\omega}{\Delta t}$<br>$\alpha = \frac{26.2\ \text{rad/s}}{5.00\ \text{s}} = 5.24\ \text{rad/s}^2$ |
| **Part (b)** | |
| 1. The angular acceleration and the initial angular velocity are known from Part (a). Find the stoppage time by using the definition of angular acceleration and solving for $\Delta t$. | $\Delta t = \frac{\Delta\omega}{\alpha}$ |
| 2. In this situation the angular velocity decreases from 26.2 rad/s (250 rpm) to zero, so that Δω is 26.2 rad/s and α is given to be – 87.3 rad/s$^2$ | $\Delta t = \frac{-26.2\ \text{rad/s}}{-87.3\ \text{rad/s}^2} = 0.300\ \text{s}$ |

## Practice Problems 7.2.2 — Angular Acceleration

1. A giant disk with radius 2.0 m is initially at rest. It is accelerated uniformly to a final angular velocity of 18 rad/s over a time of 0.90 s. Determine the angular acceleration of the disk.

2. A tire of radius 40 cm initially at rest begins to acceleration downhill at a rate of 2.0 rad/$s^2$ for 5.0 seconds. Determine its final angular velocity.

3. An engine initially at its idling speed of 600 rpm accelerates uniformly at 12.0 rad/$s^2$ to a final speed of 1200 rpm. What was the time of acceleration?

## Tangential Acceleration

If the bicycle in the sample problem above had been on its wheels instead of upside-down, it would first have accelerated along the ground and then come to a stop. It is important you explore the connection between circular motion and linear motion. For example, how are linear and angular acceleration related. In circular motion, linear acceleration is tangent to the circle at the point of interest, as seen in Figure 7.2.6. Thus, linear acceleration is called **tangential acceleration** ($a_t$).

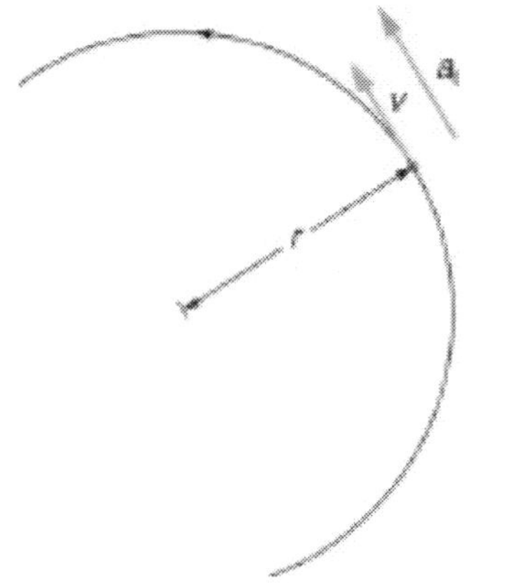


**Figure 7.2.6** *In circular motion, linear acceleration a, occurs as the magnitude of the velocity changes: a is tangent to the motion. In the context of circular motion, linear acceleration is also called tangential acceleration* $a_t$.

Linear or tangential acceleration refers to changes in the magnitude of velocity but not its direction. We know from Circular Motion and Gravitation that in circular motion centripetal acceleration, $a_c$. refers to changes in the direction of the velocity but not its magnitude. An object undergoing circular motion experiences centripetal acceleration, as seen in Figure 7.2.7. Thus, $a_t$ and $a_c$ are perpendicular and independent of one another. Tangential acceleration at is directly related to the angular acceleration α and is linked to an increase or decrease in the velocity, but not its direction.

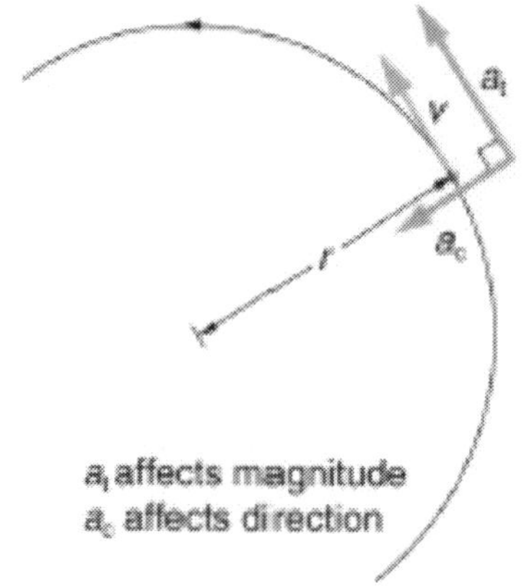


**Figure 7.2.7** *Centripetal acceleration* $a_c$ *occurs as the direction of velocity changes; it is perpendicular to the circular motion. Centripetal and tangential acceleration are thus perpendicular to each other*

Now find the exact relationship between linear acceleration $a_t$ and angular acceleration $a$. Because linear acceleration is proportional to a change in the magnitude of the velocity, $a_t$ is defined as it was in Kinematics.

$$a_t = \frac{\Delta v}{\Delta t}$$

For circular motion, note that $v = r\omega$, so

$$a_t = \frac{\Delta(r\omega)}{\Delta t}$$

The radius, r, is constant for circular motion, and $\Delta(r\omega) = r(\Delta\omega)$.

$$a_t = \frac{r(\Delta\omega)}{\Delta t}$$

And by definition, $\alpha = \frac{\Delta\omega}{\Delta t}$

$$a_t = r\alpha \text{ or } \alpha = \frac{a_t}{r}$$

These equations mean that linear acceleration and angular acceleration are directly proportional. The greater the angular acceleration is, the larger the linear (tangential) acceleration is, and vice versa. For example, the greater the angular acceleration of a car's drive wheels, the greater the acceleration of the car. The radius also matters. For example, the smaller a wheel, the smaller its linear acceleration for a given angular acceleration $\alpha$.

**Sample Problem 7.2.3 — Calculating the Angular Acceleration of a Motorcycle Wheel**

A powerful motorcycle can accelerate from 0 to 30.0 m/s in 4.20 s. What is the angular acceleration of its 0.320-m-radius wheels?

| What to Think About | How to Do It |
| --- | --- |
| We are given information about the linear velocities of the motorcycle. Thus, we can find its linear acceleration $a_t$. | $a_t = \Delta v/\Delta t$<br>$= (30.0 \text{ m/s})/(4.20 \text{ s})$<br>$= 7.14 \text{ m/s}^2$ |
| Then, the expression $\alpha = \frac{a_t}{r}$ can be used to find the angular acceleration. | $\alpha = \frac{a_t}{r}$<br>$= (7.14 \text{ m/s}^2)/(0.320 \text{ m})$<br>$= 22.3 \text{ rad/s}^2$ |

## Practice Problems 7.2.3 — Calculating Angular Acceleration

1. A motorcycle can accelerate from 0 to 100 km'/hr in 5.0 s. What is the angular acceleration of its tires given that they have a radius of 30 cm?

2. A wheel with diameter 80 cm accelerated from rest downhill at a rate of 20 m/s$^2$ until it reaches a final velocity of 20 m/s. Determine the time of acceleration.

### Rotational and Translational Quantities

So far, we have defined three rotational quantities — θ, ω and α. These quantities are analogous to the translational quantities x, v and a. Table 7.2.2 displays rotational quantities, and the analogous translational quantities, and the relationships between them.

**Table 7.2.2** *Rotational and Translational Quantities*

| Rotational | Translational | Relationship |
|---|---|---|
| $\theta$ | $x$ | $\theta = \frac{x}{r}$ |
| $\omega$ | $v$ | $\omega = \frac{v}{r}$ |
| $\alpha$ | $a$ | $\alpha = \frac{a_t}{r}$ |

## 7.2 Review Questions

1. A lemon pie with a 30 cm diameter is cut into 8 equal pieces. What angle, in radians, is between the sides of each piece?

2. At its peak, a tornado is 60.0 m in diameter and carries 500 km/h winds. What is its angular velocity in revolutions per second?

3. An ultracentrifuge accelerates from rest to 100,000 rpm in 2.00 min.

a) What is its angular acceleration in rad/s$^2$?

b) What is the tangential acceleration of a point 9.50 cm from the axis of rotation?

c) What is the radial acceleration in m/s$^2$ and multiples of $g$ of this point at full rpm?

4. You have a grindstone (a disk) that is 90.0 kg, has a 0.340-m radius, and is turning at 90.0 rpm, and you press a steel axe against it with a radial force of 20.0 N.

a) Assuming the kinetic coefficient of friction between steel and stone is 0.20, calculate the angular acceleration of the grindstone.

b) How many turns will the stone make before coming to rest?

5. You are told that a basketball player spins the ball with an angular acceleration of 100 rad/s$^2$.

a) What is the ball's final angular velocity if the ball starts from rest and the acceleration lasts 2.00 s?

b) What is unreasonable about the result?

c) Which premises are unreasonable or inconsistent?

# 7.3 Rotational Kinematics

## Warm Up

Using a broom grab the handle in several places as indicated in the image. At which locations is it the easiest to twist the broom? At which locations is it the hardest to twist the broom? Explain your reasoning.

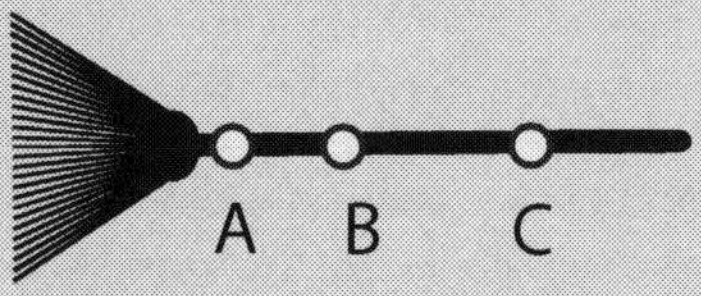


___________________________________________

___________________________________________

___________________________________________

In the last section did you notice how rotational quantities like $\theta$, $\omega$ *and* $a$ are related to one another. For example, if a motorcycle wheel has a large angular acceleration for a fairly long time, it ends up spinning rapidly and rotates through many revolutions. In more technical terms, if the wheel's angular acceleration $\alpha$ is large for a long period of time t, then the final angular velocity $\omega$ and angle of rotation $\theta$ are large. The wheel's rotational motion is exactly analogous to the fact that the motorcycle's large translational acceleration produces a large final velocity, and the distance traveled will also be large.

### Rotational Kinematics

Kinematics is the description of motion. The kinematics of rotational motion describes the relationships among rotation angle, angular velocity, angular acceleration, and time. It is important you know the relationship between $\omega$, $\alpha$, and t . To determine relationship and the subsequent equation, recall a familiar kinematic equation for translational, or straight-line, motion:

$$v = v_0 + at \quad (\text{constant } a)$$

In rotational motion $a = a_t$ , and for this book the symbol $a$ for tangential or linear acceleration will be used. As in linear kinematics, we assume $a$ is constant, which means that angular acceleration $\alpha$ is also a constant, because $a = r\alpha$. Now, let us substitute $v = r\omega$ and $a = r\alpha$ into the linear equation above:

$$r\omega = r\omega_0 + r\alpha t.$$

The radius $r$ cancels in the equation, yielding

$$\omega = \omega_0 + at \quad (\text{constant } a),$$

where $\omega_0$ is the initial angular velocity. This last equation is a kinematic relationship among $\omega$, $\alpha$, and $t$ — that is, it describes their relationship without reference to forces or masses that may affect rotation. It is also precisely analogous in form to its translational counterpart.

Starting with the four kinematic equations developed in Kinematics, we can derive the following four rotational kinematic equations. Note the similarity to their translational counterparts.

**Table 7.3.1** *Rotational Kinematic Equations*

| Rotational | Translational | |
|---|---|---|
| $\theta = \omega t$ | $x = v_{ave} t$ | |
| $\omega = \omega_o + \alpha t$ | $v = v_0 + at$ | (constant $\alpha$, a) |
| $\theta = \omega_0 + ½\alpha t^2$ | $x = v_0 t + ½at^2$ | (constant $\alpha$, a) |
| $\omega^2 = \omega_o^2 + 2\alpha\theta$ | $v^2 = v_o^2 + 2a\theta$ | (constant $\alpha$, a) |

In these equations, the subscript 0 denotes initial values ($\theta_0$, $x_0$, and $t_0$ are initial values), and the average angular velocity, $\omega_{ave}$, and average velocity $v_{ave}$ are defined as follows:

$$\omega_{ave} = \frac{\omega_0 + \omega}{2} \text{ and } v_{ave} = \frac{v_0 + v}{2}$$

The equations given above in Table 7.3.1 can be used to solve any rotational or translational kinematics problem in which *a* and $\alpha$ are constant.

## Sample Problem 7.3.1 — Rotational Kinematics

A deep-sea fisherman hooks a big fish that swims away from the boat pulling the fishing line from his fishing reel. The whole system is initially at rest and the fishing line unwinds from the reel at a radius of 4.50 cm from its axis of rotation. The reel is given an angular acceleration of 110 rad/s$^2$ for 2.00 s as seen in Figure 7.3.1.

(a) What is the final angular velocity of the reel?
(b) At what speed is fishing line leaving the reel after 2.00 s elapses?
(c) How many revolutions does the reel make?
(d) How many meters of fishing line come off the reel in this time?

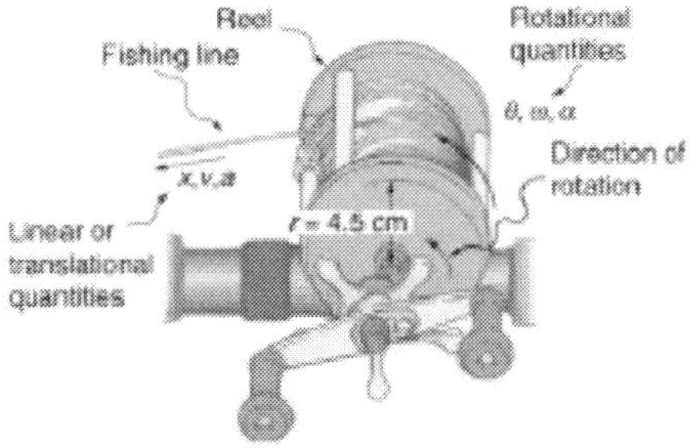


**Figure 7.3.1** *Fishing line coming off a rotating reel moves linearly.*

| What to Think About | How to Do It |
| --- | --- |
| **Part (a)** | |
| 1. $\alpha$ and $t$ are given and $\omega$ needs to be determined. The most straightforward equation to use is $\omega + \omega_0 \alpha t$ because the unknown is already on one side and all other terms are known. | $\omega = \omega_o + \alpha t$<br>$\omega = 0 + (110\ rad/s^2)(2.00s) = 220\ rad/s$ |
| **Part (b)** | |
| 1. Now that $\omega$ is known, find the speed $v$.<br>2. And we know the radius $r$ of the reel is given to be 4.50 cm. | $v = r\omega$<br>$v = (0.0450\ m)(220\ rad/s) = 9.90\ m/s$ |
| **Part (c)** | |
| 1. Next find the number of revolutions. Remember 1 rev = $2\pi$ rad. We can find the number of revolutions by finding $\theta$ in radians.<br>2. Since $\alpha$ and t are given and we know $\omega_0$ is zero, $\theta$ can be obtained using $\theta = \omega_0 t + ½at^2$<br>3. Converting radians to revolutions gives the answer in revolutions. | $\theta = \omega_o t + 1/2\ at^2$<br>$\theta = 0 + (0.500)(110\ rad/s^2)(2.00\ s)^2 = 220\ rad$<br>$\theta = (220\ rad)((1\ rev)/(2\pi\ rad)) = 35.0\ rev$ |
| **Part (d)** | |
| 1. The number of meters of fishing line is $x$, which can be obtained through its relationship with $\theta$. | $x = r\theta = (0.0450\ m)(220\ rad) = 9.90\ m$ |

### Practice Problem 7.3.1 — Rotational Kinematics

1. What happens if the fisherman applies a brake to the spinning reel in Figure 7.3.1 achieving an angular acceleration of – 300 rad/s$^2$. How long does it take the reel to come to a stop?

## 7.3 Review Questions

.1. A large freight trains accelerate very slowly. Suppose one such train accelerates from rest, giving its 0.350-m-radius wheels an angular acceleration of 0.250 rad/$s^2$. After the wheels have made 200 revolutions (assume no slippage)

(a) How far has the train moved down the track?

(b) What are the final angular velocity of the wheels and the linear velocity of the train?

2. A person decides to use a microwave oven to reheat some lunch. In the process, a pea falls off the tray and lands on the outer edge of the rotating plate and remains there. If the plate has a radius of 0.15 m and rotates at 6.0 rpm, calculate the total distance traveled by the pea during a 2.0-min cooking period. (Ignore the start-up and slow-down times.)

3. With the aid of a string, a gyroscope is accelerated from rest to 32 rad/s in 0.40 s.

(a) What is its angular acceleration in rad/$s^2$?

(b) How many revolutions does it go through in the process?

4. Suppose a piece of dust finds itself on a CD. If the spin rate of the CD is 500 rpm, and the piece of dust is 4.30 cm from the center, what is the total distance traveled by the dust in 3.00 minutes? (Ignore accelerations due to getting the CD rotating.)

5. A gyroscope slows from an initial rate of 32.0 rad/s at a rate of 0.700 rad/s$^2$.

(a) How long does it take to come to rest?

(b) How many revolutions does it make before stopping?

6. During a very quick stop, a car decelerates at 7.00 m/s$^2$.

(a) What is the angular acceleration of its 0.280-m-radius tires, assuming they do not slip on the pavement?

(b) How many revolutions do the tires make before coming to rest, given their initial angular velocity is 95.0 rad/s ?

(c) How long does the car take to stop completely?

(d) What distance does the car travel in this time?

(e) What was the car's initial velocity?

(f) Do the values obtained seem reasonable, considering that this stop happens very quickly?

7. A yo-yo has a center shaft that has a 0.250 cm radius and that its string is being pulled.

(a) If the string is stationary and the yo-yo accelerates away from it at a rate of 1.50 m/s$^2$, what is the angular acceleration of the yo-yo?

(b) What is the angular velocity after 0.750 s if it starts from rest?

(c) The outside radius of the yo-yo is 3.50 cm. What is the tangential acceleration of a point on its edge?

# 7.4 Rotational Dynamics

## Warm Up

Cut out a circle that has about a 10 cm radius from stiff cardboard. Near the edge of the circle, write numbers 1 to 12 like hours on a clock face. Position the circle so that it can rotate freely about a horizontal axis through its center, like a wheel. Hold the circle stationary and with the number 12 positioned at the top, attach a lump of putty at the number 3. Now answer the following questions:

(a) How large does the lump need to be to just rotate the circle?

(b) In what direction did the circle rotate when you added putty at the number 3 (clockwise or counterclockwise)?

(c) Was the angular velocity constant?

(d) What can we say about the direction (clockwise or counterclockwise) of the angular acceleration?

(e) How could you change the placement of the putty to create angular velocity in the opposite direction?

If you have ever spun a bike wheel or pushed a merry-go-round, you know that force is needed to change angular velocity as seen in Figure 7.4.1. In situations like these our intuition is reliable in predicting many of the factors that are involved. For example, we know that a door opens slowly if we push too close to its hinges. Or we know that the more massive the door, the more slowly it opens. The first example implies that the farther the force is applied from the pivot, the greater the angular acceleration. Another relationship implied from this example is angular acceleration is inversely proportional to mass. These relationships should seem very similar to you as they are similar to the relationships among force, mass, and acceleration from Newton's second law of motion.

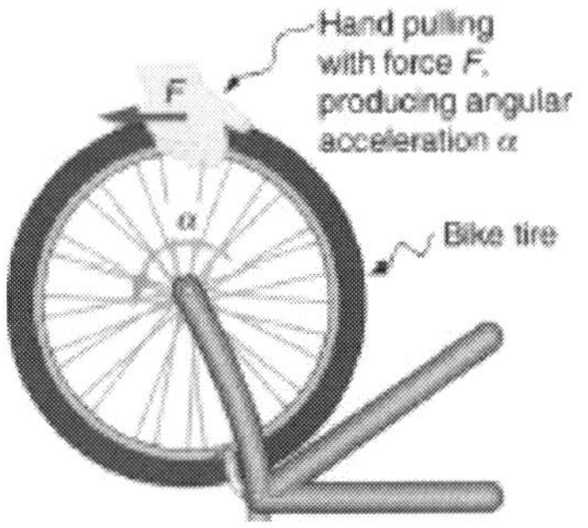


**Figure 7.4.1** *Force is required to spin the bike wheel. The greater the force, the greater the angular acceleration produced. The more massive the wheel, the smaller the angular acceleration. If you push on a spoke closer to the axle, the angular acceleration will be smaller.*

## Rotational Inertia

To develop the precise relationship among force, mass, radius, and angular acceleration, consider what happens if we exert a force *F* on a point mass m that is at a distance r from a pivot point, as shown in Figure 7.4.2. Because the force is perpendicular to *r*, an acceleration $a = F/m$ is obtained in the direction of *F*. We can rearrange this equation such that $F = ma$ and then look for ways to relate this expression to expressions for rotational quantities. We note that $a = r\alpha$, and we substitute this expression into $F = ma$, yielding

$$F=mr\alpha$$

Recall that torque is the turning effectiveness of a force. In this case, because *F* is perpendicular to *r*, torque is simply $\tau = Fr$. So, if we multiply both sides of the equation above by *r*, we get torque on the left-hand side.

$$rF=mr^2\alpha$$

Or

$$\tau=mr^2\alpha.$$

This last equation is the rotational equivalent, or analog, of Newton's second law ($F = ma$), where torque is analogous to force, angular acceleration is analogous to translational acceleration, and $mr^2$ is analogous to mass (or inertia). The quantity $mr^2$ is called the rotational inertia or moment of inertia of a point mass *m* a distance r from the center of rotation.

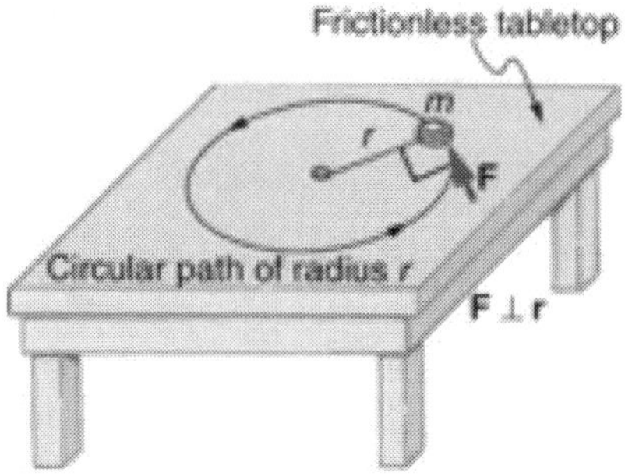


**Figure 7.4.2** *An object is supported by a horizontal frictionless table and is attached to a pivot point by a cord that supplies centripetal force. A force F is applied to the object perpendicular to the radius r, causing it to accelerate about the pivot point. The force is kept perpendicular to r.*

## Rotational Inertia and Moment of Inertia

Before we can consider the rotation of anything other than a point mass like the one in Figure 7.4.2, we must consider applying rotational inertia to all types of objects. This means we expand our concept of rotational inertia and define the **moment of inertia, *I*,** of an object to be the sum of $mr^2$ for all the point masses of which it is composed. That is, $I = \sum mr^2$. Here *I* is analogous to m in translational motion. Because of the distance *r*, the moment of inertia for any object depends on the chosen axis. Calculating *I* is beyond the scope of this text except for one simple case—that of a hoop, which has all its mass at the same distance from its axis. A hoop's moment of inertia around its axis is therefore $MR^2$, where *M* is its total mass and *R* its radius. We use *M* and *R* for an entire object to distinguish them from *m* and *r* for point masses. In all other cases, we must consult Figure 7.4.3 for formulas for *I* that have been derived from integration over the continuous body. Units for *I* are mass multiplied by distance squared ($kg \cdot m^2$).

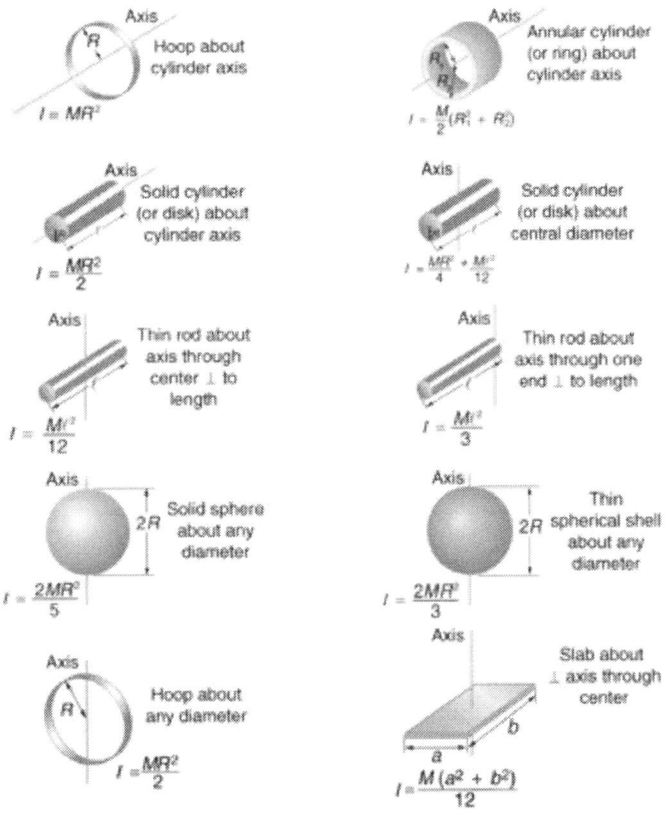


**7.4.3** *Some rotational inertias.*

The general relationship among torque, moment of inertia and angular acceleration is:

$$\text{net } \tau = I\alpha$$

or

$$\alpha = \frac{(\text{net } \tau)}{I}$$

where net τ is the total torque from all forces relative to a chosen axis. For simplicity, we will only consider torques exerted by forces in the plane of the rotation. Such torques are either positive or negative and add like ordinary numbers. The relationship in $\tau = I\alpha$, $\alpha = (\text{net } \tau)/I$ is the rotational analog to Newton's second law and is very generally applicable. This equation is actually valid for any torque, applied to any object, relative to any axis.

The larger the torque is, the larger the angular acceleration is. For example, the harder a child pushes on a merry-go-round, the faster it accelerates. It is also true that the more massive a merry-go-round, the slower it accelerates for the same torque. The basic relationship between moment of inertia and angular acceleration is that the larger the moment of inertia, the smaller is the angular acceleration. But there is an additional twist. The moment of inertia depends not only on the mass of an object, but also on its distribution of mass relative to the axis around which it rotates. For example, it will be much easier to accelerate a merry-go-round full of children if they stand close to its axis than if they all stand at the outer edge. The mass is the same in both cases; but the moment of inertia is much larger when the children are at the edge.

**Sample Problem 7.4.1 — Calculating the Effect of Mass Distribution on a Merry-Go-Round**

Consider the father pushing a playground merry-go-round in the figure below. He exerts a force of 250 N at the edge of the 50.0-kg merry-go-round, which has a 1.50 m radius. Calculate the angular acceleration produced

(a) when no one is on the merry-go-round.
(b) when an 18.0-kg child sits 1.25 m away from the center. Consider the merry-go-round itself to be a uniform disk with negligible friction.

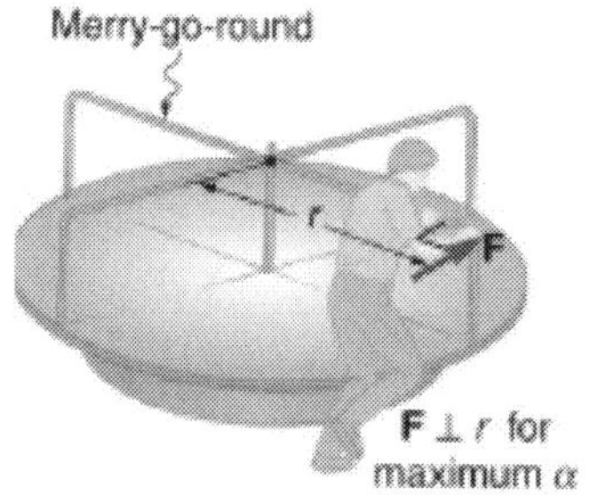


*Continued on next page*

| What to Think About | How to Do It |
|---|---|
| **Part (a)**<br>To solve for $\alpha$, we must first calculate the torque τ and moment of inertia I. To find the torque, we note that the applied force is perpendicular to the radius and friction is negligible. | $\tau = rF \sin\theta = (1.50\ m)(250\ N) = 375\ N{\cdot}m.$ |
| Next, find the moment of inertia of a solid disk about this axis. | $I = \frac{1}{2}MR^2\ (0.500)(50.0\ kg)(1.50\ m)^2$<br>$I = 56.25\ kg{\cdot}m^2$ |
| Now, substitute the known values to find the angular acceleration. | $\alpha = \frac{\tau}{I}$<br>$= (375\ N)/(56.25\ kg{\cdot}m^2) = 6.67\ rad/s^2$ |
| **Part (b)**<br>The angular acceleration for the system will be less in this part, because the moment of inertia is greater when the child is on the merry-go-round. To find the total moment of inertia I, first find the child's moment of inertia $I_c$ by considering the child to be equivalent to a point mass at a distance of 1.25 m from the axis. | $I_c = MR^2 = (18.0\ kg)(1.25\ m)^2 = 28.13\ kg \cdot m^2$ |
| The total moment of inertia is the sum of moments of inertia of the merry-go-round and the child about the same axis. | $I = 28.13\ kg{\cdot}m^2 + 56.25\ kg{\cdot}m^2 = 84.38\ kg{\cdot}m^2$ |
| Substituting known values into the equation for α. | $\alpha = \frac{\tau}{I}$<br>$= (375\ N)/(84.38\ kg{\cdot}m^2) = 4.44\ rad/s^2$ |

In Sample Problem 7.4.1 the angular acceleration is less when the child is on the merry-go-round than when the merry-go-round is empty, as expected. The angular accelerations found are quite large, partly due to the fact that friction was considered to be negligible. If, for example, the father kept pushing perpendicularly for 2.00 s, he would give the merry-go-round an angular velocity of 13.3 rad/s when it is empty but only 8.89 rad/s when the child is on it. In terms of revolutions per second, these angular velocities are 2.12 rev/s and 1.41 rev/s, respectively. The father would end up running at about 50 km/h in the first case.

# 7.4 Review Questions

1. A large potter's wheel has a diameter of 60.0 cm and a mass of 8.00 kg. It is powered by a 20.0 N motor acting on the outer edge. There is also a brake capable of exerting a 15.0 N force at a radius of 12.0 cm from the axis of rotation, on the underside. What is the angular acceleration when the motor is in use?

2. Find the moment of inertia of a 1000 gram solid disk turntable of radius 17.0 cm.

3. A constant torque of 50 Nm is applied to a 1.0 kg solid disk of radius 15 cm. What is the maximum angular acceleration that can be produced by the applied torque?

4. A wheel with moment of inertia 15 $kgm^2$ is rotating at 90 rad/s. What constant torque is required to slow it down to 40 rad/s in 20 s?

5. A constant frictional torque of 200 Nm is applied to a turbine initially rotating at 120 rad/s, and it comes to a stop in 80 s. What is the turbine's moment of inertia?

6. A tire whose moment of inertia is 2.0 $kgm^2$ has initial angular velocity of 50 rad/s. If a constant torque of 10 Nm acts on the wheel, how long will it take to be accelerated to 80 rad/s?

# 7.5 Rotational Kinetic Energy: Work and Energy Revisited

## Warm Up

Locate several cans each containing different types of food. First, predict which can will win the race down an inclined plane and explain why. See if your prediction is correct. You could also do this experiment by collecting several empty cylindrical containers of the same size and filling them with different materials such as wet or dry sand.

**Figure 7.5.1** *The motor works in spinning the grindstone, giving it rotational kinetic energy. That energy is then converted to heat, light, sound, and vibration. (credit: U.S. Navy photo by Mass Communication Specialist Seaman Zachary David Bell)*

## Rotational Kinetic Energy

Work must be done to rotate objects such as grindstones or merry-go-rounds. Work was defined in the chapter on Energy for translational motion, and we can build on that knowledge when considering work done in rotational motion. The simplest rotational situation is one in which the net force is exerted perpendicular to the radius of a disk as shown in Figure 7.5.2 and remains perpendicular as the disk starts to rotate.

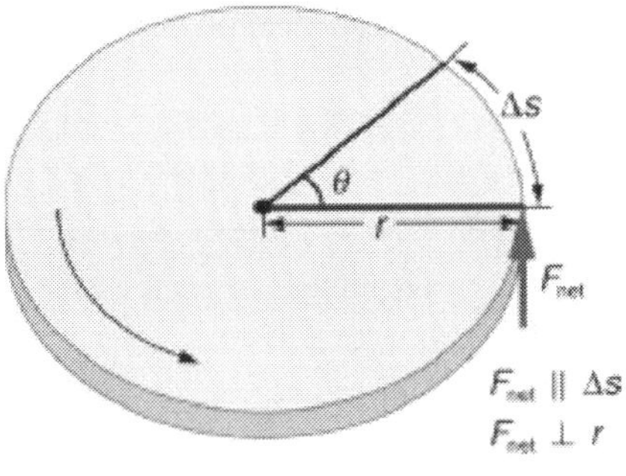


**Figure 7.5.2** *The net force on this disk is kept perpendicular to its radius as the force causes the disk to rotate. The net work done is (net F)Δs. The new work goes into rotational kinetic energy.*

The force is parallel to the displacement, and so the net work done is the product of the force times the arc length traveled:

$$\text{net } W = (\text{net } F)\,\Delta s$$

To get torque and other rotational quantities into the equation, we multiply and divide the right-hand side of the equation by $r$, and gather terms:

$$\text{net } W = (r \text{ net } F)\,\frac{\Delta s}{r}$$

We recognize that $r$ net $F$ = net $\tau$ and $\Delta s / r = \theta$, so that:

$$\text{net } W = (\text{net } \tau)\,\theta$$

This equation is the expression for rotational work. It is very similar to the familiar definition of translational work as force multiplied by distance. Here, torque is analogous to force, and angle is analogous to distance. The equation net $W$ = (net $\tau$) $\theta$ is valid in general, even though it was derived for a special case.

To get an expression for rotational kinetic energy, we must again perform some algebraic manipulations. The first step is to note that net $\tau = I\alpha$, so that:

$$\text{net } W = I\alpha\theta$$

Now, we solve one of the rotational kinematics equations for $\alpha\theta$

$$\omega^2 = \omega_0^{\,2} + 2\alpha\theta$$

Next, we solve for $\alpha\theta$:

$$\alpha\theta = \frac{\omega^2 - \omega_0^2}{2}$$

Substituting this into the equation for net W and gathering terms yields

$$\text{net } W = \frac{1}{2}I\omega^2 - \frac{1}{2}I\omega_0^2$$

This equation is the work-energy theorem for rotational motion only. As you may recall, net work changes the kinetic energy of a system. Through an analogy with translational motion, we define the term $I$ to be **rotational kinetic energy** $KE_{rot}$ for an object with a moment of inertia $I$ and an angular velocity $\omega$:

$$KE_{rot} = \frac{1}{2}I\omega^2$$

The expression for rotational kinetic energy is exactly analogous to translational kinetic energy, with $I$ being analogous to $m$ and $\omega$ to $v$. Rotational kinetic energy has important effects. Flywheels, for example, can be used to store large amounts of rotational kinetic energy in a vehicle, as seen in Figure 7.5.3.

**Figure 7.5.3** *Experimental vehicles, such as this bus, have been constructed in which rotational kinetic energy is stored in a large flywheel. When the bus goes down a hill, its transmission converts its gravitational potential energy $KE_{rot}$. It can also convert translational kinetic energy, when the bus stops, into $KE_{rot}$. The flywheel's energy can then be used to accelerate, to go up another hill, or to keep the bus from going against friction.*

## Sample Problem 7.5.1 — Calculating Work and Energy

Consider a person who spins a large grindstone by placing her hand on its edge and exerting a force through part of a revolution as shown in the figure. In this example, we verify that the work done by the torque she exerts equals the change in rotational energy.

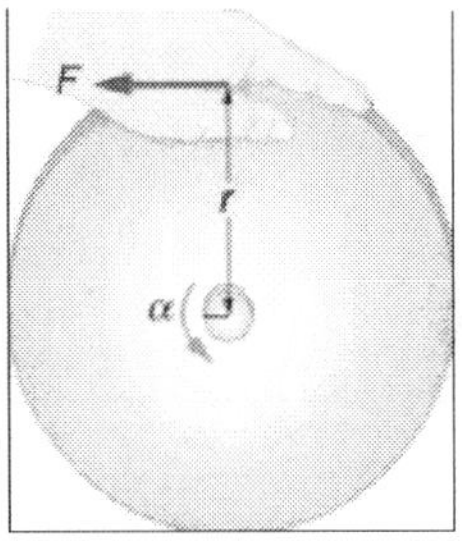


(a) How much work is done if she exerts a force of 200 N through a rotation of 1.00 rad (57.3°)? The force is kept perpendicular to the grindstone's 0.320-m radius at the point of application, and the effects of friction are negligible.
(b) What is the final angular velocity if the grindstone has a mass of 85.0 kg?
(c) What is the final rotational kinetic energy? (It should equal the work.)

| What to Think About | How to Do It |
|---|---|
| **Part (a)** | |
| 1. Need to find work. | net $W = (\text{net } \tau)\theta$ |
| 2. Net $\tau$ is the applied force multiplied by the radius ($rF$) because there is no retarding friction, and the force is perpendicular to r. | net $W = rF\theta = (0.320 \text{ m})(200 \text{ N})(1.00 \text{ rad})$ <br> $= 64.0 \text{ N} \cdot \text{m}$ or $64.0 \text{ J}$ |
| **Part (b)** | |
| 1. To find $\omega$ from the given information requires more than one step so use $\omega^2=\omega_0^2+2\alpha\theta$ to find $\omega$. | $\omega^2 = \omega_0^2 + 2\alpha\theta$ <br> $\omega = \sqrt{2\alpha\theta}$ |
| 2. But need to find α using (net π)/I | net $\pi = rF = (0.320 \text{ m})(200 \text{ N}) = 64.0 \text{ N} \cdot \text{m}$ |
| 3. Substitute the values of torque and moment of inertia for a disc (Figure 7.4.3) into the expression for α. | $I = \frac{1}{2}MR^2 = 0.5(85.0 kg)(0.320)^2 = 4.352 kg \cdot m^2$ <br> $\alpha = \frac{net\ \pi}{I} = \frac{64.0 N \cdot m}{4.352 kg \cdot m^2} = 14.7 \frac{rad}{s^2}$ |
| 4. Substitute this value and the given value for θ into the above expression for ω | $\omega = \sqrt{2\alpha\theta} = \sqrt{2(14.7 \frac{rad}{s^2})(1.00\ rad)} = 5.42 \frac{rad}{s}$ |
| **Part (c)** | |
| 1. Find final rotational kinetic energy using I and ω from Part (c) | $KE_{rot} = 1/2\, I\omega^2$ <br> $= (0.5)(4.352 \text{ kg} \cdot \text{m}^2)(5.42 \text{ rad/s})^2 = 64.0 \text{ J}$ |

**Practice Problem 7.5.1 — Calculating Work and Energy**

1. A bowling ball (solid sphere) of mass 2.0 kg and radius 10 cm is rolling across the floor at a rate of 4 rotations per second. Determine its rotational inertia, angular velocity and rotational kinetic energy.

2. A disk with rotational inertia of 16 $kgm^2$ is rotating at 90 rad/s. A constant torque slows it down to 40 rad/s in 20 seconds. Determine the rate of deceleration, the magnitude of the torque, and how much kinetic energy is lost by the disk?

3. A wheel whose moment of inertia is 0.600 $kgm^2$ is rotating at 1500 rpm.
   (a) what constant torque is required to increase its angular velocity to 2000 rpm in 8.00 s?

   (b) How many rotations does the wheel make while accelerating?

   (c) Calculate the work done on the wheel.

Helicopter pilots are quite familiar with rotational kinetic energy. They know, for example, that a point of no return will be reached if they allow their blades to slow below a critical angular velocity during flight. The blades lose lift, and it is impossible to immediately get the blades spinning fast enough to regain it. Rotational kinetic energy must be supplied to the blades to get them to rotate faster, and enough energy cannot be supplied in time to avoid a crash. Because of weight limitations, helicopter engines are too small to supply both the energy needed for lift and to replenish the rotational kinetic energy of the blades once they have slowed down. The rotational kinetic energy is put into them before takeoff and must not be allowed to drop below this crucial level. One possible way to avoid a crash is to use the gravitational potential energy of the helicopter to replenish the rotational kinetic energy of the blades by losing altitude and aligning the blades so that the helicopter is spun up in the descent. Of course, if the helicopter's altitude is too low, then there is insufficient time for the blade to regain lift before reaching the ground.

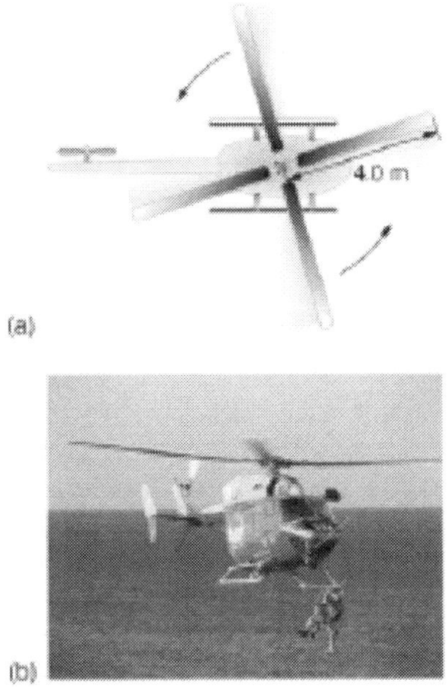


**Figure 7.5.4** *The first image shows how helicopters store large amounts of rotational kinetic energy in their blades. This energy must be put into the blades before takeoff and maintained until the end of the flight. The engines do not have enough power to simultaneously provide lift and put significant rotational energy into the blades. The second image shows a helicopter from the Auckland Westpac Rescue Helicopter Service. Over 50,000 lives have been saved since its operations beginning in 1973. Here, a water rescue operation is shown. (credit: 111 Emergency, Flickr)*

## Sample Problem 7.5.2 — Calculating Helicopter Energies

A typical small rescue helicopter, similar to the one in Figure 7.5.4, has four blades, each is 4.00 m long and has a mass of 50.0 kg. The blades can be approximated as thin rods that rotate about one end of an axis perpendicular to their length. The helicopter has a total loaded mass of 1000 kg.

(a) Calculate the rotational kinetic energy in the blades when they rotate at 300 rpm.
(b) Calculate the translational kinetic energy of the helicopter when it flies at 20.0 m/s, and compare it with the rotational energy in the blades.
(c) To what height could the helicopter be raised if all of the rotational kinetic energy could be used to lift it?

*Continued on next page*

| What to Think About | How to Do It |
|---|---|
| Rotational and translational kinetic energies can be calculated from their definitions. The last part of the problem relates to the idea that energy can change form, in this case from rotational kinetic energy to gravitational potential energy. | |
| **Part (a)** | |
| 1. First we must convert the angular velocity (ω) to radians per second and calculate the moment of inertia before we can find $KE_{rot}$. | $\omega = (300\text{ rev})/(1.00\text{ min})\cdot(2\pi\text{ rad})/(1\text{ rev})\cdot(1.00\text{ min})/(60\text{ s})$ <br> $\omega = 31.4\text{ rad/s}$ <br> $\omega = \frac{3.00\,rev}{1.00\,min} = \frac{2\pi\,rad}{1\,rev} = \frac{1.00\,min}{60.0\,s} = 31.4\frac{rad}{s}$ |
| 2. The moment of inertia of one blade will be that of a thin rod rotated about its end, found in Figure 7.4.3. The total I is four times this moment of inertia, because there are four blades. | $I = 4\frac{Ml^2}{3} = 4(\frac{(50.0\,kg)(4.00\,m)^2}{3} = 1067\,kg\cdot m^2$ |
| 3. Entering ω and I into the expression for rotational kinetic energy gives $KE_{rot}$. | $KE_{rot} = 0.5(1067\text{ kg}\cdot\text{m}^2)(31.4\text{ rad/s})^2$ <br> $KE_{rot} = 5.26 \times 10^5\text{ J}$ |
| **Part (b)** | |
| 1. Find translational kinetic energy with given mass and velocity values. Then compare kinetic energies. | $KE_{trans} = \frac{1}{2}mv^2 = (0.5)(1000\,kg)(20.0\,m/s)^2 = 2.00 \times 10^5\,J$ <br> Compare kinetic energies: <br> $\frac{KE_{trans}}{KE_{rot}} = \frac{2.00 \times 10^5\,J}{5.26 \times 10^5\,J} = 0.380$ |
| **Part (c)** | |
| 1. At the maximum height, all rotational kinetic energy will have been converted to gravitational energy. To find this height, we equate those two energies. | $KE_{rot} = PE_{grav}$ <br> Or <br> $\frac{1}{2}I\omega^2 = mgh$ |
| 2. We now solve for *h* and substitute known values into the resulting equation | $h = \frac{\frac{1}{2}I\omega^2}{mg} = \frac{5.26 \times 10^5\,J}{(1000\,kg)(9.80\,m/s^2)} = 53.7\,m$ |

## Cylinders and Ramp Rolling at Different Rates

One of the quality controls in a tomato soup factory consists of rolling filled cans down a ramp. If they roll too fast, the soup is too thin. Why should cans of identical size and mass roll down an incline at different rates? And why should the thickest soup roll the slowest?

The easiest way to answer these questions is to consider energy. Suppose each can starts down the ramp from rest. Each can starting from rest means each starts with the same gravitational potential energy $PE_{grav}$, which is converted entirely to KE, provided each rolls without slipping. KE, however, can take the form of $KE_{trans}$ or $KE_{rot}$, and total KE is the sum of the two. If a can rolls down a ramp, it puts part of its energy into rotation, leaving less for translation. Thus, the can goes slower than it would if it slid down. Furthermore, the thin soup does not rotate, whereas the thick soup does, because it sticks to the can. The thick soup thus puts more of the can's original gravitational potential energy into rotation than the thin soup, and the can rolls more slowly, as seen in Figure 7.5.5.

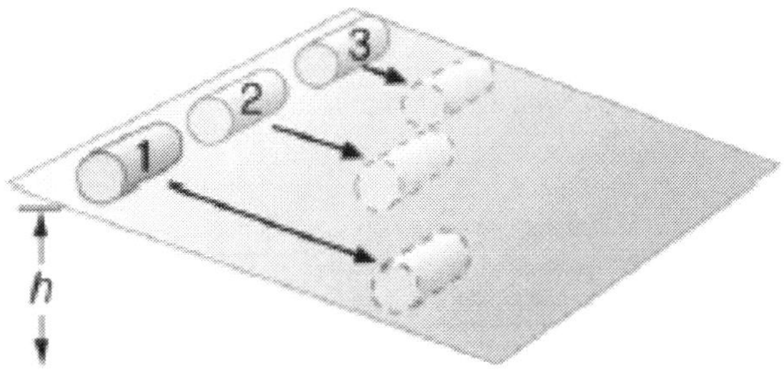


**Figure 7.5.5** *Three cans of soup with identical masses race down an incline. The first can has a low friction coating and does not roll but just slides down the incline. It wins because it converts its entire PE into translational KE. The second and third cans both roll down the incline without slipping. The second can contains thin soup and comes in second because part of its initial PE goes into rotating the can (but not the thin soup). The third can contains thick soup. It comes in third because the soup rotates along with the can, taking even more of the initial PE for rotational KE, leaving less for translational KE.*

Assuming no losses due to friction, there is only one force doing work—gravity. Therefore, the total work done is the change in kinetic energy. As the cans start moving, the potential energy is changing into kinetic energy. Conservation of energy gives

$$PE_i = KE_f.$$

More specifically,

$$PE_{grav} = KE_{trans} + KE_{rot}$$

Or

$$mgh = mv^2 + I\omega^2$$

So, the initial *mgh* is divided between translational kinetic energy and rotational kinetic energy; and the greater I is, the less energy goes into translation. If the can slides down without friction, then $\omega = 0$ and all the energy goes into translation; thus, the can goes faster.

### Sample Problem 7.5.3 — Speed of Rolling Cylinder Down an Incline

Calculate the final speed of a solid cylinder that rolls down a 2.00-m-high incline. The cylinder starts from rest, has a mass of 0.750 kg, and has a radius of 4.00 cm.

| What to Think About | How to Do It |
| --- | --- |
| We can solve for the final velocity using conservation of energy, but we must first express rotational quantities in terms of translational quantities to end up with v as the only unknown. | |
| 1. Start with the law of conservation of energy | $mgh = \frac{1}{2}mv^2 + \frac{1}{2}I\omega^2$ |
| 2. Before we can solve for v, we must get an expression for I from Figure 7.4.3. Because v and ω are related, the cylinder is rolling without slipping, we must also substitute the relationship ω = v / R into the expression. | $mgh = \frac{1}{2}mv^2 + \frac{1}{2}(\frac{1}{2}mR^2)(\frac{v^2}{R^2})$ |
| 3. Now the cylinder's radius R and mass m cancel | $gh = \frac{1}{2}v^2 + \frac{1}{4}v^2 = \frac{3}{4}v^2$ |
| 4. Solving algebraically, the equation for the final velocity v gives | $v = \sqrt{(\frac{4gh}{3})}$ |
| 5. Substituting known values into the resulting expression yields | $v = \sqrt{\frac{4(9.80 m/s^2)(2.00 m)}{3}} = 5.11 m/s$ |

**Final Thoughts**

Because *m* and *R* cancel, the result $v = \sqrt{\frac{4gh}{3}}$ is valid for any solid cylinder, implying that all solid cylinders will roll down an incline at the same rate independent of their masses and sizes. Rolling cylinders down inclines is what Galileo actually did to show that objects fall at the same rate independent of mass. If the cylinder slid without friction down the incline without rolling, then the entire gravitational potential energy would go into translational kinetic energy. Thus, $\frac{1}{2}mv^2 = mgh$ and $v=\sqrt{2gh}$, which is 22% greater than $\sqrt{\frac{4gh}{3}}$. That is, the cylinder would go faster at the bottom.

# 7.5 Review Questions

1. Refer to the Sample Problem 7.5.3. Suppose that the cylinder is replaced with a solid sphere with the same mass and radius as the cylinder. Explain how each of the following quantities is affected:

   (a) initial gravitational potential energy.

   (b) rotational Inertia.

   (c) final speed.

2. A solid cylinder rolls from rest down an inclined plane 1.2 m high. Determine its linear velocity at the bottom of the incline.

3. A bowling ball rolling at 8.0 m/s across the floor begins to roll up an inclined plane. What will be the maximum vertical displacement of the ball?

4. A 1 kg mass is suspended height $D$= 1m as shown in the mass-pulley system. The pulley has radius $R$, mass $M$, and a moment of inertia I= 0.5 $MR^2$. The mass is allowed to accelerate from rest until striking the floor. Determine the maximum velocity of the mass just before impact with the floor.

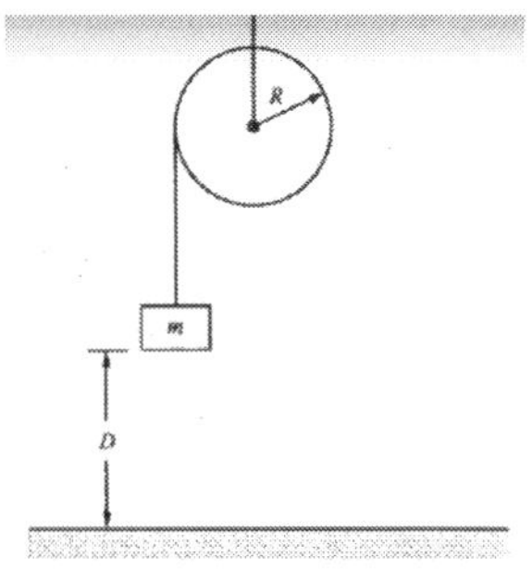

5. Derive an equation to find the velocity of the Atwood pulley system ($m_1 > m_2$) after $m_2$ has been raised through height *h*. The pulley has mass *M*, radius R, and moment of inertia $I=MR^2$. Note that the tension in the string above each mass is not the same. Express the equation in terms of the variables $m_1$, $m_2$, *M*, *R*, *h*, *g*.

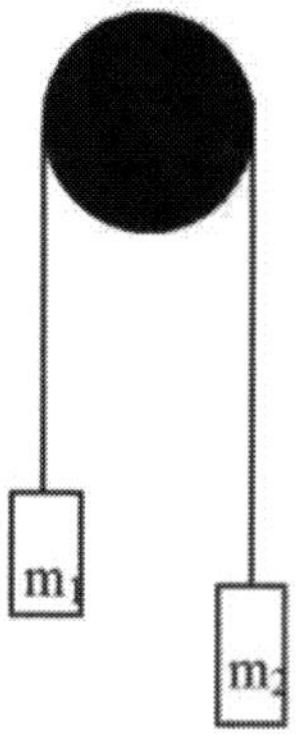


6. A spring loaded projectile launcher is used to supply the force needed to shoot a solid metal sphere across the table. The sphere has a mass of 100 g and radius 2.00 cm, and a moment of inertia of $I = \frac{2}{5}MR^2$. The spring constant k=500 N/m and the spring in the launcher is compressed 10 cm before firing. The table height *h* is 1.00 m above the floor. Find the horizontal displacement of the steel ball once it leaves the table.

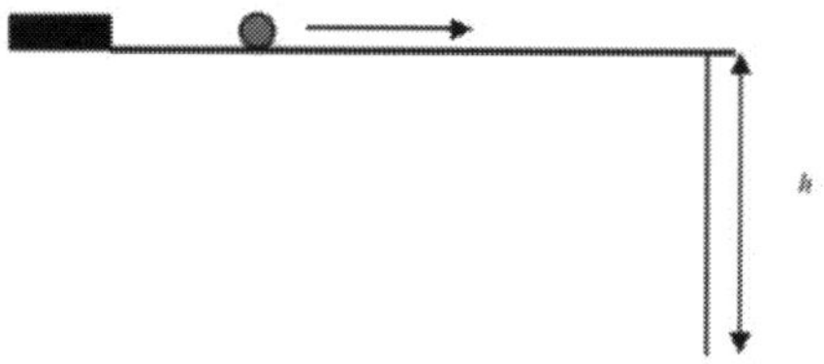

# 7.6 Angular Momentum and Its Conservation

## Warm Up

Sit down on a chair that rotates. Tuck your feet close to the seat of the chair and not touching the ground. Stick both of your arms straight out to each side like in the picture. Now have your teacher carefully spin the chair. As the chair is spinning, bring in your arms. What happens? Why do you think this happens?

### Angular Momentum

Why does Earth keep on spinning? What started it spinning to begin with? And how does an ice skater manage to spin faster and faster simply by pulling her arms in? Why does she not have to exert a torque to spin faster? Questions like these have answers based in angular momentum, the rotational analog to linear momentum. Throughout this chapter you should notice a pattern emerging — every rotational phenomenon has a direct translational analog. Continuing the pattern, momentum has a rotational equilvalent called **angular momentum.** Angular momentum, L, is defined as:

$$L=I\omega$$

This equation is an analog to the definition of linear momentum as $p = mv$. Units for linear momentum are kg·m/s while units for angular momentum are kg·m$^2$/s. An object that has a large moment of inertia $I$, such as Earth, has a very large angular momentum. An object that has a large angular velocity $\omega$, such as a centrifuge like the one in Figure 7.6.1, also has a rather large angular momentum.

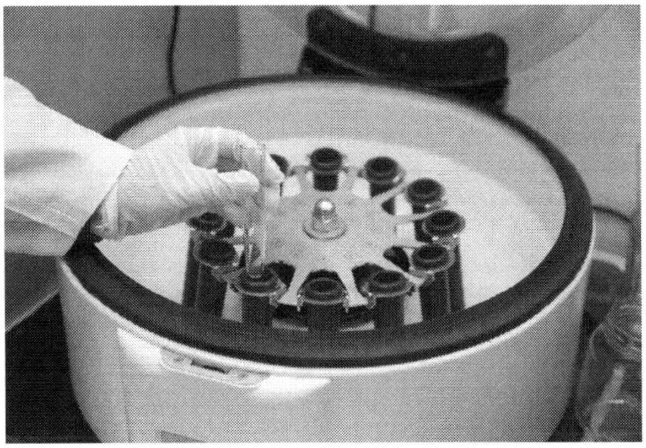

**Figure 7.6.1** *Centrifuges are common in many scientific laboratories.*

## Sample Problem 7.6.1 — Calculating the Earth's Angular Momentum

What is the angular momentum of the Earth?

| What to Think About | How to Do It |
| --- | --- |
| 1. No information is given in the statement of the problem; so we must look up pertinent data before we can calculate $L = I\omega$. | • Earth's mass M is 5.979 X 1024 kg<br>• Earth's radius R is 6.376 X 106 m<br>• Earth's angular velocity ω is one revolution per day converted to radians per second. |
| 2. Now, using Figure 7.4.3, find the formula for the moment of inertia. This will allow us to find *L*. | $I = \dfrac{2MR^2}{5}$<br>$L = I\omega = \dfrac{2MR^2\omega}{5}$ |
| 3. Substitute known information into the expression for *L* and convert ω to radians per second. | $L = 0.4(5.979 \times 10^{24}\ kg)(6.376 \times 10^{6}\ m)^2 (1\dfrac{rev}{day})$<br>$L = 9.72 \times 10^{37}\ kg \cdot m^2 \cdot \dfrac{rev}{day}$ |
| 4. Finally substituting 2π rad for 1 rev and $8.64 \times 10^4$ s for 1 day to find *L* in $kg{\cdot}m^2/s$ | $L = (9.72 \times 10^{37}\ kg \cdot m^2)\left(\dfrac{\dfrac{2\pi rad}{rev}}{\dfrac{8.64 \times 10^4\ sec}{day}}\right)(1\dfrac{rev}{day})$<br>$L = 7.07 \times 10^{33}\ kg \cdot m^2/s$<br>This number is large, demonstrating that Earth, as expected, has a tremendous angular momentum. The answer is approximate, because we have assumed a constant density for Earth in order to estimate its moment of inertia. |

### Practice Problem 7.6.1 — Calculating Angular Momentum

1. A solid metal sphere (moment of inertia $I = \frac{2}{5}MR^2$) initially at rest rolls atop a 2.00 m high incline. The mass of the sphere is 100 g and its radius is 5.00 cm. The sphere is released from rest and accelerates down the incline. Determine its final angular momentum at the bottom of the incline.

When you push a merry-go-round, spin a bike wheel, or open a door, you exert a torque. If the torque you exert is greater than opposing torques, then the rotation accelerates, and angular momentum increases. The greater the net torque, the more rapid the increase in *L*. The relationship between torque and angular momentum is:

$$\text{net } \tau = \frac{\Delta L}{\Delta t}$$

This expression is exactly analogous to the relationship between force and linear momentum, $F = \frac{\Delta p}{\Delta t}$. The equation $\text{net } \tau = \frac{\Delta L}{\Delta t}$ is fundamental and broadly applicable. It is, in fact, the rotational form of Newton's second law.

## Sample Problem 7.6.2 — Torque and Angular Momentum

The figure below shows a spinning food tray being rotated by a person. Suppose the person exerts a 2.50 N force perpendicular to the plate 0.260-m radius for 0.150 s.

(a) What is the final angular momentum of the spinning food tray if it starts from rest, assuming friction is negligible?
(b) What is the final angular velocity of the spinning food tray, given that its mass is 4.00 kg and assuming its moment of inertia is that of a disk?

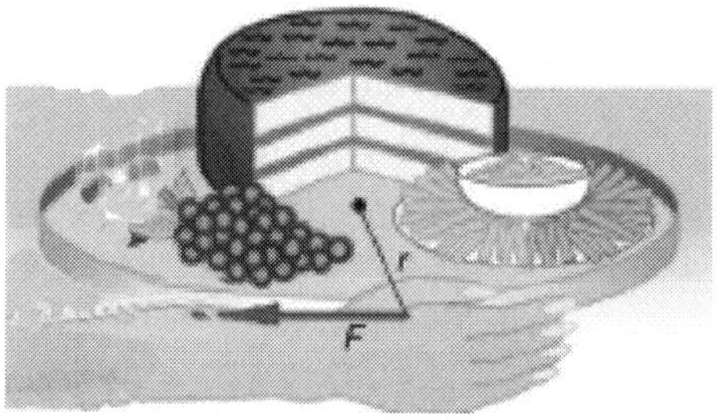


*A person exerts a torque on a spinning food tray to make it rotate. The equation net τ = ΔL/Δt gives the relationship between torque and the angular momentum produced.*

| What to Think About | How to Do It |
|---|---|
| **Part (a)** | |
| 1. Need to solve net $\tau = \Delta L/\Delta t$ for $\Delta L$ | $\Delta L = (\text{net}\,\tau)\Delta t$ |
| 2. Because the force is perpendicular to r, we see that net $\tau = rF$. | $L = rF\Delta t = (0.260\text{ m})(2.50\text{ N})(0.150\text{ s})$<br>$L = 9.75 \times 10\text{–}2\text{ kg m}^2/\text{s}$ |
| **Part (b)** | |
| 1. Calculate the final angular velocity from the definition of angular momentum. | $L = I\omega$ |
| 2. Solve for ω and substitute the formula for the moment of inertia of a disk. | $\omega = \frac{L}{I} = \frac{L}{\frac{1}{2}MR^2}$ |
| 3. Substitute known values and solve. | $\omega = \frac{9.75 \times 10^{-2}\text{ kg}\cdot\text{m}^2/\text{s}}{0.500(4.00\text{kg})(0.260\text{m})} = 0.721\text{rad}/\text{s}$ |

### Practice Problem 7.6.2 — Calculating Torque and Angular Momentum

1. A disk ($I = \frac{1}{2} MR^2$) with mass 100g, radius 5.00 cm is initially at rest. A torque of 5.00 N·m applied for 2.00 seconds. Find momentum and final angular velocity.

## Conservation of Angular Momentum

We can now explain why Earth keeps on spinning. As we saw in the previous example, $\Delta L = (\text{net } \tau)\Delta t$. This equation means that, to change angular momentum, a torque must act over some period of time. Because Earth has a large angular momentum, a large torque acting over a long time is needed to change its rate of spin. So what external torques are there? Tidal friction exerts torque that is slowing Earth's rotation, but tens of millions of years must pass before the change is very significant. Recent research indicates the length of the day was 18 h some 900 million years ago. Only the tides exert significant retarding torques on Earth, and so it will continue to spin, although ever more slowly, for many billions of years. This is another example of a conservation law. If the net torque is zero, then angular momentum is constant or conserved. We can see this rigorously by considering $\text{net } \tau = \frac{\Delta L}{\Delta t}$ for the situation in which the net torque is zero. In that case,

$$\text{net } \tau = 0$$

Implying that

$$\frac{\Delta L}{\Delta t} = 0$$

If the change in angular momentum ΔL is zero, then the angular momentum is constant; thus,

$$L = \text{constant (net } \tau = 0)$$

or

$$L = L' (\text{net } \tau = 0).$$

These expressions are the law of conservation of angular momentum. Conservation laws are as scarce as they are important.

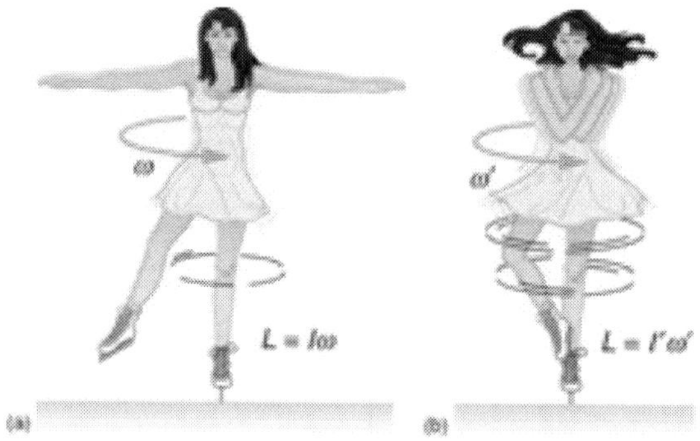


**Figure 7.6.2** *(a) An ice skater is spinning on the tip of her skate with her arms extended. Her angular momentum is conserved because the net torque on her is negligibly small. In (b) her rate of spin increases greatly when she pulls in her arms, decreasing her moment of inertia. The work she does to pull in her arms results in an increase in rotational kinetic energy*

An example of conservation of angular momentum is seen in Figure 7.6.2, in which an ice skater is executing a spin. The net torque on her is very close to zero, because there is relatively little friction between her skates and the ice and because the friction is exerted very close to the pivot point. Both *F* and *r* are small, and so τ is negligibly small. Consequently, she can spin for quite some time. She can do something else, too. She can increase her rate of spin by pulling her arms and legs in. Why does pulling her arms and legs in increase her rate of spin? The answer is that her angular momentum is constant, so that

$$L = L'$$

Expressing this equation in terms of the moment of inertia,

$$I\omega = I'\omega'$$

where the primed quantities refer to conditions after she has pulled in her arms and reduced her moment of inertia. Because $I'$ is smaller, the angular velocity $\omega'$ must increase to keep the angular momentum constant. The change can be dramatic, as the following example shows.

**Sample Problem 7.6.3 — Calculating the Angular Momentum of a Spinning Skater**

Suppose an ice skater, such as the one in Figure 7.6.2, is spinning at 0.800 rev/ s with her arms extended. She has a moment of inertia of 2.34 kg·m$^2$ with her arms extended and of 0.363 kg·m$^2$ with her arms close to her body. These moments of inertia are based on reasonable assumptions about a 60.0 kg skater.

(a) What is her angular velocity in revolutions per second after she pulls in her arms?
(b) What is her rotational kinetic energy before and after she does this?

| What to Think About | How to Do It |
|---|---|
| **Part (a)** | |
| 1. Because torque is negligible as mentioned in the caption of Figure 7.6.2, we can use the conservation of angular momentum | $L = L'$ or $I\omega = I'\omega'$ |
| 2. Solve for ω' and substitute known values. | $\omega' = \frac{I}{I'}\omega = \left(\frac{2.34\,kg\cdot m^2}{0.363\,kg\cdot m^2}\right)(0.800\,rev/s)$ <br> $\omega' = 5.16\,rev/s$ |
| **Part (b)** | $KE_{rot} = \frac{1}{2}I\omega^2$ |
| 1. The initial value for $KE_{rot}$ is found by substituting known values into the equation and converting the angular velocity to rad/s. | $KE_{rot} = 0.5(2.34\,kg\cdot m^2)(0.800\frac{rev}{s})(2\pi\frac{rad}{rev})^2$ <br> $KE_{rot} = 29.6\,J$ |
| 2. Final $KE_{rot}$ or $KE_{rot}'$ is found by substituting known values. | $KE_{rot}' = 0.5(0.363\,kg\cdot m^2)(5.16\frac{rev}{s})(2\pi\frac{rad}{rev})^2$ <br> $KE_{rot}' = 191\,J$ |

In both parts, there is an impressive increase. First, the final angular velocity is large, although most world-class skaters can achieve spin rates about this great. Second, the final kinetic energy is much greater than the initial kinetic energy. The increase in rotational kinetic energy comes from work done by the skater in pulling in her arms. This work is internal work that depletes some of the skater's food energy.

There are several other examples of objects that increase their rate of spin because something reduced their moment of inertia. Tornadoes are one example. Storm systems that create tornadoes are slowly rotating. When the radius of rotation narrows, even in a local region, angular velocity increases, sometimes to the furious level of a tornado. Earth is another example. Our planet was born from a huge cloud of gas and dust, the rotation of which came from turbulence in an even larger cloud. Gravitational forces caused the cloud to contract, and the rotation rate increased as a result.

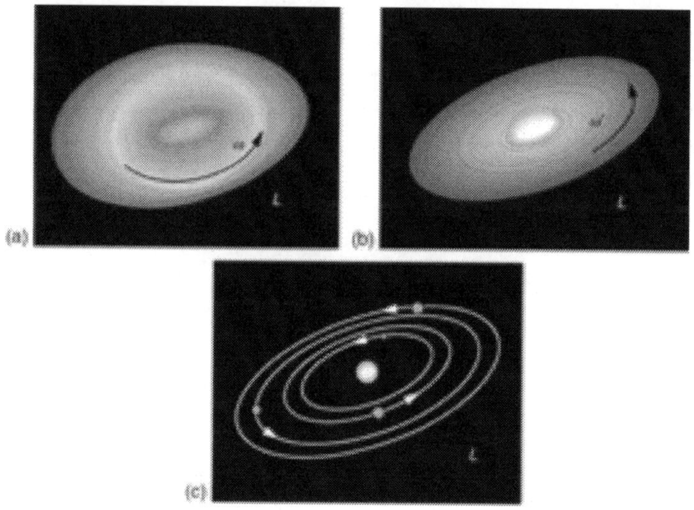


**Figure 7.6.3** *The Solar System coalesced from a cloud of gas and dust that was originally rotating. The orbital motions and spins of the planets are in the same direction as the original spin and conserve the angular momentum of the parent cloud.*

# 7.6 Review Questions

1. A solid disk with radius, $R$, mass, $M$ and moment of inertia $I = ½ MR^2$ rolls along a surface without slipping at a constant velocity $v$. Show what is the angular momentum of the disk about its own axis as it rolls.

2. A horizontal disk 1 with rotational inertia 4.25 kg·m$^2$ with respect to the axis of rotation is spinning counter clockwise at 15.5 rev/s as viewed from above. A second disk 2 with rotational inertia 1.80 kg·m$^2$ with respect to the axis of rotation, spins clockwise 14.2 rev/s as viewed from above. Disk 2 drops onto disk 1 and they stick together and rotate as one about their common rotational axis. Determine the final angular speed of the two-disk system in rev/s and rad/s.

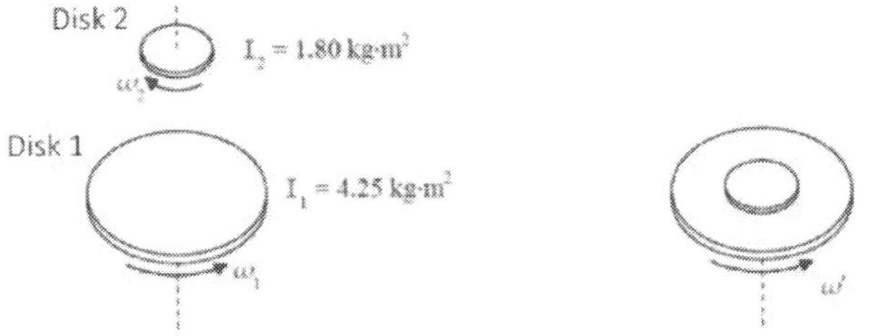


3. Comets travel in elliptical paths around the sun at a distance r from the center of the sun. They can be considered to be point-particles with rotational inertia $I=mr^2$. Explain in terms of the conservation of angular momentum, why comets speed up as they approach the sun.

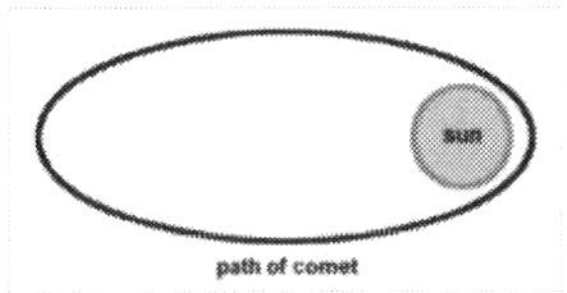

*The path of a comet*

4. A solid disk of mass 100 g and radius 5.00 cm is initially at rest atop an inclined place. The disk is released and accelerates down the incline making 6 complete revolutions in 4.00 seconds. Determine the final angular velocity and angular momentum of the disk.

5. A solid disk (moment of inertia $I = ½ MR^2$) is initially at rest rolls atop a 4.00 m high incline. The mass of the disk is 100 g and its radius is 5.00 cm. The disk is released from rest and accelerates to the bottom of the incline. Determine its final angular momentum at the bottom of the incline.

# Chapter 7 Conceptual Review Questions

1. You are at a playground with a merry-go-round. While standing at the center of the device, a friend spins you around until you reach a constant speed. You then begin to walk toward the outer edge of the platform. Describe what happens to you in terms of your angular momentum and rotational kinetic energy.

2. What will happen to the magnitude of acceleration for a propeller that goes from three blades to four blades? Assume the same net torque is placed on each propeller.

3. You are doing a laboratory investigation with the following objects: a hoop; a uniform disk; and a uniform sphere. They all have the same mass and outer radius. Your procedural plan is to roll them up an incline with the same starting speed. Rank from highest to lowest, how high each object will go up the ramp and explain your thinking.

4. When an ice skater pulls his hands into his body while spinning describe what happens in terms of angular momentum, moment of inertia and rotational speed.

5. You and three friends are watching the women's Olympic figure skating finals. If a skater with a rotational inertia of $I_o$ is spinning with an angular speed $w_o$ pulls her arms in and increases her angular speed to $4w_o$, what is her rotational inertia?

## Chapter 7 Review Questions

1. A 588 N mother sits on one side of a seesaw, 2.20 m from the pivot. Her daughter sits 2.00 m from the pivot on the other side of the seesaw. If the force of gravity on this child is 256 N, where must the mother's other child sit to balance the seesaw if the force of gravity on him is 412 N?

2. If the force exerted by the fish line on the tip of the rod is 4.0 N, what force must the person fishing exert in the direction and location shown in the drawing below? Ignore the rod's mass, and assume the rod is pivoted in the other hand.

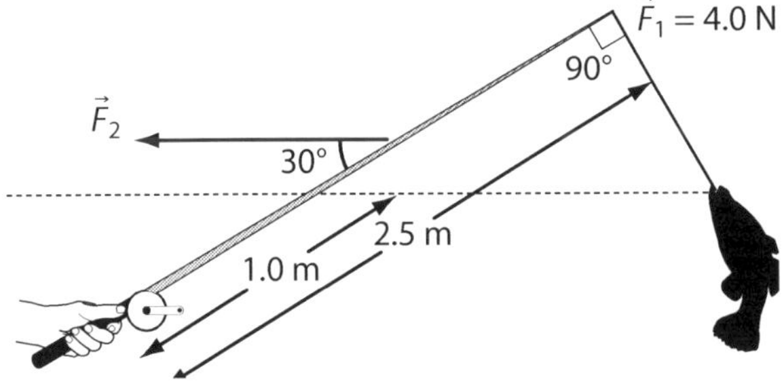


3. What upward force is exerted by the right support leg of the bench in the drawing below?

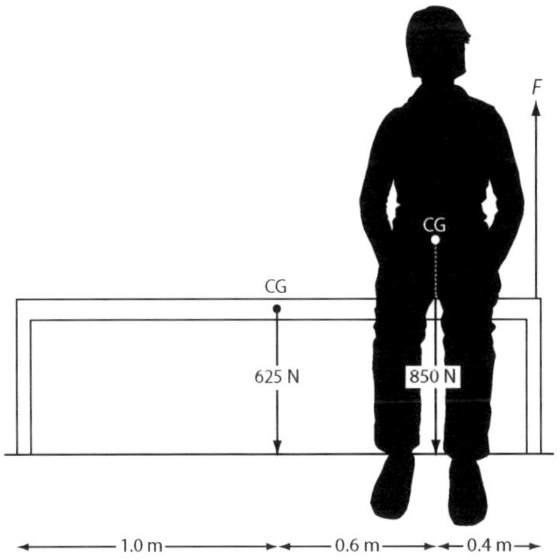


4. If the force of gravity on the beam in the diagram below is $1.2 \times 10^3$ N, what forces must be exerted at A and B to maintain equilibrium? In what direction must each force act?

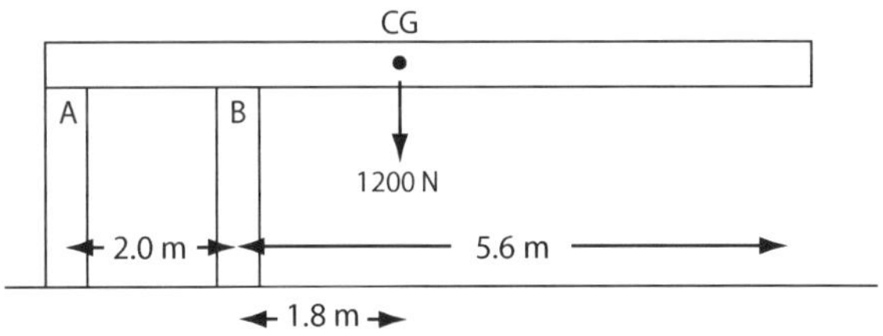

5. A giant disk with radius 2.0 m is initially at rest. It is accelerated uniformly to a final angular velocity of 18 rad/s over a time of 0.90 s. Determine its angular displacement.

6. A tire of radius 40 cm initially at rest begins to acceleration downhill at a rate of 2.0 rad/$s^2$ for 5.0 seconds. Determine its angular displacement in radians and linear displacement in meters.

7. A car engine is idling at 500 rpm. When the traffic light turns green the driver accelerates and the engines crankshaft rotation increases uniformly to 2500 rpm in 3.00 s. How many revolutions does the crankshaft make in this time?

8. A turntable initially spinning at 3.5 rad/s makes three complete rotations as is comes to a complete stop. Find its angular deceleration, and how much time it takes to stop.

9. A flywheel with moment of inertia 15 $kgm^2$ is rotating at 90 rad/s. What constant torque is required to slow it down to 40 rad/s in 20 s? What is the angular displacement of the flywheel while it is decelerated from 90 rad/s to 40 rad/s in 20 s?

10. A 100 cm long rod of mass 200 grams and moment of inertia $I = \frac{1}{3}mr^2$ is hinged at one end and connected to the wall. The rod is initially held horizontally and then released. Find the speed of the tip of the rod as it strikes the wall.

11. The engine of a small airplane provides a torque of 60 N·m and operates to spin a propeller of mass 40 kg and length $L = 2.0$ m. The propeller is similar to a rod that rotates about its center with moment of inertia $I = {}^{1}/_{12}\, mL^2$. Upon start up, how much time would it take for the propeller to be spinning at 200 rpm?

12. A disk ($I = {}^{1}/_{2} mr^2$) with mass 100 grams, radius 5.00 cm is initially at rest. A torque of 10.0 Nm applied for 4.00 seconds. Find final angular velocity, rotational KE, and momentum.

13. A solid spherical marble of mass 200 g and radius 15 cm is rolling at 40 cm/s. The moment of inertia $I = {}^{2}/_{5} mr^2$. Determine the sum of rotational and translational kinetic energies of the marble, and the ratio of rotational KE to translational KE.

14. A 450 g solid disk of radius 50 cm has an initial translational speed of 2.8 m/s as it rolls across the floor. The disk's rotational inertia $I = ½\ mr^2$. The disk rolls up the ramp that is 50 cm above the floor. Determine the translational velocity of the disk as it rolls across the horizontal level at the top of the ramp.

15. A uniform solid cylinder of mass 200 grams and radius 10.0 cm is mounted on frictionless bearings about a fixed axis through O. The moment of inertia of the cylinder is $\frac{1}{2}mr^2$. A block of mass 100 grams is suspended from the cord that wraps around the cylinder as shown. Determine the velocity of the mass when it has fallen 50.0 cm, and the angular momentum of the solid cylinder.

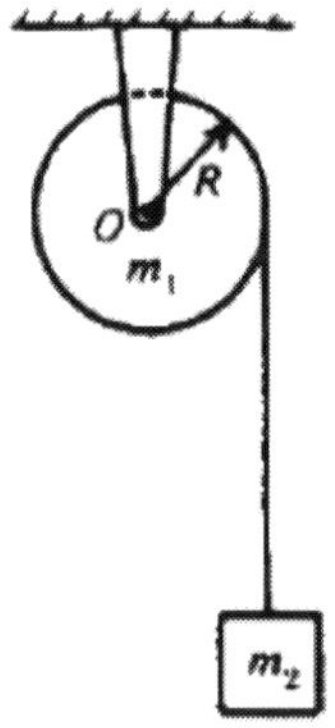


16. A merry-go-round of radius 2.00 m is rotating about a frictionless pivot. The rotating platform has $I = \frac{1}{2}mr^2$ and it makes one revolution every 5.00 s. The moment of inertia of the merry-go-round (about an axis through its center) is 500 kg·m². A child of mass 25.0 kg, originally standing at the center walks toward the outer rim. The child can be considered as a point mass ($I = mr^2$).

a) What is the new angular velocity of the merry-go-round?

b) Calculate the initial rotational KE and the final rotational KE.

# Investigation 7.1 Rotational Equilibrium

## Purpose

To investigate the conditions necessary to prevent the rotation of a loaded beam

## Procedure

1. Figure 7.1.a shows you how to find the centre of gravity of a metre stick very quickly. Hold the metre stick on your two index fingers, as in the diagram. Slowly slide your fingers toward each other. When they meet, they will have the centre of gravity "surrounded." Try this several times.

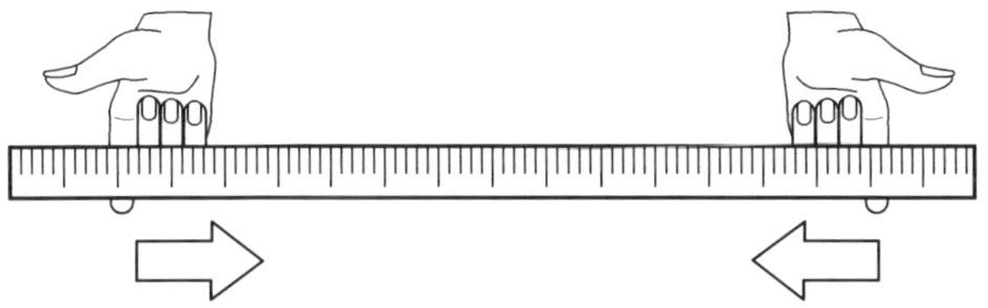

**Figure 7.1.a**

2. Mount your metre stick on a stand (Figure 7.1.b) with the pivot exactly at the centre of gravity. (Few metre sticks are perfectly uniform, so do not assume that the centre of gravity (CG) is at the 50.0 cm mark.) Adjust the pivot point precisely until the metre stick is in equilibrium. Record the position of the CG to the nearest millimetre.

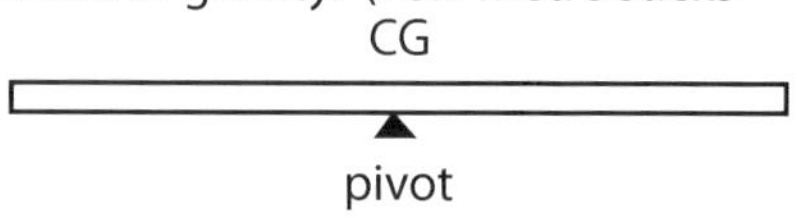


**Figure 7.1.b**

3. Use a very thin, light piece of wire to attach a 1.00 kg mass at a distance of 20.0 cm from the pivot. The force of gravity on this mass will be 9.80 N. This force is labeled $\vec{F}_1$ on Figure 7.1.c. The distance from the pivot to the point where $\vec{F}_1$ acts is called the lever arm and is labelled $\ell_1$. The torque due to $\vec{F}_1$ produces a clockwise turning effect, so it is called a clockwise torque. It is labelled $\tau_1$. ($\tau_1 = \vec{F}_1 \ell_1$).

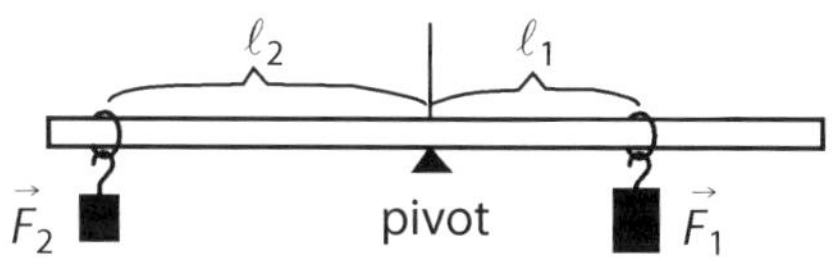


**Figure 7.1.c**

4. Suspend a 500 g mass by a light piece of wire on the other side of the metre stick. Adjust its lever arm until the metre stick is in a state of equilibrium. The force of gravity on the 500 g mass is 4.90 N. Call this force $\vec{F}_2$ and its lever arm $\ell_2$. The torque $\tau_2$ is a counterclockwise torque. ($\tau_2 = \vec{F}_2 \ell_2$) Record the forces and lever arms in a table like Table 7.1. Calculate the torques and enter them in the table for Trial 1. (Torque is expressed in N• m.)

**Table 7.1** *Observations for Investigation 7.1*

| **Trial** | $\vec{F}_1$ | $\ell_1$ | $\tau_1$ | $\vec{F}_2$ | $\ell_2$ | $\tau_2$ | $\vec{F}_3$ | $\ell_3$ | $\tau_3$ | $\tau_2 + \tau_3$ |
|---|---|---|---|---|---|---|---|---|---|---|
| | (N) | (m) | (N•m) | (N) | (m) | (N•m) | (N) | (m) | (N•m) | (N•m) |
| 1 | | | | | | | | | | |
| 2 | | | | | | | | | | |
| 3 | | | | | | | | | | |
| 4 | | | | | | | | | | |

5. Repeat the experiment, but place the 1.0 kg mass 25.0 cm from the pivot. Use *two* masses to produce counterclockwise torques and adjust their positions until the metre stick is at equilibrium. Measure and record all

the forces and lever arms in Table 7.1. Calculate torques $\tau_1$, $\tau_2$ and $\tau_3$ and record them in Table 7.1. (Trial 2.)

6. Try another combination of at least three forces of your own choosing. Record all forces and lever arms and calculate all the torques needed to produce rotational equilibrium. (Trial 3.)
7. Finally, set up your metre stick as in Figure 7.1.d so that the force of gravity on the metre stick produces a clockwise torque. Place the CG 20.0 cm to the right of the pivot. Use a 100 g mass (force of gravity 0.980 N) to balance the metre stick. Move the mass to a position where the metre stick stays balanced. Record all your data in Table 7.1 (Trial 4). Note that in this case $\vec{F}_1$ is the unknown force of gravity on the metre stick.

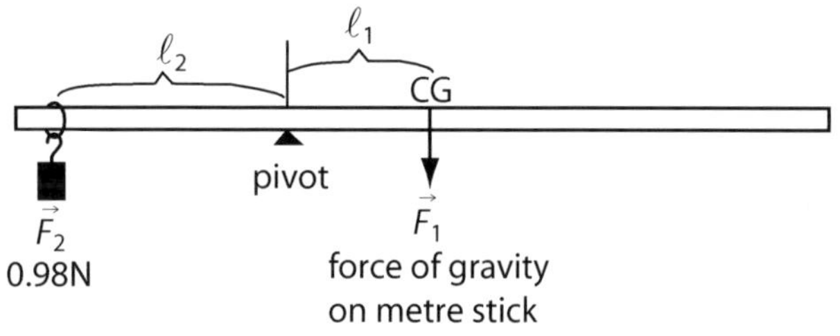


**Figure 7.1.d**

8. Hang the metre stick from a spring balance and measure the force of gravity on the metre stick, according to the spring balance. Keep a record of this force.

### Concluding Questions

1. Examine your calculated torques for each trial. When rotational equilibrium is achieved, what can you conclude regarding the clockwise torque(s) when compared with the counterclockwise torque(s)? State a general rule describing the condition(s) required for rotational equilibrium.
2. What are some likely sources of error that might cause discrepancies in your results? What is the maximum percent difference you observed when comparing the sum of the clockwise torques with the sum of the counterclockwise torques?
3. Use the general rule you described in (1) to calculate the force of gravity on your metre stick (Procedure step 7), using only the torques involved. Calculate the percentage difference between your calculated force of gravity and the force of gravity according to the spring balance. Explain any discrepancy you observe.

### Challenges

1. Explain why you can find the centre of gravity of a rod or metre stick using the method in Procedure step 1. Why do you think your fingers always meet at (or surrounding) the centre of gravity?
2. An equal-arm balance will work only if there is a gravitational field, $\vec{g}$ . Explain why such a balance will "read" the same mass whether it is used on Earth or on the Moon, where $\vec{g}$ is only 1/6 of that on Earth.
3. A golfer wishes to know where the centre of gravity of his putter face is. He can find out quickly by holding the putter face horizontal and bouncing a golf ball on the face of the putter, which is held loosely in his other hand. How does he know when he is bouncing the ball off the CG?

 

# 8 Electric Charge and Electric Force

This chapter focuses on the following AP Physics 1 Big Ideas from the College Board:

**BIG IDEA 1:** Objects and systems have properties such as mass and charge. Systems may have internal structure.

**BIG IDEA 3:** The interactions of an object with other objects can be described by forces.

**BIG IDEA 5:** Changes that occur as a result of interactions are constrained by conservation laws.

---

By the end of this chapter, you should know the meaning of these **key terms**:

- attract
- conduction
- conductors
- Coulomb's law
- electric force
- electron
- electrostatics
- elementary charge
- induction
- insulators
- law of conservation of charges
- point charge
- proton
- repel
- static electricity

---

By the end of the chapter, you should be able to use and know when to use the following formula:

$$F = k\frac{Q_1Q_2}{r^2}$$

$$Q = ne$$

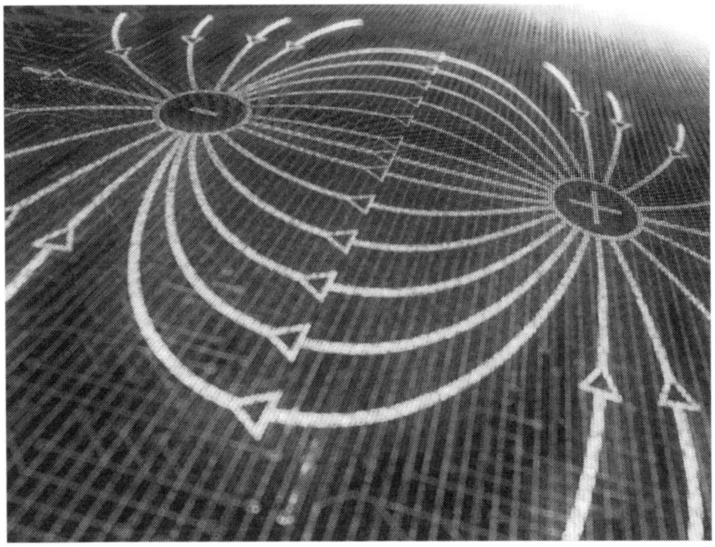

*In this chapter, you will investigate electrostatic principles, like the electric field interactions modelled in this image.*

# 8.1 Static Electric Charges

## Warm Up

Place a metre stick on a watch glass. Rub an inflated balloon on your hair and bring it close to the metre stick. Observe the result. Describe and provide a reason for what you observe.

______________________________________________________________________________

______________________________________________________________________________

______________________________________________________________________________

### Attraction and Repulsion Forces

If your hair is dry and you comb it briskly, your comb will attract not only your hair but also bits of dust, paper, or thread. The comb is probably made of plastic, but many kinds of material will produce the same effect. As long ago as 600 B.C., the Greeks observed the "attracting power" of amber when it was rubbed with cloth. Amber is a fossilized resin from trees that the Greeks used for decoration and trade. Of course, magnets also have an "attracting power," but they only attract certain metallic elements such as iron, nickel, and cobalt, and some of their alloys. Amber, if rubbed with cloth, will attract small bits of just about anything.

In the late 1500s, the Englishman Dr. William Gilbert was curious about this interesting property of amber, and he did many experiments with it and other materials. Gilbert discovered that many materials, if rubbed with certain fabrics, could be electrified. Words like *electrified, electricity, electron,* and *electronics* come from the Greek word for *amber,* which was *elektron.*

In the early 1700s, Charles du Fay, a French scientist, was probably the first person to figure out that there were two kinds of electricity**.** He observed that if two glass rods were rubbed with silk and brought near each other, they would **repel** one another. "Repel" means to push away. Two amber rods rubbed with fur would also repel one another. If, however, an "electrified" amber rod was brought close to an "electrified" glass rod, the two rods would **attract** each other. Du Fay correctly deduced that there must be two kinds of electricity. Later in the 1700s, Benjamin Franklin called these "positive electricity" and "negative electricity."

By convention, a glass rod rubbed with silk is said to have a **positive charge**. An amber rod rubbed with wool or fur has a **negative charge.**

In classroom experiments, a good way to get a positive charge is to rub an acetate plastic strip with cotton. A negative charge is easily obtained by rubbing a vinyl plastic strip with wool or fur (Figure 8.1.1).

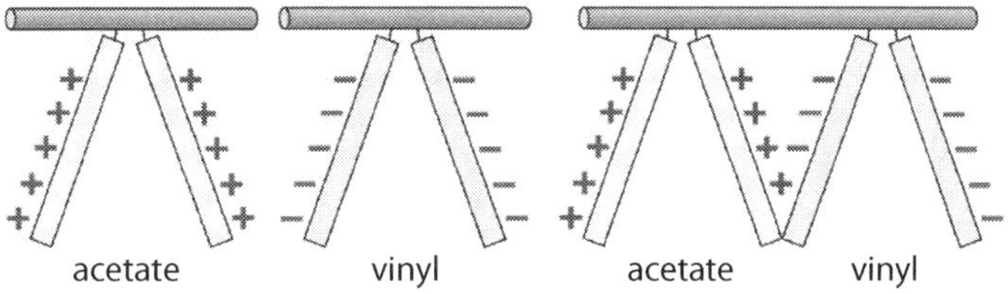


**Figure 8.1.1** *Two charged acetate plastic strips (+), hanging freely from a supporting rod, repel each other. Two charged vinyl strips (–) also repel each other. However, a charged acetate strip will attract a charged vinyl strip.*

Since the electric charges on "electrified" objects are not moving, they are referred to as **static charges** or **static electricity**. "Static" means stationary or unmoving.

A charged object will attract any **neutral** body. A neutral body is one without any charge. It will also attract an oppositely charged body, but it will repel another body carrying the same charge.

Bodies with the same charge repel each other.
Bodies with opposite charges attract one another.
A neutral body is attracted to either a positively charged body or a negatively charged body.

## Elementary Atomic Structure

John Dalton's famous atomic theory assumed that all matter was made up of indivisible particles. A very important experiment by Ernest Rutherford showed that the atom actually had some internal structure to it. He was able to show that the atom had a **nucleus**, in which positive charge was concentrated. Since the atom as a whole is neutral, there must be negatively charged matter somehow distributed around the nucleus. Negatively charged particles were first identified by English physicist J. J. Thomson. These were later called **electrons**.

A simplified view of the atom as pictured in Rutherford's "planetary" model shows the nucleus of the atom with its positive charge, surrounded by negatively charged electrons**.** The positively charged particles in the nucleus are **protons**. Figure 8.1.2 also shows **neutrons**, but these were not discovered until 1932. An English physicist named James Chadwick, a contemporary of Rutherford, added this particle to the list of subatomic particles. Neutrons carry no electric charge, and their mass is just slightly greater than that of protons. Electrons are far less massive than protons or neutrons. The mass of a proton is $1.67 \times 10^{-27}$ kg, which is 1836 times the mass of an electron.

The smallest atom is that of hydrogen. It has the simplest possible nucleus — one proton. The radius of the nucleus is approximately $10^{-15}$ m, compared with the radius of the hydrogen atom as a whole, which is approximately $10^{-10}$ m. Rutherford thought that the hydrogen nucleus might be the fundamental unit of positive charge. He was first to use the label proton for the hydrogen nucleus.

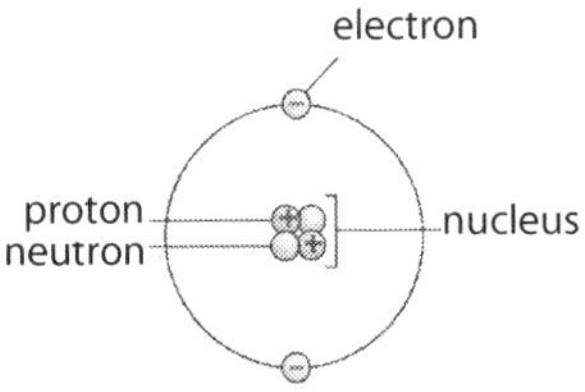


**Figure 8.1.2** *The simple "planetary" model of the atom*

The normal state of an atom is neutral. However, atoms can gain or lose electrons, in which case they become electrically charged atoms called **ions.** Since protons are safely locked away in the nucleus of an atom, only electrons are transferred from one body to another during the "electrification" of normal objects.

## Electrification of Objects

Figure 8.1.3 shows what happens when a vinyl plastic strip is rubbed on wool. Vinyl has a stronger affinity for electrons than wool. When vinyl contacts wool, some electrons leave the wool and go to the surface of the vinyl. This leaves the vinyl with an excess of electrons, so it has a negative charge. The wool, having lost electrons, has a positive charge.

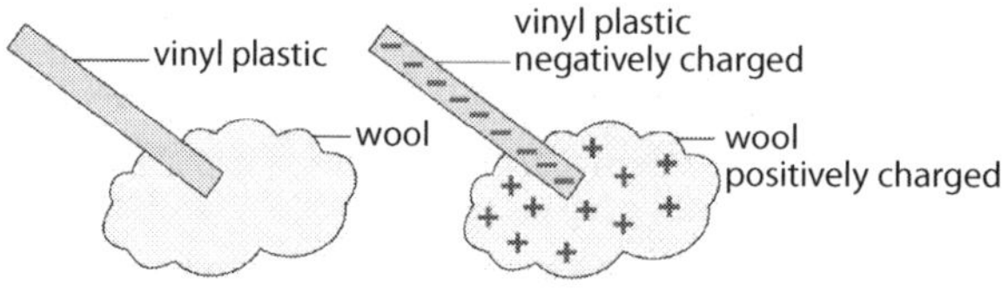


**Figure 8.1.3** *Charging a vinyl rod with wool: the vinyl becomes negatively charged and the wool becomes positively charged.*

Similarly, if acetate plastic is rubbed with cotton, the cotton gains electrons from the acetate. The acetate becomes positively charged while the cotton becomes negatively charged.

All experiments show that there is no "creation" or "destruction" of electric charge during electrification. All that happens is a transfer of electrons from one body to another.

> According to the **law of conservation of charge**, electric charge is never created and never destroyed. Electric charge, like momentum and total energy, is a conserved quantity.

## The Electrostatic or Triboelectric Series

Whether an object loses or gains electrons when rubbed with another object depends on how tightly the object holds onto its electrons. The electrostatic or triboelectric series lists various objects according to how tightly they hold onto their electrons (Figure 8.1.4). The higher up on the list the object is, the stronger its hold is on its electrons. The lower down on the list the object is, the weaker its hold is on its electrons. This means if we rub wool and amber together, electrons will be transferred from the wool to the amber. This results in the wool being positively charged and the amber being negatively charged.

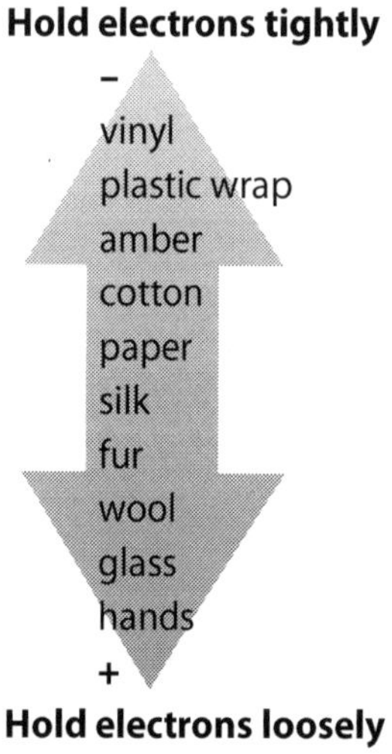


**Figure 8.1.4** *The electrostatic or triboelectric series*

## Conductors and Insulators

**Conductors** are materials that allow charged particles to pass through them easily. Metals such as silver, copper, and aluminum are excellent conductors of electricity, but all metals conduct to some extent. Atoms of metals have one or more outer electrons that are very loosely bound to their nuclei — so loosely attached that they are called "free" electrons.

In Figure 8.1.5, a metal rod is supported by a plastic cup. Plastic does not conduct electricity. A negatively charged vinyl strip is allowed to touch one end of the metal rod. When the vinyl touches the metal, a few excess electrons are conducted to the rod, so it becomes negatively charged as well. The negatively charged strip repels excess electrons to the far end of the metal rod. An initially neutral metal sphere, hanging from a silk string, is attracted to the charged rod. When the sphere touches the negatively charged rod, some of the excess electrons are conducted onto the sphere. Since the sphere is now the same charge as the rod, it is repelled from the rod.

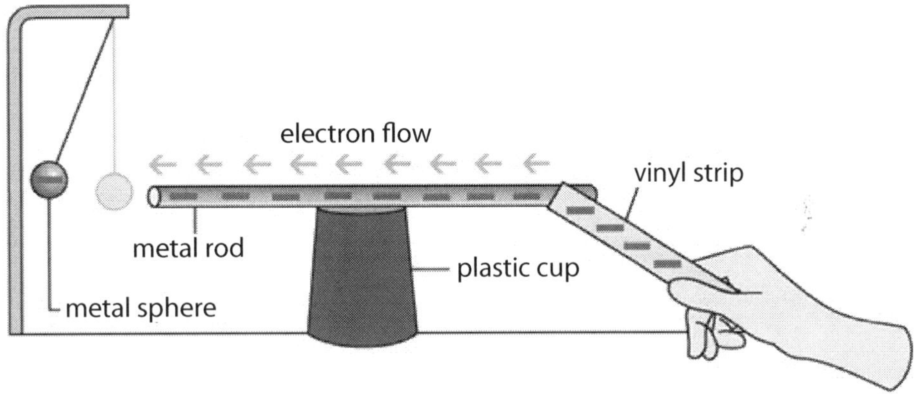


**Figure 8.1.5** *Electrons transfer from the vinyl strip to the metal rod and onto the sphere.*

Now both the rod and the sphere have an excess of electrons. If the vinyl strip is taken away, the rod and the sphere will retain their negative charge and the sphere will remain in its "repelled" position. On a dry day, it may stay there for many hours.

If the metal rod is replaced with a glass or plastic rod of similar dimensions, the metal sphere does not move. This is because glass and plastic are **insulators**. Insulators are materials that resist the flow of charged particles through them. Plastics, rubber, amber, porcelain, various textiles, mica, sulphur, and asbestos are examples of good insulators. Carbon in the form of diamond is an excellent but very expensive insulator. Carbon in the form of graphite is a good conductor.

Non-metals such as silicon and selenium find many uses in transistors and computer chips because of their "semiconductor" behavior.

It is easy to place a static charge on an insulator, because electrons are transferred only where the two objects come in contact. When an excess of charge builds up at a point on an insulator, the charge will not flow away — it remains static.

## Charging by Conduction

An **electroscope** is a device designed to detect excess electric charge. In Figure 8.1.6, a positively charged acetate strip is brought close enough to touch the neutral, metal-coated sphere of an electroscope. When they touch, the free electrons on the surface of the conducting sphere will be attracted to the positively charged acetate plastic. The acetate will gain a few electrons, but its overall charge will remain overwhelmingly positive. The sphere, however, now has a positive charge, so it is repelled by the acetate strip. We say the sphere has been charged by contact or by **conduction**. You could just as easily charge the sphere negatively by touching it with a charged vinyl strip.

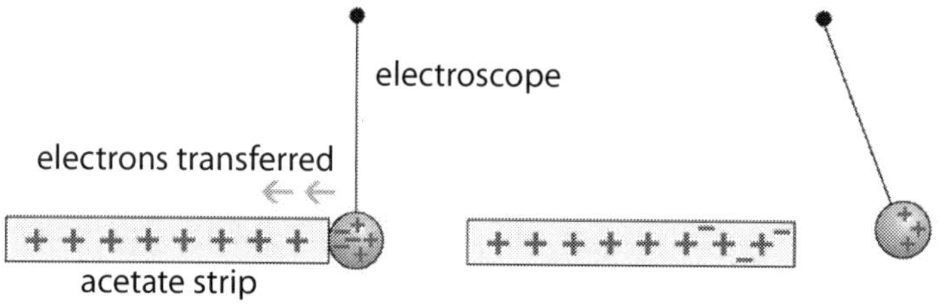


**Figure 8.1.6** *Charging by conduction*

## Charging by Induction

Objects can be charged without being touched at all, in which case we call it **charging by induction**. There are many ways to do this. Figure 8.1.7 shows one way. Two metal spheres are on insulated stands and are touching each other. A positively charged acetate strip is brought near the two spheres, but it does not touch them. Free electrons from the right sphere are attracted toward the left sphere by the positive acetate strip. Now the right sphere is pushed away using the insulated support stand. Tests with an electroscope will show that the right sphere has been charged **positively** by **induction**. The left sphere is charged **negatively** by **induction**.

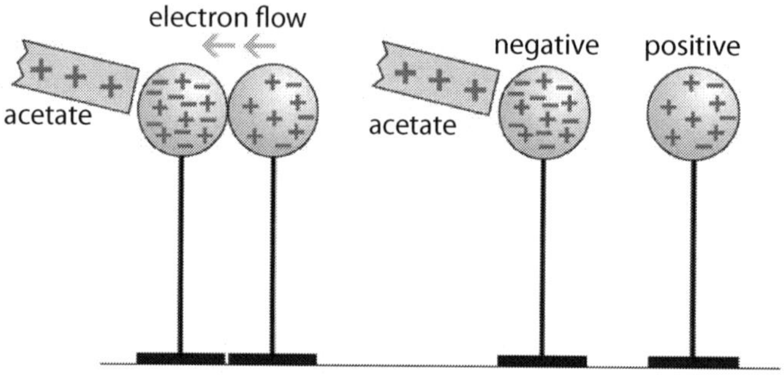


**Figure 8.1.7** *Charging by induction*

Note that charge has not been "created" during this procedure. All that has happened is this: a few electrons have been transferred from the right sphere to the left sphere. The total charge is still the same as it was before the charging by induction was attempted. The net charge is still zero.

 

## 8.1 Review Questions

1. What are the similarities and differences between the properties of an electron and a proton?

2. Describe the difference between a positive charge and a negative charge in terms of electrons.

3. Why do clothes sometimes have static on them as soon as they come out of the clothes dryer?

4. What will be the charge on a silk scarf if it is rubbed with glass? With plastic wrap?

5. A charged rod is brought near a pile of tiny plastic spheres. The spheres are attracted to the charged rod and are then fly off the rod. Why does this happen?

6. What would happen if the vinyl strip in Figure 8.1.5 was replaced with a positively charged acetate strip? Why?

7. Outline a method by which you could determine, with certainty, whether the charge on your comb after you comb your hair is positive or negative.

# 8.2 The Electric Force

## Warm Up

You have a charged acetate strip and some confetti. How could you use these two pieces of equipment to demonstrate which force is stronger — gravitational force or electric force?

______________________________________________

______________________________________________

______________________________________________

### Charles Coulomb

When you observe two objects being attracted or repelled due to electrostatic charge, you are observing non-contact forces in action. The two objects are exerting forces on each other without touching. The force exerted by one charged body on another can be measured. The force was initially measured by French scientist Charles Coulomb (1736–1806). He used an apparatus much like the Henry Cavendish's gravitational force apparatus to work out the relationship among these variables: force, distance, and quantity of charge. Figure 8.2.1 shows a setup similar to the one Coulomb used.

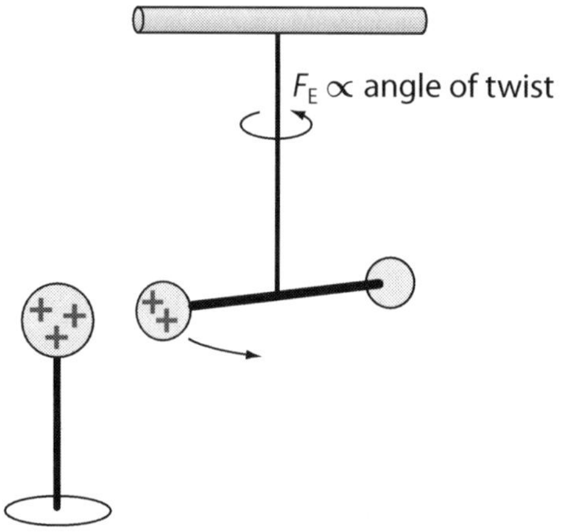


**Figure 8.2.1** *Coulomb used an apparatus similar to this to study the relationship among the variables force, distance, and quantity of charge.*

In Coulomb's apparatus, a torque caused by the repulsion of two similarly charged spheres caused a length of vertical wire to twist through an angle. The amount of twist was used to calculate the force of repulsion between the two charged spheres. The apparatus is called a **torsion balance**.

 

## Coulomb's Law

Coulomb was unable to measure the charges on the spheres directly. However, he found you can change the *relative* amount of charge in the following way: One sphere has an unknown charge $Q$ on it, and the other identical sphere has zero charge. If you touch the two spheres together, both spheres will have the charge $\frac{1}{2}Q$. This assumes that the excess charge on the original sphere will be shared equally with the second, identical sphere. This sharing of excess charge can be repeated several times to obtain spheres with charges of $\frac{1}{4}Q$, $\frac{1}{8}Q$, and so on.

Experiments by Coulomb and others led to the conclusion that the force of attraction or repulsion between two point charges depends directly on the product of the excess charges on the bodies and inversely on the square of the distance between the two point charges. This is known as **Coulomb's law**, and is written symbolically like this:

$$F = \text{constant} \cdot \frac{Q_1Q_2}{r^2} \text{, or}$$

$$F = \text{k}\frac{Q_1Q_2}{r^2}$$

The magnitude of the proportionality constant k depends on the units used to measure the excess charge. If the measuring unit is the **elementary charge** (as on one electron or one proton), then $Q$ would be measured in elementary charges, and the constant k in $F = \text{k}\frac{Q_1Q_2}{r^2}$ has a magnitude of

$$\mathbf{k = 2.306 \times 10^{-28}\ N{\cdot}m^2/(elem.\ charge)^2}$$

If the measuring unit for excess charge is the **coulomb** (named after Charles Coulomb), then $Q$ would be measured in coulombs (**C**) and the constant k becomes

$$\mathbf{k = 8.988 \times 10^{9}\ N{\cdot}m^2/C^2}$$

The value of k was worked out after Coulomb's time. At the time he did his experiments, there was not yet a unit for "quantity of charge." When scientists decided on an appropriate measuring unit for charge, they named it after Coulomb.

The wording of Coulomb's law mentions "point charges." Coulomb's law applies to very small charged bodies. If the charged bodies are large relative to the distance between them, it is difficult to know what value of $r$ to use. If the bodies are uniform spheres over which the charge is evenly spread, then you can use the distance between their centres. If two large, conducting spheres approach each other, forces between the charges will cause excess charges to rearrange themselves on the spheres in such a way that the "centres of charge" may not coincide with the "centres of mass."

## The Coulomb and the Elementary Charge

It is now known that a coulomb of charge is equivalent to the amount of charge on $6.2422 \times 10^{18}$ electrons (if the charge is negative) or on the same number of protons (if the charge is positive). The charge on one electron or one proton, called the elementary charge, is

$$\mathbf{1\ elementary\ charge\ (e) = \frac{1}{6.2422 \times 10^{18}\ /C} = 1.602 \times 10^{-19}\ C}$$

**Sample Problem 8.2.1 — Coulomb's Law**

What force would be exerted by a 1.00 C positive charge on a 1.00 C negative charge that is 1.00 m away?

| What to Think About | How to Do It |
| --- | --- |
| 1. Two charges are separated by a distance. This is a Coulomb's law question. | $F = k\frac{Q_1Q_2}{r^2}$ |
| 2. Find each charge and distance and remember to keep track of the sign. | $F = \frac{(8.988\ 10^9\ Nm^2/C^2)(1.00\ C)(-1.00\ C)}{(1.00\ m)^2}$ |
| 3. Solve. | |
| 4. As you can see, a +1.00 C charge would attract a −1.00 C charge 1 m away with a force of nearly 10 billion newtons! The coulomb is actually a *very* large amount of charge. | $F = -8.99 \times 10^9\ N$ |

**Practice Problems 8.2.1 — Coulomb's Law**

1. A small metal sphere with a charge of 3.00 $\mu$C (microcoloumbs) is brought near another metal sphere of charge 2.10 $\mu$C. The distance between the two spheres is 3.7 cm. Find the magnitude of the force of one charge acting on the other. Is it a force of attraction or repulsion?

2. What is the distance between two charges of $8.0 \times 10^{-5}$ C and $3.0 \times 10^{-5}$ C that experience a force of $2.4 \times 10^2$ N?

3. The force of repulsion between two identically charged small spheres is 4.00 N when they are 0.25 m apart. What amount of charge is on each sphere? Express your answer in microcoulombs ($\mu$C). (1 $\mu$C = $10^{-6}$ C) Use $k = 9.00 \times 10^9\ Nm^2/C^2$.

## Electric Force Due to Multiple Point Charges

When more than two charges are in the same area, the force on any one of charges can be calculated by vector adding the forces exerted on it by each of the others. Remember, the electric force is a vector and adding vectors means considering both magnitude and direction.

### Sample Problem 8.2.2(a) — Three Collinear Charges

Three tiny spheres are lined up in a row as shown in Figure 8.2.2. The first and third spheres are 4.00 cm apart and have the charges $Q_A = 2.00 \times 10^{-6}$ C and $Q_C = 1.50 \times 10^{-6}$ C. A negatively charged sphere is placed in the middle between the two positive charges. The charge on this sphere is $Q_B = -2.20 \times 10^{-6}$ C. What is the net force on the negatively charged sphere?

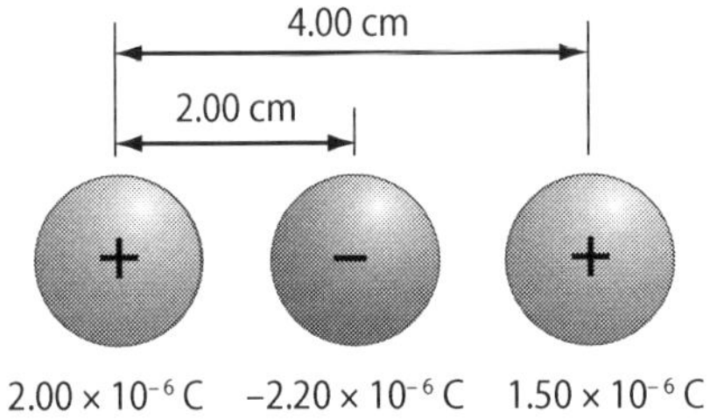


**Figure 8.2.2** *Three collinear charges*

| What to Think About | How to Do It |
|---|---|
| 1. The charge on sphere B is negative and the charge on sphere A is positive. This means the force between the two charges is attractive. The same for the force between sphere B and C. For this problem, right will be positive. | 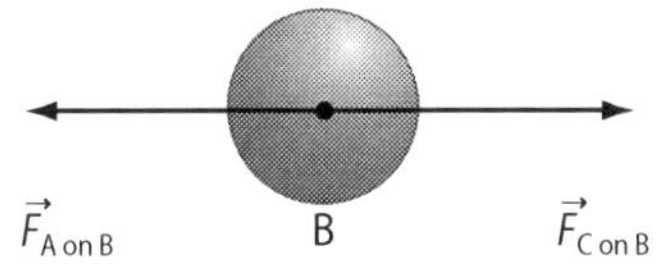  **Figure 8.2.3** |
| 2. Determine the net force on sphere B by adding the two force vectors. | $F_{net} = F_{C\ on\ B} + F_{A\ on\ B}$ <br> $F = k\dfrac{Q_C Q_B}{r^2} + k\dfrac{Q_A Q_B}{r^2}$ <br> $F = \dfrac{9.00 \times 10^9\ Nm^2/C^2\ (2.20 \times 10^{-6}\ C)(1.50 \times 10^{-6}\ C)}{(0.02\ m)(0.02\ m)}$ <br> $+ - \dfrac{9.00 \times 10^9\ Nm^2/C^2\ (2.20 \times 10^{-6}\ C)(2.00 \times 10^{-6}\ C)}{(0.02\ m)(0.02\ m)}$ |
| 3. The net force on sphere B is 24.8 N to the left. | $F = 74.2\ N + (-99.0\ N) = -24.8\ N$ |

# 8.2 Review Questions

Use the following numbers when calculating your answers:
$k = 9.00 \times 10^9$ Nm$^2$/C$^2$
1 elementary charge = $1.60 \times 10^{-19}$ C
1 C = $6.24 \times 10^{18}$ elementary charges

1. What will happen to the magnitude of the force between two charges $Q_1$ and $Q_2$ separated by a distance $r$ if:
   (a) one of the charges is doubled?
   (b) both charges are doubled?
   (c) separation distance is doubled?
   (d) separation distance is tripled?
   (e) both charges are doubled and separation distance is doubled?
   (f) both charges are doubled and separation distance is halved?

2. What force would be exerted on a 1.00 $\mu$C positive charge by a 1.00 $\mu$C negative charge that is 1.00 m away from it?

3. What is the force of repulsion between two bodies carrying 6.0 $\mu$C of charge and separated by 1.0 $\mu$m?

4. What is the force of attraction between a proton and an electron in a hydrogen atom, if they are $5.00 \times 10^{-11}$ m apart?

5. One electron has a mass of $9.1 \times 10^{-31}$ kg. How many coulombs of charge would there be in 1 kg of electrons? How much force would this charge exert on another 1 kg of electrons 1.0 km away? (This is strictly an imaginary situation!)

6. Two small spheres are located 0.50 m apart. Both have the same charge on them. If the repulsive force is 5.0 N, what charge is on the spheres, in $\mu$C?

7. Three charged objects are located at the "corners" of an equilateral triangle with sides 1.0 m long. Two of the objects carry a charge of 5.0 $\mu$C each. The third object carries a charge of –5.0 $\mu$C. What is the resultant force acting on the –5.0 $\mu$C object? Assume all three objects are very small.

8. Imagine you could place 1 g of electrons 1.0 m away from another 1 g of electrons.
   (a) Calculate
      (i) the electric force of repulsion between the two charge collections.
      (ii) the gravitational force of attraction between them.
      (iii) the *ratio* of the electric force to the gravitational force.
   (b) Discuss the practical aspects of this imaginary situation.

9. Discuss whether you think gravity would play a major part in holding atoms together. Refer to your results in question 8. Calculate the gravitational force between a proton and an electron $5.00 \times 10^{-11}$ m apart. Compare this force with the electric force calculated in question 4.

10. Two protons repel each other with a force of 1.0 piconewton ($10^{-12}$ N). How far apart are the protons?

# Chapter 8 Conceptual Review Questions

1. Four students are discussing the following statements. Which one has the correct explanation and why are the other incorrect?

a. Two charged objects attract eachother with a certain force. If the charges on both ojbects are doubled with no change in separation, what happens to the force between them?

Student 1: The force quadruples.
Student 2: The force halves.
Student 3: The force doubles
Student 4: The force increases, but there isn't enough information to determine how much of an increase.

b. Two charged objects are separated by a distance d. The first charge is larger in magnitude than the second charge.

Student 1: The first charge exerts a larger force on the second charge.
Student 2: The second charge exerts a larger force on the first charge.
Student 3: The charges exert forces on each other equal in magnitude and pointing in the same direction.
Student 4: The chrages exert forces on each other that are equal in magnitude and opposite in direction.

2. Two identical metal spheres initially carry charge of +6 Coulombs and –2 Coulombs. A conducting wire is attached to each sphere allowing charges to flow from one sphere to the other.

a. What is the final charge on each sphere?

b. How many Coulombs of charge were transferred and which sphere gained the electrons?

 

# Chapter 8 Review Questions

1. An aluminum ion carries a charge of +3 and a chloride ion carries a charge of –1. What is the coulomb charge carried by each ion?

2. Two identical metal spheres are initially 5 cm apart and carry charges of 8 C and -2 C respectively. The metal spheres are brought together and allowed to touch, resulting in electrons flowing from one sphere to the other. What is the final charge on each sphere and how many electrons were transferred?

3. An electron orbits the hydrogen nucleus containing 1 proton at a mean orbital distance of 5.3 × 10-11 m. Determine the electrostatic force of attraction between the electron and proton.

4. Two identical point charges are 10 cm apart and the electrostatic force between them is 3.6 N. Determine the magnitude of each charge.

5. Three point charges form a straight line with 10 cm between each of the charges. From left to right the charges are 2 C, –3 C, and –4 C. Determine the magnitude and direction of the net electrostatic force that acts on the middle charge.

# Investigation 8.1 Charging by Conduction and Induction

## Purpose

To experiment with two different ways of placing a charge on an object

### *Part 1 Charging by Conduction*

When you charge an object by touching it with another charged object, the electrons are conducted directly to it. In this process, you are charging by conduction.

*Styrofoam acts as an insulator.*

## Procedure

1. Set two aluminum pop cans on or in Styrofoam cups as shown in the Figure. Styrofoam is an excellent insulator, so it will keep any static charge you place on the cans from escaping to the bench.
2. Place a negative charge on one of the cans as follows:
   (a) Rub a vinyl strip with wool or fur. You may hear a crackling sound when the vinyl is being charged. The vinyl will have a negative charge on it.
   (b) Rub the charged vinyl strip over one of the insulated pop cans. Excess electrons from the vinyl will flow onto the can, giving the can a negative charge.
   (c) Repeat the process several times to make sure there is a lot of excess negative charge on the can.
3. Place a positive charge on the other can as follows:
   (a) Rub an acetate strip with cotton or paper. This will make the acetate positively charged, since electrons flow from the acetate to the cotton.
   (b) Rub the acetate strip onto the second can. The positively charged acetate strip will attract electrons from the second metal pop can, making the can positively charged.
   (c) Repeat this process several times to make sure the second can has lots of positive charge.
4. Do not touch the metal cans. Touching only their insulated Styrofoam bases, move the cans toward each other until they are about 3 cm apart.
5. Lower a graphite or pith ball between the two oppositely charged cans. Write down what you see happening.

## Concluding Questions

1. What charge was on
   (a) the first can at the start?
   (b) the second can at the start?
   (c) the graphite ball before it was lowered between the cans?
2. Explain what happened to the graphite or pith ball during the experiment. Describe what happened to the electrons going to and from the three objects involved
3. Why does the action eventually stop?

### *Part 2 Charging by Induction*

Imagine you have only a negatively charged strip, but you wish to place a positive charge on another object. If you touch the other object with a negatively charged strip, you will charge it negatively by conduction. However, if you use the induction method, you can give it a charge that is opposite to the charge on the charging body.

#### Procedure

1. Place a pop can on or in a Styrofoam cup.
2. Charge a vinyl strip negatively.
3. Bring the charged vinyl strip near and parallel to the pop can but do not let the vinyl strip touch the can.
4. Briefly touch the can with your finger, and then remove it and the vinyl strip completely. What do you think the charge is on the can? Repeat steps 2 to 4 until you can produce the same result three times in a row.
5. Work out a procedure to test for yourself whether the charge on the can is positive, negative, or neutral.

#### Concluding Questions

1. Before you brought your finger near the can,
   (a) what charge was on the vinyl strip?
   (b) what charge was on the side of the can near the vinyl strip?
   (c) what charge was on the other side of the can?
2. Your finger can conduct electrons to or from your body. In this experiment, were electrons conducted to the can from your body or from the can to your body?
3. (a) What was the final charge on the can?
   (b) Was this charge "conducted" from the vinyl strip?
   (c) How did the can obtain this charge?

# 9 DC Circuits

This chapter focuses on the following AP Physics 1 Big Ideas from the College Board:

**BIG IDEA 1:** Objects and systems have properties such as mass and charge. Systems may have internal structure

**BIG IDEA 5:** Changes that occur as a result of interactions are constrained by conservation laws.

---

By the end of this chapter, you should know the meaning of the **key terms**:

- ammeter
- ampere
- conventional electric current
- electric current
- electric power
- electromotive force (emf)
- equivalent resistance
- internal resistance
- parallel circuit
- resistance
- series circuit
- terminal voltage
- voltmeter

By the end of this chapter, you should be able to use and know when to use the following formulae:

$I = \frac{Q}{t}$ $V = IR$ $P = IV$ $V_{terminal} = \pm Ir$

*These high voltage transmission lines have an important role in transporting electrical energy to your home and school where the energy is used to power a range of electrical devices including hybrid vehicles.*

# 9.1 Current Events in History

## Warm Up

Your teacher will give you a light source, energy source, and wire. How many different ways can you arrange these three items so that the light source goes on? Draw each circuit.

### Galvani's and Volta's Experiments

Until 200 years ago, the idea of producing a steady current of electricity and putting it to use was nonexistent. The discovery of a way to produce a flow of electric charges was, in fact, accidental. In the year 1780, at the University of Bologna, Italian professor of anatomy Luigi Galvani (1737–1798) was dissecting a frog. First, he noticed that when a nearby static electricity generator made a spark while a metal knife was touching the frog's nerves, the frog's legs would jump as its muscles contracted! Galvani proceeded to look for the conditions that caused this behavior. In the course of his investigations, Galvani discovered that if two different metal objects (such as a brass hook and an iron support) touched each other, while also touching the frog's exposed flesh, the same contractions of the frog's legs occurred. Galvani thought that the source of the electricity was in the frog itself, and he called the phenomenon "animal electricity."

Another Italian scientist, physics professor Alessandro Volta (1745–1827), of the University of Pavia, set about to test Galvani's "animal electricity" theory for himself. Before long, Volta discovered that the source of the electricity was in the contact of two different metals. The animal (frog) was incidental. If any two different metals are immersed in a conducting solution of acid, base, or salt, they will produce an electric current. Volta was able to show that some pairs of metals worked better than other pairs. Of course, no ammeters or voltmeters were available in those days to compare currents and voltages. One way that Volta compared currents was to observe the response of the muscle tissue of dead frogs.

Neither Galvani nor Volta could explain their observations. (There is no truth to the rumor that the frog's leg jumped because 1780 was a leap year.) Many years later, it was learned that radio waves generated by the sparking generator induced a current in the metal scalpel that was penetrating the frog, even though the scalpel was some distance from the generator!

Volta eventually invented the first practical electric battery. Zinc and silver disks, separated by paper pads soaked with salt water, acted as electric cells. Stacked one on top of another, these cells became a "battery" that yielded more current than a single cell.

## Cells and Batteries

There are many types of electric cells in existence today. Usually when you purchase a "battery" in a store, you are actually buying a single **cell.** Strictly speaking, a battery consists of two or more cells connected together. Nine-volt batteries used in portable radios, tape recorders, calculators, and smoke alarms are true batteries. If you open up a discarded 9 V battery, you will see six small 1.5 V cells connected together, one after the other in what is called "a series."

Figure 9.1.1 shows one type of **voltaic cell** (named after Volta). The two rods, called **electrodes**, are made of carbon and zinc, as in the traditional **dry cell**, but they are immersed in a solution of ammonium chloride ($NH_4Cl$). In a real dry cell, a paste containing $NH_4Cl$, sawdust, and other ingredients is used. The chemistry of voltaic cells will be left to your chemistry courses. The reaction that occurs, however, has the effect of *removing electrons* from the carbon electrode (making it *positive*) and adding them to the zinc (making the zinc *negative*). In a real dry cell, the outer casing of the cell is made of zinc. The zinc is dissolved away as the cell is used, and may eventually leak its contents.

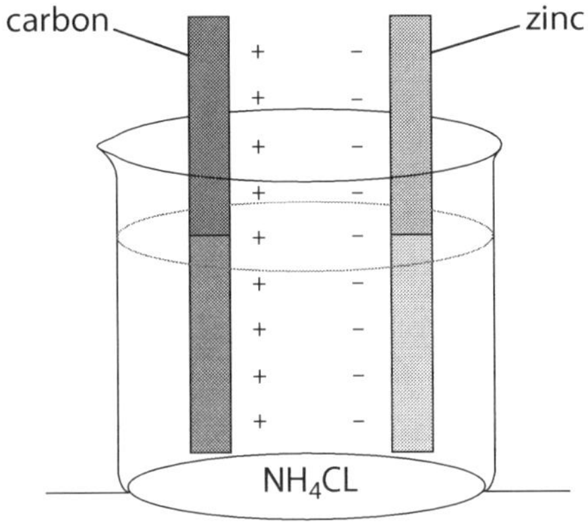


**Figure 9.1.1** *A voltaic cell*

There are many kinds of cells and batteries. Rechargeable "batteries" may use nickel and cadmium, or molybdenum and lithium, or lead and lead oxide (as in the standard car battery). There are many kinds of cells on the market today, but they all produce electric current when connected to a conducting path.

## Electromotive Force

In a carbon-zinc dry cell, forces resulting from the chemical reaction within the cell drive charges to the terminals, doing work to overcome the repulsive forces. The work done on the charges increases their potential energy. The difference in potential energy between the terminals amounts to 1.5 J for every coulomb of charge separated. We say the **potential difference** is 1.5 J/C, or 1.5 V. For a cell or battery that is not supplying current, the potential difference is at its peak value, which is called the **electromotive force (emf)**. It is given the symbol $\varepsilon$.

For a dry cell, the emf is 1.5 V. A nickel-cadmium cell is usually labelled 1.2 V or 1.25 V, but a freshly charged nickel-cadmium battery will have an even higher emf than its labelled rating. The cells in a lead storage battery have emfs of 2 V each. Six of these cells connected in series within the battery give a total emf of 12 V.

## Electric Current

When electric charges *flow*, we say a current exists**.** A current will exist as long as a continuous conducting path is created for charges to flow from and back to a source of emf, as shown in Figure 9.1.2.

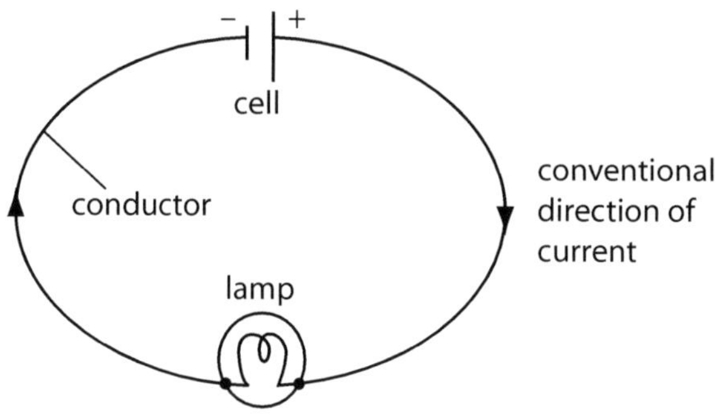


**Figure 9.1.2** *Electric charges flow as a current through a conductor as long as there is no break in the path.*

**Electric current** is defined as the amount of electric charge that passes a point in a circuit in one second. If an amount of charge Q passes a point in a circuit in a time t, then the average current I through that point is $I = \frac{Q}{t}$.

Current could quite logically be measured in coulombs per second (C/s), but this unit is called the **ampere (A)** after André Ampère (1775–1836**)**, a French physicist.

**1 A = 1 C/s**

One ampere is the sort of current that exists in a 100 W light bulb in a lamp in your home. (A 100 W lamp in a 110 V circuit would draw approximately 0.9 A.) In terms of electrons,

$$1\text{ A} = 6.24 \times 10^{18}\text{ electrons/s}$$

## Current Direction

The direction of current was defined arbitrarily by André Ampère to be the direction that positive charges would move between two points where there is a difference of potential energy. In many simple circuits, we now know it is negative charges (electrons) that actually move. In solid conductors, the positive charges are locked in the nuclei of atoms, which are fixed in their location in the crystal. Loosely attached electrons can move through the conductor from atom to atom. In liquids and gases, however, the flow of charges may consist of positively charged ions as well as negatively charged ions and electrons.

Throughout this book, we shall use conventional current direction: the direction that positive charges would move between two points where there is a potential difference between the points.

## Drift Velocity

How fast do electrons move in a wire carrying a current of, for example, 1 A? When a switch is closed in a circuit, the effect of the current can be detected immediately throughout the entire circuit. This might lead you to conclude that the electric charges (usually electrons) travel at very high velocity through the circuit. In fact, this is not so!

 

The average **drift velocity** of electrons in a given set of circumstances can be calculated.

Within a length of metal wire, there are many, many loosely attached electrons (sometimes called "free electrons"). These electrons move about much like the molecules in a container of gas might move.

Let's consider the movement of electrons in a silver wire. Silver is an excellent conductor. Let's assume there is one free electron for every silver atom in a piece of wire. When the wire is connected to a source of emf, the potential difference (voltage) will cause electrons to move from the negative terminal of the source of emf toward the positive terminal. This movement is *superimposed* on the random motion of the electrons that is going on all the time with or without a source of emf.

The trip the electrons make from the negative to the positive terminal is not a smooth one (as it is, for example, in the vacuum of a CRT). Electrons in the metal wire collide with positive silver ions on the way, and transfer some of their kinetic energy to the silver ions. The increased thermal energy of the silver ions will show up as an increase in temperature of the silver conductor.

Assume the current in the silver wire in Figure 9.1.3 is 1.0 A. Then there are $6.24 \times 10^{18}$ electrons passing the observer each second. This is because

$$\mathbf{1.0\ A = 1.0\ C/s = 6.24 \times 10^{18}\ e/s}$$

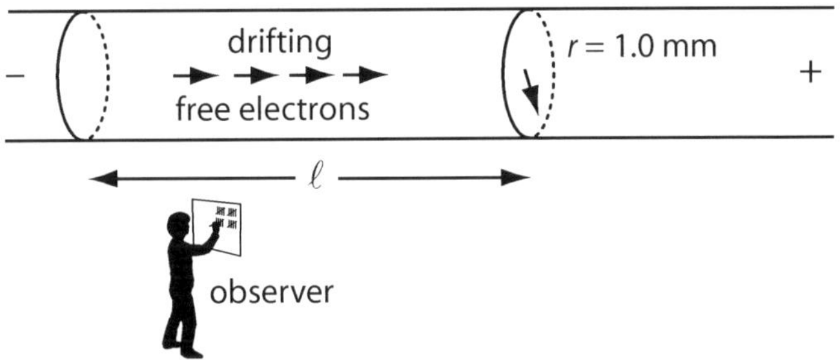


**Figure 9.1.3** *Calculating the average drift velocity of electrons through a silver wire*

To calculate the average drift velocity of the electrons, we start by again assuming that there is *one free electron for every silver atom*, a reasonable assumption, since chemists tell us that silver usually forms ions with a charge of +1.

All we need to know is what length of the silver wire in Figure 9.1.3 would contain $6.24 \times 10^{18}$ silver atoms (and therefore $6.24 \times 10^{18}$ free electrons). We can find this out in three steps, as follows:

1. The mass of silver needed to have $6.24 \times 10^{18}$ free electrons is

$$\text{mass} = \frac{6.24 \times 10^{18}\ \text{atoms}}{6.02 \times 10^{23}\ \text{atoms/mole}} \times 108\ \text{g/mole} = 1.12 \times 10^{-3}\ \text{g}$$

2. The volume of silver wire needed to have $6.24 \times 10^{18}$ free electrons is

$$\text{volume} = \frac{\text{mass}}{\text{density}} = \frac{1.12 \times 10^{-3}\ \text{g}}{10.5\ \text{g/cm}^3} = 1.07 \times 10^{-4}\ \text{cm}^3$$

3. The radius of the silver wire in Figure 9.1.3 is 1.0 mm, or 1.0 x $10^{-1}$ cm. Its cross-sectional area is $\pi r^2$, so the length, ℓ, can be found as follows:

$$\text{length}, \ell = \frac{\text{volume}}{\text{area}} = \frac{1.07 \times 10^{-4}\ \text{cm}^3}{\pi(1.0 \times 10^{-1}\ \text{cm})^2} = 3.4 \times 10^{-3}\ \text{cm}$$

Since a length of 3.4 x $10^{-3}$ cm contains 6.24 x $10^{18}$ electrons, and this many electrons pass the observer in 1 s, the average drift velocity of the conducting electrons is 3.4 x $10^{-3}$ cm/s, or 0.034 mm/s! This is true only for the stated conditions, of course. If the amount of current, the nature of the material in the conductor, or the dimensions of the conductor change, then the drift velocity will also change.

When you turn on a switch to light a lamp using a battery, the change in the electric field may travel at the speed of light, but the electrons themselves drift ever so slowly through the wire, under the influence of the electric field.

## Representing Electric Circuits

Figure 9.1.4 shows a simple electric circuit. There is an energy source or battery, a device to use the electrical energy (such as a lamp), a switch or control, and wires to carry the energy.

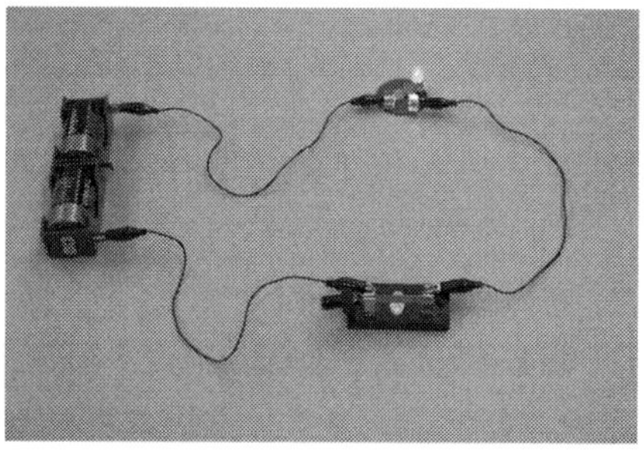

**Figure 9.1.4** *A simple electric circuit*

Any circuit can be represented with a schematic diagram using a set of common symbols. Table 9.1.1 lists some of the more common symbols used for drawing electrical circuits. You will need to know each of these symbols so you can draw electrical circuits.

**Table 9.1.1** *Common Symbols Used in Circuit Diagrams*

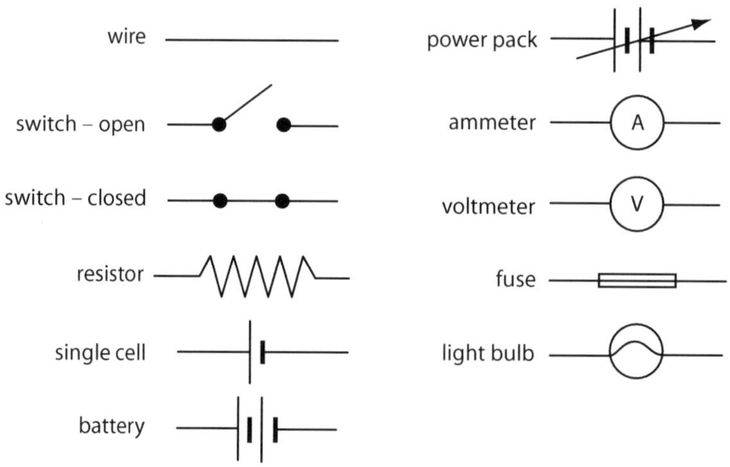


 

The circuit in Figure 9.1.4 can be represented as shown in Figure 9.1.5.

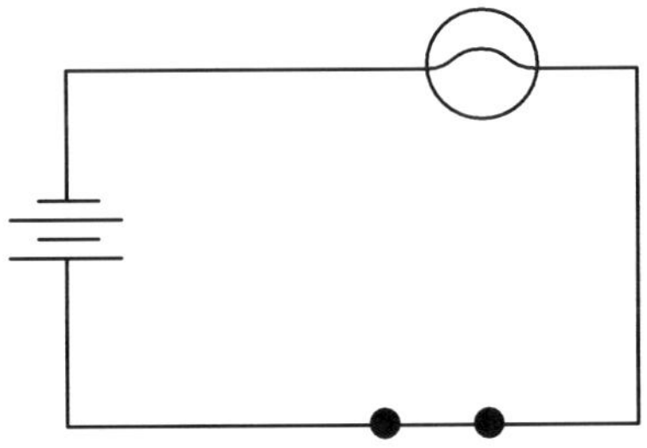

**Figure 9.1.5** *A schematic drawing of the circuit shown in Figure 9.1.4*

## Quick Check

1. Draw a circuit that has two light bulbs, a battery, a fuse, and closed switch.

2. Design a circuit that has a switch that can turn off two light bulbs at the same time.

3. Design a circuit that has two light bulbs and one switch that can turn one light bulb on and off while keeping the other light bulb on.

## How to Read the Scale on an Ammeter

Figure 9.1.6 shows the face of a typical milliammeter. There are three scales printed on the face, but there are eight different ranges for this meter. When you connect the meter into a circuit, the terminal post labeled "C" is always connected to the negative terminal of the power source or to a part of the circuit that eventually leads to the negative terminal.

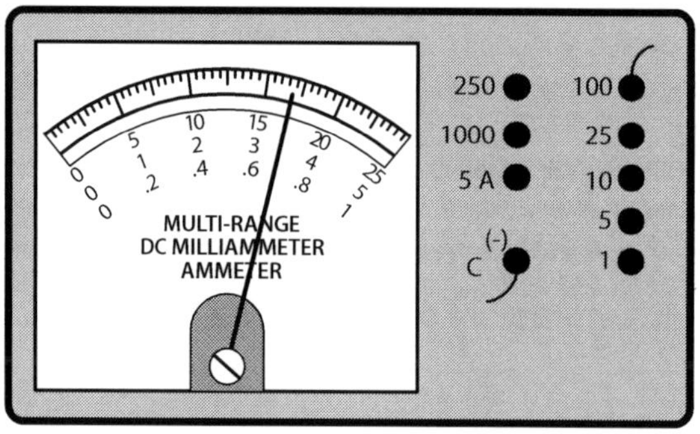


**Figure 9.1.6** *An ammeter*

You must choose a suitable range for the current you have to measure. If you are not sure what range to use, try the red 5A terminal post first. This is the least sensitive range for the meter, so it can handle the most current safely. On this range, the milliammeter can handle up to 5 A.

What do the numbers on the terminal posts mean?

If you connect to the 5 A range, the meter reads anywhere from 0 A up to a maximum of 5 A. Read the middle scale of your meter. The markings mean exactly what they say: 0 A, 1 A, 2 A, 3 A, 4 A, and 5 A. On this range, the needle in Figure 9.1.6 is at 3.3 A.

If you connect to the 1000 range, the meter reads anywhere between 0 mA and 1000 mA. Read the bottom scale, but read the 1 on the scale as 1000 mA. Read 0.2 as 200 mA, 0.4 as 400 mA, 0.6 as 600 mA, and 0.8 as 800 mA. On this range, the needle in Figure 9.1.6 reads 660 mA.

If you connect to the 250 range, the meter reads anywhere from 0 mA up to 250 mA. Use the top scale but 25 reads as 250 mA. Read 5 as 50 mA, 10 as 100 mA, 15 as 150 mA, and 20 as 200 mA. On this range, the needle in Figure 9.1.6 reads 170 mA.

### Quick Check

1. Look at the 100 scale on the meter in Figure 9.1.6.
   (a) What is the highest reading the scale will measure?

   (b) What is the needle reading in Figure 9.1.6?

2. What is the needle reading in Figure 9.1.6 for each of the following scales?

   (a) the 25 mA scale
   (c) the 5 mA scale

   (b) the 10 mA scale
   (d) the 1 mA scale

# 9.1 Review Questions

1. If the current in a wire is 5.0 A, how many coulombs of charge pass a point in the wire in 1 min?

2. What is the current if $6.0 \times 10^3$ C pass a point in a circuit in 10.0 min?

3. If the current in a circuit is 12 A, how many electrons pass a point in 1 h?

4. The drift speed of electrons in a copper wire running from a battery to a light bulb and back is approximately 0.020 mm/s. The battery is at the front of a classroom and wires run around the perimeter of the room to the light bulb. The total length of wire is 40.0 m. How long would it take a single electron to drift from the negative terminal of the battery back to the positive terminal? Express your answer in days.

5. How much copper would be plated by a current of 1.5 A in a time of 1.0 h?

6. How much silver is deposited by a current of 1.000 A in 1.000 h? The mass of one mole of silver atoms is 107.9 g.

$$Ag^+ + 1e^- \rightarrow Ag^0$$

7. Draw a circuit with three light bulbs and two switches, and show the different combinations where one, two, and three light bulbs are lit.

8. What is the reading of the milliammeter below?

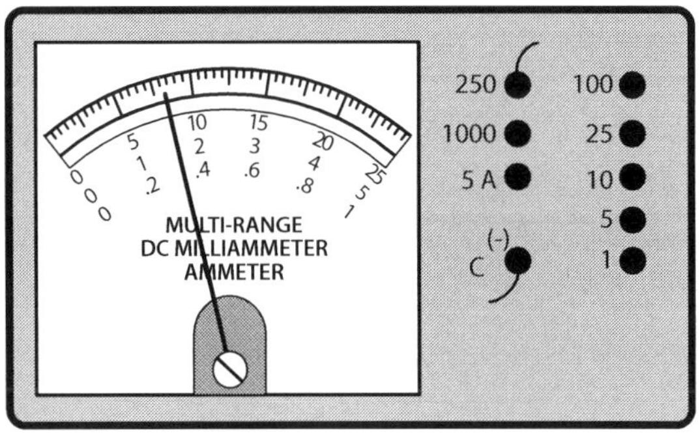

# 9.2 Ohm's Law

## Warm Up

If you draw a line with a graphite pencil, it will conduct electricity. Why does more current go through a 5.0 cm line of graphite than a 10.0 cm line?

______________________________________________

______________________________________________

______________________________________________

### Resistance

Georg Simon Ohm (1787–1854) experimented with current in wires using variations in voltage to produce different currents. He found that for metal conductors at a given temperature, the current was directly proportional to the voltage between the ends of the wire.

$$I \propto V$$

$$\text{Therefore, } \frac{V}{I} = \text{constant.}$$

For example, the potential difference (voltage) between the ends of a wire is 1.50 V and the current is 2.00 A. If the potential difference is increased to 3.00 V, the current will also double to 4.00 A.

The constant of proportionality is called the **resistance** (*R*) of the length of wire. The relationship among current, voltage, and resistance is written:

$$\frac{V}{I} = R$$

where *R* is the resistance, in **ohms** (Ω)**.** This is called **Ohm's law.** Ohm's law can be written in two other forms, but all three forms are equivalent.

$$\frac{V}{I} = R \qquad V = IR \qquad \frac{V}{R} = I$$

**Sample Problem 9.2.1 — Ohm's Law**

The current in a portable stove's heating element is 12.0 A when the potential difference between the ends of the element is 120 V. What is the resistance of the stove element?

| What to Think About | How to Do It |
|---|---|
| 1. Determine what you know from the problem. | $I = 12.0\ \text{A}$<br>$V = 120\ \text{V}$ |
| 2. Determine the appropriate formula. | $R = \frac{V}{I}$ |
| 3. Solve. | $R = \frac{120\ \text{V}}{12.0\ \text{A}} = 1.0 \times 10^{1}\ \Omega$ |

 

## Practice Problems 9.2.1 — Ohm's Law

1. A resistor allows 1.0 mA to exist within it when a potential difference of 1.5 V is applied to its ends. What is the resistance of the resistor, in kilohms? ($1 k\Omega = 10^3 \Omega$)

2. If a 10.0 Ω kettle element is plugged into a 120 V outlet, how much current will it draw?

3. A current of 1.25 mA exists in a 20.0 kΩ resistor. What is the potential difference between the ends of the resistor?

### Resistors

Under normal circumstances, every conductor of electricity offers some resistance to the flow of electric charges and is therefore a **resistor**. However, when we use the term "resistors," we are usually referring to devices manufactured specifically to control the amount of current in a circuit.

There are two main kinds of resistor: (1) wire-wound resistors, made of a coil of insulated, tightly wound fine wire and (2) carbon resistor (Figure 9.2.1). Carbon resistors consist of a cylinder of carbon, with impurities added to control the amount of resistance. Metal wire leads are attached to each end of the carbon cylinder, and the whole assembly is enclosed in an insulating capsule.

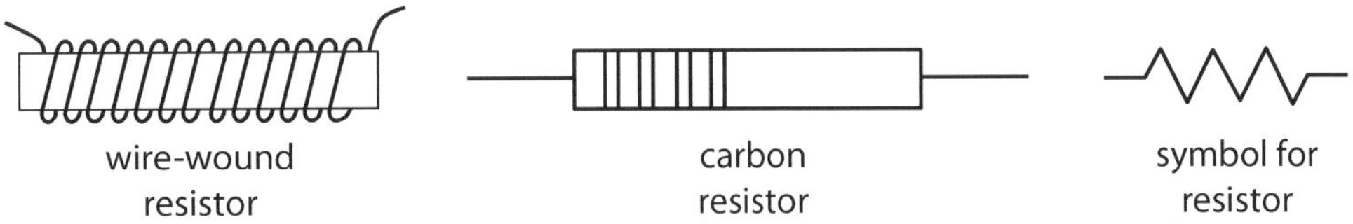


**Figure 9.2.1** *Types of resistors and the symbol for resistors used in circuit diagrams*

In any resistor, electrical energy is transformed into thermal energy. There are some materials which, if cooled to temperatures approaching 0 K, offer no resistance to the flow of charges. These materials are called **superconductors**.

## Limitations of Ohm's Law

Ohm's law applies to metal resistors and metal-like resistors such as those made of compressed carbon. The ratio of potential difference to current, which is resistance, is constant for this class of material, providing that the temperature of the material remains constant.

Ohm's law only applies to metallic or metal-like conductors at a specific temperature. It does *not* apply to just any conductor in a circuit. For example, Ohm's law would not apply to a conducting solution or to a gas discharge tube.

## Joule's Law

The English physicist James Prescott Joule (1818–1889) did experiments to measure the amount of heat released by various resistors under different conditions. He found that, for a particular resistor, the amount of thermal energy released in a unit of time by a resistor is proportional to the square of the current. The rate at which energy is released with respect to time is called **power**, so Joule's results can be expressed as follows:

$$P \propto I^2$$

$$\text{or } P = \text{constant}\cdot I^2$$

The constant in this equation will have units with the dimensions $W/A^2$, since constant = $P/I^2$. Consider the following simplification of these measuring units ($W/A^2$):

$$1\frac{W}{A^2} = 1\frac{\frac{J}{s}}{\frac{C^2}{s^2}} = 1\frac{\frac{J}{C}}{\frac{C}{s}} = 1\frac{V}{A} = 1\,\Omega$$

The ohm (Ω) is the unit for resistance. In fact, the constant of proportionality in the relationship discovered by Joule is the same constant of proportionality that is in Ohm's law. The ratio $P/I^2$ is the resistance of the resistor.

**Joule's law** can be written as follows: $P = RI^2$. By combining Joule's law with Ohm's law for resistors, other expressions for electrical power can be derived:

$$P = RI^2 = \frac{V}{I}I^2 = VI$$

$$\text{And } P = VI = V \times \frac{V}{R} = \frac{V^2}{R}$$

In summary, $$P = RI^2 = VI = \frac{V^2}{R}$$

## Quick Check

1. What is the resistance of a 60.0 W lamp, if the current in it is 0.50 A?

2. A 600 W coffee percolator is operated at 120 V.
   (a) What is the resistance of the heating element of the percolator?

   (b) How much thermal energy does it produce in 6.0 min?

3. How much thermal energy is released by a 1500 W kettle in 5.0 min?

## EMF, Terminal Voltage, and Internal Resistance

In Figure 9.2.2, the dry cell has a rated emf of 1.50 V. Assume you are using a high quality voltmeter to measure the potential difference between the terminals A and B of the cell, when essentially no current is being drawn from the cell other than a tiny amount going through the voltmeter itself. In that case, the voltage between the terminals will be nearly equal to the ideal value of the emf. That is, with no current, the terminal voltage of the battery, $V_{AB}$, will equal the emf, $\mathcal{E}$.

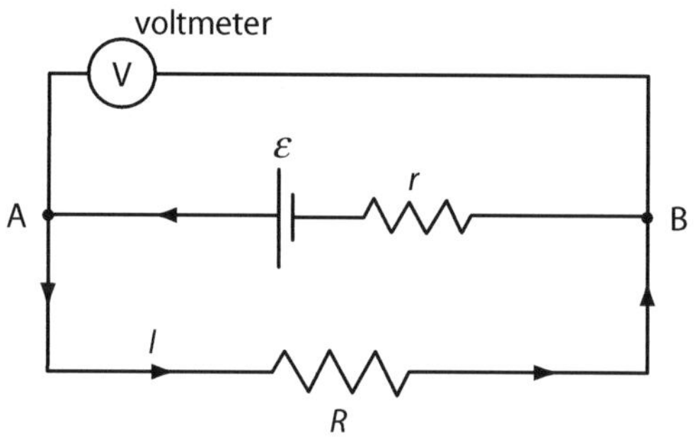


**Figure 9.2.2** *The dry cell in this circuit has a rated emf of 1.50 V.*

If, however, the cell is connected to a resistor *R* so that a current *I* exists in the simple circuit including in the cell itself, then the terminal voltage is *less than* the cell emf.

$$V_{AB} < \mathcal{E}$$

This is because the cell itself has an internal resistance of its own, symbolized by *r*. According to Ohm's law, the loss of potential energy per coulomb between the terminals is *Ir*. The measured terminal voltage of the cell will be less than the ideal emf by an amount equal to *Ir*.

$$V_{AB} = \mathcal{E} - Ir$$

### Sample Problem 9.2.3 — Terminal Voltage and Internal Resistance

A dry cell with an emf of 1.50 V has an internal resistance of 0.050 Ω. What is the terminal voltage of the cell when it is connected to a 2.00 Ω resistor?

| What to Think About | How to Do It |
|---|---|
| 1. Determine what you know from the problem. | $\mathcal{E} = 1.50$ V<br>$R = 2.00\ \Omega$<br>$r = 0.050\ \Omega$ |
| 2. To solve, apply Ohm's law to the circuit as a whole, and consider the internal resistance *r* to be in series with the external resistance *R*. This means you will solve for the current in the circuit. | $I = \dfrac{\mathcal{E}}{R + r} = \dfrac{1.50\text{ V}}{2.05\ \Omega} = 0.732\text{ A}$ |
| 3. Now find the terminal voltage. | $V_{AB} = \mathcal{E} - Ir$<br>$V_{AB} = 1.50\text{ V} - (0.732\text{ A})(0.050\ \Omega)$<br>$V_{AB} = 1.50\text{ V} - 0.037\text{ V}$<br>$V_{AB} = 1.46\text{ V}$ |

## Practice Problems 9.2.3 — Terminal Voltage and Internal Resistance

1. A dry cell with an emf of 1.50 V and an internal resistance of 0.050 Ω Is "shorted out" with a piece of wire with a resistance of only 0.20 Ω. What will a voltmeter read if it is connected to the terminals of the dry cell at this time?

2. A battery has an emf of 12.50 V. When a current of 35 A is drawn from it, its terminal voltage is 11.45 V. What is the internal resistance of the battery?

## 9.2 Review Questions

1. A current of 1.2 mA exists in a resistor when a potential difference of 4.8 V is applied to its ends. What is the resistance of the resistor? Express your answer in kilohms (1 kΩ = 1000 Ω).

2. A current of 3.0 mA exists in a 2.0 kΩ resistor. What is the voltage between the ends of the resistor?

3. What current will exist in a 30 Ω resistor if a 120 V voltage is applied to its ends?

4. A 3.0 V battery is connected to a carbon resistor.
   (a) If the current is 3.0 mA, what is the resistance of the resistor?

   (b) If a 6.0 V battery is connected to the same resistor, what will the current be?

   (c) What is the resistance of the resistor when the 6.0 V battery replaces the 3.0 V battery?

5. A 12 V battery sends a current of 2.0 A through a car's circuit to the headlights. What is the resistance of the filament in a headlight?

6. What voltage is needed to send 0.5 A through a 220 Ω light bulb filament?

7. What current exists in a 120 V coffee percolator, if the resistance of its heating element is 24 Ω?

8. What is the resistance of the element of a 1500 W kettle if it draws 12.5 A?

9. A 1500 W kettle is connected to a 110 V source. What is the resistance of the kettle element?

10. When you pay your electricity bill, you are charged not for power but for the energy used. The unit for measuring the energy used is the kilowatt•hour (kW•h).
    (a) How many joules are there in one kW•h?

    (b) How much energy, in kW•h, does a 400-W TV set use in a month (30 days), if it is used an average of 6.0 h each day?

    (c) If electrical energy costs \$0.06/kW•h, what will it cost you to operate the TV set for one month?

11. How many kW•h of energy does a 900 W toaster use in 3.0 min?

12. A 1.0 kΩ resistor is rated ½ W. This rating means the resistor will be destroyed if more than than ½ W passes through it. What is the maximum voltage you can apply to this resistor without risking damage to it?

13. A battery with an emf of 6.00 V has an internal resistance of 0.20 Ω. What current does the battery deliver when the terminal voltage reads only 5.00 V?

# 9.3 Kirchhoff's Laws

## Warm Up

What will happen to the brightness of the remaining six light bulbs in a parallel circuit if the seventh bulb in the circuit is unhooked?

______________________________________________

______________________________________________

______________________________________________

### Resistors in Series

In Figure 9.3.1, four resistors are connected end-to-end so that there is one continuous conducting path for electrons coming from the source of emf, through the resistors, and back to the source. Electrons move through the resistors, one after the other. The same current exists in each resistor. Resistors arranged like this are said to be "in **series**" with each other. Figure 9.3.1 shows a typical series circuit.

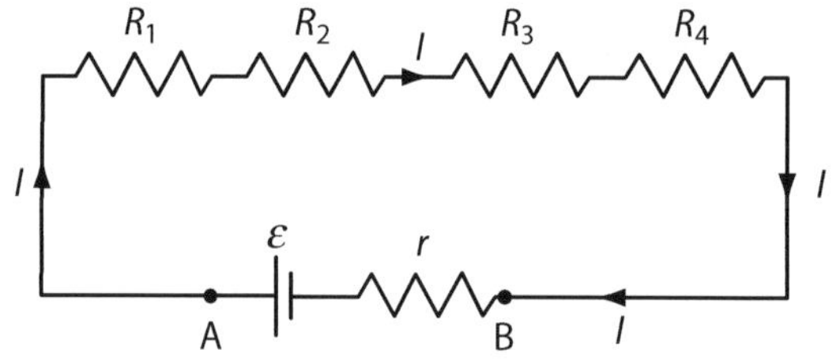


**Figure 9.3.1** *A series circuit*

Within the cell, the gain in potential energy per unit charge is equal to the emf, ε. When a current $I$ exists, energy will be lost in resistors $R_1$, $R_2$, $R_3$, $R_4$, and $r$. The loss of potential energy per unit charge in each resistor is the voltage $V$ across that resistor. From Ohm's law, we know that $V = IR$. The law of conservation of energy requires that the total gain in energy in the cell(s) must equal the total loss of energy in the resistors in the circuit. It follows that the total gain in energy per unit charge ($E$) must equal the total loss of energy per unit charge in the circuit.

$$E = Ir + IR_1 + IR_2 + IR_3 + IR_4$$

$$\therefore\ E - Ir = IR_1 + IR_2 + IR_3 + IR_4$$

Recalling that terminal voltage $V_{AB} = E - Ir$,

$$V_{AB} = IR_1 + IR_2 + IR_3 + IR_4 = V_S$$

where $V_S$ is the sum of voltages across the resistors in the external part of the circuit.

Another way of writing this is: $V_{AB} = V_1 + V_2 + V_3 + V_4 = V_S$

 

## Equivalent Resistance

What is the total resistance of a series circuit like the one in Figure 9.3.1? In other words, what single resistance, called the **equivalent resistance** $R_S$, could be used to replace $R_1$, $R_2$, $R_3$, and $R_4$ without changing current $I$?

If $V_S = IR_S$ and $V_S = IR_1 + IR_2 + IR_3 + IR_4$, then

$$IR_S = IR_1 + IR_2 + IR_3 + IR_4$$

$$\therefore\ R_S = R_1 + R_2 + R_3 + R_4$$

**Summary: For a Series Circuit**

1. Current ($I$) is the same everywhere throughout the circuit.
2. The net gain in potential energy per coulomb in the circuit equals the net loss of potential energy per coulomb in the circuit. That is, for a circuit like the one in Figure 9.3.1, with a single source of emf,
$$V_{AB} = V_1 + V_2 + V_3 + V_4 + ... + V_n$$
3. The equivalent resistance of all the resistors in series with each other is equal to the sum of all their resistances.
$$R_S = R_1 + R_2 + R_3 + R_4 + ... + R_n$$

## Resistors in Parallel

The resistors in Figure 9.3.2 are connected in **parallel**. The current divides into three branches. Electrons coming from the cell take one of three paths, which meet at a junction where the electrons all converge to one path again and return to the battery.

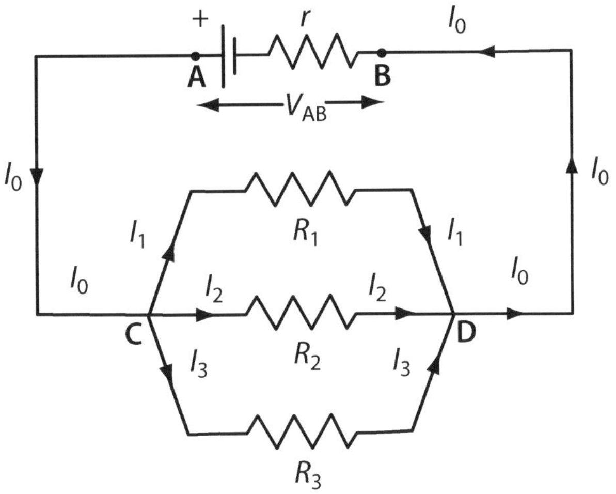


**Figure 9.3.2** *Resistors $R_1$, $R_2$, and $R_3$ are placed in parallel in this circuit.*

Electric charge is a conserved quantity. The electrons are not "created" or "lost" during their journey through the parallel network of resistors. The number of electrons entering a junction (such as D) per second will equal the number of electrons leaving that junction per second. Likewise, the number of electrons entering junction C per second will equal the number of electrons leaving C per second. (The actual direction of electron flow is opposite to the conventional current direction shown in Figure 9.3.2.) If we express current in C/s or in A, as is normally the case,

$$I_0 = I_1 + I_2 + I_3$$

The net gain in potential energy per unit charge in the cell, which is $V_{AB}$, is equal to the loss in potential energy per unit charge between C and D. If you think of C as an extension of terminal A and D as an extension of terminal B of the cell, you can see that the difference in potential between C and D is the same no matter which of the three paths the electrons take to get from one terminal to the other. In fact,

$$V_{AB} = V_1 = V_2 = V_3$$

where $V_{AB}$ is the terminal voltage of the cell, and $V_1$, $V_2$, and $V_3$ are the voltages across resistors $R_1$, $R_2$, and $R_3$ respectively.

Since the voltages are the same in each branch, we shall use the label $V_p$ for the voltage in *any* branch of the parallel network.

## Equivalent Resistance

What single resistance could be used in place of the parallel network of resistors, and draw the same total current? Call this the **equivalent resistance** $R_p$.

If the voltage across the parallel network is $V_p$, and the equivalent single resistance is $R_p$, we can apply Ohm's law as follows to find the total current $I_0$ entering the network:

$$I_0 = \frac{V_p}{R_p}$$

However, $I_0 = I_1 + I_2 + I_3$

Using Ohm's law again: $$\frac{V_p}{R_p} = \frac{V_p}{R_1} + \frac{V_p}{R_2} + \frac{V_p}{R_3}$$

Eliminating $V_p$: $$\frac{1}{R_p} = \frac{1}{R_1} + \frac{1}{R_2} + \frac{1}{R_3}$$

**Summary: For a Parallel Circuit Network**

1. Voltage is the same between the ends of each branch of a parallel network.
2. The total current entering a junction of a parallel network is equal to the total current leaving the same junction. As a result, the total current entering a parallel network of resistors or leaving the same network is equal to the sum of the currents in the branches.
3. The reciprocal of the single equivalent resistance that will replace all the resistance in a parallel network, and draw the same current, is equal to the sum of the reciprocals of the resistances in the branches.

$$\frac{1}{R_p} = \frac{1}{R_1} + \frac{1}{R_2} + \frac{1}{R_3} + \dots + \frac{1}{R_n}$$

## Combined Series and Parallel Circuits

Figure 9.3.3 shows a combined **series-parallel circuit**. The rules you have learned for series and parallel circuits can be applied to this problem. A logical approach for finding the equivalent resistance and current for the circuit in Figure 9.3.3 is to first reduce the parallel network to a single equivalent resistance, then treat the circuit as a series circuit.

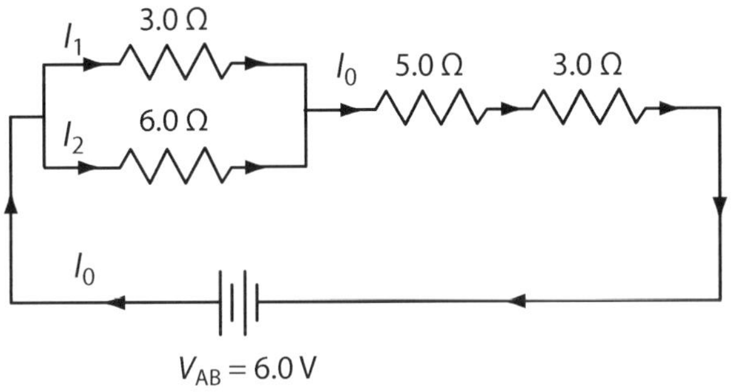


**Figure 9.3.3** *A combined series-parallel circuit*

### Sample Problem 9.3.1 — Resistors in Parallel

(a) What is the equivalent resistance of the circuit in Figure 9.3.3?
(b) What is the voltage across the 6.0 Ω resistor?

| What to Think About | How to Do It |
|---|---|
| **(a)** | |
| 1. First, reduce the parallel network to an equivalent single resistance. | $\frac{1}{R_p} = \frac{1}{3.0\ \Omega} + \frac{1}{6.0\ \Omega} = \frac{2+1}{6.0\ \Omega} = \frac{3}{6.0\ \Omega} = \frac{1}{2.0\ \Omega}$ <br> $R_p = 2.0\ \Omega$ |
| 2. Next, add the three resistances that are in series with one another. | $R_s = 2.0\ \Omega + 5.0\ \Omega + 3.0\ \Omega = 10.0\ \Omega$ |
| 3. Then, find the current using Ohm's law with the total equivalent resistance and the battery terminal voltage. | $I_0 = \frac{V_{AB}}{R_s} = \frac{6.0\ V}{10.0\ \Omega} = 0.60\ A$ |
| **(b)** | |
| 1. Find the voltage across the parallel network by using Ohm's law on the parallel network by itself. | $V_p = I_0 R_p = (0.60\ A)(2.0\ \Omega) = 1.2\ V$ |

## Practice Problems 9.3.1 — Resistors in Parallel

1. (a) Draw a circuit showing a 6.0 V battery with an internal resistance of 0.50 Ω connected to a parallel network consisting of a 25.0 Ω resistor in parallel with a 6.25 Ω resistor.

   (b) Calculate the current in the battery.

2. Calculate the equivalent resistance of each of the networks of resistors in Figure 9.3.4.

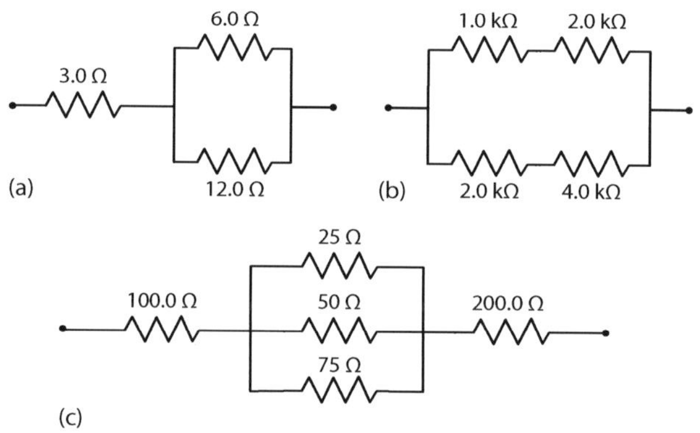


**Figure 9.3.4**

   (a)

   (b)

   (c)

 

## Kirchhoff's Laws for Electric Circuits

So far, we have looked at series and parallel circuits from the points of view of (a) conservation of energy, (b) conservation of charge, and (c) Ohm's law. Most simple circuits can be analyzed using the rules worked out for series and parallel circuits in this section. For more complicated circuits, a pair of rules called **Kirchhoff's rules** or **Kirchhoff's laws** can be applied.

> **Kirchhoff's Current Rule**
> At any junction in a circuit, the sum of all the currents entering that junction equals the sum of all the currents leaving that junction.

Kirchhoff's current rule follows from the law of conservation of electric charge. Charged particles are not "lost" or "created" in a circuit. The number of charged particles (usually electrons) that enter a junction point equals the number that leave that junction point.

> **Kirchhoff's Voltage Rule**
> The algebraic sum of all the changes in potential around a closed path in a circuit is zero.

Kirchhoff's voltage rule is really a restatement of the law of conservation of energy. In Investigation 9.3, you will examine several circuits from the point of view of Kirchhoff's laws.

### Quick Check

1. Calculate the current in the cell in the circuit in Figure 9.3.5.

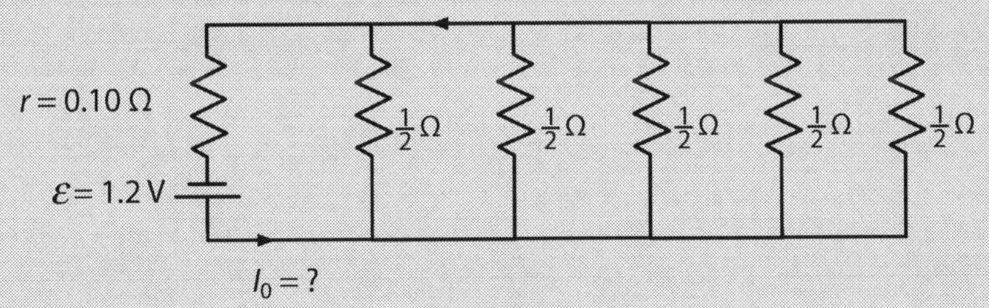


**Figure 9.3.5**

*Quick Check continues*

2. A wire has length $\ell$ and resistance $R$. It is cut into four identical pieces, and these pieces are arranged in parallel. What will be the resistance of this parallel network?

3. Four identical resistors are connected in parallel, as shown in Figure 9.3.6. The current is 2.0 A with all four resistors in the circuit. What will be the current if the wire at X is cut?

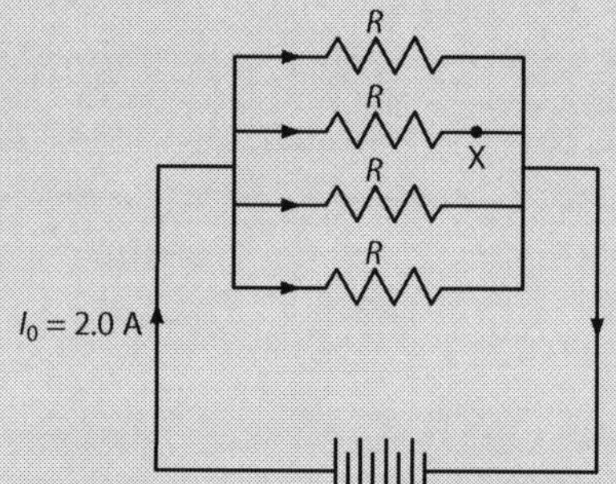


**Figure 9.3.6**

4. (a) What is the equivalent resistance of the network of resistors in Figure 9.3.7?

   (b) What current exists in the 3.0 Ω resistor?

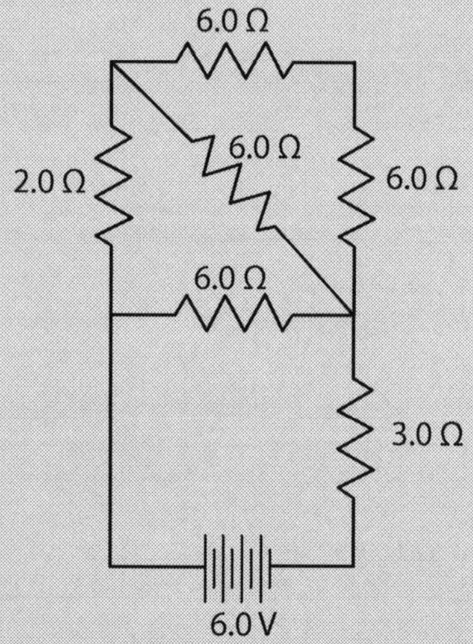


**Figure 9.3.7**

 

## 9.3 Review Questions

1. The current through A is 0.50 A when the switch S is open. What will the current be through A when the switch S is closed?

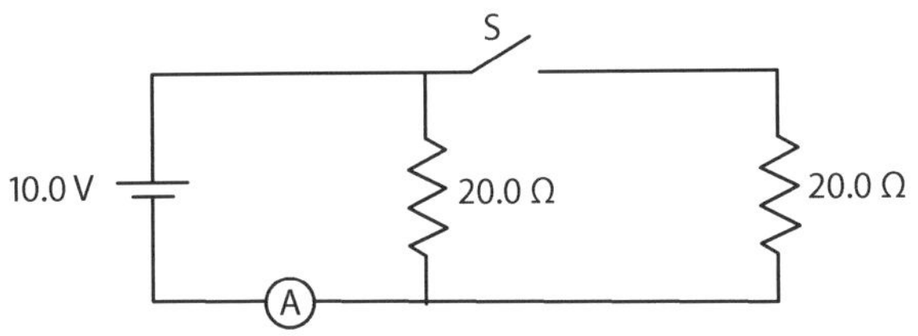


2. Which one of the following arrangements of four identical resistors will have the least resistance?

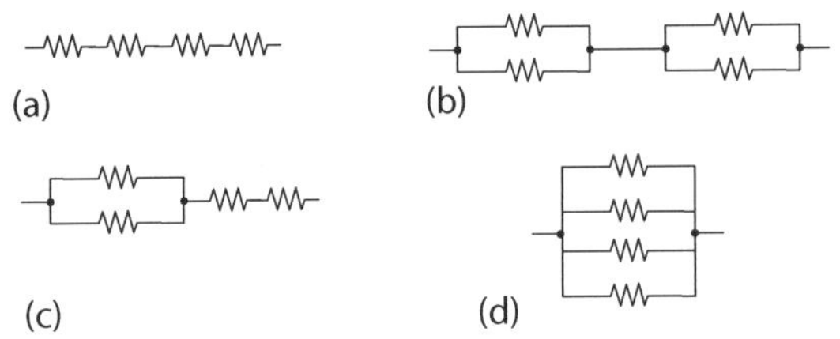


3. Use this circuit diagram to answer the questions below.

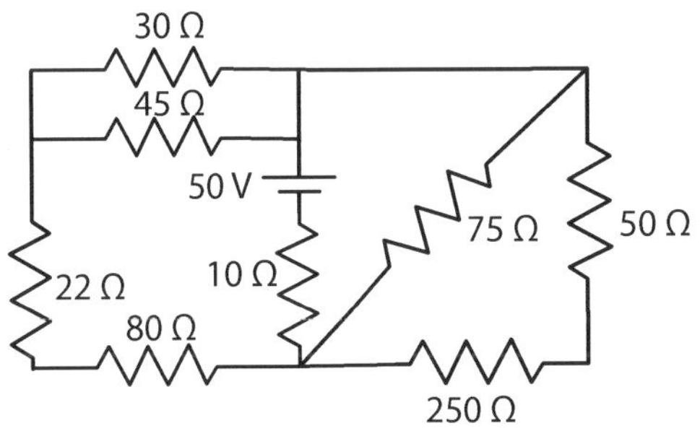


(a) What is the equivalent resistance of the entire circuit?

(b) What current is drawn from the battery?

(c) What is the current in the 50 Ω resistor?

(d) What is the voltage across the 22 Ω resistor?

4. What is the current in the ammeter A in this circuit?

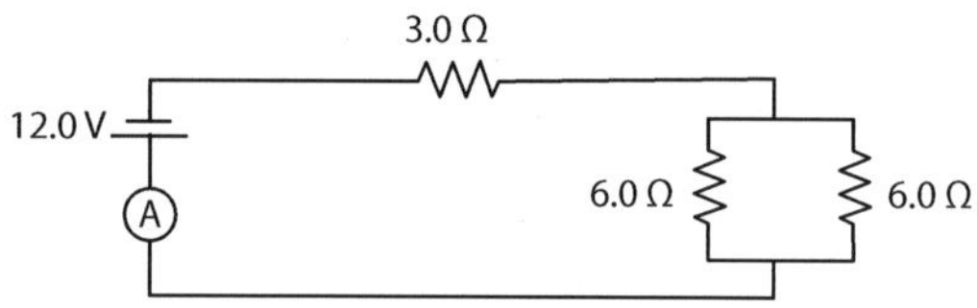


5. What is the emf of the battery if the current in A is 1.2 A and the internal resistance of the battery is 0.0833 Ω in this circuit?

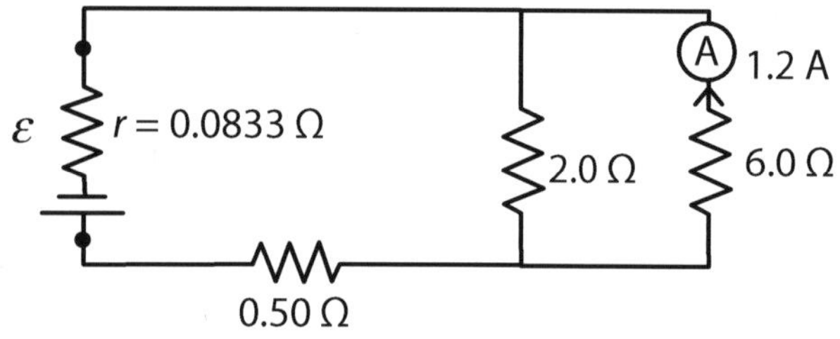


6. What is the voltage $V$ of the power supply in the circuit below?

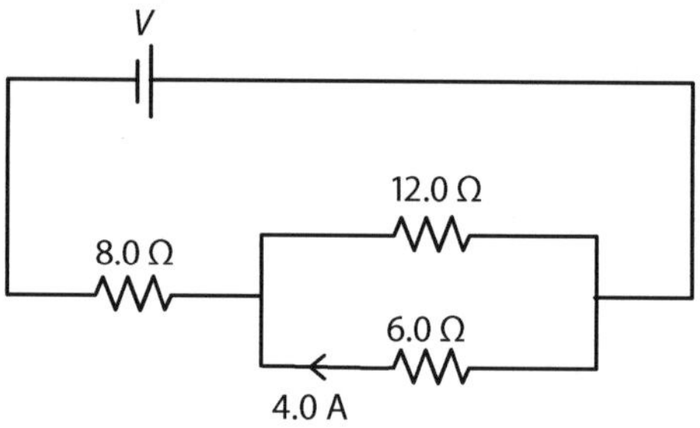


7. What is the internal resistance of the battery shown here?

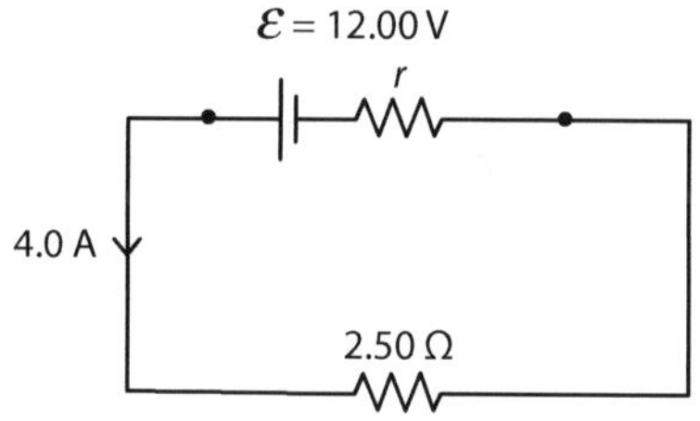

8. Use this circuit diagram to answer the questions below.

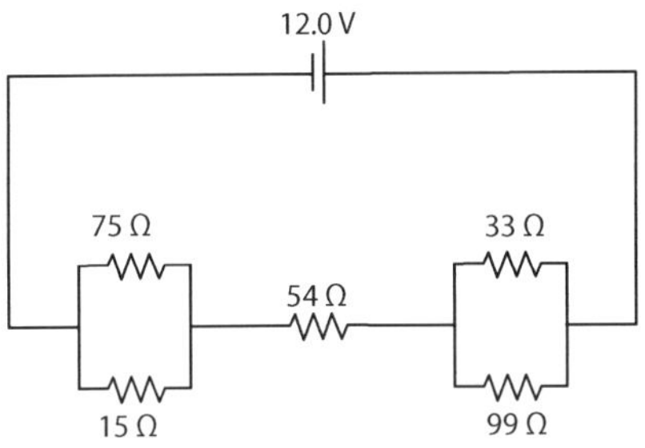


(a) What is the equivalent resistance of this circuit?

(b) What is the current through the 54 Ω resistor?

(c) How much power is dissipated in the 54 Ω resistor?

9. Use this circuit diagram to answer the questions below.

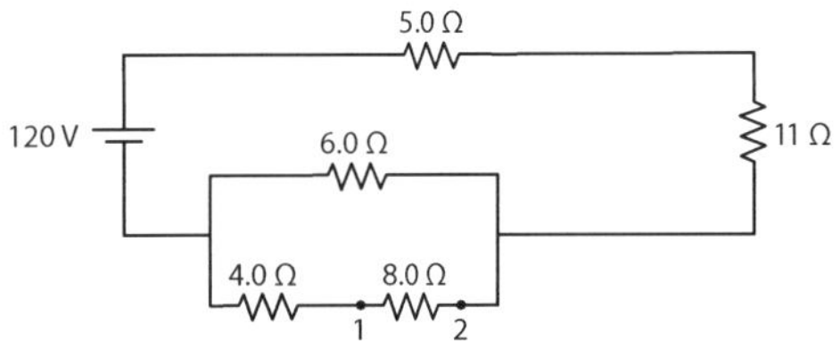


(a) What is the voltage across the 8.0 Ω resistor (between 1 and 2)?

(b) How much power is dissipated in the 5.0 Ω resistor?

# Chapter 9 Conceptual Review Questions

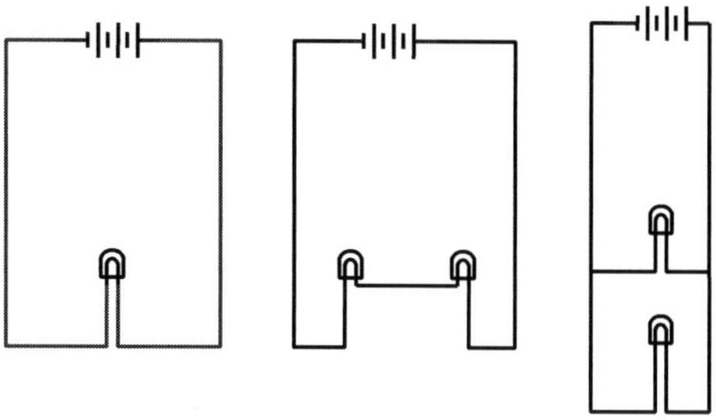

Circuit A Circuit B Circuit C

1a. In the image above similar batteries and light bulbs are used to arrange the three circuits. In which circuit will the light bulb(s) be the brightest? Explain your answer.

1b. Which circuit will the light bulbs burn out last? Explain your reasoning.

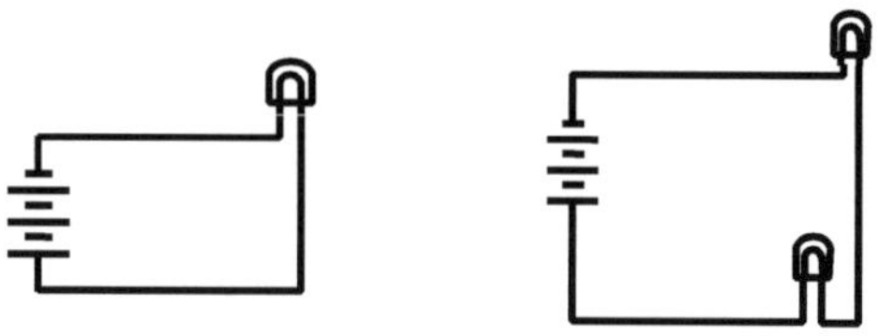

A B

2. Assuming batteries and light bulbs are identical, which of the above circuits will carry less current? Explain.

# Chapter 9 Review Questions

1. What is the difference between the terminal voltage of a battery and its emf?

2. What current exists in a wire if $2.4 \times 10^3$ C of charge pass through a point in the wire in a time of $6.0 \times 10^1$ s?

3. The current through an ammeter is 5.0 A. In one day, how many electrons will pass through the ammeter?

4. How much silver will be electroplated by a current of 0.255 A in one day?

5. A mercury cell has an emf of 1.35 V and an internal resistance of 0.041 Ω. If it is used in a circuit that draws 1.50 A, what will its terminal voltage be?

6. A set of eight decorative light bulbs is plugged into a 120 V wall receptacle. What is the potential difference across each light bulb filament, if the eight light bulbs are connected:

   (a) in series?

   (b) in parallel?

7. What is the resistance of a resistor if a potential difference of 36 V between its ends results in a current of 1.20 mA?

8. What is the potential difference (voltage) between the ends of a resistor if 24.0 J of work must be done to drive 0.30 C of charge through the resistor?

9. A 2.2 kΩ resistor is rated at ½ W. What is the highest voltage you could safely apply to the resistor without risking damage to it from overheating?

10. What current will a 1500 W kettle draw from a 120 V source?

11. A toaster draws 8.0 A on a 120 V circuit. What is its power rating?

12. A 60.0 W light bulb and a 40.0 W light bulb are connected in parallel in a 120 V circuit. What is the equivalent resistance of the two light bulbs?

13. A circuit in your house has the following appliances plugged into it: a 1500 W kettle, a 150 W light, and a 900 W toaster. The circuit is protected by a 20 A circuit breaker. If the house voltage is 120 V, will the circuit breaker be activated? Explain your answer.

14. How many kW•h of energy will a 400 W television set use in one month, if it is turned on for an average of 5.0 h per day? What will it cost you at \$0.06/kW•h?

15. The cell in the diagram below is short-circuited with a wire of resistance 0.10 Ω. What is the terminal voltage under these conditions?

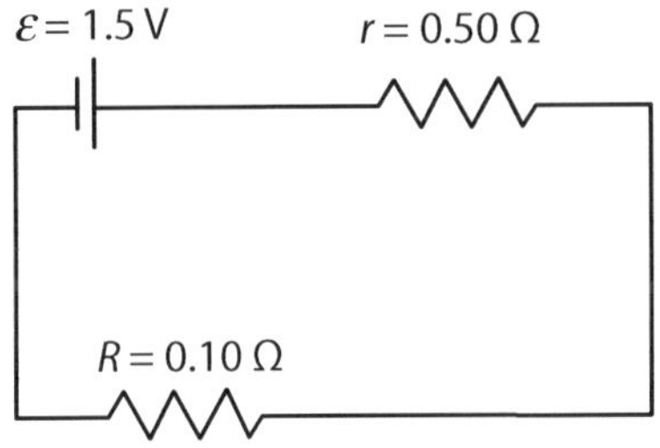


16. A storage battery has an emf of 12.0 V. What is the terminal voltage if a current of 150 A is drawn just as the starter motor is turned on? The internal resistance is 0.030 Ω.

17. What is the equivalent resistance of resistors of 8.0 Ω, 12.0 Ω, and 24.0 Ω if they are connected

(a) in series?

(b) in parallel?

18. A resistor is intended to have a resistance of 60.00 Ω, but when checked it is found to be 60.07 Ω. What resistance might you put in parallel with it to obtain an equivalent resistance of 60.00 Ω?

19. A 12.0 Ω resistor and a 6.0 Ω resistor are connected in series with a 9.0 V battery. What is the voltage across the 6.0 Ω resistor?

20. What is the resistance $R$ in diagram below, if the current through the battery is 5.0 A?

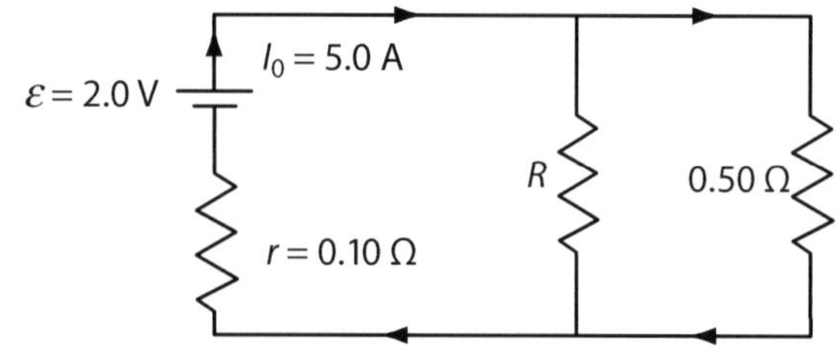


21. You have three 6.0 kΩ resistors. By combining these three resistors in different combinations, how many different equivalent resistances can you obtain with them? (All three must be used.)

22. For each circuit, find
(i) the equivalent resistance of the entire circuit, and
(ii) the current at the point marked $I$.

(a)

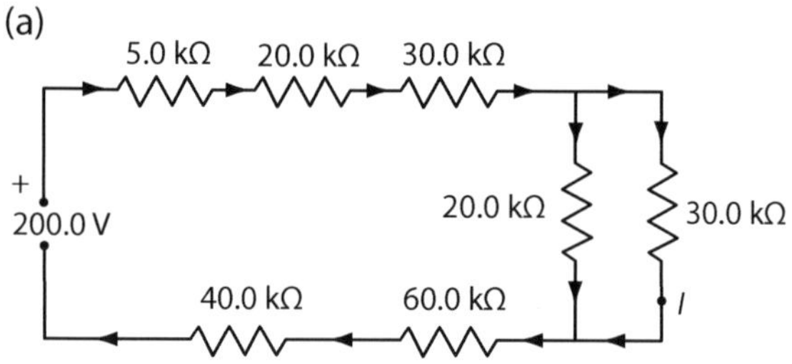


(b)

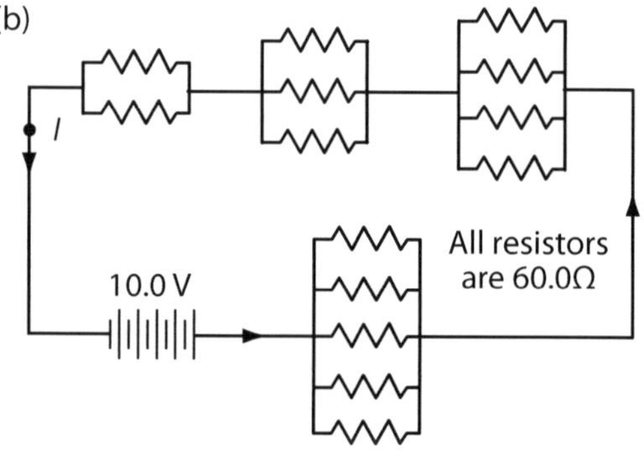


(c)

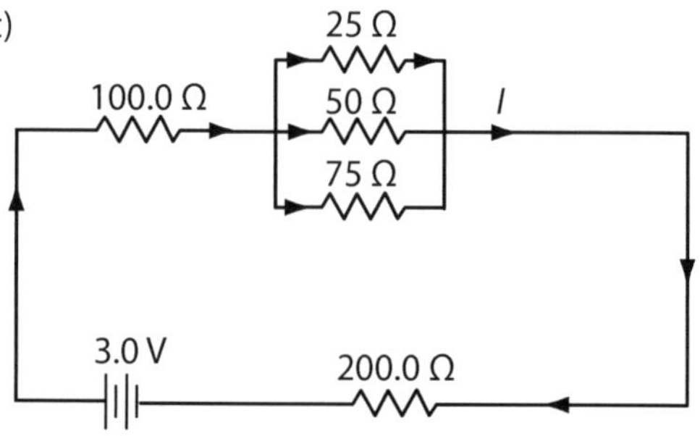

23. What is the voltage across the 6.0 Ω resistor in the diagram below?

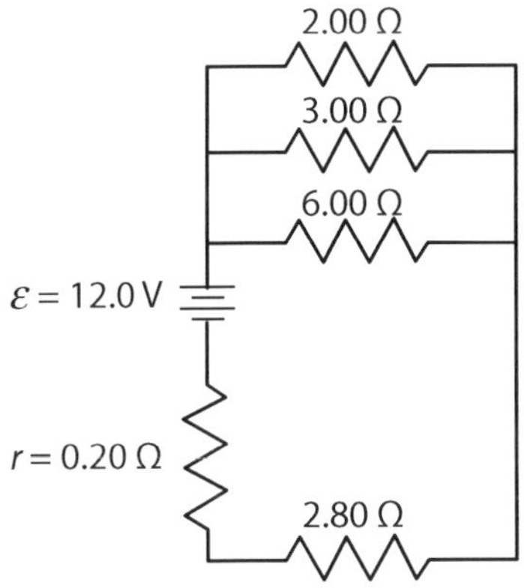


24. Twelve identical pieces of resistance wire, each of resistance 1.0 Ω, are formed into a cubical resistance network, shown in the diagram below. If a current of 12 A enters one corner of the cube and leaves at the other corner, what is the equivalent resistance of the cube between the opposite corners? Use Kirchhoff's laws.

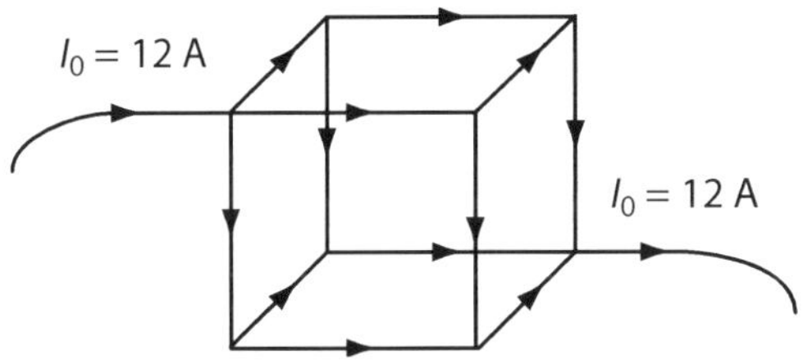

# Investigation 9.1 Measuring Current Using Electroplating

### Purpose

To measure current by counting copper atoms deposited on a carbon rod in a measured amount of time

### Introduction

A solution of copper II sulfate contains two kinds of ions: $Cu^{2+}$ ions, which give the solution its blue color, and $SO_4^{2-}$ ions, which are colorless (see Figure below). Two electrodes are immersed in the copper II sulfate solution and connected to a source of emf. The electrode connected to the positive terminal of the cell will attract $SO_4^{2-}$ ions, and the electrode connected to the negative terminal of the cell will attract $Cu^{2+}$ ions.

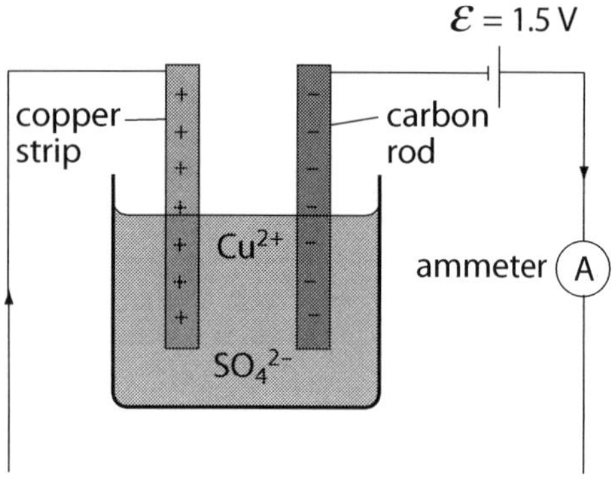


$Cu^{2+}$ ions attracted to the negative electrode pick up two electrons, and deposit themselves on the negative electrode as copper atoms, $Cu^0$.

$$Cu^{2+} + 2e^- \rightarrow Cu^0$$

Meanwhile, at the positive electrode, which is made of copper, copper atoms *lose* two electrons and become copper ions, thus replenishing the $Cu^{2+}$ ions in the solution.

$$Cu^0 \rightarrow Cu^{2+} + 2e^-$$

The two electrons return to the source of emf, the cell.

In this experiment, you allow the copper atoms to plate onto a negatively charged carbon electrode. If you measure the increase in mass of the carbon electrode after, say, 20 min of copper plating, you can calculate the mass of copper plated. This will give you the number of copper atoms plated, and from this, the number of electrons that were transferred in the 20 min. Finally you can calculate the current in amperes. You can also compare your calculated current with the current measured with an ammeter placed in the same circuit.

### Procedure

1. Measure the mass of a dry, clean carbon rod as precisely as you can.
2. Set up the circuit shown in the Figure above. Make sure the carbon rod is connected to the negative terminal of the dry cell or other DC power source. The red binding post of the ammeter should be connected to the positive terminal of the cell, and an appropriate current range chosen as quickly as possible when the current is turned on. *Let the current run for a carefully measured time, such as 20 min.* Record current frequently, and *average* it.
3. As soon as the current is turned off, carefully remove the carbon electrode. Dip it in a beaker of methyl hydrate, and allow it time to dry. A heat lamp can be used to speed drying.

**Caution! Methyl hydrate is both highly toxic and flammable!**

4. Measure the mass of the plated carbon rod precisely, and calculate the amount of copper that has plated on its surface. Record the mass of copper.
5. To remove the copper, set up the circuit once more, but *reverse the connections* to the cell so that the copper plates back onto the copper strip.

### Concluding Questions

1. One mole of copper atoms (63.5 g) contains $6.02 \times 10^{23}$ atoms. Using this information and the mass of copper plated on the carbon rod, calculate
   (a) the number of copper atoms plated
   (b) the number of electrons transferred
   (c) the number of coulombs transferred in 20 min
2. If 1 A = 1 C/s, what was the current in amperes?
3. Compare your calculated current with the measured current by calculating the percent difference between the two currents.

# Investigation 9.2 Ohm's Law

**Purpose**

To investigate the relationship between the voltage applied to a resistor and the current in the resistor

**Procedure**

1. Set up the circuit shown in the Figure below. Start with one cell, an ammeter, and a carbon resistor. These are all in series as they form one path. A voltmeter is connected in parallel with the resistor, as there are two paths for the current to travel.

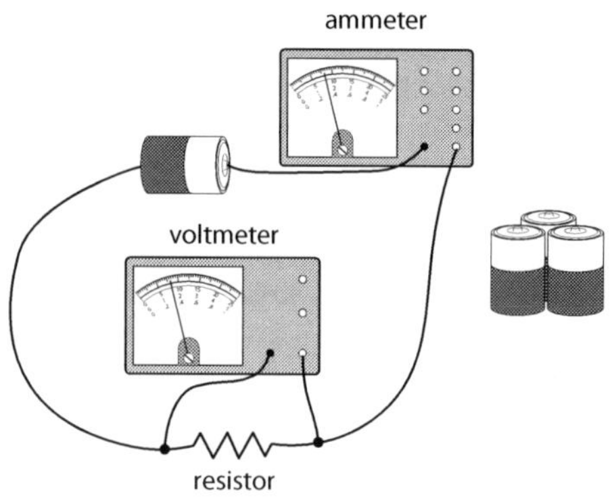


2. Prepare a copy of the Table below.

**Sample Data Table**

| Number of Cells Used | Voltage across Resistor (V) | Current in Resistor (A) | Calculated Resistance (Ω) |
|---|---|---|---|
| 1 | | | |
| 2 | | | |
| 3 | | | |
| 4 | | | |

**Resistor rating:** ______________________

3. With one cell in the circuit, measure the current in milliamperes (mA) and the voltage in volts (V). Convert the current from mA to A by dividing by l000. (Move the decimal three places to the left. For example, 2.4 mA is equal to 0.0024 A.) Enter the current and voltage in your copy of the Sample Data Table.
4. Add a second cell in series with the first cell. Record the current and the voltage in your copy of the Sample Data Table.
5. Repeat with three cells, then with four cells. Enter your results in your copy of the Sample Data Table.
6. Complete the final column of your copy of the Sample Data Table. Divide voltage ($V$) by current ($I$) for each trial. This ratio, $V/I$, is the resistance ($R$) of the resistor, measured in ohms.
7. Replace the resistor with one of a different color and repeat Procedure steps 1 to 6.

### Concluding Questions

1. What happens to the voltage across a resistor when the number of cells in series with it is (a) doubled? (b) tripled? (c) quadrupled?
2. What happens to the current across a resistor when the number of cells in series with it is (a) doubled? (b) tripled? (c) quadrupled?
3. What happens to the resistance ($R = V/I$) across a resistor when the number of cells in series with it is (a) doubled? (b) tripled? (c) quadrupled?
4. What is the resistance in ohms (Ω) of (a) the first resistor you used? (b) the second resistor you used?
5. Determine the manufacturer's rating of your resistors. Record these resistances in your notes. Why is the measured value different from the manufacturer's rating?

# Investigation 9.3 Kirchhoff's Laws for Circuits

## Purpose

To examine several circuits from the point of view of Kirchhoff's laws

### *Part 1 — A Series Circuit*

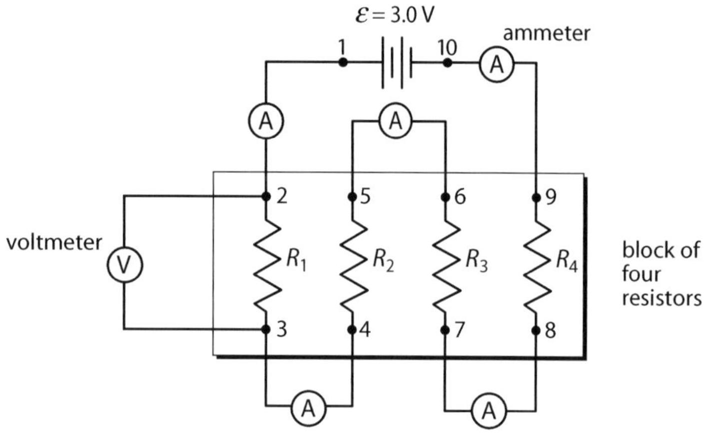


## Procedure

1. To check Kirchhoff's current law, wire a series circuit like the one in the Figure above, and insert your ammeter in *each* of the locations, in turn, where the symbol A for ammeter is shown in the diagram. Record each current in your notebook (possibly on a diagram like the Figure above).

   $I_{1-2}$ = ______ $I_{3-4}$ = ______ $I_{5-6}$ = ______ $I_{7-8}$ = ______ $I_{9-10}$ = ______

2. To check Kirchhoff's voltage law, measure the terminal voltage of the battery or power supply, $V_{1-10}$. Then measure the voltages between the ends of each resistor. Remember that the voltmeter is not in the same conducting path as the circuit. An example is shown in the Figure above, where the voltmeter is connected correctly across the ends of resistor $R_1$. The symbol for the voltmeter is V. Record all the voltages in your notebook.

   $V_{1-10}$ = ______ $V_{2-3}$ = ______ $V_{4-5}$ = ______ $V_{6-7}$ = ______ $V_{8-9}$ = ______

## Concluding Questions

1. Do your current readings support Kirchhoff's current law? How would you describe the current at various junctions in your series circuit?
2. Compare the potential gain in the battery (terminal voltage) with the potential drop in the resistors in the circuit. Do your results suggest that $\sum V = 0$?
3. What are some sources of error in this investigation? For example, how might the ammeter itself affect the results for current, and how might the voltmeter affect the results for voltage?
4. Calculate the resistance of each resistor using Ohm's law and the current and voltage readings for each individual resistor. Compare your calculated resistances with the manufacturer's ratings. Organize your results in a table like Sample Data Table on the next page.

*Sample Data Table*

| | $R_1$ | $R_2$ | $R_3$ | $R_4$ |
|---|---|---|---|---|
| Measured Voltage, *V* | V | V | V | V |
| Measured Current, *I* | A | A | A | A |
| Calculated Resistance, *R* | Ω | Ω | Ω | Ω |
| Color Code Rating, *R* | Ω | Ω | Ω | Ω |

5. Calculate the equivalent resistance $R_S$ of the whole series circuit by using Ohm's law and dividing the terminal voltage of the battery or power supply by the current in the battery. Compare this value with the sum of the individual calculated resistances.
6. What is the percent difference between $R_S$ and $\sum [R_1 + R_2 + R_3 + R_4]$?

***Part 2 — A Parallel Circuit***

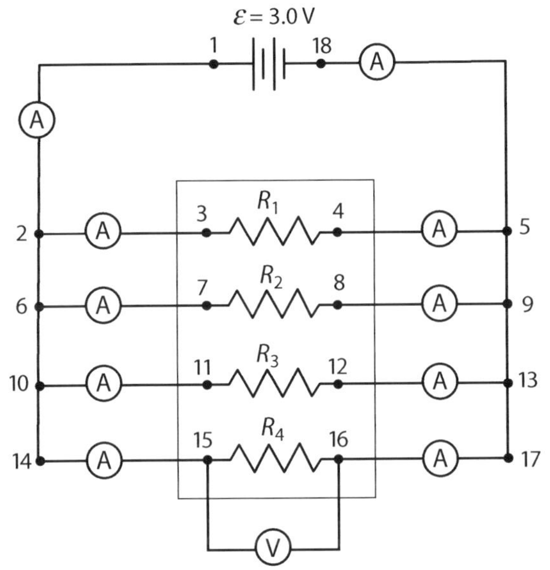


**Figure 9.3.a**

## Procedure

1. Set up the circuit shown in Figure 9.3.a. To simplify recording your data, copy the diagram into your notebook. When you measure the current at each point labeled A, record the current right on the diagram in the ammeter circle.
2. Measure the voltage of the battery ($V_{1-18}$) and also the voltage across each resistor. Record the voltages in your notebook.

$V_{1-18}$ = _____ $V_{3-4}$ = _____ $V_{7-8}$ = _____ $V_{11-12}$ = _____ $V_{15-16}$ = _____

## Concluding Questions

1. Examine the currents at each of the eight junctions of the parallel network of resistors. Do your results confirm Kirchhoff's current law?
2. Compare the potential gain in the battery (terminal voltage) with the potential drop across each branch of the circuit, in turn. Do your measurements seem to confirm Kirchhoff's voltage law?

3. What are some sources of error in this experiment?
4. Use the measured voltage across each resistor, and the measured current in each resistor, to calculate $R_1$, $R_2$, $R_3$, and $R_4$. Calculate the resistance of the parallel network:

$$\frac{1}{R_p} = \frac{1}{R_1} + \frac{1}{R_2} + \frac{1}{R_3} + \frac{1}{R_4}$$

Organize your data in a table like Data Table below.

**Data Table**

| | $R_1$ | $R_2$ | $R_3$ | $R_4$ |
|---|---|---|---|---|
| Measured Voltage, $V$ | V | V | V | V |
| Measured Current, $I$ | A | A | A | A |
| Calculated Resistance, $R$ | Ω | Ω | Ω | Ω |

| | |
|---|---|
| (a) $R_p$ calculated in Concluding Question 4 = | Ω |
| (b) $R_p$ calculated from $\frac{V_{1-18}}{I_0}$ = | Ω |
| Percent difference between (a) and (b) = | % |

5. Calculate the equivalent resistance of the parallel network by dividing the terminal voltage of the battery by the current in the battery. What is the percent difference between this $R_p$ and the result from Procedure step 4?

## Challenge

1. Set up a series-parallel circuit like the one in Figure 9.3.b. Test Kirchhoff's two laws for this circuit.

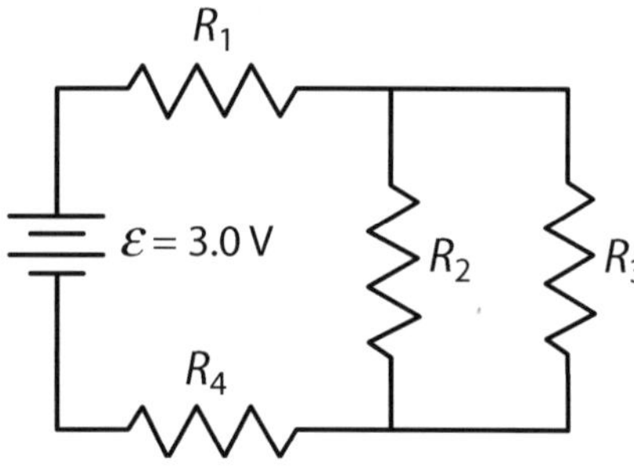


**Figure 9.3.b**

# 10 Mechanical Waves and Sound

This chapter focuses on the following AP Physics 1 Big Ideas from the College Board:

**BIG IDEA 6:** Waves can transfer energy and momentum from one location to another without the permanent transfer of mass and serve as a mathematical model for the description of other phenomena.

---

By the end of this chapter, you should know the meaning of these **key terms**:

- amplitude
- constructive interference
- crests
- destructive interference
- diffraction
- Doppler effect
- frequency
- hertz
- longitudinal wave
- nodal lines
- period
- periodic wave
- pulse
- reflection
- refraction
- sonic boom
- sound barrier
- transverse wave
- troughs
- wavelength

---

By the end of this chapter, you should be able to use and know when to use the following formulae:

$T = \frac{1}{f}$ $v = f\lambda$

*A tiny drop creates a pattern of circular waves.*

# 10.1 Wave Properties

## Warm Up

Fill a wine glass with water. Dip your finger in the water and run your wet finger around the edge of the glass until the glass starts to emit a high-pitched sound. While you are doing this, watch the surface of the water near where your finger is making the glass vibrate. Try the same activity with varying depths of water.

1. What effect does adding water to the glass have on the pitch of the sound you hear?

_______________________________________________

2. Will the glass vibrate when it is empty? Why or why not?

_______________________________________________

_______________________________________________

### Good Vibrations

There are many kinds of waves in nature. You have heard of light waves, sound waves, radio waves, earthquake waves, water waves, shock waves, brain waves and the familiar wave created by a cheering crowd at a sports event. Wave motion is an important phenomenon because it is so common and it is one of the major ways in which energy can be transmitted from one place to another.

There are two basic kinds of waves. First, there is the **pulse,** which is a non-repeating wave. A single disturbance sends a pulse from the source outward, but there is no repetition of the event. For example, you may give a garden hose a quick "yank" to one side, causing a pulse to travel the length of the hose.

Second, there is the **periodic wave.** Periodic waves are probably more familiar to you. You have watched water waves moving across a pond. The waves arrive at the shore of the pond at regularly repeated time intervals. Periodic means recurring at regular intervals. Water waves are caused by a disturbance of the water somewhere in the pond.

Whether the wave is a pulse or a periodic wave, a disturbance is spread by the wave, usually through a material substance. An exception is the medium for electromagnetic radiation (light, radio, X-rays, ultraviolet, infrared, gamma radiation, etc.). The medium for electromagnetic radiation is electric and magnetic fields created by charged particles.

To have a regularly repeating wave, there must be regularly repeating vibrations. For example, the regularly repeating sound waves from a tuning fork are caused by the vibrations of the two tines of the fork disturbing the air. Vibrating electrons disturb the electric field around them to create the microwaves that cook your supper or measure the speed of your car in a radar trap.

## Describing Waves

### Wavelength ($\lambda$)

Figure 10.1.1 depicts waves emanating from a vibrating source. They could be water waves. The highest points on the waves are called **crests** and the lowest points are called **troughs**. The distance between successive crests or between successive troughs is called the **wavelength** ($\lambda$) of the wave. The symbol $\lambda$ is the Greek letter lambda. The **amplitude** or height of the wave is measured from its displacement from the horizontal line in the diagram to the crest or trough. The amplitude is shown on the diagram.

Wavelengths may be measured in metres, in the case of water waves, or in nanometres (1 nm = $10^{-9}$), in the case of visible light. Microwaves may be measured in centimetres, while the waves produced by AC power lines may be kilometres long. Wavelengths of audible sounds range from millimetres up to metres.

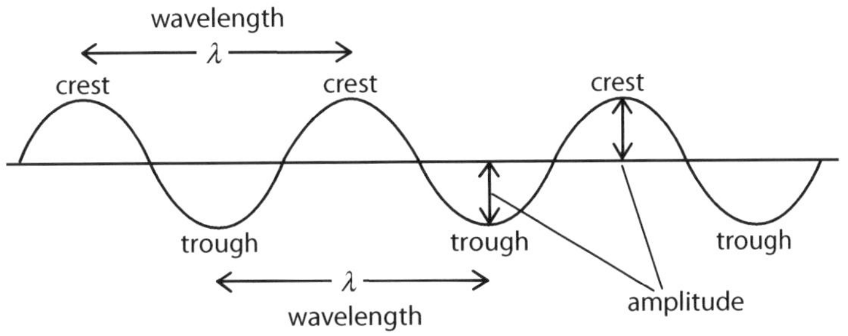


**Figure 10.1.1** *Terms used for describing waves*

### Frequency ($f$)

Another important aspect of waves is their **frequency**. The frequency of the waves tells you how often or frequently they and their source vibrate. If you are listening to a tuning fork, sound waves reach your ear with the same frequency as the vibrating fork. For example, the fork's tines vibrate back and forth 256 times in 1 s if the frequency of the fork is 256 vibrations per second. Frequency is measured in a unit called the **hertz (Hz)**. The unit is named after Heinrich Hertz (1857–1894), who was the first scientist to detect radio waves. One hertz is one vibration per second: 1 Hz $= 1\ s^{-1}$.

A pendulum 24.8 cm long has a frequency of 1 Hz. Electrons vibrating to and fro in an alternating current circuit have a frequency of 60 Hz. Radio waves may be several kilohertz (kHz), where 1 kHz = 1 000 Hz, or they may be in the megahertz (MHz) range, where 1 MHz is equal to 1 000 000 Hz.

### Period ($T$)

Related to the frequency of a vibration is the **period** of the vibration. The period is the time interval between vibrations. For example, if the period of a vibration is 1/2 s, then the frequency must be $2\ s^{-1}$ or 2 Hz. Consider a pendulum with a length of 24.8 cm. It will have a frequency of 1 Hz and a period of 1 s. A pendulum 99.2 cm long will have a frequency of 1/2 Hz and a period of 2 s. A pendulum 223 cm long will have a frequency of 1/3 Hz and a period of 3 s. As you can see, frequency and period are reciprocals of each other.

$$\text{frequency} = \frac{1}{\text{period}}$$

$$f = \frac{1}{T} \text{ or } \boldsymbol{T} = \frac{\mathbf{1}}{\boldsymbol{f}}$$

## Quick Check

1. A dog's tail wags 50.0 times in 40.0 s.
   (a) What is the frequency of the tail?

   (b) What is the period of vibration of the tail?

2. A certain tuning fork makes 7680 vibrations in 30 s.
   (a) What is the frequency of the tuning fork?

   (b) What is the period of vibration of the tuning fork?

3. Tarzan is swinging back and forth on a vine. If each complete swing takes 4.0 s, what is the frequency of the swings?

## Transverse and Longitudinal Waves

Figure 10.1.2 illustrates two ways to send a pulse through a long length of spring or a long Slinky. In method (a), the spring is pulled sideways, so that the disturbance is at right angles to the direction that the pulse will travel. This produces a **transverse wave.** In method (b), several turns of the spring are compressed and let go. The disturbance is in the same direction as the direction the pulse will travel. This produces a **longitudinal wave.** Transverse means *across* and longitudinal means *lengthwise*.

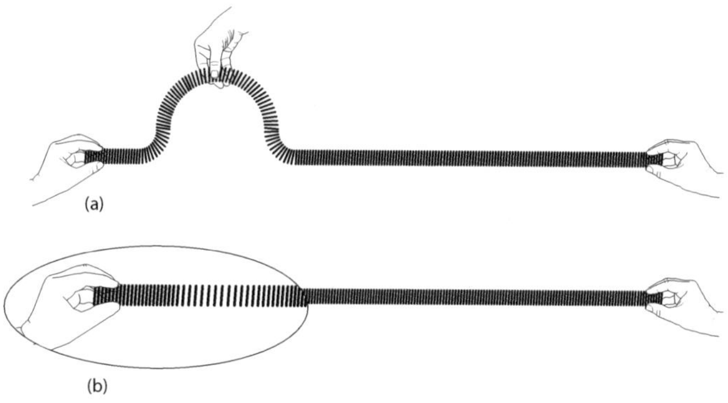


**Figure 10.1.2** (**a**) *A transverse wave;* (**b**) *A longitudinal wave*

## Wave Reflection and Refraction

When a wave encounters a boundary like a shoreline, wall or another medium, several things can happen. The two most common things are the wave will reflect or refract. **Reflection** occurs when a wave hits an object or another boundary and the wave is reflected back. If you attach or hold one end of a spring and send a wave down the spring, you will see it reflect off the end. Usually not all the wave is reflected back as some can be absorbed or refracted. **Refraction** is a bending of the wave and occurs when the wave hits an object at an angle or the wave enters a new medium. Refraction results from the change in the waves speed. The changing speed causes the wave to bend.

## The Wave Equation

The wave shown in Figure10.1.3 is moving through water in a wave tank. The waves in the wave tank are produced by a wave generator, which vibrates up and down with a frequency $f$ and a period $T$ where $T = 1/f$.

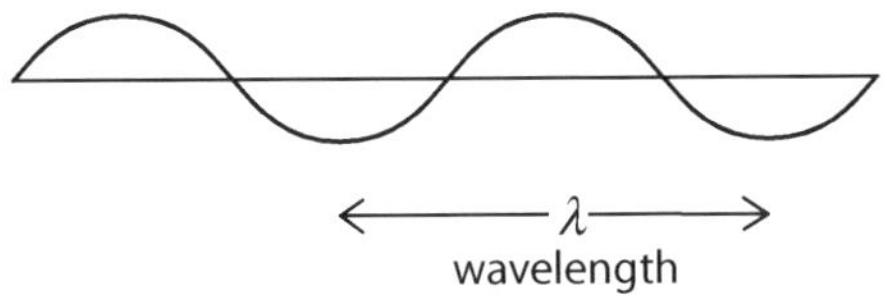


**Figure 10.1.3** *A wave in a wave tank*

What is the speed of the wave? If you could see the wave tank, you could watch a wave travel its own length, or wavelength $\lambda$, and time exactly how long the wave takes to travel its own length. Since the waves are generated once every $T$ seconds by the generator, then this $T$ should be the period of the waves. To calculate the speed $v$ of the waves, all you have to do is divide the wavelength by the period of the wave.

$$v = \lambda/T$$

Since $$T = 1/f \text{ or } f = 1/T$$

$$\mathbf{v = f\lambda}$$

This relationship is a very important one, because it is true for any kind of wave. This includes sound waves, earthquake waves, waves in the strings of musical instruments or any kind of electromagnetic wave (light, infrared, radio, X-radiation, ultraviolet, gamma radiation, etc.)! In words, the wave equation says

**wave speed = wavelength × frequency**

**Sample Problem 10.1.1 — Calculating Wave Speed**

What is the speed of a sound wave if its frequency is 256 Hz and its wavelength is 1.29 m?

| What to Think About | How to Do It |
|---|---|
| 1. Determine what you need to find. | speed of sound |
| 2. Select appropriate formula. | $v = \lambda f$ |
| 3. Find the speed of sound | $v = (1.29\ \text{m})(256\ \text{s}^{-1}) = 330\ \text{m/s}$ |

**Practice Problems 10.1.1 — Calculating Wave Speed**

1. If waves maintain a constant speed, what will happen to their wavelength if the frequency of the waves is
   (a) doubled?

   (b) halved?

2. What is the frequency of a sound wave if its speed is 340 m/s and its wavelength is 1.70 m?

3. Waves of frequency 2.0 Hz are generated at the end of a long steel spring. What is their wavelength if the waves travel along the spring with a speed of 3.0 m/s?

## 10.1 Review Questions

1. What is the source of all wave motion?

2. What kind of wave has no amplitude and no frequency?

3. How many vibrations per second are there from a radio signal from 107.3 MHz?

4. What is the period of a wave that has a frequency of 25 Hz?

5. What is the frequency of a wave that has the period of 2.0 s?

6. When a salmon fishing boat captain describes waves as being 8 m high, what is the approximate amplitude of these waves? Explain your answer.

7. What is the frequency of one revolution of the second hand on a clock?

8. What is the frequency of one revolution of the hour hand on a clock?

9. If the frequency of a sound is tripled, what will happen to the period of the sound waves?

10. A student measures the speed of water waves in her tank to be 25 cm/s. If the wavelength is 2.5 cm, what is the frequency of the waves?

11. Some microwaves have a frequency of $3.0 \times 10^{10}$ Hz. How long is a microwave of this frequency? (Microwave radiation travels at the speed of light.)

12. While fishing, a girl notices the wave crests passing her bob once every 6 s. She thinks the distance between crests is about 12 m. What is the speed of the water waves?

# 10.2 Wave Phenomena

## Warm Up

You and a friend both throw rocks into a lake. The rocks enter the water 1.0 m apart. If you were looking down from above, draw what you think the wave pattern for each of the rocks will look like. Place the letter X at the point or points where the waves would be the highest.

### Properties of Waves

You already know several properties of waves. Waves can be reflected and refracted. All waves conform to the wave equation. There are other important properties of waves, such as constructive and destructive interference, that lead to interesting natural phenomena.

### Constructive and Destructive Interference

Figure 10.2.1 shows waves coming from two different sources — A and B. What happens if the two sets of waves arrive simultaneously at the same place? The result is shown in the third diagram. The amplitudes of the two sets of waves are additive. Since the waves from source A are in phase with the waves from source B, the resultant waves have twice the amplitude of the individual waves from A or B. This is an example of what is called **constructive interference.** Notice that crests are twice as high and troughs are twice as deep in the combined waves.

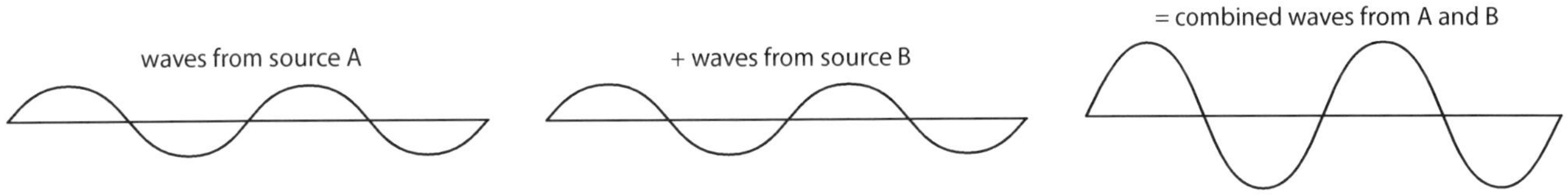


**Figure 10.2.1** *Constructive interference*

In Figure 10.2.2, the waves from source A are exactly out of phase with the waves from source B. A crest from source A arrives simultaneously with a trough from source B. The two sets of waves exactly cancel each other. This is an example of **destructive interference.**

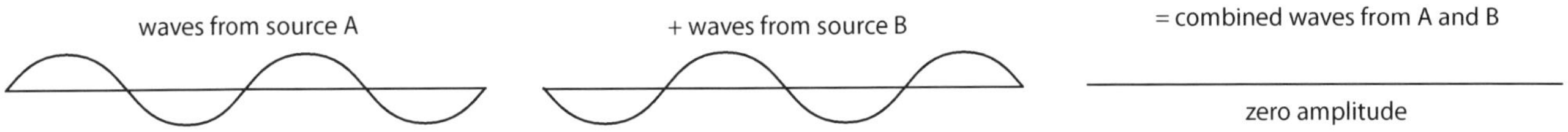


**Figure 10.2.2** *Destructive interference*

Interference of waves occurs with all sorts of waves. You may have seen interference of water waves in the wave tank. You can hear interference of sound waves if you simply listen to a tuning fork as you rotate it slowly near your ear. Each tine of the fork produces a set of sound waves. Listen for constructive interference. It's the extra loud sound. Destructive interference is the minimum sound you hear as you slowly rotate the tuning fork.

## Diffraction

You hear someone talking from around a corner. Light leaks through a crack in a closed door. These are both examples of another property of waves called diffraction. **Diffraction** is when a wave spreads out as it passes through narrow openings, around corners or small obstacles.

You have probably seen examples of diffraction many times, perhaps without knowing what it was. If you look out at streetlights through a window screen or a fine mesh curtain, the *starburst* effect you see is due to diffraction of light waves as they pass by the screen. Diffraction is often used in television programs to obtain starburst effects in musical productions. Diffraction is commonplace with sound. Figure 10.2.5 shows the diffraction of red laser light around a razor blade.

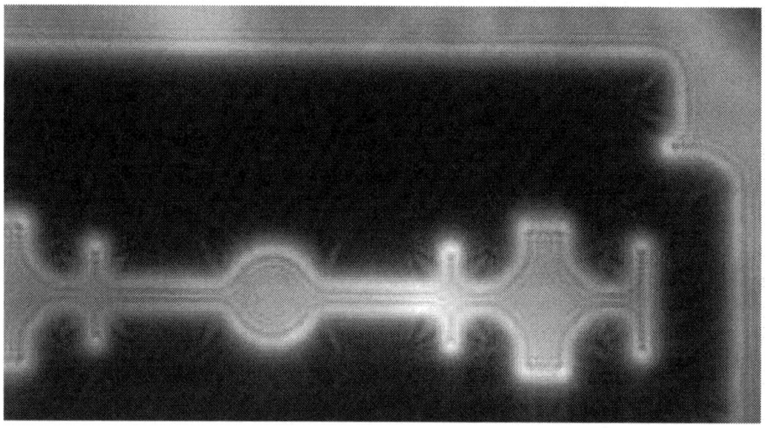

**Figure 10.2.5** *Using the interference pattern to calculate the wavelength of light*

## The Doppler Effect

When a fast car or motorbike approaches you, the pitch of its sound rises. As the vehicle goes by, the pitch lowers. The effect is quite noticeable if you watch a high-speed automobile race on television. What causes this change in pitch? Austrian physicist C. J. Doppler (1803–1853) was the first to explain the effect in terms of waves, and therefore the effect is called the **Doppler effect**.

Figure 10.2.6 illustrates sound waves coming from a moving source. The vehicle is moving to the left. Sound waves coming from the vehicle are bunched in front of the vehicle, which tends to catch up with its own sound. (This diagram exaggerates the effect.) The wave fronts or compressions are closer together in front of the vehicle and farther apart behind the vehicle.

The observer at A hears a higher pitch than normal, since more compressions and rarefactions pass his ear per second than pass the observer at B. Observer B hears the normal pitch of the vehicle's sound. Behind the vehicle, compressions are spaced out, since the vehicle is travelling away from the sound it sends in that direction. The observer at C hears a lower pitch than normal. Fewer compressions and rarefactions pass his ear per second than if he was at A or B. As the vehicle passes observer A, he will hear the pitch go from high to normal to low in a very short time interval. He will hear the Doppler effect.

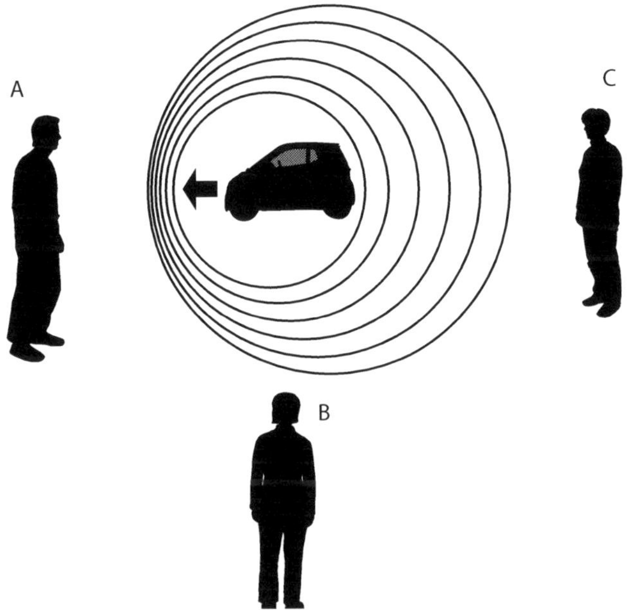


**Figure 10.2.6** *The wave fronts are closer together at the front of the moving vehicle as it moves forward and more spread out behind.*

## The Sound Barrier

An extreme case of the Doppler effect occurs when an aircraft or bullet travels at the same speed as the sound it is producing. At the leading edges of the aircraft, the compressions it creates tend to bunch up and superimpose on each other (Figure 10.2.7(a)). This creates a wall or barrier of compressed air called the **sound barrier**. Great thrust is needed from the plane's engines to enable the plane to penetrate the sound barrier. Once through the barrier, the plane experiences much less resistance to its movement through the air. The plane, once through the sound barrier, is then supersonic. Its speed is now greater than Mach 1!

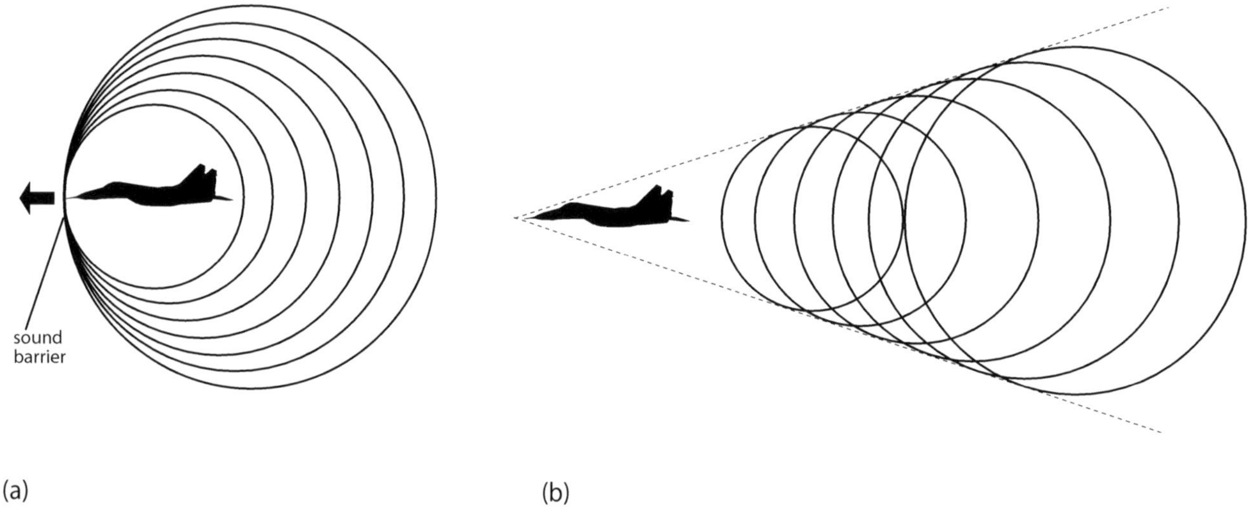


**Figure 10.2.7** *(**a**) The airplane travelling at the speed of sound creates a wall of compressed called the sound barrier; (**b**) An airplane travelling faster than the speed of sound creates a shock wave that you hear as a sonic boom.*

### Shock Waves and the Sonic Boom

If a plane travels *faster* than sound, it gets ahead of the compressions and rarefactions it produces. In two dimensions (Figure 10.2.7(b)), overlapping circular waves form a V-shaped bow wave, somewhat like what you see from the air looking down at a speedboat travelling through still water. In three dimensions, there is a cone of compressed air trailing the aircraft. This cone is called a shock wave. When the shock wave passes you, you hear a loud, sharp crack called the **sonic boom.** Aircraft are not the only producers of sonic booms. Cracking whips and rifle bullets causes miniature sonic booms!

# 10.2 Review Questions

Complete these diagrams to show what happens to waves after they encounter the barrier or other obstacle. Name the phenomenon that occurs in each situation.

1.

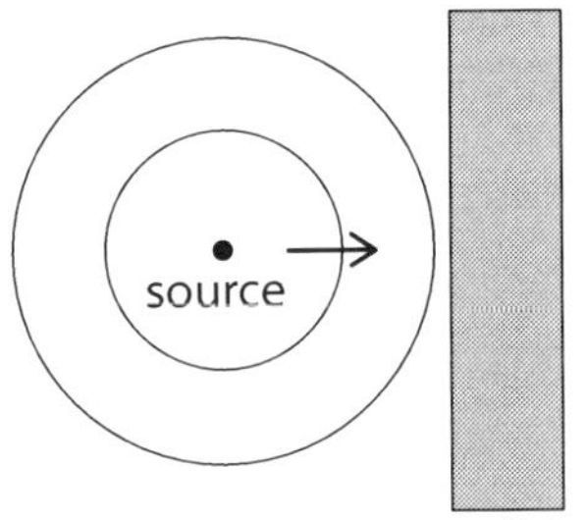


_______________
phenomenon

2.

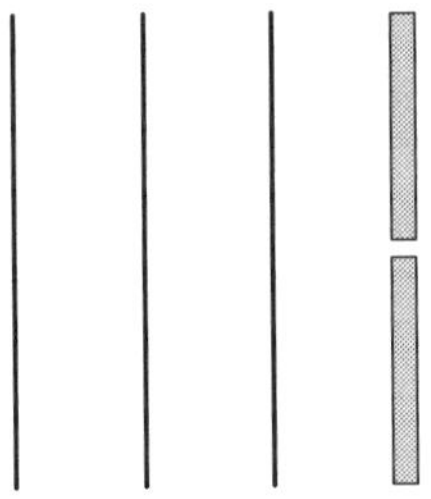

_______________
phenomenon

3. If you look at streetlights through a fine mesh curtain, you will see a "starburst" effect. What phenomenon is involved in this situation?

_______________
phenomenon

4. Use the following diagram to answer the questions below.

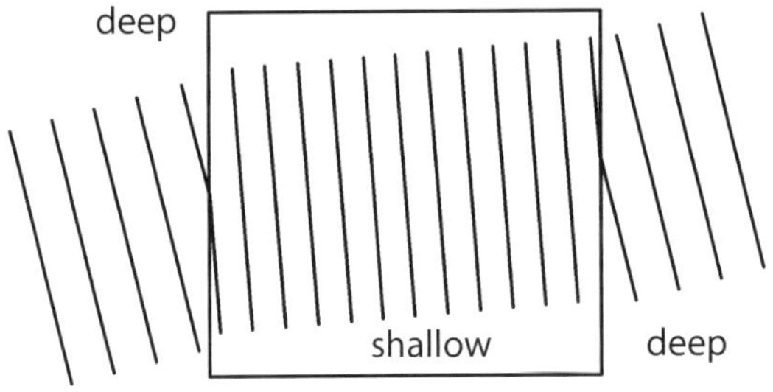


(a) The diagram shows water waves in a wave tank moving from deep water into shallow water and then back into deep water. What property of waves does this model illustrate?

(b) According to the diagram, what can you conclude happens to the waves when they enter the shallow water?

5. For the following situations, is there a point where the amplitude will be zero everywhere? If so, mark that point.

(a) 

(b) 

(c) 

(d) 

(e) 

(f) 

6. For which of the following waves can wave interference occur?

   ______ sound

   ______ light

   ______ water

7. For which of the following waves can the Doppler effect occur?

   ______ sound

   ______ light

   ______ water

8. Does the Doppler effect occur if you are moving and the object making the noise is stationary? Explain your answer.

9. What can you conclude about the speed of an airplane overhead if you hear a sonic boom?

10. Draw two waves travelling toward each other that will create destructive interference when they meet.

11. What is the difference between a sonic boom and the sound barrier?

# Chapter 10 Conceptual Review Questions

1. How do sound vibrations of atoms differ from thermal motion?

2. Six members of a synchronized swim team wear earplugs to protect themselves against water pressure at depths, but they can still hear the music and perform the combinations in the water perfectly. One day, they were asked to leave the pool so the dive team could practice a few dives, and they tried to practice on a mat, but seemed to have a lot more difficulty. Why might this be?

3. Is the Doppler shift real or just a sensory illusion?

4. When you hear a sonic boom, you often cannot see the plane that made it. Why is that?

5. It is more difficult to obtain a high-resolution ultrasound image in the abdominal region of someone who is overweight than for someone who has a slight build. Explain why this statement is accurate.

# Chapter 10 Review Questions

1. What is the difference between a pulse and periodic waves?

2. Explain, with the help of a sketch, what each of these terms means with respect to waves:
   (a) crest

   (b) trough

   (c) wavelength

   (d) frequency

   (e) amplitude

3. What is a hertz?

4. How are frequency and period related?

5. A dog wags its tail 50 times in 20 s. What are (a) the frequency and (b) the period of vibration of the tail?

6. What is the difference between a transverse wave and a longitudinal wave?

7. For any kind of wave motion, how are wave speed, wavelength, and frequency related to one another?

8. Alternating current in power lines produces electromagnetic waves of frequency 60 Hz that travel outward at the speed of light, which is $3.0 \times 10^8$ m/s. What is the wavelength of these waves?

9. If the speed of sound is 330 m/s, what wavelength does a sound of frequency 512 Hz have?

11. Explain the difference between refraction and diffraction. Give an example of each phenomenon from everyday experience.

12. When waves slow down on entering a new medium, what happens to
(a) their wavelength?

(b) their frequency?

(c) their direction?

(d) Under what conditions will the direction *not* change?

13. (a) What is constructive interference?

(b) What is destructive interference?

14. In a wave tank, what causes a nodal line? A maximum?

15. The following diagram shows two parabolic reflectors. A small source of infrared heat is placed at the focus of one of the mirrors. Soon after, a match at the focus of the other reflector lights on fire. Draw a diagram showing how the wave model explains this.

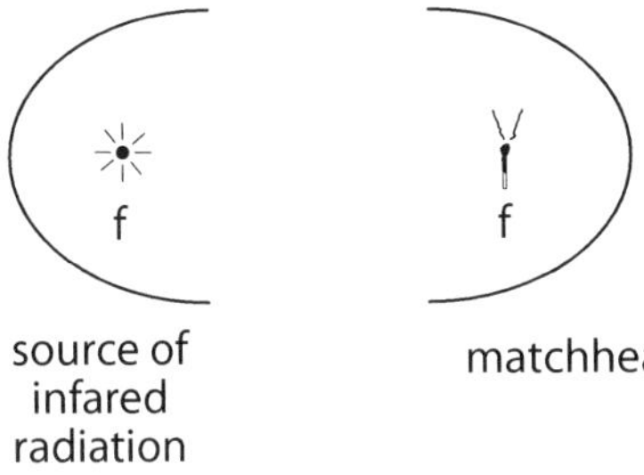


16. The sonar on a navy submarine produces ultrasonic waves at a frequency of 2.2 MHz and a wavelength of $5.10 \times 10^{-4}$ m. If a sonar technician sends one wave pulse from underneath the submarine toward the bottom of the ocean floor and it takes 8.0 s to return, how deep is the ocean at this point?

# Investigation 10-1 Observing Transverse and Longitudinal Waves

**Purpose**

To observe pulses travelling in springs of different diameters

**Procedure**

1. With your partner's help, stretch a long spring about 2.5 cm in diameter to a length of 9 or 10 m. Hold on firmly as both you and the spring can be damaged if it is let go carelessly.
2. Create a transverse pulse by pulling a section of the spring to one side and letting it go suddenly. Observe the motion of the pulse and its reflection from your partner's hand.
3. Try increasing the amplitude of the pulse. Does this affect the speed of the wave through the spring?
4. Try tightening the spring. How does increasing the tension affect the speed of the pulse?
5. Observe the pulse as it reflects. Does a crest reflect as a crest or as a trough?
6. Have your partner create a pulse simultaneously with yours. Do the two pulses affect each other as they pass through each other?
7. Repeat Procedure steps 1 to 6 using a long Slinky, which is a spring with a much larger diameter.
8. Try sending a longitudinal pulse through each spring. To do this, bunch up a dozen or so turns of the spring, then let the compressed section go. Do longitudinal waves reflect at your partner's hand?

**Concluding Questions**

1. In which spring did the transverse waves travel faster — the small diameter spring or the Slinky?
2. In which spring did the longitudinal waves travel faster?
3. Does the amplitude of the waves affect their speed through the spring?
4. Does spring tension affect wave speed? Explain.
5. When a wave travels through the medium, like the spring, does the medium travel or just the disturbance in the medium?
6. When a wave reflects from a fixed end of the medium, does a crest reflect as a crest or is it reflected as a trough? In other words, is the wave inverted?

# Answer Key

For the most current version of the answer key, scan the appropriate QR code with your mobile device or go to edvantagescience.com, login and select AP Physics 1.

Introductory Chapter

Chapter 1

Chapter 2

Chapter 3

Chapter 4

Chapter 5

Chapter 6

Chapter 7

Chapter 8

Chapter 9

Chapter 10

Made in the USA
Columbia, SC
21 August 2021

43204251R00237